MASS CALENDAR FOR 2016-2017

Using this Book in Prayer

You can use this book to help your prayer,
alone or with your family and friends:

- Read the Gospel or other readings for last Sunday, and pray about them.

- Read the Gospel or other readings for next Sunday, and begin to pray about them.

- Think about God's Word: what is the Holy Spirit telling you?

- Pray the Responsorial Psalm from any of the Masses in the book.

- Reflect on the Collect from last Sunday's Mass, and pray it slowly.

- Use some of the prayers in the treasury.

- Say the Lord's Prayer slowly (page 72).

This Missal belongs to

....

New *Saint Joseph*

SUNDAY MISSAL
PRAYERBOOK AND HYMNAL

CANADIAN MISSAL

For 2016 - 2017

Year A

How easy it is to use this Missal

- Refer to the Calendar inside the front cover for the page of the Sunday Mass (the "Proper").

- This arrow (↓) means continue to read. This arrow (→) indicates a reference back to the Order of Mass ("Ordinary") or to another part of the "Proper."

- Boldface type always indicates the people's parts that are to be recited aloud.

"Take this, all of you, and eat of it, for this is my Body, which will be given up for you."

CANADIAN EDITION

New . . . St. Joseph

SUNDAY MISSAL

PRAYERBOOK AND HYMNAL

For 2016 - 2017

THE COMPLETE MASSES FOR
SUNDAYS and the
SACRED PASCHAL TRIDUUM

With the People's Parts Printed in Boldface Type
and Arranged for Parish Participation

The liturgical texts are approved by
the Canadian Conference of Catholic Bishops.

IN ACCORD WITH THE THIRD TYPICAL EDITION
OF THE ROMAN MISSAL

With the
"NEW REVISED STANDARD VERSION" Text

Dedicated to St. Joseph
Patron of the Universal Church

CATHOLIC BOOK PUBLISHING CORP.
New Jersey

The *St. Joseph Sunday Missal for 2016-2017* is approved for use in Canada by the National Liturgy Office, Canadian Conference of Catholic Bishops.

Acknowledgements:

The St. Joseph Missals have been diligently prepared with the invaluable assistance of a special Board of Editors, including specialists in Liturgy and Sacred Scripture, Catechetics, and Sacred Music and Art.

Excerpts from the English translation and chants of *The Roman Missal* © 2010, International Commission on English in the Liturgy Corporation (ICEL); the English translation of the Psalm Responses, Alleluia Verses and Titles of the Readings from *Lectionary for Mass* © 1969, 1981, 1997, ICEL; excerpts from the English translation of *Rite of Christian Initiation of Adults* © 1985, ICEL. All rights reserved.

The lectionary texts contained herein are from the *Lectionary, Sundays and Solemnities* of the Canadian Conference of Catholic Bishops, copyright © Concacan Inc., 1992, 2009. All rights reserved. Used by permission of the Canadian Conference of Catholic Bishops.

This revised edition of the *Lectionary, Sundays and Solemnities* follows the *Ordo Lectionum Missae, editio typica altera*, Typis Polyglottis Vaticanus, 1981.

The Scripture quotations contained herein (including the texts of the readings, the Psalms, the Psalm refrains and the Gospel verses) are based on the New Revised Standard Version of the Bible, copyright © 1989 National Council of the Churches of Christ in the USA. Adapted and used by permission. All rights reserved.

Adaptations for liturgical use have been made to selected Scripture texts. These adaptations have been made to bring the readings into conformity with the *Ordo Lectionum Missae, editio typica altera*, the *Lectionarium* and *Liturgiam Authenticam*, as well as to facilitate proclamation. These adaptations were prepared by and are the sole responsibility of the Canadian Conference of Catholic Bishops. Adaptations copyright © 2009 National Council of the Churches of Christ in the USA. Used by permission. All rights reserved.

English translation of the Sequence for Easter, copyright © Peter J. Scagnelli. All rights reserved. English translation of the Sequence for Pentecost, Edward Caswell (+1878); adaptations, copyright © Peter J. Scagnelli. All rights reserved.

Texts on pages 637-650 in the "Treasury of Prayers"—copyright © Concacan Inc., 1983. Used by permission.

All other texts and illustrations © Copyright by Catholic Book Publishing Corp., N.J.

(T-2117)

ISBN 978-1-941243-59-6

PREFACE

IN the words of the Second Vatican Council in the *Constitution on the Sacred Liturgy*, the Mass "is an action of Christ the priest and of his body which is the Church; it is a sacred action surpassing all others; no other action of the Church can equal its efficacy by the same title and to the same degree" (art. 7). Hence the Mass is a sacred sign, something visible which brings the invisible reality of Christ to us in the worship of the Father.

The Mass was first instituted as a meal at the Last Supper and became a living memorial of Christ's sacrifice on the Cross:

"At the Last Supper, on the night when he was betrayed, our Saviour instituted the Eucharistic sacrifice of his body and blood. He did this in order to perpetuate the sacrifice of the Cross throughout the centuries until he should come again, and so to entrust to his beloved spouse, the Church, a memorial of his death and resurrection: a sacrament of love, a sign of unity, a bond of charity, a Paschal banquet in which Christ is eaten, the mind is filled with grace, and a pledge of future glory is given to us.

"The Church, therefore, earnestly desires that Christ's faithful, when present at this mystery of faith, should not be there as strangers or silent spectators; on the contrary, through a good understanding of the rites and prayers they should take part in the sacred action conscious of what they are doing, with devotion and full collaboration. They should be instructed by God's word and be nourished at the table of the Lord's body; they should give thanks to God; by offering the immaculate Victim, not only through the hands of the priest, but also with him, they should learn also to offer themselves; through Christ the Mediator, they should be drawn day by day into ever more perfect union with God and with each other, so that . . . God may be all in all" (art. 47-48).

A simple method of identifying the various parts of the Mass has been designed using different typefaces:

(1) **boldface type**—clearly identifies all people's parts

(2) lightface type—indicates the Priest's, Deacon's, or lector's parts.

In order to enable the faithful to prepare for each Mass at home and so participate more actively at Mass, the editors have added short helpful explanations of the scripture readings, geared to the spiritual needs of daily life. A large selection of hymns for congregational singing has been included as well as a treasury of personal prayers.

We trust that all these special features will help Catholics who use this new St. Joseph Missal to be led—in keeping with the desire of the Church—"to that full, conscious, and active participation in liturgical celebrations which is demanded by the very nature of the liturgy. Such participation by the Christian people as a chosen race, a royal priesthood, a holy nation, a redeemed people (1 Pt 2, 9; cf. 2, 4-5), is their right and duty by reason of their baptism" (art. 14).

PLAN OF THE MASS

THE INTRODUCTORY RITES
1. Entrance Chant
2. Greeting
3. Rite for the Blessing and Sprinkling of Water
4. Penitential Act
5. Kyrie
6. Gloria
7. Collect (**Proper**)

THE LITURGY OF THE WORD
8. First Reading (**Proper**)
9. Responsorial Psalm (**Proper**)
10. Second Reading (**Proper**)
11. Gospel Acclamation (**Proper**)
12. Gospel Dialogue
13. Gospel Reading (**Proper**)
14. Homily
15. Profession of Faith (**Creed**)
16. Universal Prayer

THE LITURGY OF THE EUCHARIST
17. Presentation and Preparation of the Gifts
18. Invitation to Prayer
19. Prayer over the Offerings (**Proper**)
20. Eucharistic Prayer
21. Preface Dialogue
22. Preface
23. Preface Acclamation
    Eucharistic Prayer
    1, 2, 3, 4
    Reconciliation 1, 2
    Various Needs 1, 2, 3, 4

The Communion Rite
24. The Lord's Prayer
25. Sign of Peace
26. Lamb of God
27. Invitation to Communion
28. Communion
29. Prayer after Communion (**Proper**)

THE CONCLUDING RITES
30. Solemn Blessing
31. Final Blessing
32. Dismissal

THE ORDER OF MASS

Options are indicated by A, B, C, D in the margin.

THE INTRODUCTORY RITES

Acts of prayer and penitence prepare us to meet Christ as he comes in Word and Sacrament. We gather as a worshipping community to celebrate our unity with him and with one another in faith.

1 ENTRANCE CHANT   `STAND`

If it is not sung, it is recited by all or some of the people.

Joined together as Christ's people, we open the celebration by raising our voices in praise of God who is present among us. This song should deepen our unity as it introduces the Mass we celebrate today.

→ `Turn to Today's Mass`

2 GREETING (3 forms)

When the Priest comes to the altar, he makes the customary reverence with the ministers and kisses the altar. Then, with the ministers, he goes to his chair. After the Entrance Chant, all make the Sign of the Cross:

Priest: **In the name of the Father, and of the Son, and of the Holy Spirit.**

PEOPLE: **Amen.**

The Priest welcomes us in the name of the Lord. We show our union with God, our neighbour, and the Priest by a united response to his greeting.

A

Priest: The grace of our Lord Jesus Christ,
and the love of God,
and the communion of the Holy Spirit
be with you all.

PEOPLE: **And with your spirit.**

B ——————— OR ———————

Priest: Grace to you and peace from God our Father
and the Lord Jesus Christ.

PEOPLE: **And with your spirit.**

C ——————— OR ———————

Priest: The Lord be with you.

PEOPLE: **And with your spirit.**

[Bishop: Peace be with you.

PEOPLE: **And with your spirit.**]

3 RITE FOR the BLESSING and SPRINKLING of WATER

From time to time on Sundays, especially in Easter Time, instead of the customary Penitential Act, the Blessing and Sprinkling of Water may take place (see pp. 78-81) as a reminder of Baptism.

4 PENITENTIAL ACT (3 forms)

(Omitted when the Rite for the Blessing and Sprinkling of Water [see pp. 78-81] has taken place or some part of the liturgy of the hours has preceded.)

Before we hear God's word, we acknowledge our sins humbly, ask for mercy, and accept his pardon.

Invitation to repent:

After the introduction to the day's Mass, the Priest invites the people to recall their sins and to repent of them in silence:

Priest: Brethren (brothers and sisters), let us acknowledge our sins,
and so prepare ourselves to celebrate the sacred mysteries.

Then, after a brief silence, one of the following forms is used.

A

Priest and **PEOPLE:**

I confess to almighty God
and to you, my brothers and sisters,
that I have greatly sinned,
in my thoughts and in my words,
in what I have done and in what I have failed to do,

They strike their breast:

through my fault, through my fault,
through my most grievous fault;

Then they continue:

therefore I ask blessed Mary ever-Virgin,
all the Angels and Saints,
and you, my brothers and sisters,
to pray for me to the Lord our God.

B ———————— OR ————————

Priest: Have mercy on us, O Lord.

PEOPLE: For we have sinned against you.

Priest: Show us, O Lord, your mercy.

PEOPLE: And grant us your salvation.

C ———————— OR ————————

Priest, or a Deacon or another minister:

You were sent to heal the contrite of heart:
Lord, have mercy.

PEOPLE: Lord, have mercy.

Priest or other minister:

You came to call sinners:
Christ, have mercy.

PEOPLE: Christ, have mercy.

Priest or other minister:

You are seated at the right hand of the
Father to intercede for us:

Lord, have mercy.

PEOPLE: Lord, have mercy.

————————

Absolution:

At the end of any of the forms of the Penitential Act:

Priest: May almighty God have mercy on us,
forgive us our sins,
and bring us to everlasting life.

PEOPLE: Amen.

5 KYRIE

Unless included in the Penitential Act, the Kyrie is sung or said by all, with alternating parts for the choir or cantor and for the people:

℣. Lord, have mercy.

℟. **Lord, have mercy.**

℣. Christ, have mercy.

℟. **Christ, have mercy.**

℣. Lord, have mercy.

℟. **Lord, have mercy.**

6 GLORIA

As the Church assembled in the Spirit we praise and pray to the Father and the Lamb.

When the Gloria is sung or said, the Priest or the cantors or everyone together may begin it:

**Glory to God in the highest,
and on earth peace to people of good will.**

**We praise you,
we bless you,
we adore you,
we glorify you,
we give you thanks for your great glory,
Lord God, heavenly King,
O God, almighty Father.**

**Lord Jesus Christ, Only Begotten Son,
Lord God, Lamb of God, Son of the Father,
you take away the sins of the world,
      have mercy on us;**

you take away the sins of the world,
    receive our prayer;
you are seated at the right hand of the Father,
    have mercy on us.

For you alone are the Holy One,
you alone are the Lord,
you alone are the Most High,
Jesus Christ,
with the Holy Spirit,
in the glory of God the Father.
Amen.

7 COLLECT

The Priest invites us to pray silently for a moment and then, in our name, expresses the theme of the day's celebration and petitions God the Father through the mediation of Christ in the Holy Spirit.

Priest: Let us pray.

→ **Turn to Today's Mass**

Priest and people pray silently for a while. Then the Priest says the Collect prayer, at the end of which the people acclaim:

PEOPLE: Amen.

Liturgy of the WORD

The proclamation of God's Word is always centred on Christ, present through his Word. Old Testament writings prepare for him; New Testament books speak of him directly. All of scripture calls us to believe once more and to follow. After the reading we reflect on God's words and respond to them.

As in Today's Mass   **SIT**

8 FIRST READING

At the end of the reading: Reader: **The word of the Lord.**

PEOPLE: Thanks be to God.

9 RESPONSORIAL PSALM

The people repeat the response sung by the cantor the first time and then after each verse.

10 SECOND READING

At the end of the reading: Reader: **The word of the Lord.**

PEOPLE: Thanks be to God.

11 GOSPEL ACCLAMATION   **STAND**

Jesus will speak to us in the Gospel. We rise now out of respect and prepare for his message with the Alleluia.

The people repeat the Alleluia after the the cantor's Alleluia and then after the verse. During Lent one of the following invocations is used as a response instead of the Alleluia:

(a) **Glory and praise to you, Lord Jesus Christ!**
(b) **Glory to you, Lord Jesus Christ, Wisdom of God the Father!**
(c) **Glory to you, Word of God, Lord Jesus Christ!**
(d) **Glory to you, Lord Jesus Christ, Son of the living God!**

(e) **Praise and honour to you, Lord Jesus Christ!**
(f) **Praise to you, Lord Jesus Christ, King of endless glory!**
(g) **Marvellous and great are your works, O Lord!**
(h) **Salvation, glory, and power to the Lord Jesus Christ!**

12 GOSPEL DIALOGUE

Before proclaiming the Gospel, the Deacon asks the Priest: Your blessing, Father. *The Priest says:*

May the Lord be in your heart and on your lips,
that you may proclaim his Gospel worthily and well,
in the name of the Father, and of the Son, ✚ and of
the Holy Spirit. *The Deacon answers:* Amen.

If there is no Deacon, the Priest says inaudibly:

Cleanse my heart and my lips, almighty God,
that I may worthily proclaim your holy Gospel.

13 GOSPEL READING

Deacon (or Priest):
          The Lord be with you.

PEOPLE: And with your spirit.

Deacon (or Priest):

✚ A reading from the holy Gospel according to N.

PEOPLE: Glory to you, O Lord.

At the end:

Deacon (or Priest):
          The Gospel of the Lord.

PEOPLE: Praise to you, Lord Jesus Christ.

Then the Deacon (or Priest) kisses the book, saying inaudibly: Through the words of the Gospel may our sins be wiped away.

14 HOMILY   `SIT`

God's word is spoken again in the Homily. The Holy Spirit speaking through the lips of the preacher explains and applies today's biblical readings to the needs of this particular congregation. He calls us to respond to Christ through the life we lead.

15 PROFESSION OF FAITH (CREED) `STAND`

As a people we express our acceptance of God's message in the Scriptures and Homily. We summarize our faith by proclaiming a creed handed down from the early Church.

All say the Profession of Faith on Sundays.

——————— **THE NICENE CREED** ———————

I believe in one God,
the Father almighty,
maker of heaven and earth,
of all things visible and invisible.

I believe in one Lord Jesus Christ,
the Only Begotten Son of God,
born of the Father before all ages.
God from God, Light from Light,
true God from true God,
begotten, not made, consubstantial with the Father;
through him all things were made.
For us men and for our salvation
he came down from heaven,
and by the Holy Spirit was incarnate of the Virgin ⎫
*   Mary,*   ⎬ *bow*
and became man.   ⎭

For our sake he was crucified under Pontius Pilate,
he suffered death and was buried,
and rose again on the third day
in accordance with the Scriptures.
He ascended into heaven
and is seated at the right hand of the Father.
He will come again in glory
to judge the living and the dead
and his kingdom will have no end.

I believe in the Holy Spirit, the Lord, the giver of life,
who proceeds from the Father and the Son,
who with the Father and the Son is adored and
    glorified,
who has spoken through the prophets.

I believe in one, holy, catholic and apostolic Church.
I confess one Baptism for the forgiveness of sins
and I look forward to the resurrection of the dead
and the life of the world to come. Amen.

OR ———————— APOSTLES' CREED ————————

*Especially during Lent and Easter Time, the Apostles'
Creed may be said after the Homily.*

I believe in God,
the Father almighty,
Creator of heaven and earth,
and in Jesus Christ, his only Son, our Lord,
who was conceived by the Holy Spirit,⎫ *bow*
born of the Virgin Mary,   ⎭
suffered under Pontius Pilate,
was crucified, died and was buried;
he descended into hell;
on the third day he rose again from the dead;
he ascended into heaven,
and is seated at the right hand of God the Father
      almighty;
from there he will come to judge the living and the dead.

I believe in the Holy Spirit,
the holy catholic Church,
the communion of saints,
the forgiveness of sins,
the resurrection of the body,
and life everlasting. Amen.

16 UNIVERSAL PRAYER   (Prayer of the Faithful)

As a priestly people we unite with one another to pray for today's
needs in the Church and the world.

*After the Priest gives the introduction the Deacon or other
minister sings or says the invocations.*

PEOPLE: Lord, hear our prayer.

(or other response, according to local custom)
At the end the Priest says the concluding prayer:

PEOPLE: Amen.

THE LITURGY OF THE EUCHARIST

17 PRESENTATION AND PREPARATION `SIT` OF THE GIFTS

While the people's gifts are brought forward to the Priest and are placed on the altar, the Offertory Chant is sung.

Before placing the bread on the altar, the Priest says inaudibly:

Blessed are you, Lord God of all creation,
for through your goodness we have received
the bread we offer you:
fruit of the earth and work of human hands,
it will become for us the bread of life.

If there is no singing, the Priest may say this prayer aloud, and the people may respond:

PEOPLE: **Blessed be God for ever.**

When he pours wine and a little water into the chalice, the Deacon (or the Priest) says inaudibly:

By the mystery of this water and wine
may we come to share in the divinity of Christ
who humbled himself to share in our humanity.

Before placing the chalice on the altar, he says:

Blessed are you, Lord God of all creation,
for through your goodness we have received
the wine we offer you:
fruit of the vine and work of human hands,
it will become our spiritual drink.

If there is no singing, the Priest may say this prayer aloud, and the people may respond:

20

PEOPLE: Blessed be God for ever.

The Priest says inaudibly:

With humble spirit and contrite heart
may we be accepted by you, O Lord,
and may our sacrifice in your sight this day
be pleasing to you, Lord God.

Then he washes his hands, saying:

Wash me, O Lord, from my iniquity
and cleanse me from my sin.

18 INVITATION TO PRAYER

Priest: Pray, brethren (brothers and sisters),
that my sacrifice and yours
may be acceptable to God,
the almighty Father.

`STAND`

PEOPLE:

**May the Lord accept the sacrifice at your hands
for the praise and glory of his name,
for our good
and the good of all his holy Church.**

19 PRAYER OVER THE OFFERINGS

*The Priest, speaking in our name, asks the Father to
bless and accept these gifts.*

→ `Turn to Today's Mass`

At the end, **PEOPLE: Amen.**

20 EUCHARISTIC PRAYER

We begin the eucharistic service of praise and thanksgiving, the centre of the entire celebration, the central prayer of worship. We lift our hearts to God, and offer praise and thanks as the Priest addresses this prayer to the Father through Jesus Christ. Together we join Christ in his sacrifice, celebrating his memorial in the holy meal and acknowledging with him the wonderful works of God in our lives.

21 PREFACE DIALOGUE

Priest: The Lord be with you.
PEOPLE: And with your spirit.
Priest: Lift up your hearts.
PEOPLE: We lift them up to the Lord.
Priest: Let us give thanks to the Lord our God.
PEOPLE: It is right and just.

22 PREFACE

As indicated in the individual Masses of this Missal, the Priest may say one of the following Prefaces (listed in numerical order).

23   PREFACE ACCLAMATION

Priest and **PEOPLE:**
Holy, Holy, Holy Lord, God of hosts.
Heaven and earth are full of your glory.
Hosanna in the highest.
Blessed is he who comes in the name of the Lord.
Hosanna in the highest.   `KNEEL`

Then the Priest continues with one of the following Eucharistic Prayers.

EUCHARISTIC PRAYER	**Choice of ten**
1	To you, therefore, most merciful Father..............p. 24
2	You are indeed Holy, O Lord, the fount...............p. 31
3	You are indeed Holy, O Lord, and all...................p. 34
4	We give you praise, Father most holy ....p. 39
R1	You are indeed Holy, O Lord, and from...............p. 44
R2	You, therefore, almighty Father...........................p. 49
V1	You are indeed Holy and to be glorified..............p. 53
V2	You are indeed Holy and to be glorified..............p. 58
V3	You are indeed Holy and to be glorified..............p. 63
V4	You are indeed Holy and to be glorified..............p. 68

EUCHARISTIC PRAYER No. 1

The Roman Canon

(This Eucharistic Prayer is especially suitable for Sundays and Masses with proper Communicantes *and* Hanc igitur.*)*

[The words within parentheses may be omitted.]

To you, therefore, most merciful Father,
we make humble prayer and petition
through Jesus Christ, your Son, our Lord:
that you accept
and bless ✠ these gifts, these offerings,
these holy and unblemished sacrifices,
which we offer you firstly
for your holy catholic Church.
Be pleased to grant her peace,
to guard, unite and govern her
throughout the whole world,
together with your servant N. our Pope,
and N. our Bishop,
and all those who, holding to the truth,
hand on the catholic and apostolic faith.

Remember, Lord, your servants N. and N.
and all gathered here,
whose faith and devotion are known to you.
For them, we offer you this sacrifice of praise
or they offer it for themselves
and all who are dear to them:
for the redemption of their souls,
in hope of health and well-being,
and paying their homage to you,
the eternal God, living and true.

1

In communion with those whose memory we
   venerate,
especially the glorious ever-Virgin Mary,
Mother of our God and Lord, Jesus Christ,
† and blessed Joseph, her Spouse,
your blessed Apostles and Martyrs
Peter and Paul, Andrew,
(James, John,
Thomas, James, Philip,
Bartholomew, Matthew,
Simon and Jude;
Linus, Cletus, Clement, Sixtus,
Cornelius, Cyprian,
Lawrence, Chrysogonus,
John and Paul,
Cosmas and Damian)
and all your Saints;
we ask that through their merits and prayers,
in all things we may be defended
by your protecting help.
(Through Christ our Lord. Amen.)

Therefore, Lord, we pray:*
graciously accept this oblation of our service,
that of your whole family;
order our days in your peace,
and command that we be delivered from eternal
   damnation
and counted among the flock of those you have
   chosen.
(Through Christ our Lord. Amen.)

Be pleased, O God, we pray,
to bless, acknowledge,
and approve this offering in every respect;

† * See p. 95 for proper Communicantes and Hanc igitur.

1 make it spiritual and acceptable,
so that it may become for us
the Body and Blood of your most beloved Son,
our Lord Jesus Christ.

On the day before he was to suffer,
he took bread in his holy and venerable hands,
and with eyes raised to heaven
to you, O God, his almighty Father,
giving you thanks, he said the blessing,
broke the bread
and gave it to his disciples, saying:

Take this, all of you, and eat of it,
for this is my Body,
which will be given up for you.

In a similar way when supper was ended,
he took this precious chalice
in his holy and venerable hands,
and once more giving you thanks, he said the
    blessing
and gave the chalice to his disciples, saying:

Take this, all of you, and drink from it,
for this is the chalice of my Blood,
the Blood of the new and eternal covenant,
which will be poured out for you and for many
for the forgiveness of sins.
Do this in memory of me.

Priest: **The mystery of faith.** *(Memorial Acclamation)*
PEOPLE:

A **We proclaim your Death, O Lord,**
     and profess your Resurrection
     until you come again.

B   **When we eat this Bread and drink this Cup,**   **1**
  we proclaim your Death, O Lord,
  until you come again.

C   **Save us, Saviour of the world,**
  for by your Cross and Resurrection
  you have set us free.

Therefore, O Lord,
as we celebrate the memorial of the blessed Passion,
the Resurrection from the dead,
and the glorious Ascension into heaven
of Christ, your Son, our Lord,
we your servants and your holy people,
offer to your glorious majesty
from the gifts that you have given us,
this pure victim,
this holy victim,
this spotless victim,
the holy Bread of eternal life
and the Chalice of everlasting salvation.

Be pleased to look upon these offerings
with a serene and kindly countenance,
and to accept them,
as once you were pleased to accept
the gifts of your servant Abel the just,
the sacrifice of Abraham, our father in faith,
and the offering of your high priest Melchizedek,
a holy sacrifice, a spotless victim.

In humble prayer we ask you, almighty God:
command that these gifts be borne
by the hands of your holy Angel
to your altar on high
in the sight of your divine majesty,

1 so that all of us, who through this participation at
the altar
receive the most holy Body and Blood of your Son,
may be filled with every grace and heavenly
blessing.
(Through Christ our Lord. Amen.)

Remember also, Lord, your servants, N. and N.,
who have gone before us with the sign of faith
and rest in the sleep of peace.
Grant them, O Lord, we pray,
and all who sleep in Christ,
a place of refreshment, light and peace.
(Through Christ our Lord. Amen.)

To us, also your servants, who, though sinners,
hope in your abundant mercies,
graciously grant some share
and fellowship with your holy Apostles and
Martyrs:
with John the Baptist, Stephen,
Matthias, Barnabas,
(Ignatius, Alexander,
Marcellinus, Peter,
Felicity, Perpetua,
Agatha, Lucy,
Agnes, Cecilia, Anastasia)
and all your Saints;
admit us, we beseech you,
into their company,
not weighing our merits,
but granting us your pardon,
through Christ our Lord.

Through whom
you continue to make all these good things,
    O Lord;
you sanctify them, fill them with life,
bless them, and bestow them upon us.

(Concluding Doxology)

Through him, and with him, and in him,
O God, almighty Father,
in the unity of the Holy Spirit,
all glory and honour is yours,
for ever and ever.

All reply: **Amen.**

Continue with the Mass, as on p. 72.

2 EUCHARISTIC PRAYER No. 2

(This Eucharistic Prayer is particularly suitable on Weekdays or for special circumstances.)

STAND

℣. The Lord be with you.

℟. **And with your spirit.**

℣. Lift up your hearts.

℟. **We lift them up to the Lord.**

℣. Let us give thanks to the Lord our God.

℟. **It is right and just.**

It is truly right and just, our duty and our salvation,
always and everywhere to give you thanks, Father most holy,
through your beloved Son, Jesus Christ,
your Word through whom you made all things,
whom you sent as our Saviour and Redeemer,
incarnate by the Holy Spirit and born of the Virgin.

Fulfilling your will
    and gaining for you a holy people,
he stretched out his hands
    as he endured his Passion,
so as to break the bonds of death
    and manifest the resurrection.

And so, with the Angels and all the Saints
we declare your glory,
as with one voice we acclaim:

2

Holy, Holy, Holy Lord God of hosts.
Heaven and earth are full of your glory.
Hosanna in the highest.
Blessed is he who comes in the name of the Lord.
Hosanna in the highest.

`KNEEL`

You are indeed Holy, O Lord,
the fount of all holiness.

Make holy, therefore, these gifts, we pray,
by sending down your Spirit upon them like the
    dewfall,
so that they may become for us
the Body and ✠ Blood of our Lord Jesus Christ.

At the time he was betrayed
and entered willingly into his Passion,
he took bread and, giving thanks, broke it,
and gave it to his disciples, saying:

Take this, all of you, and eat of it,
for this is my Body,
which will be given up for you.

In a similar way, when supper was ended,
he took the chalice
and, once more giving thanks,
he gave it to his disciples, saying:

Take this, all of you, and drink from it,
for this is the chalice of my Blood,
the Blood of the new and eternal covenant,
which will be poured out for you and for many
for the forgiveness of sins.
Do this in memory of me.

2 Priest: **The mystery of faith.** *(Memorial Acclamation)*
PEOPLE:

A We proclaim your Death, O Lord,
   and profess your Resurrection
   until you come again.

B When we eat this Bread and drink this Cup,
   we proclaim your Death, O Lord,
   until you come again.

C Save us, Saviour of the world,
   for by your Cross and Resurrection
   you have set us free.

Therefore, as we celebrate
the memorial of his Death and Resurrection,
we offer you, Lord,
the Bread of life and the Chalice of salvation,
giving thanks that you have held us worthy
to be in your presence and minister to you.

Humbly we pray
that, partaking of the Body and Blood of Christ,
we may be gathered into one by the Holy Spirit.

Remember, Lord, your Church,
spread throughout the world,
and bring her to the fullness of charity,
together with *N.* our Pope and *N.* our Bishop
and all the clergy.

In Masses for the Dead the following may be added:

Remember your servant *N.*,
whom you have called (today)
from this world to yourself.

2

Grant that he (she) who was united with your Son in a
    death like his,
may also be one with him in his Resurrection.

Remember also our brothers and sisters
who have fallen asleep in the hope of the
    resurrection,
and all who have died in your mercy:
welcome them into the light of your face.
Have mercy on us all, we pray,
that with the Blessed Virgin Mary, Mother of God,
with blessed Joseph, her Spouse,
with the blessed Apostles,
and all the Saints who have pleased you
    throughout the ages,
we may merit to be co-heirs to eternal life,
and may praise and glorify you
through your Son, Jesus Christ.

(Concluding Doxology)

Through him, and with him, and in him,
O God, almighty Father,
in the unity of the Holy Spirit,
all glory and honour is yours,
for ever and ever.

All reply: **Amen.**

Continue with the Mass, as on p. 72.

(This Eucharistic Prayer may be used with any Preface and preferably on Sundays and feast days.)

KNEEL

You are indeed Holy, O Lord,
and all you have created
rightly gives you praise,
for through your Son our Lord Jesus Christ,
by the power and working of the Holy Spirit,
you give life to all things and make them holy,
and you never cease to gather a people to yourself,
so that from the rising of the sun to its setting
a pure sacrifice may be offered to your name.

Therefore, O Lord, we humbly implore you:
by the same Spirit graciously make holy
these gifts we have brought to you for
    consecration,
that they may become the Body and ✠ Blood
of your Son our Lord Jesus Christ,
at whose command we celebrate these mysteries.

For on the night he was betrayed
he himself took bread,
and, giving you thanks, he said the blessing,
broke the bread and gave it to his disciples,
    saying:

Take this, all of you, and eat of it,
for this is my Body,
which will be given up for you.

In a similar way, when supper was ended,
he took the chalice,

and, giving you thanks, he said the blessing,
and gave the chalice to his disciples, saying:

Take this, all of you, and drink from it,
for this is the chalice of my Blood,
the Blood of the new and eternal covenant,
which will be poured out for you and for many
for the forgiveness of sins.

Do this in memory of me.

Priest: The mystery of faith. *(Memorial Acclamation)*

PEOPLE:

A We proclaim your Death, O Lord,
and profess your Resurrection
until you come again.

B When we eat this Bread and drink this Cup,
we proclaim your Death, O Lord,
until you come again.

C Save us, Saviour of the world,
for by your Cross and Resurrection
you have set us free.

Therefore, O Lord, as we celebrate the memorial
of the saving Passion of your Son,
his wondrous Resurrection
and Ascension into heaven,
and as we look forward to his second coming,
we offer you in thanksgiving
this holy and living sacrifice.

Look, we pray, upon the oblation of your Church
and, recognizing the sacrificial Victim by whose
     death
you willed to reconcile us to yourself,

3 grant that we, who are nourished
by the Body and Blood of your Son
and filled with his Holy Spirit,
may become one body, one spirit in Christ.

May he make us
an eternal offering to you,
so that we may obtain an inheritance with your
    elect,
especially with the most Blessed Virgin Mary,
    Mother of God,
with blessed Joseph, her Spouse,
with your blessed Apostles and glorious Martyrs
(with Saint N.: the Saint of the day or Patron Saint)
and with all the Saints,
on whose constant intercession in your presence
we rely for unfailing help.

May this Sacrifice of our reconciliation,
we pray, O Lord,
advance the peace and salvation of all the world.
Be pleased to confirm in faith and charity
your pilgrim Church on earth,
with your servant N. our Pope and N. our Bishop,
the Order of Bishops, all the clergy,
and the entire people you have gained for your own.

Listen graciously to the prayers of this family,
whom you have summoned before you:
in your compassion, O merciful Father,
gather to yourself all your children
scattered throughout the world.

† To our departed brothers and sisters
and to all who were pleasing to you
at their passing from this life,
give kind admittance to your Kingdom.

3

There we hope to enjoy for ever the fullness of
    your glory
through Christ our Lord,
through whom you bestow on the world all that
    is good. †

(Concluding Doxology)

Through him, and with him, and in him,
O God, almighty Father,
in the unity of the Holy Spirit,
all glory and honour is yours,
for ever and ever.

All reply: **Amen.**

Continue with the Mass, as on p. 72.

---

* In Masses for the Dead the following may be said:

† Remember your servant N.
whom you have called (today)
from this world to yourself.
Grant that he (she) who was united with your Son in a
    death like his,
may also be one with him in his Resurrection,
when from the earth
he will raise up in the flesh those who have died,
and transform our lowly body
after the pattern of his own glorious body.
To our departed brothers and sisters, too,
and to all who were pleasing to you
at their passing from this life,
give kind admittance to your Kingdom.
There we hope to enjoy for ever the fullness of your glory,
when you will wipe away every tear from our eyes.
For seeing you, our God, as you are,
we shall be like you for all the ages
and praise you without end,
through Christ our Lord,
through whom you bestow on the world all that is good. †

℣. The Lord be with you.

STAND

℟. **And with your spirit.**

℣. Lift up your hearts.

℟. **We lift them up to the Lord.**

℣. Let us give thanks to the Lord our God.

℟. **It is right and just.**

It is truly right to give you thanks,
truly just to give you glory, Father most holy,
for you are the one God living and true,
existing before all ages and abiding for all eternity,
dwelling in unapproachable light;
yet you, who alone are good, the source of life,
have made all that is,
so that you might fill your creatures with blessings
and bring joy to many of them by the glory of your
    light.

And so, in your presence are countless hosts of
    Angels,
who serve you day and night
and, gazing upon the glory of your face,
glorify you without ceasing.

With them we, too, confess your name in exultation,
giving voice to every creature under heaven,
as we acclaim:

Holy, Holy, Holy Lord God of hosts.
Heaven and earth are full of your glory.
Hosanna in the highest.

**Blessed is he who comes in the name of the Lord. 4
Hosanna in the highest.**

KNEEL

We give you praise, Father most holy,
for you are great
and you have fashioned all your works
in wisdom and in love.
You formed man in your own image
and entrusted the whole world to his care,
so that in serving you alone, the Creator,
he might have dominion over all creatures.
And when through disobedience he had lost your
    friendship,
you did not abandon him to the domain of death.
For you came in mercy to the aid of all,
so that those who seek might find you.
Time and again you offered them covenants
and through the prophets
taught them to look forward to salvation.

And you so loved the world, Father most holy,
that in the fullness of time
you sent your Only Begotten Son to be our Saviour.
Made incarnate by the Holy Spirit
and born of the Virgin Mary,
he shared our human nature
in all things but sin.
To the poor he proclaimed the good news of
    salvation,
to prisoners, freedom,
and to the sorrowful of heart, joy.
To accomplish your plan,
he gave himself up to death,
and, rising from the dead,
he destroyed death and restored life.

4 And that we might live no longer for ourselves
but for him who died and rose again for us,
he sent the Holy Spirit from you, Father,
as the first fruits for those who believe,
so that, bringing to perfection his work in the world,
he might sanctify creation to the full.

Therefore, O Lord, we pray:
may this same Holy Spirit
graciously sanctify these offerings,
that they may become
the Body and ✠ Blood of our Lord Jesus Christ
for the celebration of this great mystery,
which he himself left us
as an eternal covenant.

For when the hour had come
for him to be glorified by you, Father most holy,
having loved his own who were in the world,
he loved them to the end:
and while they were at supper,
he took bread, blessed and broke it,
and gave it to his disciples, saying:

Take this, all of you, and eat of it,
for this is my Body,
which will be given up for you.

In a similar way,
taking the chalice filled with the fruit of the vine,
he gave thanks,
and gave the chalice to his disciples, saying:

Take this, all of you, and drink from it,
for this is the chalice of my Blood,
the Blood of the new and eternal covenant,

4

which will be poured out for you and for many for the forgiveness of sins.

Do this in memory of me.

Priest: **The mystery of faith.** *(Memorial Acclamation)*

PEOPLE:

A We proclaim your Death, O Lord,
and profess your Resurrection
until you come again.

B When we eat this Bread and drink this Cup,
we proclaim your Death, O Lord,
until you come again.

C Save us, Saviour of the world,
for by your Cross and Resurrection
you have set us free.

Therefore, O Lord,
as we now celebrate the memorial of our redemption,
we remember Christ's Death
and his descent to the realm of the dead,
we proclaim his Resurrection
and his Ascension to your right hand,
and, as we await his coming in glory,
we offer you his Body and Blood,
the sacrifice acceptable to you
which brings salvation to the whole world.

Look, O Lord, upon the Sacrifice
which you yourself have provided for your Church,
and grant in your loving kindness
to all who partake of this one Bread and one Chalice
that, gathered into one body by the Holy Spirit,

4 they may truly become a living sacrifice in Christ
to the praise of your glory.

Therefore, Lord, remember now
all for whom we offer this sacrifice:
especially your servant *N.* our Pope,
N. our Bishop, and the whole Order of Bishops,
all the clergy,
those who take part in this offering,
those gathered here before you,
your entire people,
and all who seek you with a sincere heart.

Remember also
those who have died in the peace of your Christ
and all the dead,
whose faith you alone have known.

To all of us, your children,
grant, O merciful Father,
that we may enter into a heavenly inheritance
with the Blessed Virgin Mary, Mother of God,
with blessed Joseph, her Spouse,
and with your Apostles and Saints in your
    Kingdom.
There, with the whole of creation,
freed from the corruption of sin and death,
may we glorify you through Christ our Lord,
through whom you bestow on the world all that
    is good.

(Concluding Doxology)

Through him, and with him, and in him,
O God, almighty Father,
in the unity of the Holy Spirit,
all glory and honour is yours,
for ever and ever.
All reply: **Amen.**

Continue with the Mass, as on p. 72.

EUCHARISTIC PRAYER FOR RECONCILIATION I

℣. The Lord be with you.
℟. **And with your spirit.**

℣. Lift up your hearts.
℟. **We lift them up to the Lord.**

℣. Let us give thanks to the Lord our God.
℟. **It is right and just.**

It is truly right and just
that we should always give you thanks,
Lord, holy Father, almighty and eternal God.

For you do not cease to spur us on
to possess a more abundant life
and, being rich in mercy,
you constantly offer pardon
and call on sinners
to trust in your forgiveness alone.

Never did you turn away from us,
and, though time and again we have broken your
    covenant,
you have bound the human family to yourself
through Jesus your Son, our Redeemer,
with a new bond of love so tight
that it can never be undone.

Even now you set before your people
a time of grace and reconciliation,
and, as they turn back to you in spirit,
you grant them hope in Christ Jesus
and a desire to be of service to all,

43

R 1 while they entrust themselves
more fully to the Holy Spirit.

And so, filled with wonder,
we extol the power of your love,
and, proclaiming our joy
at the salvation that comes from you,
we join in the heavenly hymn of countless hosts,
as without end we acclaim:

**Holy, Holy, Holy Lord God of hosts.
Heaven and earth are full of your glory.
Hosanna in the highest.
Blessed is he who comes in the name of the Lord.
Hosanna in the highest.**

KNEEL

You are indeed Holy, O Lord,
and from the world's beginning
are ceaselessly at work,
so that the human race may become holy,
just as you yourself are holy.

Look, we pray, upon your people's offerings
and pour out on them the power of your Spirit,
that they may become the Body and ✠ Blood
of your beloved Son, Jesus Christ,
in whom we, too, are your sons and daughters.

Indeed, though we once were lost
and could not approach you,
you loved us with the greatest love:
for your Son, who alone is just,
handed himself over to death,

and did not disdain to be nailed for our sake
to the wood of the Cross.

But before his arms were outstretched between
    heaven and earth,
to become the lasting sign of your covenant,
he desired to celebrate the Passover with his
    disciples.

As he ate with them,
he took bread
and, giving you thanks, he said the blessing,
broke the bread and gave it to them, saying:

Take this, all of you, and eat of it,
for this is my Body,
which will be given up for you.

In a similar way, when supper was ended,
knowing that he was about to reconcile all things
    in himself
through his Blood to be shed on the Cross,
he took the chalice, filled with the fruit of the
    vine,
and once more giving you thanks,
handed the chalice to his disciples, saying:

Take this, all of you, and drink from it,
for this is the chalice of my Blood,
the Blood of the new and eternal covenant,
which will be poured out for you and for many
for the forgiveness of sins.
Do this in memory of me.

R1

Priest: **The mystery of faith.** *(Memorial Acclamation)*

PEOPLE:

A **We proclaim your Death, O Lord,**
and profess your Resurrection
until you come again.

B **When we eat this Bread and drink this Cup,**
we proclaim your Death, O Lord,
until you come again.

C **Save us, Saviour of the world,**
for by your Cross and Resurrection
you have set us free.

Therefore, as we celebrate
the memorial of your Son Jesus Christ,
who is our Passover and our surest peace,
we celebrate his Death and Resurrection from the
    dead,
and looking forward to his blessed Coming,
we offer you, who are our faithful and merciful
    God,
this sacrificial Victim
who reconciles to you the human race.

Look kindly, most compassionate Father,
on those you unite to yourself
by the Sacrifice of your Son,
and grant that, by the power of the Holy Spirit,
as they partake of this one Bread and one
    Chalice,
they may be gathered into one Body in Christ,
who heals every division.

Be pleased to keep us always
in communion of mind and heart,
together with N. our Pope and N. our Bishop.
Help us to work together
for the coming of your Kingdom,
until the hour when we stand before you,
Saints among the Saints in the halls of heaven,
with the Blessed Virgin Mary, Mother of God,
the blessed Apostles and all the Saints,
and with our deceased brothers and sisters,
whom we humbly commend to your mercy.

Then, freed at last from the wound of corruption
and made fully into a new creation,
we shall sing to you with gladness
the thanksgiving of Christ,
who lives for all eternity.

(Concluding Doxology)

Through him, and with him, and in him,
O God, almighty Father,
in the unity of the Holy Spirit,
all glory and honour is yours,
for ever and ever.

The people respond: **Amen.**

Continue with the Mass, as on p. 72.

EUCHARISTIC PRAYER FOR RECONCILIATION II

STAND

℣. The Lord be with you.

℟. **And with your spirit.**

℣. Lift up your hearts.

℟. **We lift them up to the Lord.**

℣. Let us give thanks to the Lord our God.

℟. **It is right and just.**

It is truly right and just
that we should give you thanks and praise,
O God, almighty Father,
for all you do in this world,
through our Lord Jesus Christ.

For though the human race
is divided by dissension and discord,
yet we know that by testing us
you change our hearts
to prepare them for reconciliation.

Even more, by your Spirit you move human hearts
that enemies may speak to each other again,
adversaries join hands,
and peoples seek to meet together.

By the working of your power
it comes about, O Lord,
that hatred is overcome by love,
revenge gives way to forgiveness,
and discord is changed to mutual respect.

Therefore, as we give you ceaseless thanks
with the choirs of heaven,

R 2

we cry out to your majesty on earth,
and without end we acclaim:

**Holy, Holy, Holy Lord God of hosts.
Heaven and earth are full of your glory.
Hosanna in the highest.
Blessed is he who comes in the name of the Lord.
Hosanna in the highest.**

`KNEEL`

You, therefore, almighty Father,
we bless through Jesus Christ your Son,
who comes in your name.
He himself is the Word that brings salvation,
the hand you extend to sinners,
the way by which your peace is offered to us.
When we ourselves had turned away from you
on account of our sins,
you brought us back to be reconciled, O Lord,
so that, converted at last to you,
we might love one another
through your Son,
whom for our sake you handed over to death.

And now, celebrating the reconciliation
Christ has brought us,
we entreat you:
sanctify these gifts by the outpouring of your
    Spirit,
that they may become the Body and ✠ Blood of
    your Son,
whose command we fulfill
when we celebrate these mysteries.

For when about to give his life to set us free,
as he reclined at supper,

R 2 he himself took bread into his hands,
and, giving you thanks, he said the blessing,
broke the bread and gave it to his disciples, saying:

Take this, all of you, and eat of it,
for this is my Body,
which will be given up for you.

In a similar way, on that same evening,
he took the chalice of blessing in his hands,
confessing your mercy,
and gave the chalice to his disciples, saying:

Take this, all of you, and drink from it,
for this is the chalice of my Blood,
the Blood of the new and eternal covenant,
which will be poured out for you and for many
for the forgiveness of sins.

Do this in memory of me.

Priest: The mystery of faith. *(Memorial Acclamation)*

PEOPLE:

A We proclaim your Death, O Lord,
and profess your Resurrection
until you come again.

B When we eat this Bread and drink this Cup,
we proclaim your Death, O Lord,
until you come again.

C Save us, Saviour of the world,
for by your Cross and Resurrection
you have set us free.

Celebrating, therefore, the memorial
of the Death and Resurrection of your Son,
who left us this pledge of his love,
we offer you what you have bestowed on us,
the Sacrifice of perfect reconciliation.

R 2

Holy Father, we humbly beseech you
to accept us also, together with your Son,
and in this saving banquet
graciously to endow us with his very Spirit,
who takes away everything
that estranges us from one another.

May he make your Church a sign of unity
and an instrument of your peace among all people
and may he keep us in communion
with N. our Pope and N. our Bishop
and all the Bishops
and your entire people.

Just as you have gathered us now at the table of
  your Son,
so also bring us together,
with the glorious Virgin Mary, Mother of God,
with your blessed Apostles and all the Saints,
with our brothers and sisters
and those of every race and tongue
who have died in your friendship.
Bring us to share with them the unending banquet
  of unity
in a new heaven and a new earth,
where the fullness of your peace will shine forth
in Christ Jesus our Lord.

(Concluding Doxology)

Through him, and with him, and in him,
O God, almighty Father,
in the unity of the Holy Spirit,
all glory and honour is yours,
for ever and ever.

The people respond: **Amen.**

Continue with the Mass, as on p. 72.

V 1 EUCHARISTIC PRAYER FOR USE IN MASSES FOR VARIOUS NEEDS I

STAND

℣. The Lord be with you.
℟. **And with your spirit.**

℣. Lift up your hearts.
℟. **We lift them up to the Lord.**

℣. Let us give thanks to the Lord our God.
℟. **It is right and just.**

It is truly right to give you thanks
and raise to you a hymn of glory and praise,
O Lord, Father of infinite goodness.

For by the word of your Son's Gospel
you have brought together one Church
from every people, tongue, and nation,
and, having filled her with life by the power of
    your Spirit,
you never cease through her
to gather the whole human race into one.

Manifesting the covenant of your love,
she dispenses without ceasing
the blessed hope of your Kingdom
and shines bright as the sign of your faithfulness,
which in Christ Jesus our Lord
you promised would last for eternity.

And so, with all the Powers of heaven,
we worship you constantly on earth,
while, with all the Church,
as one voice we acclaim:

V
1

Holy, Holy, Holy Lord God of hosts.
Heaven and earth are full of your glory.
Hosanna in the highest.
Blessed is he who comes in the name of the Lord.
Hosanna in the highest.

KNEEL

You are indeed Holy and to be glorified, O God,
who love the human race
and who always walk with us on the journey of life.
Blessed indeed is your Son,
present in our midst
when we are gathered by his love,
and when, as once for the disciples, so now for us,
he opens the Scriptures and breaks the bread.

Therefore, Father most merciful,
we ask that you send forth your Holy Spirit
to sanctify these gifts of bread and wine,
that they may become for us
the Body and ✠ Blood
of our Lord Jesus Christ.

On the day before he was to suffer,
on the night of the Last Supper,
he took bread and said the blessing,
broke the bread and gave it to his disciples, saying:

Take this, all of you, and eat of it,
for this is my Body,
which will be given up for you.

In a similar way, when supper was ended,
he took the chalice, gave you thanks
and gave the chalice to his disciples, saying:

V1 *Take this, all of you, and drink from it,*
for this is the chalice of my Blood,
the Blood of the new and eternal covenant,
which will be poured out for you and for many
for the forgiveness of sins.

Do this in memory of me.

Priest: The mystery of faith. *(Memorial Acclamation)*

PEOPLE:

A We proclaim your Death, O Lord,
   and profess your Resurrection
   until you come again.

B When we eat this Bread and drink this Cup,
   we proclaim your Death, O Lord,
   until you come again.

C Save us, Saviour of the world,
   for by your Cross and Resurrection
   you have set us free.

Therefore, holy Father,
as we celebrate the memorial of Christ your Son,
   our Saviour,
whom you led through his Passion and Death on
   the Cross
to the glory of the Resurrection,
and whom you have seated at your right hand,
we proclaim the work of your love until he comes
   again
and we offer you the Bread of life
and the Chalice of blessing.

Look with favour on the oblation of your Church,
in which we show forth

V1

the paschal Sacrifice of Christ that has been handed
   on to us,
and grant that, by the power of the Spirit of your
   love,
we may be counted now and until the day of
   eternity
among the members of your Son,
in whose Body and Blood we have communion.

Lord, renew your Church (which is in N.)
by the light of the Gospel.
Strengthen the bond of unity
between the faithful and the pastors of your
   people,
together with N. our Pope, N. our Bishop,
and the whole Order of Bishops,
that in a world torn by strife
your people may shine forth
as a prophetic sign of unity and concord.

Remember our brothers and sisters (N. and N.),
who have fallen asleep in the peace of your Christ,
and all the dead, whose faith you alone have
   known.
Admit them to rejoice in the light of your face,
and in the resurrection give them the fullness of
   life.

Grant also to us,
when our earthly pilgrimage is done,
that we may come to an eternal dwelling place
and live with you for ever;
there, in communion with the Blessed Virgin Mary,
   Mother of God,
with the Apostles and Martyrs,

V1 (with Saint *N.*: the Saint of the day or Patron)
and with all the Saints,
we shall praise and exalt you
through Jesus Christ, your Son.

(Concluding Doxology)

Through him, and with him, and in him,
O God, almighty Father,
in the unity of the Holy Spirit,
all glory and honour is yours,
for ever and ever.

The people respond: **Amen.**

Continue with the Mass, as on p. 72.

EUCHARISTIC PRAYER FOR USE IN MASSES FOR VARIOUS NEEDS II

STAND

℣. The Lord be with you.
℟. **And with your spirit.**

℣. Lift up your hearts.
℟. **We lift them up to the Lord.**

℣. Let us give thanks to the Lord our God.
℟. **It is right and just.**

It is truly right and just, our duty and our
    salvation,
always and everywhere to give you thanks,
Lord, holy Father,
creator of the world and source of all life.

For you never forsake the works of your wisdom,
but by your providence are even now at work in
    our midst.
With mighty hand and outstretched arm
you led your people Israel through the desert.
Now, as your Church makes her pilgrim journey
    in the world,
you always accompany her
by the power of the Holy Spirit
and lead her along the paths of time
to the eternal joy of your Kingdom,
through Christ our Lord.

And so, with the Angels and Saints,
we, too, sing the hymn of your glory,
as without end we acclaim:

**V
2**

**Holy, Holy, Holy Lord God of hosts.
Heaven and earth are full of your glory.
Hosanna in the highest.
Blessed is he who comes in the name of the Lord.
Hosanna in the highest.**

KNEEL

You are indeed Holy and to be glorified, O God,
who love the human race
and who always walk with us on the journey of life.
Blessed indeed is your Son,
present in our midst
when we are gathered by his love,
and when, as once for the disciples, so now for us,
he opens the Scriptures and breaks the bread.

Therefore, Father most merciful,
we ask that you send forth your Holy Spirit
to sanctify these gifts of bread and wine,
that they may become for us
the Body and ✠ Blood
of our Lord Jesus Christ.

On the day before he was to suffer,
on the night of the Last Supper,
he took bread and said the blessing,
broke the bread and gave it to his disciples, saying:

*Take this, all of you, and eat of it,
for this is my Body,
which will be given up for you.*

In a similar way, when supper was ended,
he took the chalice, gave you thanks
and gave the chalice to his disciples, saying:

**V
2**

Take this, all of you, and drink from it,
for this is the chalice of my Blood,
the Blood of the new and eternal covenant,
which will be poured out for you and for many
for the forgiveness of sins.

Do this in memory of me.

Priest: **The mystery of faith.** *(Memorial Acclamation)*

PEOPLE:

A **We proclaim your Death, O Lord,**
   and profess your Resurrection
   until you come again.

B **When we eat this Bread and drink this Cup,**
   we proclaim your Death, O Lord,
   until you come again.

C **Save us, Saviour of the world,**
   for by your Cross and Resurrection
   you have set us free.

Therefore, holy Father,
as we celebrate the memorial of Christ your Son,
   our Saviour,
whom you led through his Passion and Death on
   the Cross
to the glory of the Resurrection,
and whom you have seated at your right hand,
we proclaim the work of your love until he comes
   again
and we offer you the Bread of life
and the Chalice of blessing.

Look with favour on the oblation of your Church,
in which we show forth

**V
2** the paschal Sacrifice of Christ that has been handed
on to us,
and grant that, by the power of the Spirit of your
love,
we may be counted now and until the day of
eternity
among the members of your Son,
in whose Body and Blood we have communion.

And so, having called us to your table, Lord,
confirm us in unity,
so that, together with *N.* our Pope and *N.* our
Bishop,
with all Bishops, Priests and Deacons,
and your entire people,
as we walk your ways with faith and hope,
we may strive to bring joy and trust into the world.

Remember our brothers and sisters (*N.* and *N.*),
who have fallen asleep in the peace of your Christ,
and all the dead, whose faith you alone have
known.
Admit them to rejoice in the light of your face,
and in the resurrection give them the fullness of
life.

Grant also to us,
when our earthly pilgrimage is done,
that we may come to an eternal dwelling place
and live with you for ever;
there, in communion with the Blessed Virgin Mary,
Mother of God,
with the Apostles and Martyrs,
(with Saint *N.*: the Saint of the day or Patron)

and with all the Saints,
we shall praise and exalt you
through Jesus Christ, your Son.

(Concluding Doxology)

Through him, and with him, and in him,
O God, almighty Father,
in the unity of the Holy Spirit,
all glory and honour is yours,
for ever and ever.

The people respond: **Amen.**

Continue with the Mass, as on p. 72.

V 3 EUCHARISTIC PRAYER FOR USE IN MASSES FOR VARIOUS NEEDS III

STAND

℣. The Lord be with you.

℟. **And with your spirit.**

℣. Lift up your hearts.

℟. **We lift them up to the Lord.**

℣. Let us give thanks to the Lord our God.

℟. **It is right and just.**

It is truly right and just, our duty and our salvation,
always and everywhere to give you thanks,
holy Father, Lord of heaven and earth,
through Christ our Lord.

For by your Word you created the world
and you govern all things in harmony.
You gave us the same Word made flesh as Mediator,
and he has spoken your words to us
and called us to follow him.
He is the way that leads us to you,
the truth that sets us free,
the life that fills us with gladness.

Through your Son
you gather men and women,
whom you made for the glory of your name,
into one family,
redeemed by the Blood of his Cross
and signed with the seal of the Spirit.

Therefore, now and for ages unending,
with all the Angels,

V
3

we proclaim your glory,
as in joyful celebration we acclaim:

Holy, Holy, Holy Lord God of hosts.
Heaven and earth are full of your glory.
Hosanna in the highest.
Blessed is he who comes in the name of the Lord.
Hosanna in the highest.

KNEEL

You are indeed Holy and to be glorified, O God,
who love the human race
and who always walk with us on the journey of life.
Blessed indeed is your Son,
present in our midst
when we are gathered by his love,
and when, as once for the disciples, so now for us,
he opens the Scriptures and breaks the bread.

Therefore, Father most merciful,
we ask that you send forth your Holy Spirit
to sanctify these gifts of bread and wine,
that they may become for us
the Body and ✠ Blood
of our Lord Jesus Christ.

On the day before he was to suffer,
on the night of the Last Supper,
he took bread and said the blessing,
broke the bread and gave it to his disciples, saying:

Take this, all of you, and eat of it,
for this is my Body,
which will be given up for you.

V 3 In a similar way, when supper was ended,
he took the chalice, gave you thanks
and gave the chalice to his disciples, saying:

Take this, all of you, and drink from it,
for this is the chalice of my Blood,
the Blood of the new and eternal covenant,
which will be poured out for you and for many
for the forgiveness of sins.

Do this in memory of me.

Priest: The mystery of faith. *(Memorial Acclamation)*

PEOPLE:

A We proclaim your Death, O Lord,
and profess your Resurrection
until you come again.

B When we eat this Bread and drink this Cup,
we proclaim your Death, O Lord,
until you come again.

C Save us, Saviour of the world,
for by your Cross and Resurrection
you have set us free.

Therefore, holy Father,
as we celebrate the memorial of Christ your Son,
    our Saviour,
whom you led through his Passion and Death on
    the Cross
to the glory of the Resurrection,
and whom you have seated at your right hand,
we proclaim the work of your love until he comes
    again
and we offer you the Bread of life
and the Chalice of blessing.

V 3

Look with favour on the oblation of your Church,
in which we show forth
the paschal Sacrifice of Christ that has been handed
   on to us,
and grant that, by the power of the Spirit of your
   love,
we may be counted now and until the day of
   eternity
among the members of your Son,
in whose Body and Blood we have communion.

By our partaking of this mystery, almighty Father,
give us life through your Spirit,
grant that we may be conformed to the image of
   your Son,
and confirm us in the bond of communion,
together with N. our Pope and N. our Bishop,
with all other Bishops,
with Priests and Deacons,
and with your entire people.

Grant that all the faithful of the Church,
looking into the signs of the times by the light of
   faith,
may constantly devote themselves
to the service of the Gospel.

Keep us attentive to the needs of all
that, sharing their grief and pain,
their joy and hope,
we may faithfully bring them the good news of
   salvation
and go forward with them
along the way of your Kingdom.

**V
3** Remember our brothers and sisters (N. and N.),
who have fallen asleep in the peace of your Christ,
and all the dead, whose faith you alone have known.
Admit them to rejoice in the light of your face,
and in the resurrection give them the fullness of
    life.

Grant also to us,
when our earthly pilgrimage is done,
that we may come to an eternal dwelling place
and live with you for ever;
there, in communion with the Blessed Virgin Mary,
    Mother of God,
with the Apostles and Martyrs,
(with Saint N.: the Saint of the day or Patron)
and with all the Saints,
we shall praise and exalt you
through Jesus Christ, your Son.

(Concluding Doxology)

Through him, and with him, and in him,
O God, almighty Father,
in the unity of the Holy Spirit,
all glory and honour is yours,
for ever and ever.

The people respond: **Amen.**

Continue with the Mass, as on p. 72.

EUCHARISTIC PRAYER FOR USE IN MASSES FOR VARIOUS NEEDS IV

STAND

℣. The Lord be with you.

℟. **And with your spirit.**

℣. Lift up your hearts.

℟. **We lift them up to the Lord.**

℣. Let us give thanks to the Lord our God.

℟. **It is right and just.**

It is truly right and just, our duty and our salvation,
always and everywhere to give you thanks,
Father of mercies and faithful God.

For you have given us Jesus Christ, your Son,
as our Lord and Redeemer.

He always showed compassion
for children and for the poor,
for the sick and for sinners,
and he became a neighbour
to the oppressed and the afflicted.

By word and deed he announced to the world
that you are our Father
and that you care for all your sons and daughters.

And so, with all the Angels and Saints,
we exalt and bless your name
and sing the hymn of your glory,
as without end we acclaim:

V 4 Holy, Holy, Holy Lord God of hosts.
Heaven and earth are full of your glory.
Hosanna in the highest.
Blessed is he who comes in the name of the Lord.
Hosanna in the highest.

KNEEL

You are indeed Holy and to be glorified, O God,
who love the human race
and who always walk with us on the journey of life.
Blessed indeed is your Son,
present in our midst
when we are gathered by his love
and when, as once for the disciples, so now for us,
he opens the Scriptures and breaks the bread.

Therefore, Father most merciful,
we ask that you send forth your Holy Spirit
to sanctify these gifts of bread and wine,
that they may become for us
the Body and ✠ Blood
of our Lord Jesus Christ.

On the day before he was to suffer,
on the night of the Last Supper,
he took bread and said the blessing,
broke the bread and gave it to his disciples, saying:

Take this, all of you, and eat of it,
for this is my Body,
which will be given up for you.

In a similar way, when supper was ended,
he took the chalice, gave you thanks
and gave the chalice to his disciples, saying:

**V
4**

Take this, all of you, and drink from it,
for this is the chalice of my Blood,
the Blood of the new and eternal covenant,
which will be poured out for you and for many
for the forgiveness of sins.

Do this in memory of me.

Priest: The mystery of faith. *(Memorial Acclamation)*

PEOPLE:

A We proclaim your Death, O Lord,
　　and profess your Resurrection
　　until you come again.

B When we eat this Bread and drink this Cup,
　　we proclaim your Death, O Lord,
　　until you come again.

C Save us, Saviour of the world,
　　for by your Cross and Resurrection
　　you have set us free.

Therefore, holy Father,
as we celebrate the memorial of Christ your Son,
　　our Saviour,
whom you led through his Passion and Death on
　　the Cross
to the glory of the Resurrection,
and whom you have seated at your right hand,
we proclaim the work of your love until he comes
　　again
and we offer you the Bread of life
and the Chalice of blessing.

Look with favour on the oblation of your Church,
in which we show forth

V 4 the paschal Sacrifice of Christ that has been handed
on to us,
and grant that, by the power of the Spirit of your
love,
we may be counted now and until the day of
eternity
among the members of your Son,
in whose Body and Blood we have communion.

Bring your Church, O Lord,
to perfect faith and charity,
together with N. our Pope and N. our Bishop,
with all Bishops, Priests and Deacons,
and the entire people you have made your own.

Open our eyes
to the needs of our brothers and sisters;
inspire in us words and actions
to comfort those who labour and are burdened.
Make us serve them truly,
after the example of Christ and at his command.
And may your Church stand as a living witness
to truth and freedom,
to peace and justice,
that all people may be raised up to a new hope.

Remember our brothers and sisters (N. and N.),
who have fallen asleep in the peace of your Christ,
and all the dead, whose faith you alone have
known.
Admit them to rejoice in the light of your face,
and in the resurrection give them the fullness of
life.

V 4

Grant also to us,
when our earthly pilgrimage is done,
that we may come to an eternal dwelling place
and live with you for ever;
there, in communion with the Blessed Virgin Mary,
    Mother of God,
with the Apostles and Martyrs,
(with Saint N.: the Saint of the day or Patron)
and with all the Saints,
we shall praise and exalt you
through Jesus Christ, your Son.

(Concluding Doxology)

Through him, and with him, and in him,
O God, almighty Father,
in the unity of the Holy Spirit,
all glory and honour is yours,
for ever and ever.

The people respond: **Amen.**

Continue with the Mass, as on p. 72.

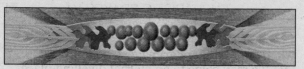

THE COMMUNION RITE

To prepare for the paschal meal, to welcome the Lord, we pray for forgiveness and exchange a sign of peace. Before eating Christ's Body and drinking his Blood, we must be one with him and with all our brothers and sisters in the Church.

24 THE LORD'S PRAYER

`STAND`

Priest: At the Saviour's command
and formed by divine teaching,
we dare to say:

Priest and **PEOPLE**:
**Our Father, who art in heaven,
hallowed be thy name;
thy kingdom come;
thy will be done
on earth as it is in heaven.
Give us this day our daily bread,
and forgive us our trespasses,
as we forgive those who trespass against us;
and lead us not into temptation,
but deliver us from evil.**

Priest: Deliver us, Lord, we pray, from every evil,
graciously grant us peace in our days,
that, by the help of your mercy,
we may be always free from sin
and safe from all distress,
as we await the blessed hope
and the coming of our Saviour, Jesus
Christ.

PEOPLE: **For the kingdom,**
the power and the glory are yours
now and for ever.

25 SIGN OF PEACE

The Church is a community of Christians joined by the Spirit
in love. It needs to express, deepen, and restore its peaceful
unity before eating the one Body of the Lord and drinking from
the one cup of salvation. We do this by a sign of peace.

The Priest says the prayer for peace:

Lord Jesus Christ,
who said to your Apostles:
Peace I leave you, my peace I give you,
look not on our sins,
but on the faith of your Church,
and graciously grant her peace and unity
in accordance with your will.
Who live and reign for ever and ever.

PEOPLE: **Amen.**

Priest: The peace of the Lord be with you always.

PEOPLE: **And with your spirit.**

Deacon (or Priest):
  Let us offer each other the sign of peace.

The people exchange a sign of peace, communion and
charity, according to local customs.

26 LAMB OF GOD

Christians are gathered for the "breaking of the bread," another
name for the Mass. In Communion, though many we are made
one body in the one bread, which is Christ.

The Priest breaks the host over the paten and places a small piece in the chalice, saying quietly:

May this mingling of the Body and Blood
of our Lord Jesus Christ
bring eternal life to us who receive it.

Meanwhile the following is sung or said:

PEOPLE:

> **Lamb of God, you take away the sins of the world,**
> **have mercy on us.**
> **Lamb of God, you take away the sins of the world,**
> **have mercy on us.**
> **Lamb of God, you take away the sins of the world,**
> **grant us peace.**

The invocation may even be repeated several times if the breaking of the bread is prolonged. Only the final time, however, is grant us peace *said.*

We pray in silence and then voice words of humility and hope
as our final preparation before meeting Christ in the Eucharist.

Before Communion, the Priest says quietly one of the following prayers:

Lord Jesus Christ, Son of the living God,
who, by the will of the Father
and the work of the Holy Spirit,
through your Death gave life to the world,
free me by this, your most holy Body and Blood,
from all my sins and from every evil;
keep me always faithful to your commandments,
and never let me be parted from you.

——————— **OR** ———————

May the receiving of your Body and Blood,
Lord Jesus Christ,
not bring me to judgment and condemnation,
but through your loving mercy
be for me protection in mind and body
and a healing remedy.

27 INVITATION TO COMMUNION

The Priest genuflects, takes the host and, holding it slightly raised above the paten or above the chalice, while facing the people, says aloud:

Priest: Behold the Lamb of God,
behold him who takes away the sins of the world.
Blessed are those called to the supper of the Lamb.

Priest and **PEOPLE** (once only):

**Lord, I am not worthy
that you should enter under my roof,
but only say the word
and my soul shall be healed.**

Before reverently consuming the Body of Christ, the Priest says quietly:

May the Body of Christ
keep me safe for eternal life.

Then, before reverently consuming the Blood of Christ, he takes the chalice and says quietly:

May the Blood of Christ
keep me safe for eternal life.

28 COMMUNION

He then gives Communion to the people.

Priest: **The Body of Christ.** Communicant: **Amen.**
Priest: **The Blood of Christ.** Communicant: **Amen.**

The Communion Psalm or other appropriate chant is sung while Communion is given to the faithful. If there is no singing, the Communion Antiphon is said.

→ **Turn to Today's Mass**

The vessels are purified by the Priest or Deacon or acolyte. Meanwhile he says quietly:

What has passed our lips as food, O Lord,
may we possess in purity of heart,
that what has been given to us in time
may be our healing for eternity.

After Communion there may be a period of sacred silence, or a canticle of praise or a hymn may be sung.

29 PRAYER AFTER COMMUNION   STAND

The Priest prays in our name that we may live the life of faith since we have been strengthened by Christ himself. Our *Amen* makes his prayer our own.

Priest: **Let us pray.**

Priest and people may pray silently for a while unless silence has just been observed. Then the Priest says the Prayer after Communion.

→ **Turn to Today's Mass**

At the end, **PEOPLE: Amen.**

THE CONCLUDING RITES

We have heard God's Word and eaten the Body of Christ. Now it is time for us to leave, to do good works, to praise and bless the Lord in our daily lives.

30 SOLEMN BLESSING   `STAND`

After any brief announcements, the Blessing and Dismissal follow:

Priest: The Lord be with you.

PEOPLE: And with your spirit.

31 FINAL BLESSING

Priest: May almighty God bless you,
the Father, and the Son, ✠ and the Holy Spirit.

PEOPLE: Amen.

On certain days or occasions, this formula of blessing is preceded, in accordance with the rubrics, by another more solemn formula of blessing (pp. 97-105) or by a prayer over the people (pp. 105-110).

32 DISMISSAL

Deacon (or Priest):

A Go forth, the Mass is ended.

B Go and announce the Gospel of the Lord.

C Go in peace, glorifying the Lord by your life.

D Go in peace.

PEOPLE: Thanks be to God.

If any liturgical service follows immediately, the rites of dismissal are omitted.

RITE FOR THE BLESSING
AND SPRINKLING OF WATER

*If this rite is celebrated during Mass, it takes the place of
the usual Penitential Act at the beginning of Mass.*

*After the greeting, the Priest stands at his chair and
faces the people. With a vessel containing the water to
be blessed before him, he calls upon the people to pray in
these or similar words:*

Dear brethren (brothers and sisters),
let us humbly beseech the Lord our God
to bless this water he has created,
which will be sprinkled on us
as a memorial of our Baptism.
May he help us by his grace
to remain faithful to the Spirit we have received.

*And after a brief pause for silence, he continues with
hands joined:*

Almighty ever-living God,
who willed that through water,
the fountain of life and the source of purification,
even souls should be cleansed
and receive the gift of eternal life;
be pleased, we pray, to ✠ bless this water,
by which we seek protection on this your day, O Lord.
Renew the living spring of your grace within us
and grant that by this water we may be defended
from all ills of spirit and body,
and so approach you with hearts made clean
and worthily receive your salvation.
Through Christ our Lord. ℟. **Amen.**

Or:

Almighty Lord and God,
who are the source and origin of all life,

whether of body or soul,
we ask you to ✠ bless this water,
which we use in confidence
to implore forgiveness for our sins
and to obtain the protection of your grace
against all illness and every snare of the enemy.
Grant, O Lord, in your mercy,
that living waters may always spring up for our
    salvation,
and so may we approach you with a pure heart
and avoid all danger to body and soul.
Through Christ our Lord. ℟. **Amen.**

Or (during Easter Time):

Lord our God,
in your mercy be present to your people's prayers,
and, for us who recall the wondrous work of our
    creation
and the still greater work of our redemption,
graciously ✠ bless this water.
For you created water to make the fields fruitful
and to refresh and cleanse our bodies.
You also made water the instrument of your mercy:
for through water you freed your people from slavery
and quenched their thirst in the desert;
through water the Prophets proclaimed the new
    covenant
you were to enter upon with the human race;
and last of all,
through water, which Christ made holy in the Jordan,
you have renewed our corrupted nature
in the bath of regeneration.
Therefore, may this water be for us
a memorial of the Baptism we have received,
and grant that we may share
in the gladness of our brothers and sisters
who at Easter have received their Baptism.
Through Christ our Lord. ℟. **Amen.**

Where the circumstances of the place or the custom of the people suggest that the mixing of salt be preserved in the blessing of water, the Priest may bless salt, saying:

We humbly ask you, almighty God:
be pleased in your faithful love to bless ✠ this salt
you have created,
for it was you who commanded the prophet Elisha
to cast salt into water,
that impure water might be purified.
Grant, O Lord, we pray,
that, wherever this mixture of salt and water is sprinkled,
every attack of the enemy may be repulsed
and your Holy Spirit may be present
to keep us safe at all times.
Through Christ our Lord. ℟. **Amen.**

Then he pours the salt into the water, without saying anything.

Afterward, taking the aspergillum, the Priest sprinkles himself and the ministers, then the clergy and people, moving through the church, if appropriate.

Meanwhile, one of the following chants, or another appropriate chant is sung.

Outside Easter Time

ANTIPHON 1 Ps. 51(50).9
Sprinkle me with hyssop, O Lord, and I shall be cleansed; wash me and I shall be whiter than snow.

ANTIPHON 2 Ez. 36.25-26
I will pour clean water upon you, and you will be made clean of all your impurities, and I shall give you a new spirit, says the Lord.

HYMN Cf. 1 Pt. 1.3-5
Blessed be the God and Father of our Lord Jesus Christ, who in his great mercy has given us new birth into a living hope through the Resurrection of Jesus Christ from

the dead, into an inheritance that will not perish, preserved for us in heaven for the salvation to be revealed in the last time!

During Easter Time

ANTIPHON 1 Cf. Ez. 47.1-2, 9

I saw water flowing from the Temple, from its right-hand side, alleluia: and all to whom this water came were saved and shall say: Alleluia, alleluia.

ANTIPHON 2 Cf. Zeph. 3.8; Ez. 36.25

On the day of my resurrection, says the Lord, alleluia, I will gather the nations and assemble the kingdoms and I will pour clean water upon you, alleluia.

ANTIPHON 3 Cf. Dn. 3.77, 79

You springs and all that moves in the waters, sing a hymn to God, alleluia.

ANTIPHON 4 1 Pt. 2.9

O chosen race, royal priesthood, holy nation, proclaim the mighty works of him who called you out of darkness into his wonderful light, alleluia.

ANTIPHON 5

From your side, O Christ, bursts forth a spring of water, by which the squalor of the world is washed away and life is made new again, alleluia.

When he returns to his chair and the singing is over, the Priest stands facing the people and, with hands joined, says:

May almighty God cleanse us of our sins,
and through the celebration of this Eucharist
make us worthy to share at the table of his Kingdom.
℟. **Amen**.

Then, when it is prescribed, the hymn Gloria in excelsis (Glory to God in the highest) *is sung or said.*

PREFACES

PREFACE I OF ADVENT (1)

The two comings of Christ

(From the First Sunday of Advent to December 16)

It is truly right and just, our duty and our salvation,
always and everywhere to give you thanks,
Lord, holy Father, almighty and eternal God,
through Christ our Lord.

For he assumed at his first coming
the lowliness of human flesh,
and so fulfilled the design you formed long ago,
and opened for us the way to eternal salvation,
that, when he comes again in glory and majesty
and all is at last made manifest,
we who watch for that day
may inherit the great promise
in which now we dare to hope.

And so, with Angels and Archangels,
with Thrones and Dominions,
and with all the hosts and Powers of heaven,
we sing the hymn of your glory,
as without end we acclaim:

➜ No. 23, p. 23

PREFACE II OF ADVENT (2)

The twofold expectation of Christ

(From December 17 to December 24)

It is truly right and just, our duty and our salvation,
always and everywhere to give you thanks,
Lord, holy Father, almighty and eternal God,
through Christ our Lord.

For all the oracles of the prophets foretold him,
the Virgin Mother longed for him
with love beyond all telling,

82

John the Baptist sang of his coming
and proclaimed his presence when he came.

It is by his gift that already we rejoice
at the mystery of his Nativity,
so that he may find us watchful in prayer
and exultant in his praise.

And so, with Angels and Archangels,
with Thrones and Dominions,
and with all the hosts and Powers of heaven,
we sing the hymn of your glory,
as without end we acclaim: → No. 23, p. 23

PREFACE I OF THE NATIVITY OF THE LORD (3)

Christ the Light

(For the Nativity of the Lord, its Octave Day and within the Octave)

It is truly right and just, our duty and our salvation,
always and everywhere to give you thanks,
Lord, holy Father, almighty and eternal God.

For in the mystery of the Word made flesh
a new light of your glory has shone upon the eyes of our
   mind,
so that, as we recognize in him God made visible,
we may be caught up through him in love of things invisible.

And so, with Angels and Archangels,
with Thrones and Dominions,
and with all the hosts and Powers of heaven,
we sing the hymn of your glory,
as without end we acclaim: → No. 23, p. 23

PREFACE II OF THE NATIVITY OF THE LORD (4)

The restoration of all things in the Incarnation

(For the Nativity of the Lord, its Octave Day and within the Octave)

It is truly right and just, our duty and our salvation,
always and everywhere to give you thanks,
Lord, holy Father, almighty and eternal God,
through Christ our Lord.

For on the feast of this awe-filled mystery,
though invisible in his own divine nature,

he has appeared visibly in ours;
and begotten before all ages,
he has begun to exist in time;
so that, raising up in himself all that was cast down,
he might restore unity to all creation
and call straying humanity back to the heavenly Kingdom.

And so, with all the Angels, we praise you,
as in joyful celebration we acclaim: → No. 23, p. 23

PREFACE III OF THE NATIVITY OF THE LORD (5)

The exchange in the Incarnation of the Word

(For the Nativity of the Lord, its Octave Day and within the Octave)

It is truly right and just, our duty and our salvation,
always and everywhere to give you thanks,
Lord, holy Father, almighty and eternal God,
through Christ our Lord.

For through him the holy exchange that restores our life
has shone forth today in splendour:
when our frailty is assumed by your Word
not only does human mortality receive unending honour
but by this wondrous union we, too, are made eternal.

And so, in company with the choirs of Angels,
we praise you, and with joy we proclaim: → No. 23, p. 23

PREFACE I OF LENT (8)

The spiritual meaning of Lent

It is truly right and just, our duty and our salvation,
always and everywhere to give you thanks,
Lord, holy Father, almighty and eternal God,
through Christ our Lord.

For by your gracious gift each year
your faithful await the sacred paschal feasts
with the joy of minds made pure,
so that, more eagerly intent on prayer
and on the works of charity,
and participating in the mysteries
by which they have been reborn,

they may be led to the fullness of grace
that you bestow on your sons and daughters.

And so, with Angels and Archangels,
with Thrones and Dominions,
and with all the hosts and Powers of heaven,
we sing the hymn of your glory,
as without end we acclaim: → No. 23, p. 23

PREFACE II OF LENT (9)

Spiritual penance

It is truly right and just, our duty and our salvation,
always and everywhere to give you thanks,
Lord, holy Father, almighty and eternal God.

For you have given your children a sacred time
for the renewing and purifying of their hearts,
that, freed from disordered affections,
they may so deal with the things of this passing world
as to hold rather to the things that eternally endure.

And so, with all the Angels and Saints,
we praise you, as without end we acclaim: → No. 23, p. 23

PREFACE I OF EASTER I (21)

The Paschal Mystery

(Easter Vigil, Easter Sunday and during the Octave and Easter Time)

(At the Easter Vigil, is said "on this night"; on Easter Sunday and throughout the Octave
of Easter, is said "on this day"; on other days of Easter Time, is said "in this time.")

It is truly right and just, our duty and our salvation,
at all times to acclaim you, O Lord,
but (on this night / on this day / in this time) above all
to laud you yet more gloriously,
when Christ our Passover has been sacrificed.

For he is the true Lamb
who has taken away the sins of the world;
by dying he has destroyed our death,
and by rising, restored our life.

Therefore, overcome with paschal joy,
every land, every people exults in your praise
and even the heavenly Powers, with the angelic hosts,
sing together the unending hymn of your glory,
as they acclaim: → No. 23, p. 23

PREFACE II OF EASTER (22)

New life in Christ

It is truly right and just, our duty and our salvation,
at all times to acclaim you, O Lord,
but in this time above all to laud you yet more gloriously,
when Christ our Passover has been sacrificed.

Through him the children of light rise to eternal life
and the halls of the heavenly Kingdom
are thrown open to the faithful;
for his Death is our ransom from death,
and in his rising the life of all has risen.

Therefore, overcome with paschal joy,
every land, every people exults in your praise
and even the heavenly Powers, with the angelic hosts,
sing together the unending hymn of your glory,
as they acclaim: → No. 23, p. 23

PREFACE III OF EASTER (23)

Christ living and always interceding for us

It is truly right and just, our duty and our salvation,
at all times to acclaim you, O Lord,
but in this time above all to laud you yet more gloriously,
when Christ our Passover has been sacrificed.

He never ceases to offer himself for us
but defends us and ever pleads our cause before you:
he is the sacrificial Victim who dies no more,
the Lamb, once slain, who lives for ever.

Therefore, overcome with paschal joy,
every land, every people exults in your praise
and even the heavenly Powers, with the angelic hosts,
sing together the unending hymn of your glory,
as they acclaim: → No. 23, p. 23

PREFACE IV OF EASTER (24)

The restoration of the universe through the Paschal Mystery

It is truly right and just, our duty and our salvation,
at all times to acclaim you, O Lord,

but in this time above all to laud you yet more gloriously,
when Christ our Passover has been sacrificed.

For, with the old order destroyed,
a universe cast down is renewed,
and integrity of life is restored to us in Christ.

Therefore, overcome with paschal joy,
every land, every people exults in your praise
and even the heavenly Powers, with the angelic hosts,
sing together the unending hymn of your glory,
as they acclaim: → No. 23, p. 23

PREFACE V OF EASTER (25)

Christ, Priest and Victim

It is truly right and just, our duty and our salvation,
at all times to acclaim you, O Lord,
but in this time above all to laud you yet more gloriously,
when Christ our Passover has been sacrificed.

By the oblation of his Body,
he brought the sacrifices of old to fulfillment
in the reality of the Cross
and, by commending himself to you for our salvation,
showed himself the Priest, the Altar, and the Lamb of
sacrifice.

Therefore, overcome with paschal joy,
every land, every people exults in your praise
and even the heavenly Powers, with the angelic hosts,
sing together the unending hymn of your glory,
as they acclaim: → No. 23, p. 23

PREFACE I OF THE ASCENSION OF THE LORD (26)

The mystery of the Ascension
(Ascension to the Saturday before Pentecost inclusive)

It is truly right and just, our duty and our salvation,
always and everywhere to give you thanks,
Lord, holy Father, almighty and eternal God.

For the Lord Jesus, the King of glory,
conqueror of sin and death,

ascended (today) to the highest heavens,
as the Angels gazed in wonder.

Mediator between God and man,
judge of the world and Lord of hosts,
he ascended, not to distance himself from our lowly state
but that we, his members, might be confident of following
where he, our Head and Founder, has gone before.

Therefore, overcome with paschal joy,
every land, every people exults in your praise
and even the heavenly Powers, with the angelic hosts,
sing together the unending hymn of your glory,
as they acclaim: ➔ No. 23, p. 23

PREFACE II OF THE ASCENSION OF THE LORD (27)

The mystery of the Ascension
(Ascension to the Saturday before Pentecost inclusive)

It is truly right and just, our duty and our salvation,
always and everywhere to give you thanks,
Lord, holy Father, almighty and eternal God,
through Christ our Lord.

For after his Resurrection
he plainly appeared to all his disciples
and was taken up to heaven in their sight,
that he might make us sharers in his divinity.

Therefore, overcome with paschal joy,
every land, every people exults in your praise
and even the heavenly Powers, with the angelic hosts,
sing together the unending hymn of your glory,
as they acclaim: ➔ No. 23, p. 23

PREFACE I OF THE SUNDAYS IN ORDINARY TIME (29)

The Paschal Mystery and the People of God

It is truly right and just, our duty and our salvation,
always and everywhere to give you thanks,
Lord, holy Father, almighty and eternal God,
through Christ our Lord.

For through his Paschal Mystery,
he accomplished the marvellous deed,

by which he has freed us from the yoke of sin and death,
summoning us to the glory of being now called
a chosen race, a royal priesthood,
a holy nation, a people for your own possession,
to proclaim everywhere your mighty works,
for you have called us out of darkness
into your own wonderful light.

And so, with Angels and Archangels,
with Thrones and Dominions,
and with all the hosts and Powers of heaven,
we sing the hymn of your glory,
as without end we acclaim: → No. 23, p. 23

PREFACE II OF THE SUNDAYS IN ORDINARY TIME (30)

The mystery of salvation

It is truly right and just, our duty and our salvation,
always and everywhere to give you thanks,
Lord, holy Father, almighty and eternal God,
through Christ our Lord.

For out of compassion for the waywardness that is ours,
he humbled himself and was born of the Virgin;
by the passion of the Cross he freed us from unending
    death,
and by rising from the dead he gave us life eternal.

And so, with Angels and Archangels,
with Thrones and Dominions,
and with all the hosts and Powers of heaven,
we sing the hymn of your glory,
as without end we acclaim: → No. 23, p. 23

PREFACE III OF THE SUNDAYS IN ORDINARY TIME (31)

The salvation of man by a man

It is truly right and just, our duty and our salvation,
always and everywhere to give you thanks,
Lord, holy Father, almighty and eternal God.

For we know it belongs to your boundless glory,
that you came to the aid of mortal beings with your divinity
and even fashioned for us a remedy out of mortality itself,
that the cause of our downfall

might become the means of our salvation,
through Christ our Lord.

Through him the host of Angels adores your majesty
and rejoices in your presence for ever.
May our voices, we pray, join with theirs
in one chorus of exultant praise, as we acclaim:

➜ No. 23, p. 23

PREFACE IV OF THE SUNDAYS IN ORDINARY TIME (32)
The history of salvation

It is truly right and just, our duty and our salvation,
always and everywhere to give you thanks,
Lord, holy Father, almighty and eternal God,
through Christ our Lord.

For by his birth he brought renewal
to humanity's fallen state,
and by his suffering, cancelled out our sins;
by his rising from the dead
he has opened the way to eternal life,
and by ascending to you, O Father,
he has unlocked the gates of heaven.

And so, with the company of Angels and Saints,
we sing the hymn of your praise,
as without end we acclaim: ➜ No. 23, p. 23

PREFACE V OF THE SUNDAYS IN ORDINARY TIME (33)
Creation

It is truly right and just, our duty and our salvation,
always and everywhere to give you thanks,
Lord, holy Father, almighty and eternal God.

For you laid the foundations of the world
and have arranged the changing of times and seasons;
you formed man in your own image
and set humanity over the whole world in all its wonder,
to rule in your name over all you have made
and for ever praise you in your mighty works,
through Christ our Lord.

And so, with all the Angels, we praise you,
as in joyful celebration we acclaim: ➔ No. 23, p. 23

PREFACE VI OF THE SUNDAYS IN ORDINARY TIME (34)

The pledge of the eternal Passover

It is truly right and just, our duty and our salvation,
always and everywhere to give you thanks,
Lord, holy Father, almighty and eternal God.

For in you we live and move and have our being,
and while in this body
we not only experience the daily effects of your care,
but even now possess the pledge of life eternal.

For, having received the first fruits of the Spirit,
through whom you raised up Jesus from the dead,
we hope for an everlasting share in the Paschal Mystery.

And so, with all the Angels, we praise you,
as in joyful celebration we acclaim: ➔ No. 23, p. 23

PREFACE VII OF THE SUNDAYS IN ORDINARY TIME (35)

Salvation through the obedience of Christ

It is truly right and just, our duty and our salvation,
always and everywhere to give you thanks,
Lord, holy Father, almighty and eternal God.

For you so loved the world
that in your mercy you sent us the Redeemer,
to live like us in all things but sin,
so that you might love in us what you loved in your Son,
by whose obedience we have been restored to those gifts
    of yours
that, by sinning, we had lost in disobedience.

And so, Lord, with all the Angels and Saints,
we, too, give you thanks, as in exultation we acclaim:
➔ No. 23, p. 23

PREFACE VIII OF THE SUNDAYS IN ORDINARY TIME (36)

The Church united by the unity of the Trinity

It is truly right and just, our duty and our salvation,
always and everywhere to give you thanks,
Lord, holy Father, almighty and eternal God.

For, when your children were scattered afar by sin,
through the Blood of your Son and the power of the Spirit,
you gathered them again to yourself,
that a people, formed as one by the unity of the Trinity,
made the body of Christ and the temple of the Holy Spirit,
might, to the praise of your manifold wisdom,
be manifest as the Church.

And so, in company with the choirs of Angels,
we praise you, and with joy we proclaim: → No. 23, p. 23

PREFACE I OF THE MOST HOLY EUCHARIST (47)
The Sacrifice and the Sacrament of Christ

It is truly right and just, our duty and our salvation,
always and everywhere to give you thanks,
Lord, holy Father, almighty and eternal God,
through Christ our Lord.

For he is the true and eternal Priest,
who instituted the pattern of an everlasting sacrifice
and was the first to offer himself as the saving Victim,
commanding us to make this offering as his memorial.
As we eat his flesh that was sacrificed for us,
we are made strong,
and, as we drink his Blood that was poured out for us,
we are washed clean.

And so, with Angels and Archangels,
with Thrones and Dominions,
and with all the hosts and Powers of heaven,
we sing the hymn of your glory,
as without end we acclaim: → No. 23, p. 23

PREFACE II OF THE MOST HOLY EUCHARIST (48)
The fruits of the Most Holy Eucharist

It is truly right and just, our duty and our salvation,
always and everywhere to give you thanks,
Lord, holy Father, almighty and eternal God,
through Christ our Lord.

For at the Last Supper with his Apostles,
establishing for the ages to come the saving memorial of
the Cross,
he offered himself to you as the unblemished Lamb,
the acceptable gift of perfect praise.

Nourishing your faithful by this sacred mystery,
you make them holy, so that the human race,
bounded by one world,
may be enlightened by one faith
and united by one bond of charity.

And so, we approach the table of this wondrous Sacrament,
so that, bathed in the sweetness of your grace,
we may pass over to the heavenly realities here
foreshadowed.

Therefore, all creatures of heaven and earth
sing a new song in adoration,
and we, with all the host of Angels,
cry out, and without end we acclaim: → No. 23, p. 23

PREFACE I FOR THE DEAD (77)
The hope of resurrection in Christ

It is truly right and just, our duty and our salvation,
always and everywhere to give you thanks,
Lord, holy Father, almighty and eternal God,
through Christ our Lord.

In him the hope of blessed resurrection has dawned,
that those saddened by the certainty of dying
might be consoled by the promise of immortality to come.
Indeed for your faithful, Lord,
life is changed not ended,
and, when this earthly dwelling turns to dust,
an eternal dwelling is made ready for them in heaven.

And so, with Angels and Archangels,
with Thrones and Dominions,
and with all the hosts and Powers of heaven,
we sing the hymn of your glory,
as without end we acclaim: → No. 23, p. 23

PREFACE II FOR THE DEAD (78)
Christ died so that we might live

It is truly right and just, our duty and our salvation,
always and everywhere to give you thanks,
Lord, holy Father, almighty and eternal God,
through Christ our Lord.

For as one alone he accepted death,
so that we might all escape from dying;
as one man he chose to die,
so that in your sight we all might live for ever.

And so, in company with the choirs of Angels,
we praise you, and with joy we proclaim: ➝ No. 23, p. 23

PREFACE III FOR THE DEAD (79)
Christ, the salvation and the life

It is truly right and just, our duty and our salvation,
always and everywhere to give you thanks,
Lord, holy Father, almighty and eternal God,
through Christ our Lord.

For he is the salvation of the world,
the life of the human race,
the resurrection of the dead.

Through him the host of Angels adores your majesty
and rejoices in your presence for ever.
May our voices, we pray, join with theirs
in one chorus of exultant praise, as we acclaim:
➝ No. 23, p. 23

PREFACE IV FOR THE DEAD (80)
From earthly life to heavenly glory

It is truly right and just, our duty and our salvation,
always and everywhere to give you thanks,
Lord, holy Father, almighty and eternal God.

For it is at your summons that we come to birth,
by your will that we are governed,
and at your command that we return,
on account of sin,
to that earth from which we came.

And when you give the sign,
we who have been redeemed by the Death of your Son
shall be raised up to the glory of his Resurrection.

And so, with the company of Angels and Saints,
we sing the hymn of your praise,
as without end we acclaim: ➜ No. 23, p. 23

PREFACE V FOR THE DEAD (81)

Our resurrection through the victory of Christ

It is truly right and just, our duty and our salvation,
always and everywhere to give you thanks,
Lord, holy Father, almighty and eternal God.

For even though by our own fault we perish,
yet by your compassion and your grace,
when seized by death according to our sins,
we are redeemed through Christ's great victory,
and with him called back into life.

And so, with the Powers of heaven,
we worship you constantly on earth,
and before your majesty
without end we acclaim: ➜ No. 23, p. 23

PROPER COMMUNICANTES AND HANC IGITUR

FOR EUCHARISTIC PRAYER I (THE ROMAN CANON)

Communicantes for the Nativity of the Lord and throughout the Octave

Celebrating the most sacred night (day)
on which blessed Mary the immaculate Virgin
brought forth the Saviour for this world,
and in communion with those whose memory we venerate,
especially the glorious ever-Virgin Mary,
Mother of our God and Lord, Jesus Christ,† etc., p. 25.

Communicantes for the Epiphany of the Lord

Celebrating the most sacred day
on which your Only Begotten Son,
eternal with you in your glory,
appeared in a human body, truly sharing our flesh,

and in communion with those whose memory we venerate,
especially the glorious ever-Virgin Mary,
Mother of our God and Lord, Jesus Christ,† etc., p. 25.

Communicantes for Easter

Celebrating the most sacred night (day)
of the Resurrection of our Lord Jesus Christ in the flesh,
and in communion with those whose memory we venerate,
especially the glorious ever-Virgin Mary,
Mother of our God and Lord, Jesus Christ,† etc., p. 25.

Hanc Igitur for the Easter Vigil
until the Second Sunday of Easter

Therefore, Lord, we pray:
graciously accept this oblation of our service,
that of your whole family,
which we make to you
also for those to whom you have been pleased to give
the new birth of water and the Holy Spirit,
granting them forgiveness of all their sins;
order our days in your peace,
and command that we be delivered from eternal damnation
and counted among the flock of those you have chosen.
(Through Christ our Lord. Amen.)   → *Canon*, p. 25.

Communicantes for the Ascension of the Lord

Celebrating the most sacred day
on which your Only Begotten Son, our Lord,
placed at the right hand of your glory
our weak human nature,
which he had united to himself,
and in communion with those whose memory we venerate,
especially the glorious ever-Virgin Mary,
Mother of our God and Lord, Jesus Christ,† etc., p. 25.

Communicantes for Pentecost Sunday

Celebrating the most sacred day of Pentecost,
on which the Holy Spirit
appeared to the Apostles in tongues of fire,
and in communion with those whose memory we venerate,
especially the glorious ever-Virgin Mary,
Mother of our God and Lord, Jesus Christ,† etc., p. 25.

BLESSINGS AT THE END OF MASS AND PRAYERS OVER THE PEOPLE

SOLEMN BLESSINGS

The following blessings may be used, at the discretion of the Priest, at the end of the celebration of Mass, or of a Liturgy of the Word, or of the Office, or of the Sacraments.

The Deacon or, in his absence, the Priest himself, says the invitation: Bow down for the blessing. *Then the Priest, with hands extended over the people, says the blessing, with all responding:* **Amen**.

I. For Celebrations in the Different Liturgical Times

1. ADVENT

May the almighty and merciful God,
by whose grace you have placed your faith
in the First Coming of his Only Begotten Son
and yearn for his coming again,
sanctify you by the radiance of Christ's Advent
and enrich you with his blessing. ℟. **Amen.**

As you run the race of this present life,
may he make you firm in faith,
joyful in hope and active in charity. ℟. **Amen.**

So that, rejoicing now with devotion.
at the Redeemer's coming in the flesh,
you may be endowed with the rich reward of eternal life
when he comes again in majesty. ℟. **Amen.**

And may the blessing of almighty God,
the Father, and the Son, ✛ and the Holy Spirit,
come down on you and remain with you for ever. ℟. **Amen.**

2. THE NATIVITY OF THE LORD

May the God of infinite goodness,
who by the Incarnation of his Son has driven darkness
from the world

and by that glorious Birth has illumined this most holy
    night (day),
drive far from you the darkness of vice
and illumine your hearts with the light of virtue. ℟. **Amen.**

May God, who willed that the great joy
of his Son's saving Birth
be announced to shepherds by the Angel,
fill your minds with the gladness he gives
and make you heralds of his Gospel. ℟. **Amen.**

And may God, who by the Incarnation
brought together the earthly and heavenly realm,
fill you with the gift of his peace and favour
and make you sharers with the Church in heaven. ℟. **Amen.**

And may the blessing of almighty God,
the Father, and the Son, ✠ and the Holy Spirit,
come down on you and remain with you for ever. ℟. **Amen.**

3. THE BEGINNING OF THE YEAR

May God, the source and origin of all blessing,
grant you grace,
pour out his blessing in abundance,
and keep you safe from harm throughout the year.
    ℟. **Amen.**

May he give you integrity in the faith,
endurance in hope,
and perseverance in charity
with holy patience to the end. ℟. **Amen.**

May he order your days and your deeds in his peace,
grant your prayers in this and in every place,
and lead you happily to eternal life. ℟. **Amen.**

And may the blessing of almighty God,
the Father, and the Son, ✠ and the Holy Spirit,
come down on you and remain with you for ever. ℟. **Amen.**

4. THE EPIPHANY OF THE LORD

May God, who has called you
out of darkness into his wonderful light,
pour out in kindness his blessing upon you
and make your hearts firm
in faith, hope and charity. ℟. **Amen.**

And since in all confidence you follow Christ,
who today appeared in the world
as a light shining in darkness,
may God make you, too,
a light for your brothers and sisters. ℟. **Amen.**

And so when your pilgrimage is ended,
may you come to him
whom the Magi sought as they followed the star
and whom they found with great joy, the Light from Light,
who is Christ the Lord. ℟. **Amen.**

And may the blessing of almighty God,
the Father, and the Son, ✠ and the Holy Spirit,
come down on you and remain with you for ever. ℟. **Amen.**

5. THE PASSION OF THE LORD

May God, the Father of mercies,
who has given you an example of love
in the Passion of his Only Begotten Son,
grant that, by serving God and your neighbour,
you may lay hold of the wondrous gift of his blessing.
   ℟. **Amen.**

So that you may receive the reward of everlasting life from
   him,
through whose earthly Death
you believe that you escape eternal death. ℟. **Amen.**

And by following the example of his self-abasement,
may you possess a share in his Resurrection. ℟. **Amen.**

And may the blessing of almighty God,
the Father, and the Son, ✠ and the Holy Spirit,
come down on you and remain with you for ever. ℟. **Amen.**

6. EASTER TIME

May God, who by the Resurrection of his Only Begotten
   Son
was pleased to confer on you
the gift of redemption and of adoption,
give you gladness by his blessing. ℟. **Amen.**

May he, by whose redeeming work
you have received the gift of everlasting freedom,
make you heirs to an eternal inheritance. ℟. **Amen.**

And may you, who have already risen with Christ
in Baptism through faith,
by living in a right manner on this earth,
be united with him in the homeland of heaven. ℟. **Amen.**

And may the blessing of almighty God,
the Father, and the Son, ✠ and the Holy Spirit,
come down on you and remain with you for ever. ℟. **Amen.**

7. THE ASCENSION OF THE LORD

May almighty God bless you,
for on this very day his Only Begotten Son
pierced the heights of heaven
and unlocked for you the way
to ascend to where he is. ℟. **Amen.**

May he grant that,
as Christ after his Resurrection
was seen plainly by his disciples,
so when he comes as Judge
he may show himself merciful to you for all eternity.
　℟. **Amen.**

And may you, who believe he is seated
with the Father in his majesty,
know with joy the fulfillment of his promise
to stay with you until the end of time. ℟. **Amen.**

And may the blessing of almighty God,
the Father, and the Son, ✠ and the Holy Spirit,
come down on you and remain with you for ever. ℟. **Amen.**

8. THE HOLY SPIRIT

May God, the Father of lights,
who was pleased to enlighten the disciples' minds
by the outpouring of the Spirit, the Paraclete,
grant you gladness by his blessing
and make you always abound with the gifts of the same
　Spirit. ℟. **Amen.**

May the wondrous flame that appeared above the disciples,
powerfully cleanse your hearts from every evil
and pervade them with its purifying light. ℟. **Amen.**

And may God, who has been pleased to unite many
   tongues
in the profession of one faith,
give you perseverance in that same faith
and, by believing, may you journey from hope to clear
   vision. ℟. **Amen.**

And may the blessing of almighty God,
the Father, and the Son, ✝ and the Holy Spirit,
come down on you and remain with you for ever. ℟. **Amen.**

9. ORDINARY TIME I

May the Lord bless you and keep you. ℟. **Amen.**

May he let his face shine upon you
and show you his mercy. ℟. **Amen.**

May he turn his countenance towards you
and give you his peace. ℟. **Amen.**

And may the blessing of almighty God,
the Father, and the Son, ✝ and the Holy Spirit,
come down on you and remain with you for ever. ℟. **Amen.**

10. ORDINARY TIME II

May the peace of God,
which surpasses all understanding,
keep your hearts and minds
in the knowledge and love of God,
and of his Son, our Lord Jesus Christ. ℟. **Amen.**

And may the blessing of almighty God,
the Father, and the Son, ✝ and the Holy Spirit,
come down on you and remain with you for ever. ℟. **Amen.**

11. ORDINARY TIME III

May almighty God bless you in his kindness
and pour out saving wisdom upon you. ℟. **Amen.**

May he nourish you always with the teachings of the faith
and make you persevere in holy deeds. ℟. **Amen.**

May he turn your steps towards himself
and show you the path of charity and peace. ℟. **Amen.**

And may the blessing of almighty God,
the Father, and the Son, ✛ and the Holy Spirit,
come down on you and remain with you for ever. ℟. **Amen.**

12. ORDINARY TIME IV

May the God of all consolation order your days in his peace
and grant you the gifts of his blessing. ℟. **Amen.**

May he free you always from every distress
and confirm your hearts in his love. ℟. **Amen.**

So that on this life's journey
you may be effective in good works,
rich in the gifts of hope, faith and charity,
and may come happily to eternal life. ℟. **Amen.**

And may the blessing of almighty God,
the Father, and the Son, ✛ and the Holy Spirit,
come down on you and remain with you for ever. ℟. **Amen.**

13. ORDINARY TIME V

May almighty God always keep every adversity far from
　　you
and in his kindness pour out upon you the gifts of his
　　blessing. ℟. **Amen.**

May God keep your hearts attentive to his words,
that they may be filled with everlasting gladness. ℟. **Amen.**

And so, may you always understand what is good and right,
and be found ever hastening along
in the path of God's commands,
made co-heirs with the citizens of heaven. ℟. **Amen.**

And may the blessing of almighty God,
the Father, and the Son, ✛ and the Holy Spirit,
come down on you and remain with you for ever. ℟. **Amen.**

14. ORDINARY TIME VI

May God bless you with every heavenly blessing,
make you always holy and pure in his sight,
pour out in abundance upon you the riches of his glory,
and teach you with the words of truth;
may he instruct you in the Gospel of salvation,
and ever endow you with fraternal charity.
Through Christ our Lord. ℟. **Amen.**

And may the blessing of almighty God,
the Father, and the Son, ✚ and the Holy Spirit,
come down on you and remain with you for ever. ℟. **Amen.**

II. For Celebrations of the Saints

15. THE BLESSED VIRGIN MARY

May God, who through the childbearing of the Blessed
    Virgin Mary
willed in his great kindness to redeem the human race,
be pleased to enrich you with his blessing. ℟. **Amen.**

May you know always and everywhere the protection
    of her,
through whom you have been found worthy to receive the
    author of life. ℟. **Amen.**

May you, who have devoutly gathered on this day,
carry away with you the gifts of spiritual joys and heavenly
    rewards. ℟. **Amen.**

And may the blessing of almighty God,
the Father, and the Son, ✚ and the Holy Spirit,
come down on you and remain with you for ever. ℟. **Amen.**

16. SAINTS PETER AND PAUL, APOSTLES

May almighty God bless you,
for he has made you steadfast in Saint Peter's saving
    confession
and through it has set you on the solid rock of the Church's
    faith. ℟. **Amen.**

And having instructed you
by the tireless preaching of Saint Paul,
may God teach you constantly by his example
to win brothers and sisters for Christ. ℟. **Amen.**

So that by the keys of Saint Peter and the words of Saint
    Paul,
and by the support of their intercession,
God may bring us happily to that homeland
that Peter attained on a cross
and Paul by the blade of a sword. ℟. **Amen.**

And may the blessing of almighty God,
the Father, and the Son, ✠ and the Holy Spirit,
come down on you and remain with you for ever. ℟. **Amen.**

17. THE APOSTLES

May God, who has granted you
to stand firm on apostolic foundations,
graciously bless you through the glorious merits
of the holy Apostles N. and N. (the holy Apostle N.).
    ℟. **Amen.**

And may he, who endowed you
with the teaching and example of the Apostles,
make you, under their protection,
witnesses to the truth before all. ℟. **Amen.**

So that through the intercession of the Apostles,
you may inherit the eternal homeland,
for by their teaching you possess firmness of faith. ℟. **Amen.**

And may the blessing of almighty God,
the Father, and the Son, ✠ and the Holy Spirit,
come down on you and remain with you for ever. ℟. **Amen.**

18. ALL SAINTS

May God, the glory and joy of the Saints,
who has caused you to be strengthened
by means of their outstanding prayers,
bless you with unending blessings. ℟. **Amen.**

Freed through their intercession from present ills
and formed by the example of their holy way of life,
may you be ever devoted
to serving God and your neighbour. ℟. **Amen.**

So that, together with all,
you may possess the joys of the homeland,
where Holy Church rejoices
that her children are admitted in perpetual peace
to the company of the citizens of heaven. ℟. **Amen.**

And may the blessing of almighty God,
the Father, and the Son, ✠ and the Holy Spirit,
come down on you and remain with you for ever. ℟. **Amen.**

III. Other Blessings

19. FOR THE DEDICATION OF A CHURCH

May God, the Lord of heaven and earth,
who has gathered you today for the dedication of this
    church,
make you abound in heavenly blessings. ℟. **Amen.**

And may he, who has willed that all his scattered children
should be gathered together in his Son,
grant that you may become his temple
and the dwelling place of the Holy Spirit. ℟. **Amen.**

And so, when you are thoroughly cleansed,
may God dwell within you
and grant you to possess with all the Saints
the inheritance of eternal happiness. ℟. **Amen.**

And may the blessing of almighty God,
the Father, ✛ and the Son, ✛ and the Holy ✛ Spirit,
come down on you and remain with you for ever. ℟. **Amen.**

20. IN CELEBRATIONS FOR THE DEAD

May the God of all consolation bless you,
for in his unfathomable goodness he created the human
    race,
and in the Resurrection of his Only Begotten Son
he has given believers the hope of rising again. ℟. **Amen.**

To us who are alive, may God grant pardon for our sins,
and to all the dead, a place of light and peace. ℟. **Amen.**

So may we all live happily for ever with Christ,
whom we believe truly rose from the dead. ℟. **Amen.**

And may the blessing of almighty God,
the Father, and the Son, ✛ and the Holy Spirit,
come down on you and remain with you for ever. ℟. **Amen.**

PRAYERS OVER THE PEOPLE

*The following prayers may be used, at the discretion
of the Priest, at the end of the celebration of Mass,
or of a Liturgy of the Word, or of the Office, or of the
Sacraments.*

The Deacon or, in his absence, the Priest himself, says the invitation: Bow down for the blessing. *Then the Priest, with hands outstretched over the people, says the prayer, with all responding:* **Amen**.

After the prayer, the Priest always adds: And may the blessing of almighty God, the Father, and the Son, ✛ and the Holy Spirit, come down on you and remain with you for ever. ℟. **Amen.**

1. Be gracious to your people, O Lord,
   and do not withhold consolation on earth
   from those you call to strive for heaven.
   Through Christ our Lord.

2. Grant, O Lord, we pray,
   that the Christian people
   may understand the truths they profess
   and love the heavenly liturgy
   in which they participate.
   Through Christ our Lord.

3. May your people receive your holy blessing,
   O Lord, we pray,
   and, by that gift,
   spurn all that would harm them
   and obtain what they desire.
   Through Christ our Lord.

4. Turn your people to you with all their heart,
   O Lord, we pray,
   for you protect even those who go astray,
   but when they serve you with undivided heart,
   you sustain them with still greater care.
   Through Christ our Lord.

5. Graciously enlighten your family, O Lord, we pray,
   that by holding fast to what is pleasing to you,
   they may be worthy to accomplish all that is good.
   Through Christ our Lord.

6. Bestow pardon and peace, O Lord, we pray,
   upon your faithful,
   that they may be cleansed from every offence

and serve you with untroubled hearts.
Through Christ our Lord.

7. May your heavenly favour, O Lord, we pray,
   increase in number the people subject to you
   and make them always obedient to your commands.
   Through Christ our Lord.

8. Be propitious to your people, O God,
   that, freed from every evil,
   they may serve you with all their heart
   and ever stand firm under your protection.
   Through Christ our Lord.

9. May your family always rejoice together, O God,
   over the mysteries of redemption they have celebrated,
   and grant its members the perseverance
   to attain the effects that flow from them.
   Through Christ our Lord.

10. Lord God, from the abundance of your mercies
    provide for your servants and ensure their safety,
    so that, strengthened by your blessings,
    they may at all times abound in thanksgiving
    and bless you with unending exultation.
    Through Christ our Lord.

11. Keep your family, we pray, O Lord,
    in your constant care,
    so that, under your protection,
    they may be free from all troubles
    and by good works show dedication to your name.
    Through Christ our Lord.

12. Purify your faithful, both in body and in mind,
    O Lord, we pray,
    so that, feeling the compunction you inspire,
    they may be able to avoid harmful pleasures
    and ever feed upon your delights.
    Through Christ our Lord.

13. May the effects of your sacred blessing, O Lord,
    make themselves felt among your faithful,

to prepare with spiritual sustenance the minds of all,
that they may be strengthened by the power of your love
to carry out works of charity.
Through Christ our Lord.

14. The hearts of your faithful submitted to your name,
entreat your help, O Lord,
and since without you they can do nothing that is just,
grant by your abundant mercy
that they may both know what is right
and receive all that they need for their good.
Through Christ our Lord.

15. Hasten to the aid of your faithful people
who call upon you, O Lord, we pray,
and graciously give strength in their human weakness,
so that, being dedicated to you in complete sincerity,
they may find gladness in your remedies
both now and in the life to come.
Through Christ our Lord.

16. Look with favour on your family, O Lord,
and bestow your endless mercy on those who seek it:
and just as without your mercy
they can do nothing truly worthy of you,
so through it,
may they merit to obey your saving commands.
Through Christ our Lord.

17. Bestow increase of heavenly grace
on your faithful, O Lord;
may they praise you with their lips,
with their souls, with their lives;
and since it is by your gift that we exist,
may our whole lives be yours.
Through Christ our Lord.

18. Direct your people, O Lord, we pray,
with heavenly instruction,
that by avoiding every evil
and pursuing all that is good,
they may earn not your anger

but your unending mercy.
Through Christ our Lord.

19. Be near to those who call on you, O Lord,
and graciously grant your protection
to all who place their hope in your mercy,
that they may remain faithful in holiness of life
and, having enough for their needs in this world,
they may be made full heirs of your promise for eternity.
Through Christ our Lord.

20. Bestow the grace of your kindness
upon your supplicant people, O Lord,
that, formed by you, their Creator,
and restored by you, their sustainer,
through your constant action they may be saved.
Through Christ our Lord.

21. May your faithful people, O Lord, we pray,
always respond to the promptings of your love
and, moved by wholesome compunction,
may they do gladly what you command,
so as to receive the things you promise.
Through Christ our Lord.

22. May the weakness of your devoted people
stir your compassion, O Lord, we pray,
and let their faithful pleading win your mercy,
that what they do not presume upon by their merits
they may receive by your generous pardon.
Through Christ our Lord.

23. In defence of your children, O Lord, we pray,
stretch forth the right hand of your majesty,
so that, obeying your fatherly will,
they may have the unfailing protection
of your fatherly care.
Through Christ our Lord.

24. Look, O Lord, on the prayers of your family,
and grant them the assistance they humbly implore,
so that, strengthened by the help they need,
they may persevere in confessing your name.
Through Christ our Lord.

25. Keep your family safe, O Lord, we pray,
    and grant them the abundance of your mercies,
    that they may find growth
    through the teachings and the gifts of heaven.
    Through Christ our Lord.

26. May your faithful people rejoice, we pray, O Lord,
    to be upheld by your right hand,
    and, progressing in the Christian life,
    may they delight in good things
    both now and in the time to come.
    Through Christ our Lord.

ON FEASTS OF SAINTS

27. May the Christian people exult, O Lord,
    at the glorification of the illustrious members of your
       Son's Body,
    and may they gain a share in the eternal lot
    of the Saints on whose feast day
    they reaffirm their devotion to you,
    rejoicing with them for ever in your glory.
    Through Christ our Lord.

28. Turn the hearts of your people
    always to you, O Lord, we pray,
    and, as you give them the help of such great patrons as
       these,
    grant also the unfailing help of your protection.
    Through Christ our Lord.

"Before the flood they were eating and drinking. . . ."

YEAR A

NOVEMBER 27, 2016

1st SUNDAY OF ADVENT

ENTRANCE ANTIPHON Cf. Ps. 24.1-3   [Hope]

To you, I lift up my soul, O my God. In you, I have trusted; let me not be put to shame. Nor let my enemies exult over me; and let none who hope in you be put to shame.

→ No. 2, p. 10 (Omit Gloria)

COLLECT   [Meeting Christ]

Grant your faithful, we pray, almighty God,
the resolve to run forth to meet your Christ
with righteous deeds at his coming,
so that, gathered at his right hand,
they may be worthy to possess the heavenly
  Kingdom.
Through our Lord Jesus Christ, your Son,

who lives and reigns with you in the unity of the
   Holy Spirit,
one God, for ever and ever. R/. **Amen.** ↓

FIRST READING Isa. 2.1-5   [The Messianic Time]

In a vision the prophet sees the promise of salvation
being fulfilled. The Lord will judge us. Let us walk in
the light of the Lord.

A reading from the book of the Prophet Isaiah.

THE word that Isaiah son of Amoz saw
   concerning Judah and Jerusalem.

In days to come
the mountain of the Lord's house
shall be established as the highest of the mountains,
and shall be raised above the hills;
all the nations shall stream to it.

Many peoples shall come and say,
"Come, let us go up to the mountain of the Lord,
to the house of the God of Jacob;
that he may teach us his ways
and that we may walk in his paths."

For out of Zion shall go forth instruction,
and the word of the Lord from Jerusalem.
He shall judge between the nations,
and shall arbitrate for many peoples;
they shall beat their swords into ploughshares,
and their spears into pruning hooks;
nation shall not lift up sword against nation,
neither shall they learn war any more.

O house of Jacob, come,
let us walk in the light of the Lord!

The word of the Lord. ↓
R̶). **Thanks be to God.** ↓

RESPONSORIAL PSALM Ps. 122

[Joy in the Lord's House]

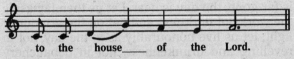

R̶). Let   us   go   re - joic - ing

to the   house___   of   the   Lord.

I was glad when they said to me,
"Let us go to the house of the Lord!"
Our feet are standing
within your gates, O Jerusalem.—R̶).

To it the tribes go up, the tribes of the Lord,
as was decreed for Israel, to give thanks to the
    name of the Lord.
For there the thrones for judgment were set up,
the thrones of the house of David.—R̶).

Pray for the peace of Jerusalem:
"May they prosper who love you.
Peace be within your walls,
and security within your towers."—R̶).

For the sake of my relatives and friends
I will say, "Peace be within you."
For the sake of the house of the Lord our God,
I will seek your good.—R̶). ↓

SECOND READING Rom. 13.11-14   [Put on the Lord]

The apostle urges us to come out of the darkness of sin
into the protective light—Jesus is the light.

A reading from the Letter of Saint Paul
to the Romans.

BROTHERS and sisters, you know what time
it is, how it is now the moment for you to
wake from sleep. For salvation is nearer to us
now than when we became believers; the night
is far gone, the day is near. Let us then lay aside
the works of darkness and put on the armour of
light; let us live honourably as in the day, not in
revelling and drunkenness, not in debauchery
and licentiousness, not in quarrelling and jealousy. Instead, put on the Lord Jesus Christ, and
make no provision for the flesh, to gratify its desires.—The word of the Lord. ℟. **Thanks be to
God.** ↓

GOSPEL ACCLAMATION Ps. 85.7   [Mercy and Love]

(If the Alleluia is not sung, the acclamation is omitted.)

℣. Alleluia. ℟. **Alleluia.**
℣. Show us your steadfast love, O Lord,
and grant us your salvation.
℟. **Alleluia.** ↓

GOSPEL Mt. 24.37-44   [Stay Awake]

We must always be prepared for the coming of Christ,
for no one knows the day or hour. His coming will be
unexpected; we must not be caught off guard.

℣. The Lord be with you. ℟. **And with your spirit.**
✚ A reading from the holy Gospel according to
Matthew. ℟. **Glory to you, O Lord.**

JESUS spoke to his disciples: "As the days of Noah were, so will be the coming of the Son of Man. For as in those days before the flood they were eating and drinking, marrying and giving in marriage, until the day Noah entered the ark, and they knew nothing until the flood came and swept them all away, so too will be the coming of the Son of Man. Then two will be in the field; one will be taken and one will be left. Two women will be grinding meal together; one will be taken and one will be left.

"Keep awake, therefore, for you do not know on what day your Lord is coming. But understand this: if the owner of the house had known in what part of the night the thief was coming, he would have stayed awake and would not have let his house be broken into. Therefore you also must be ready, for the Son of Man is coming at an unexpected hour."—The Gospel of the Lord. ℟. **Praise to you, Lord Jesus Christ.**

➜ No. 15, p. 18

PRAYER OVER THE OFFERINGS

[Eternal Redemption]

Accept, we pray, O Lord, these offerings we make,
gathered from among your gifts to us,
and may what you grant us to celebrate devoutly
   here below
gain for us the prize of eternal redemption.
Through Christ our Lord.
℟. **Amen.**   ➜ No. 21, p. 22 (Pref. 1)

COMMUNION ANTIPHON Ps. 84.13   [God's Bounty]

The Lord will bestow his bounty, and our earth shall yield its increase. ↓

PRAYER AFTER COMMUNION   [Love for Heaven]

May these mysteries, O Lord,
in which we have participated,
profit us, we pray,
for even now, as we walk amid passing things,
you teach us by them
to love the things of heaven
and hold fast to what endures.
Through Christ our Lord.
R⁄. **Amen.**   → No. 30, p. 77

Optional Solemn Blessings, p. 97, and Prayers over the People, p. 105

"Repent, for the kingdom of heaven has come near."

DECEMBER 4
2nd SUNDAY OF ADVENT

ENTRANCE ANTIPHON Cf. Isa. 30.19, 30   [Saving Lord]

O people of Sion, behold, the Lord will come to

save the nations, and the Lord will make the
glory of his voice heard in the joy of your heart.

→ No. 2, p. 10 (Omit Gloria)

COLLECT   [Heavenly Wisdom]

Almighty and merciful God,
may no earthly undertaking hinder those
who set out in haste to meet your Son,
but may our learning of heavenly wisdom
gain us admittance to his company.
Who lives and reigns with you in the unity of the
    Holy Spirit,
one God, for ever and ever. ℟. **Amen.** ↓

FIRST READING Isa. 11.1-10   [Messiah of Peace]

**Jesse, the father of David, is the ancestor of the Mes-
siah. All nations will turn to him.**

A reading from the book of the Prophet Isaiah.

O N that day:
    A shoot shall come out from the stump of
        Jesse,
and a branch shall grow out of his roots.
The spirit of the Lord shall rest on him,
the spirit of wisdom and understanding,
the spirit of counsel and might,
the spirit of knowledge and the fear of the Lord.
His delight shall be in the fear of the Lord.

He shall not judge by what his eyes see,
or decide by what his ears hear;
but with righteousness he shall judge the poor,
and decide with equity for the meek of the
    earth;
he shall strike the earth with the rod of his mouth,

and with the breath of his lips he shall kill the
    wicked.
Righteousness shall be the belt around his waist,
and faithfulness the belt around his loins.

The wolf shall live with the lamb,
the leopard shall lie down with the kid,
the calf and the lion and the fatling together,
and a little child shall lead them.
The cow and the bear shall graze,
their young shall lie down together;
and the lion shall eat straw like the ox.
The nursing child shall play over the hole of the
    asp,
and the weaned child shall put its hand on the
    adder's den.
They will not hurt or destroy
on all my holy mountain;
for the earth will be full of the knowledge of the
    Lord
as the waters cover the sea.

On that day the root of Jesse shall stand as a sig-
nal to the peoples; the nations shall inquire of him,
and his dwelling shall be glorious.—The word of
the Lord. ℟. **Thanks be to God.** ↓

RESPONSORIAL PSALM Ps. 72   [Justice and Peace]

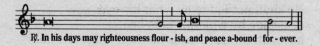

℟. In his days may righteousness flour - ish, and peace a-bound for - ever.

Give the king your justice, O God,
and your righteousness to a king's son.
May he judge your people with righteous-
    ness,
and your poor with justice.—R̲/.

In his days may righteousness flourish
and peace abound, until the moon is no more.
May he have dominion from sea to sea,
and from the River to the ends of the earth.—R̲/.

For he delivers the needy one who calls,
the poor and the one who has no helper.
He has pity on the weak and the needy,
and saves the lives of the needy.—R̲/.

May his name endure forever,
his fame continue as long as the sun.
May all nations be blessed in him;
may they pronounce him happy.—R̲/. ↓

SECOND READING Rom. 15.4-9   [For Our Instruction]

**Remember that the Scriptures are written for our instruc-
tion. In Christ the promise of the Scriptures is fulfilled.**

A reading from the Letter of Saint Paul
        to the Romans.

BROTHERS and sisters: Whatever was written
in former days was written for our instruction, so that by steadfastness and by the encouragement of the Scriptures we might have hope.
May the God of steadfastness and encouragement grant you to live in harmony with one another, in accordance with Christ Jesus, so that

together you may with one voice glorify the God and Father of our Lord Jesus Christ.

Welcome one another, therefore, just as Christ has welcomed you, for the glory of God. For I tell you that Christ has become a servant of the circumcised on behalf of the truth of God in order that he might confirm the promises given to the patriarchs, and in order that the Gentiles might glorify God for his mercy. As it is written,

"Therefore I will confess you among the Gentiles,

and sing praises to your name."

The word of the Lord. ℟. **Thanks be to God.** ↓

GOSPEL ACCLAMATION Lk. 3.4, 6   [Prepare the Way]

(If the Alleluia is not sung, the acclamation is omitted.)

℣. Alleluia. ℟. **Alleluia.**

℣. Prepare the way of the Lord, make straight his paths:

all flesh shall see the salvation of God.

℟. **Alleluia.** ↓

GOSPEL Mt. 3.1-12   [Prepare for the Lord]

John the Baptist calls the people to prepare for the Messiah. He urges a change in lifestyle and calls for repentance.

℣. The Lord be with you. ℟. **And with your spirit.**
✤ A reading from the holy Gospel according to Matthew. ℟. **Glory to you, O Lord.**

IN those days John the Baptist appeared in the wilderness of Judea, proclaiming, "Repent, for the kingdom of heaven has come near." This is the one of whom the Prophet Isaiah spoke when he said,

> "The voice of one crying out in the wilderness:
> 'Prepare the way of the Lord,
>   make his paths straight.'"

Now John wore clothing of camel's hair with a leather belt around his waist, and his food was locusts and wild honey. Then the people of Jerusalem and all Judea were going out to him, and all the region along the Jordan, and they were baptized by him in the river Jordan, confessing their sins.

But when he saw many Pharisees and Sadducees coming for baptism, John said to them, "You brood of vipers! Who warned you to flee from the wrath to come?

Bear fruit worthy of repentance. Do not presume to say to yourselves, 'We have Abraham as our father'; for I tell you, God is able from these stones to raise up children to Abraham. Even now the axe is lying at the root of the trees; every tree therefore that does not bear good fruit is cut down and thrown into the fire.

I baptize you with water for repentance, but one who is more powerful than I is coming after me; I am not worthy to carry his sandals. He will baptize you with the Holy Spirit and fire. His winnowing fork is in his hand, and he will clear his threshing floor and will gather his wheat into the granary; but the chaff he will burn with unquenchable fire."—The Gospel of the Lord. ℟.
Praise to you, Lord Jesus Christ.   ➜ No. 15, p. 18

PRAYER OVER THE OFFERINGS   [Our Offering]

Be pleased, O Lord, with our humble prayers and
    offerings,
and, since we have no merits to plead our cause,
come, we pray, to our rescue
with the protection of your mercy.
Through Christ our Lord.
R̷. **Amen.**   → No. 21, p. 22 (Pref. 1)

COMMUNION ANTIPHON Bar. 5.5; 4.36   [Coming Joy]
**Jerusalem, arise and stand upon the heights, and
behold the joy which comes to you from God.** ↓

PRAYER AFTER COMMUNION   [Wise Judgment]

Replenished by the food of spiritual nourishment,
we humbly beseech you, O Lord,
that, through our partaking in this mystery,
you may teach us to judge wisely the things of
    earth
and hold firm to the things of heaven.
Through Christ our Lord.
R̷. **Amen.**   → No. 30, p. 77

Optional Solemn Blessings, p. 97, and Prayers over the People, p. 105

"When John the Baptist heard in prison about the deeds of the Christ, he sent word by his disciples. . . ."

DECEMBER 11

3rd SUNDAY OF ADVENT

ENTRANCE ANTIPHON Phil. 4.4-5   [Mounting Joy]

Rejoice in the Lord always; again I say, rejoice. Indeed, the Lord is near.

→ No. 2, p. 10 (Omit Gloria)

COLLECT   [Joy of Salvation]

O God, who see how your people
faithfully await the feast of the Lord's Nativity,
enable us, we pray,
to attain the joys of so great a salvation
and to celebrate them always
with solemn worship and glad rejoicing.
Through our Lord Jesus Christ, your Son,
who lives and reigns with you in the unity of the
    Holy Spirit,
one God, for ever and ever. ℟. **Amen.** ↓

FIRST READING Isa. 35.1-6a, 10   [Here Is Your God]

This vision of the Messiah describes his work—not only
in restoring health and well-being to the infirm, but also
in bringing the mercy and forgiveness of salvation.

A reading from the book of the Prophet Isaiah.

THE wilderness and the dry land shall be glad,
the desert shall rejoice and blossom;
like the crocus it shall blossom abundantly,
and rejoice with joy and singing.
The glory of Lebanon shall be given to it,
the majesty of Carmel and Sharon.
They shall see the glory of the Lord,
the majesty of our God.

Strengthen the weak hands,
and make firm the feeble knees.
Say to those who are of a fearful heart,
"Be strong, do not fear!
Here is your God.
He will come with vengeance,
with terrible recompense.
He will come and save you."
Then the eyes of the blind shall be opened,
and the ears of the deaf unstopped;
then the lame shall leap like a deer,
and the tongue of the mute sing for joy.

And the ransomed of the Lord shall return,
and come to Zion with singing;
everlasting joy shall be upon their heads;
they shall obtain joy and gladness,
and sorrow and sighing shall flee away.

The word of the Lord. ℟. **Thanks be to God.** ↓

RESPONSORIAL PSALM Ps. 146   [Our Saviour]

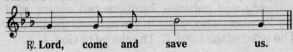

℟. Lord, come and save us.

Or: ℟. **Alleluia!**

It is the Lord who keeps faith forever,
who executes justice for the oppressed;
who gives food to the hungry.
The Lord sets the prisoners free.—℟.

The Lord opens the eyes of the blind
and lifts up those who are bowed down;
the Lord loves the righteous
and watches over the strangers.—℟.

The Lord upholds the orphan and the widow,
but the way of the wicked he brings to ruin.
The Lord will reign forever,
your God, O Zion, for all generations. —℟. ↓

SECOND READING Jas. 5.7-10 [Lord's Coming Is at Hand]

Look to the example of prophets and learn patience
under severe hardships.

A reading from the Letter of Saint James.

BE patient, brothers and sisters, until the coming of the Lord. The farmer waits for the precious crop from the earth, being patient with it until it receives the early and the late rains. You also must be patient. Strengthen your hearts, for the coming of the Lord is near.

Brothers and sisters, do not grumble against one another, so that you may not be judged. See, the

Judge is standing at the doors! As an example of suffering and patience, brothers and sisters, take the Prophets who spoke in the name of the Lord.— The word of the Lord. ℟. **Thanks be to God.** ↓

GOSPEL ACCLAMATION Lk. 4.18 (see Isa. 61.1)

[Witness]

(If the Alleluia is not sung, the acclamation is omitted.)

℣. Alleluia. ℟. **Alleluia.**

℣. The Spirit of the Lord is upon me;
he has sent me to bring good news to the poor.
℟. **Alleluia.** ↓

GOSPEL Mt. 11.2-11   [Effects of the Lord's Coming]

Jesus applies the words of Isaiah to himself. He proclaims the good news of salvation, freedom, and joy.

℣. The Lord be with you. ℟. **And with your spirit.**
✟ A reading from the holy Gospel according to Matthew. ℟. **Glory to you, O Lord.**

WHEN John the Baptist heard in prison about the deeds of the Christ, he sent word by his disciples who said to Jesus, "Are you the one who is to come, or are we to wait for another?" Jesus answered them, "Go and tell John what you hear and see: the blind receive their sight, the lame walk, the lepers are cleansed, the deaf hear, the dead are raised, and the poor have good news brought to them. And blessed is anyone who takes no offence at me."

As they went away, Jesus began to speak to the crowds about John: "What did you go out into the wilderness to look at? A reed shaken by the wind? What then did you go out to see? Someone dressed in soft robes? Look, those who wear soft robes are in royal palaces. What then did you go out to see? A Prophet? Yes, I tell you, and more than a Prophet. This is the one about whom it is written, 'See, I am sending my messenger ahead of you, who will prepare your way before you.'

Truly I tell you, among those born of women no one has arisen greater than John the Baptist; yet the least in the kingdom of heaven is greater than he."—The Gospel of the Lord. ℟. **Praise to you, Lord Jesus Christ.**   ➜ No. 15, p. 18

PRAYER OVER THE OFFERINGS [Unceasing Sacrifice]

May the sacrifice of our worship, Lord, we pray, be offered to you unceasingly, to complete what was begun in sacred mystery and powerfully accomplish for us your saving work.
Through Christ our Lord.
℟. **Amen.**   ➜ No. 21, p. 22 (Pref. 1 or 2)

COMMUNION ANTIPHON Cf. Isa. 35.4   [Trust in God]

Say to the faint of heart: Be strong and do not fear. Behold, our God will come, and he will save us. ↓

PRAYER AFTER COMMUNION   [Preparation for Christ]

We implore your mercy, Lord, that this divine sustenance may cleanse us of our faults and prepare us for the coming feasts.
Through Christ our Lord.
℟. **Amen.**   ➜ No. 30, p. 77

Optional Solemn Blessings, p. 97, and Prayers over the People, p. 105

"Joseph . . . took [Mary] as his wife."

DECEMBER 18

4th SUNDAY OF ADVENT

ENTRANCE ANTIPHON Cf. Isa. 45.8 **[The Advent Plea]**
**Drop down dew from above, you heavens, and let
the clouds rain down the Just One; let the earth
be opened and bring forth a Saviour.**

→ No. 2, p. 10 (Omit Gloria)

COLLECT [From Suffering to Glory]
Pour forth, we beseech you, O Lord,
your grace into our hearts,
that we, to whom the Incarnation of Christ your
 Son
was made known by the message of an Angel,
may by his Passion and Cross
be brought to the glory of his Resurrection.
Who lives and reigns with you in the unity of the
 Holy Spirit,
one God, for ever and ever. ℟. **Amen.** ↓

FIRST READING Isa. 7.10-14   [The Virgin with Child]

The words of the prophet spoken to the king are applied to the birth of the Saviour.

A reading from the book of the Prophet Isaiah.

THE Lord spoke to Ahaz, saying, "Ask a sign of the Lord your God; let it be deep as Sheol or high as heaven." But Ahaz said, "I will not ask, and I will not put the Lord to the test."

Then Isaiah said: "Hear then, O house of David! Is it too little for you to weary the people, that you weary my God also? Therefore the Lord himself will give you a sign. Look, the young woman is with child and shall bear a son, and shall name him Emmanuel."—The word of the Lord. ℟. **Thanks be to God.** ↓

RESPONSORIAL PSALM Ps. 24   [The King of Glory]

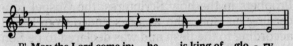

℟. **May the Lord come in;   he   is king of glo - ry.**

The earth is the Lord's and all that is in it,
the world, and those who live in it;
for he has founded it on the seas,
and established it on the rivers.—℟.

Who shall ascend the hill of the Lord?
And who shall stand in his holy place?
Someone who has clean hands and a pure
    heart,
who does not lift up their soul to what is false.—℟.

That person will receive blessing from the Lord,
and vindication from the God of their salvation.
Such is the company of those who seek him,
who seek the face of the God of Jacob.
℟. **May the Lord come in;**
    he is king of glory. ↓

SECOND READING Rom. 1.1-7   [Jesus the Saviour]

**The Christ is a descendant of David according to the
flesh and the Son of God according to the Spirit. His salvation is for all the world's people.**

A reading from the Letter of Saint Paul
to the Romans.

FROM Paul, a servant of Jesus Christ, called to
be an Apostle, set apart for the Gospel of God,
which God promised beforehand through his
Prophets in the holy Scriptures: the Gospel concerning his Son, who was descended from David
according to the flesh and was declared to be Son
of God with power according to the spirit of holiness by resurrection from the dead, Jesus Christ
our Lord.

Through Christ we have received grace and
apostleship to bring about the obedience of faith
among all the Gentiles for the sake of his name,
including yourselves who are called to belong to
Jesus Christ.

To all God's beloved in Rome, who are called to
be saints: Grace to you and peace from God our
Father and the Lord Jesus Christ.—The word of
the Lord. ℟. **Thanks be to God.** ↓

GOSPEL ACCLAMATION Mt. 1.23   [Emmanuel]

(If the Alleluia is not sung, the acclamation is omitted.)

℣. Alleluia. ℟. **Alleluia.**

℣. The virgin shall be with child and bear a son; and they shall name him Emmanuel: God is with us.

℟. **Alleluia.** ↓

GOSPEL Mt. 1.18-24   [God-with-Us]

> Emmanuel means God is with us. Jesus is conceived by the Holy Spirit and born of the Virgin Mary.

℣. The Lord be with you. ℟. **And with your spirit.**
✝ A reading from the holy Gospel according to Matthew. ℟. **Glory to you, O Lord.**

THE birth of Jesus the Christ took place in this way. When his mother Mary had been engaged to Joseph, but before they lived together, she was found to be with child from the Holy Spirit. Her husband Joseph, being a righteous man and unwilling to expose her to public disgrace, planned to dismiss her quietly.

But just when he had resolved to do this, an Angel of the Lord appeared to him in a dream and said, "Joseph, son of David, do not be afraid to take Mary as your wife, for the child conceived in her is from the Holy Spirit. She will bear a son, and you are to name him Jesus, for he will save his people from their sins."

All this took place to fulfill what had been spoken by the Lord through the Prophet:

"Look, the virgin shall conceive and bear a son, and they shall name him Emmanuel,"

which means, "God is with us." When Joseph
awoke from sleep, he did as the Angel of the Lord
commanded him; he took her as his wife.—The
Gospel of the Lord. ℟. **Praise to you, Lord Jesus
Christ.**   → No. 15, p. 18

PRAYER OVER THE OFFERINGS [Power of the Spirit]

May the Holy Spirit, O Lord,
sanctify these gifts laid upon your altar,
just as he filled with his power the womb of the
    Blessed Virgin Mary.
Through Christ our Lord.
℟. **Amen.**   → No. 21, p. 22 (Pref. 2)

COMMUNION ANTIPHON Isa. 7.14 [The Virgin Mother]

**Behold, a Virgin shall conceive and bear a son;
and his name will be called Emmanuel.** ↓

PRAYER AFTER COMMUNION   [Worthy Celebration]

Having received this pledge of eternal redemption,
we pray, almighty God,
that, as the feast day of our salvation draws ever
    nearer,
so we may press forward all the more eagerly
to the worthy celebration of the mystery of your
    Son's Nativity.
Who lives and reigns for ever and ever.
℟. **Amen.**   → No. 30, p. 77

Optional Solemn Blessings, p. 97, and Prayers over the People, p. 105

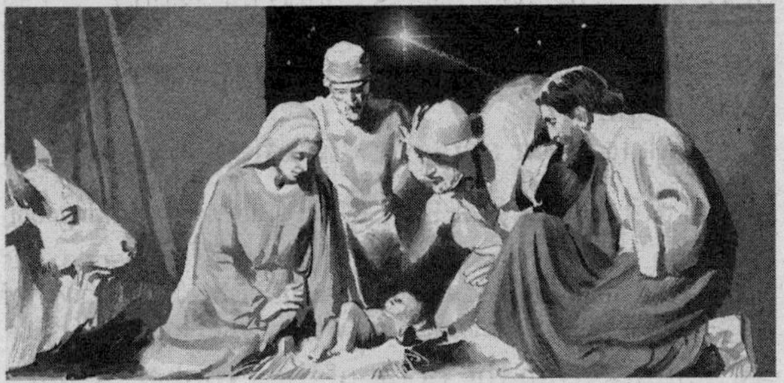

The Word is made flesh.

DECEMBER 25

CHRISTMAS: THE NATIVITY OF THE LORD

Solemnity

AT THE MASS DURING THE NIGHT

ENTRANCE ANTIPHON Ps. 2.7 [Son of God]

The Lord said to me: You are my Son. It is I who have begotten you this day. → No. 2, p. 10

OR [True Peace]

Let us all rejoice in the Lord, for our Saviour has been born in the world. Today true peace has come down to us from heaven. → No. 2, p. 10

COLLECT [Eternal Goodness]

O God, who have made this most sacred night
radiant with the splendour of the true light,
grant, we pray, that we, who have known the mysteries of his light on earth,
may also delight in his gladness in heaven.

Who lives and reigns with you in the unity of the
   Holy Spirit,
one God, for ever and ever. ℟. **Amen.** ↓

FIRST READING Isa. 9.2-4, 6-7   [The Messiah's Kingdom]

> The Messiah is a promise of peace for the world. His
> reign shall be vast and filled with justice. The power of
> God is revealed through the weakness of humans.

A reading from the book of the Prophet Isaiah.

T HE people who walked in darkness have
   seen a great light;
those who lived in a land of deep darkness—
on them light has shone.
You have multiplied the nation,
you have increased its joy;
they rejoice before you
as with joy at the harvest,
as people exult when dividing plunder.

For the yoke of their burden,
and the bar across their shoulders,
the rod of their oppressor,
you have broken as on the day of Midian.

For a child has been born for us,
a son given to us;
authority rests upon his shoulders;
and he is named
Wonderful Counsellor, Mighty God,
Everlasting Father, Prince of Peace.
His authority shall grow continually,
and there shall be endless peace
for the throne of David and his kingdom.
He will establish and uphold it
with justice and with righteousness

from this time onward and forevermore.
The zeal of the Lord of hosts will do this.

The word of the Lord. ℟. **Thanks be to God.** ↓

RESPONSORIAL PSALM Ps. 96   [Bless the Lord]

℟. Today   is   born   our   Sav - iour, Christ the Lord.

O sing to the Lord a new song;
sing to the Lord, all the earth.
Sing to the Lord, bless his name;
tell of his salvation from day to day. —℟.

Declare his glory among the nations,
his marvellous works among all the peoples.
For great is the Lord, and greatly to be praised;
he is to be revered above all gods.—℟.

Let the heavens be glad, and let the earth re-
     joice;
let the sea roar, and all that fills it;
let the field exult, and everything in it.
Then shall all the trees of the forest sing for
     joy.—℟.

Rejoice before the Lord; for he is coming,
for he is coming to judge the earth.
He will judge the world with righteous-
     ness,
and the peoples with his truth.—℟. ↓

SECOND READING Tit. 2.11-14   [Salvation for All]

God offers salvation to all people. His way asks us to reject worldly desires—to live temperately and justly. He even asked the only Son to sacrifice himself to redeem us.

A reading from the Letter of Saint Paul to Titus.

BELOVED: The grace of God has appeared, bringing salvation to all, training us to renounce impiety and worldly passions, and in the present age to live lives that are self-controlled, upright, and godly, while we wait for the blessed hope and the manifestation of the glory of our great God and Saviour, Jesus Christ.

He it is who gave himself for us that he might redeem us from all iniquity and purify for himself a people of his own who are zealous for good deeds.—The word of the Lord. ℟. **Thanks be to God.** ↓

GOSPEL ACCLAMATION Lk. 2.10-11   [Great Joy]
(*If the Alleluia is not sung, the acclamation is omitted.*)
℣. Alleluia. ℟. **Alleluia.**
℣. Good news and great joy to all the world:
today is born our Saviour, Christ the Lord.
℟. **Alleluia.** ↓

GOSPEL Lk. 2.1-16   [Birth of Christ]

Caesar Augustus desired a world census. Joseph and Mary go to Bethlehem where Jesus, the Lord of the universe, is born in a stable. Glory to God and peace on earth!

℣. The Lord be with you. ℟. **And with your spirit.**
✣ A reading from the holy Gospel according to Luke. ℟. **Glory to you, O Lord.**

IN those days a decree went out from Caesar Augustus that all the world should be registered. This was the first registration and was taken while Quirinius was governor of Syria. All went to their own towns to be registered. Joseph also went from the town of Nazareth in Galilee to Judea, to the city of David called Bethlehem, because he was descended from the house and family of David. He went to be registered with Mary, to whom he was engaged and who was expecting a child.

While they were there, the time came for her to deliver her child. And she gave birth to her first-born son and wrapped him in swaddling clothes, and laid him in a manger, because there was no place for them in the inn.

In that region there were shepherds living in the fields, keeping watch over their flock by night. Then an Angel of the Lord stood before them, and the glory of the Lord shone around them, and they were terrified. But the Angel said to them, "Do not be afraid; for see—I am bringing you good news of great joy for all the people: to you is born this day in the city of David a Saviour, who is the Christ, the Lord. This will be a sign for you: you will find a child wrapped in swaddling clothes and lying in a manger."

And suddenly there was with the Angel a multitude of the heavenly host, praising God and saying,

"Glory to God in the highest heaven,
    and on earth peace among those whom he favours!"

When the Angels had left them and gone into heaven, the shepherds said to one another, "Let us go now to Bethlehem and see this thing that has taken place, which the Lord has made known to us." So they went with haste and found Mary and Joseph, and the child lying in the manger.—The Gospel of the Lord. ℟. **Praise to you, Lord Jesus Christ.**   ➜ No. 15, p. 18

The Creed is said. All kneel at the words and by the Holy Spirit was incarnate.

PRAYER OVER THE OFFERINGS [Become Like Christ]

May the oblation of this day's feast
be pleasing to you, O Lord, we pray,
that through this most holy exchange
we may be found in the likeness of Christ,
in whom our nature is united to you.
Who lives and reigns for ever and ever.
℟. **Amen.**   ➜ No. 21, p. 22 (Pref. 3-5)

When the Roman Canon is used, the proper form of the Communicantes (In communion with those) *is said.*

COMMUNION ANTIPHON Jn. 1.14   [Glory of Christ]

The Word became flesh, and we have seen his glory. ↓

PRAYER AFTER COMMUNION   [Union with Christ]

Grant us, we pray, O Lord our God,
that we, who are gladdened by participation
in the feast of our Redeemer's Nativity,
may through an honourable way of life become
    worthy of union with him.
Who lives and reigns for ever and ever.
℟. **Amen.**   ➜ No. 30, p. 77

Optional Solemn Blessings, p. 97, and Prayers over the People, p. 105

AT THE MASS AT DAWN

ENTRANCE ANTIPHON Cf. Isa. 9.1, 5; Lk. 1.33
[Prince of Peace]

Today a light will shine upon us, for the Lord is born for us; and he will be called Wondrous God, Prince of peace, Father of future ages: and his reign will be without end.   → No. 2, p. 10

COLLECT   [Light of Faith]

Grant, we pray, almighty God,
that, as we are bathed in the new radiance of your
    incarnate Word,
the light of faith, which illumines our minds,
may also shine through in our deeds.
Through our Lord Jesus Christ, your Son,
who lives and reigns with you in the unity of the
    Holy Spirit,
one God, for ever and ever. ℟. **Amen.** ↓

FIRST READING Isa. 62.11-12   [The Saviour's Birth]

Isaiah foretells the birth of the Saviour who will come to Zion. These people will be called holy, and they shall be redeemed.

A reading from the book of the Prophet Isaiah.

THE Lord has proclaimed to the end of the
    earth:
"Say to daughter Zion,
See, your salvation comes;
his reward is with him,
and his recompense before him.

They shall be called 'The Holy People,'
'The Redeemed of the Lord';

and you shall be called 'Sought Out,'
'A City Not Forsaken.'"
The word of the Lord. ℟. **Thanks be to God.** ↓

RESPONSORIAL PSALM Ps. 97   [Be Glad]

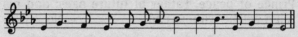

℟. **A light will shine on us this day: The Lord is born for us.**

The Lord is king! Let the earth rejoice;
let the many coastlands be glad!
Clouds and thick darkness are all around him;
righteousness and justice are the foundation of
   his throne.—℟.

The mountains melt like wax before the Lord,
before the Lord of all the earth.
The heavens proclaim his righteousness;
and all the peoples behold his glory.—℟.

Light dawns for the righteous,
and joy for the upright in heart.
Rejoice in the Lord, O you righteous,
and give thanks to his holy name!—℟. ↓

SECOND READING Tit. 3.4-7   [Saved by God's Mercy]

**Christians are saved not because of their own merits but
because of the mercy of God. We are saved through
baptism and renewal in the Holy Spirit.**

A reading from the Letter of Saint Paul to Titus.

WHEN the goodness and loving kindness of
God our Saviour appeared, he saved us, not

because of any works of righteousness that we had done, but according to his mercy, through the water of rebirth and renewal by the Holy Spirit. This Spirit he poured out on us richly through Jesus Christ our Saviour, so that, having been justified by his grace, we might become heirs according to the hope of eternal life.—The word of the Lord. ℟. **Thanks be to God.** ↓

GOSPEL ACCLAMATION Lk. 2.14   [Glory to God]
(If the Alleluia is not sung, the acclamation is omitted.)

℣. Alleluia. ℟. **Alleluia.**
℣. Glory to God in the highest heaven;
peace on earth to people of good will.
℟. **Alleluia.** ↓

GOSPEL Lk. 2.15-20   [Jesus, the God-Man]

The shepherds, the poor of the people of God, come to pay homage to Jesus. Mary ponders and prays over the great event of God becoming one of us.

℣. The Lord be with you. ℟. **And with your spirit.**
✠ A reading from the holy Gospel according to Luke. ℟. **Glory to you, O Lord.**

WHEN the Angels had left them and gone into heaven, the shepherds said to one another, "Let us go now to Bethlehem and see this thing that has taken place, which the Lord has made known to us."

So they went with haste and found Mary and Joseph, and the child lying in the manger. When they saw this, they made known what had been told them about this child; and all who heard it were amazed at what the shepherds told them.

But Mary treasured all these words and pondered them in her heart. The shepherds returned, glorifying and praising God for all they had heard and seen, as it had been told them.—The Gospel of the Lord. ℟. **Praise to you, Lord Jesus Christ.**

➙ No. 15, p. 18

The Creed is said. All kneel at the words and by the Holy Spirit was incarnate.

PRAYER OVER THE OFFERINGS [Gift of Divine Life]

May our offerings be worthy, we pray, O Lord,
of the mysteries of the Nativity this day,
that, just as Christ was born a man and also
　　shone forth as God,
so these earthly gifts may confer on us what is
　　divine.
Through Christ our Lord.
℟. **Amen.**　　　➙ No. 21, p. 22 (Pref. 3-5)

When the Roman Canon is used, the proper form of the Communicantes (In communion with those) *is said.*

COMMUNION ANTIPHON Cf. Zech. 9.9 [The Holy One]

Rejoice, O Daughter Sion; lift up praise, Daughter Jerusalem: Behold, your King will come, the Holy One and Saviour of the world. ↓

PRAYER AFTER COMMUNION [Hidden Depths]

Grant us, Lord, as we honour with joyful devotion
the Nativity of your Son,
that we may come to know with fullness of faith
the hidden depths of this mystery
and to love them ever more and more.
Through Christ our Lord.
℟. **Amen.**　　　➙ No. 30, p. 77

Optional Solemn Blessings, p. 97, and Prayers over the People, p. 105

AT THE MASS DURING THE DAY

ENTRANCE ANTIPHON Cf. Isa. 9.5 [The Gift of God's Son]

A child is born for us, and a son is given to us; his sceptre of power rests upon his shoulder, and his name will be called Messenger of great counsel.

→ No. 2, p. 10

COLLECT   [Share in Christ's Divinity]

O God, who wonderfully created the dignity of
  human nature
and still more wonderfully restored it,
grant, we pray,
that we may share in the divinity of Christ,
who humbled himself to share in our humanity.
Who lives and reigns with you in the unity of the
  Holy Spirit,
one God, for ever and ever. ℟. **Amen.** ↓

FIRST READING Isa. 52.7-10   [Your God Is King]

God shows salvation to all people. God brings peace and
good news. God comforts and redeems the faithful.

 A reading from the book of the Prophet Isaiah.

HOW beautiful upon the mountains
  are the feet of the messenger who announces
  peace,
who brings good news,
who announces salvation,
who says to Zion, "Your God reigns."

Listen! Your watchmen lift up their voices,
together they sing for joy;
for in plain sight they see
the return of the Lord to Zion.

Break forth together into singing,
you ruins of Jerusalem;
for the Lord has comforted his people,
he has redeemed Jerusalem.
The Lord has bared his holy arm
before the eyes of all the nations;
and all the ends of the earth shall see the salva-
    tion of our God.
The word of the Lord. ℟. **Thanks be to God.** ↓

RESPONSORIAL PSALM Ps. 98   [Sing a New Song]

℟. All the ends of the earth have seen   the   victory   of our God.

O sing to the Lord a new song,
for he has done marvellous things.
His right hand and his holy arm
have brought him victory.— ℟.

The Lord has made known his victory;
he has revealed his vindication in the sight of the
    nations.
He has remembered his steadfast love
and faithfulness to the house of Israel.— ℟.

All the ends of the earth have seen
the victory of our God.
Make a joyful noise to the Lord, all the earth;
break forth into joyous song and sing praises.— ℟.

Sing praises to the Lord with the lyre,
with the lyre and the sound of melody.
With trumpets and the sound of the horn
make a joyful noise before the King, the Lord.— ℟.

SECOND READING Heb. 1.1-6 [God Speaks through Jesus]

God now speaks through Jesus, the Son, who reflects God's glory. The Son cleanses us from sin. Heaven and earth should worship him.

A reading from the Letter to the Hebrews.

LONG ago God spoke to our ancestors in many and various ways by the Prophets, but in these last days he has spoken to us by the Son, whom he appointed heir of all things, through whom he also created the ages.

He is the reflection of God's glory and the exact imprint of God's very being, and he sustains all things by his powerful word. When he had made purification for sins, he sat down at the right hand of the Majesty on high, having become as much superior to Angels as the name he has inherited is more excellent than theirs.

For to which of the Angels did God ever say,

"You are my Son;

today I have begotten you"?

Or again,

"I will be his Father,

and he will be my Son"?

And again, when he brings the firstborn into the world, he says,

"Let all God's Angels worship him."

The word of the Lord. ℞. **Thanks be to God.** ↓

GOSPEL ACCLAMATION   [Adore the Lord]

(*If the Alleluia is not sung, the acclamation is omitted.*)

℣. Alleluia. ℞. **Alleluia.**

℣. A holy day has dawned upon us.

Come you nations and adore the Lord.

Today a great light has come down upon the earth.
℟. **Alleluia.** ↓

GOSPEL Jn. 1.1-18 or 1.1-5, 9-14   [The True Light]

John's opening words parallel the Book of Genesis.
Jesus is the Word made flesh, the light of the world,
who always was and will ever be.

[If the "Shorter Form" is used, the indented text in brackets is omitted.]

℣. The Lord be with you. ℟. **And with your spirit.**
✠ A reading from the holy Gospel according to
John. ℟. **Glory to you, O Lord.**

IN the beginning was the Word, and the Word
was with God, and the Word was God. He was
in the beginning with God. All things came into
being through him, and without him not one thing
came into being. What has come into being in
him was life, and the life was the light of the
human race.

The light shines in the darkness, and the darkness did not overcome it.

[There was a man sent from God, whose
name was John. He came as a witness to testify to the light, so that all might believe
through him. He himself was not the light,
but he came to testify to the light.]

The true light, which enlightens everyone, was
coming into the world. He was in the world, and
the world came into being through him; yet the
world did not know him. He came to what was his
own, and his own people did not accept him. But
to all who received him, who believed in his

name, he gave power to become children of God, who were born, not of blood or of the will of the flesh or of the will of man, but of God. And the Word became flesh and lived among us, and we have seen his glory, the glory as of a father's only-begotten son, full of grace and truth.

[John testified to him and cried out, "This was he of whom I said, 'He who comes after me ranks ahead of me because he was before me.'"

From his fullness we have all received, grace upon grace. The law indeed was given through Moses; grace and truth came through Jesus Christ. No one has ever seen God. It is God the only-begotten Son, who is close to the Father's heart, who has made him known.]

The Gospel of the Lord. ℟. **Praise to you, Lord Jesus Christ.**   ➙ No. 15, p. 18

The Creed is said. All kneel at the words and by the Holy Spirit was incarnate.

PRAYER OVER THE OFFERINGS   [Reconciliation]

Make acceptable, O Lord, our oblation on this solemn day,
when you manifested the reconciliation
that makes us wholly pleasing in your sight
and inaugurated for us the fullness of divine worship.
Through Christ our Lord.
℟. **Amen.**   ➙ No. 21, p. 22 (Pref. 3-5)

When the Roman Canon is used, the proper form of the Communicantes (In communion with those) *is said.*

COMMUNION ANTIPHON Cf. Ps. 97.3   [Salvation]
All the ends of the earth have seen the salvation of our God. ↓

PRAYER AFTER COMMUNION [Giver of Immortality]
Grant, O merciful God,
that, just as the Saviour of the world, born this day,
is the author of divine generation for us,
so he may be the giver even of immortality.
Who lives and reigns for ever and ever.
℟. **Amen.**   → No. 30, p. 77

Optional Solemn Blessings, p. 97, and Prayers over the People, p. 105

"He was called Jesus. . . ."

JANUARY 1, 2017

The Octave Day of the Nativity of the Lord
SOLEMNITY OF MARY, THE HOLY MOTHER OF GOD

ENTRANCE ANTIPHON   [Hail, Holy Mother]

Hail, Holy Mother, who gave birth to the King who rules heaven and earth for ever.   ➙ No. 2, p. 10

OR Cf. Isa. 9.1, 5; Lk. 1.33   [Wondrous God]

Today a light will shine upon us, for the Lord is born for us; and he will be called Wondrous God, Prince of peace, Father of future ages: and his reign will be without end.   ➙ No. 2, p. 10

COLLECT   [Mary's Intercession]

O God, who through the fruitful virginity of
   Blessed Mary
bestowed on the human race

the grace of eternal salvation,
grant, we pray,
that we may experience the intercession of her,
through whom we were found worthy
to receive the author of life,
our Lord Jesus Christ, your Son.
Who lives and reigns with you in the unity of the
    Holy Spirit,
one God, for ever and ever. ℟. **Amen.** ↓

FIRST READING Num. 6.22-27   [The Aaronic Blessing]

**Aaron and the Israelites are to pray that God will answer
their prayers with blessings.**

A reading from the book of Numbers.

THE Lord spoke to Moses:
Speak to Aaron and his sons, saying,
Thus you shall bless the children of Israel:
You shall say to them,

The Lord bless you and keep you;
the Lord make his face to shine upon you,
and be gracious to you;
the Lord lift up his countenance upon you,
and give you peace.

So they shall put my name on the children of
    Israel,
and I will bless them.
The word of the Lord. ℟. **Thanks be to God.** ↓

RESPONSORIAL PSALM Ps. 67   [God Bless Us]

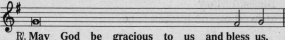

℟. **May God be gracious to us and bless us.**

May God be gracious to us and bless us
and make his face to shine upon us,
that your way may be known upon earth,
your saving power among all nations.—℟.

Let the nations be glad and sing for joy,
for you judge the peoples with equity
and guide the nations upon earth.
Let the peoples praise you, O God;
let all the peoples praise you.—℟.

The earth has yielded its increase;
God, our God, has blessed us.
May God continue to bless us;
let all the ends of the earth revere him.—℟. ↓

SECOND READING Gal. 4.4-7   [Heirs by God's Design]

God sent Jesus, his Son, born of Mary, to deliver all people from the bondage of sin and slavery of the law. By
God's choice we are heirs of heaven.

A reading from the Letter of Saint Paul
to the Galatians.

BROTHERS and sisters: When the fullness of
time had come, God sent his Son, born of a
woman, born under the law, in order to redeem
those who were under the law, so that we might
receive adoption to sonship.

And because you are sons and daughters,
God has sent the Spirit of his Son into our
hearts, crying, "Abba! Father!" So you are no
longer slave but son, and if son then also heir,
through God.—The word of the Lord. ℟. **Thanks
be to God.** ↓

GOSPEL ACCLAMATION Heb. 1.1-2   [God Speaks]

(If the Alleluia is not sung, the acclamation is omitted.)

℣. Alleluia. ℟. **Alleluia.**

℣. Long ago God spoke to our ancestors by the
   Prophets;

in these last days he has spoken to us by the
   Son.

℟. **Alleluia.** ↓

GOSPEL Lk. 2.16-21   [The Name of Jesus]

When the shepherds came to Bethlehem, they began to
understand the message of the angels. Mary prayed
about this great event. Jesus received his name according
to the Jewish ritual of circumcision.

℣. The Lord be with you. ℟. **And with your spirit.**
✝ A reading from the holy Gospel according to
Luke. ℟. **Glory to you, O Lord.**

THE shepherds went with haste to Bethlehem
and found Mary and Joseph, and the child
lying in the manger. When they saw this, they
made known what had been told them about this
child; and all who heard it were amazed at what
the shepherds told them. But Mary treasured all
these words and pondered them in her heart.

The shepherds returned, glorifying and praising God for all they had heard and seen, as it had
been told them.

After eight days had passed, it was time to cir-
cumcise the child; and he was called Jesus, the
name given by the Angel before he was conceived
in the womb.—The Gospel of the Lord. ℟. **Praise
to you, Lord Jesus Christ.**   → No. 15, p. 18

PRAYER OVER THE OFFERINGS   [Rejoice in Grace]

O God, who in your kindness begin all good
   things
and bring them to fulfillment,
grant to us, who find joy in the Solemnity of the
   holy Mother of God,
that, just as we glory in the beginnings of your
   grace,
so one day we may rejoice in its completion.
Through Christ our Lord. ℟. **Amen.** ↓

PREFACE (56)   [Mary, Virgin and Mother]

℣. The Lord be with you. ℟. **And with your spirit.**
℣. Lift up your hearts. ℟. **We lift them up to the
Lord.**
℣. Let us give thanks to the Lord our God. ℟. **It is
right and just.**

It is truly right and just, our duty and our
   salvation,
always and everywhere to give you thanks,
Lord, holy Father, almighty and eternal God,
and to praise, bless, and glorify your name
on the Solemnity of the Motherhood
of the Blessed ever-Virgin Mary.

For by the overshadowing of the Holy Spirit
she conceived your Only Begotten Son,
and without losing the glory of virginity,
brought forth into the world the eternal Light,
Jesus Christ our Lord.

Through him the Angels praise your majesty,
Dominions adore and Powers tremble before you.

Heaven and the Virtues of heaven and the blessed
  Seraphim
worship together with exultation.
May our voices, we pray, join with theirs
in humble praise, as we acclaim: → No. 23, p. 23

When the Roman Canon is used, the proper form of the
Communicantes (In communion with those) *is said.*

COMMUNION ANTIPHON Heb. 13.8   [Jesus Forever]

**Jesus Christ is the same yesterday, today, and for
ever.** ↓

PRAYER AFTER COMMUNION

[Mother of the Church]

We have received this heavenly Sacrament with
  joy, O Lord:
grant, we pray,
that it may lead us to eternal life,
for we rejoice to proclaim the blessed ever-Virgin
  Mary
Mother of your Son and Mother of the Church.
Through Christ our Lord.
℞. **Amen.**   → No. 30, p. 77

Optional Solemn Blessings, p. 97, and Prayers over the People, p. 105

"They knelt down and paid him homage."

JANUARY 8

THE EPIPHANY OF THE LORD

Solemnity

AT THE VIGIL MASS (January 7)

ENTRANCE ANTIPHON Cf. Bar. 5.5   [Arise, Jerusalem]

Arise, Jerusalem, and look to the East and see your children gathered from the rising to the setting of the sun.   → No. 2, p. 10

COLLECT   [Splendour of God's Majesty]

May the splendour of your majesty, O Lord, we
    pray,
shed its light upon our hearts,
that we may pass through the shadows of this
    world
and reach the brightness of our eternal home.
Through our Lord Jesus Christ, your Son,
who lives and reigns with you in the unity of the
    Holy Spirit,
one God, for ever and ever. ℟. **Amen.** ↓

The readings for this Mass can be found beginning on p. 158.

PRAYER OVER THE OFFERINGS   [Render Praise]

Accept we pray, O Lord, our offerings,
in honour of the appearing of your Only Begotten
    Son
and the first fruits of the nations,
that to you praise may be rendered
and eternal salvation be ours.
Through Christ our Lord. ℞. **Amen.** ↓

PREFACE (6)   [Jesus Revealed to All]

℣. The Lord be with you. ℞. **And with your spirit.**
℣. Lift up your hearts. ℞. **We lift them up to the Lord.**
℣. Let us give thanks to the Lord our God. ℞. **It is right and just.**

It is truly right and just, our duty and our
    salvation,
always and everywhere to give you thanks,
Lord, holy Father, almighty and eternal God.

For today you have revealed the mystery
of our salvation in Christ
as a light for the nations,
and, when he appeared in our mortal nature,
you made us new by the glory of his immortal
    nature.

And so, with Angels and Archangels,
with Thrones and Dominions,
and with all the hosts and Powers of heaven,
we sing the hymn of your glory,
as without end we acclaim: ➔ No. 23, p. 23

COMMUNION ANTIPHON Cf. Rev. 21.23

[Walking by God's Light]

The brightness of God illumined the holy city Jerusalem, and the nations will walk by its light. ↓

PRAYER AFTER COMMUNION [True Treasure]

Renewed by sacred nourishment,
we implore your mercy, O Lord,
that the star of your justice
may shine always bright in our minds
and that our true treasure may ever consist in our
    confession of you.
Through Christ our Lord.
R̸. **Amen.** ➝ No. 30, p. 77

Optional Solemn Blessings, p. 97, and Prayers over the People, p. 105

AT THE MASS DURING THE DAY

ENTRANCE ANTIPHON Cf. Mal. 3.1; 1 Chron. 29.12

[Lord and Ruler]

Behold, the Lord, the Mighty One, has come; and kingship is in his grasp, and power and dominion. ➝ No. 2, p. 10

COLLECT [Behold Glory]

O God, who on this day
revealed your Only Begotten Son to the nations
by the guidance of a star,
grant in your mercy
that we, who know you already by faith,
may be brought to behold the beauty of your
    sublime glory.

Through our Lord Jesus Christ, your Son,
who lives and reigns with you in the unity of the
　Holy Spirit,
one God, for ever and ever. ℟. **Amen.** ↓

FIRST READING Isa. 60.1-6   [Glory of God's Church]

　　Jerusalem is favoured by the Lord. Kings and peoples will come
　　there, and the riches of the earth will be placed at its gates.

A reading from the book of the Prophet Isaiah.

A RISE, shine, for your light has come,
　and the glory of the Lord has risen upon you!
For darkness shall cover the earth,
and thick darkness the peoples;
but the Lord will arise upon you,
and his glory will appear over you.

Nations shall come to your light,
and kings to the brightness of your dawn.
Lift up your eyes and look around;
they all gather together, they come to you;
your sons shall come from far away,
and your daughters shall be carried on their
　nurses' arms.

Then you shall see and be radiant;
your heart shall thrill and rejoice,
because the abundance of the sea shall be
　brought to you,
the wealth of the nations shall come to you.
A multitude of camels shall cover you,
the young camels of Midian and Ephah;
all those from Sheba shall come.
They shall bring gold and frankincense,
and shall proclaim the praise of the Lord.

The word of the Lord. ℟. **Thanks be to God.** ↓

RESPONSORIAL PSALM Ps. 72   [Messiah-King]

℟. **Lord, every nation on earth will adore you.**

Give the king your justice, O God,
and your righteousness to a king's son.
May he judge your people with righteousness,
and your poor with justice.—℟.

In his days may righteousness flourish
and peace abound, until the moon is no more.
May he have dominion from sea to sea,
and from the River to the ends of the earth.—℟.

May the kings of Tarshish and of the isles render
    him tribute,
may the kings of Sheba and Seba bring gifts.
May all kings fall down before him,
all nations give him service.—℟.

For he delivers the needy one who calls,
the poor and the one who has no helper.
He has pity on the weak and the needy,
and saves the lives of the needy.—℟. ↓

SECOND READING Eph. 3.2-3a, 5-6   [Good News for All]

Paul admits that God has revealed the divine plan of salvation to him. Not only the Jews, but also the whole world will share in the good news.

A reading from the Letter of Saint Paul
        to the Ephesians.

BROTHERS and sisters: Surely you have already heard of the commission of God's grace that was given me for you, and how the mystery was made known to me by revelation.

In former generations this mystery was not made known to humankind as it has now been revealed to his holy Apostles and Prophets by the Spirit: that is, the Gentiles have become fellow heirs, members of the same body, and sharers in the promise in Christ Jesus through the Gospel.— The word of the Lord. ℟. **Thanks be to God.** ↓

GOSPEL ACCLAMATION See Mt. 2.2　　[Leading Star]
(*If the Alleluia is not sung, the acclamation is omitted.*)

℣. Alleluia. ℟. **Alleluia.**
℣. We observed his star at its rising,
and have come to pay homage to the Lord.
℟. **Alleluia.** ↓

GOSPEL Mt. 2.1-12　　　　　　　　　[Wise Men]

> King Herod, being jealous of his earthly crown, was threatened by the coming of another king. The wise men from the East followed the star to Bethlehem, from which a ruler was to come.

℣. The Lord be with you. ℟. **And with your spirit.**
✤ A reading from the holy Gospel according to Matthew. ℟. **Glory to you, O Lord.**

IN the time of King Herod, after Jesus was born in Bethlehem of Judea, wise men from the East came to Jerusalem, asking, "Where is the child who has been born king of the Jews? For we observed his star at its rising, and have come to pay him homage."

When King Herod heard this, he was frightened, and all Jerusalem with him; and calling together all the chief priests and scribes of the people, he inquired of them where the Messiah was to be born. They told him, "In Bethlehem of Judea; for so it has been written by the Prophet:

'And you, Bethlehem, in the land of Judah,
  are by no means least among the rulers of Judah;
for from you shall come a ruler
  who is to shepherd my people Israel.'"

Then Herod secretly called for the wise men and learned from them the exact time when the star had appeared. Then he sent them to Bethlehem, saying, "Go and search diligently for the child; and when you have found him, bring me word so that I may also go and pay him homage."

When they had heard the king, they set out; and there, ahead of them, went the star that they had seen at its rising, until it stopped over the place where the child was.When they saw that the star had stopped, they were overwhelmed with joy.

On entering the house, they saw the child with Mary his mother; and they knelt down and paid him homage. Then, opening their treasure chests, they offered him gifts of gold, frankincense, and myrrh. And having been warned in a dream not to return to Herod, they left for their own country by another road.—The Gospel of the Lord. ℟.
Praise to you, Lord Jesus Christ.   ➔ No. 15, p. 18

PRAYER OVER THE OFFERINGS   [Offering of Jesus]

Look with favour, Lord, we pray,
on these gifts of your Church,
in which are offered now not gold or
    frankincense or myrrh,
but he who by them is proclaimed,
sacrificed and received, Jesus Christ.
Who lives and reigns for ever and ever. ℟. **Amen.**

➔ Pref. 6, p. 156

When the Roman Canon is used, the proper form of the
Communicantes *(In communion with those) is said.*

COMMUNION ANTIPHON Cf. Mt. 2.2   [Adore the Lord]

**We have seen his star in the East, and have come
with gifts to adore the Lord.** ↓

PRAYER AFTER COMMUNION   [Heavenly Light]

Go before us with heavenly light, O Lord,
always and everywhere,
that we may perceive with clear sight
and revere with true affection
the mystery in which you have willed us to
    participate.
Through Christ our Lord.
℟. **Amen.**

➔ No. 30, p. 77

Optional Solemn Blessings, p. 97, and Prayers over the People, p. 105

"Here is the Lamb of God who takes away the sin of the world!"

JANUARY 15

2nd SUNDAY IN ORDINARY TIME

ENTRANCE ANTIPHON Ps. 65.4   [Proclaim His Glory]

All the earth shall bow down before you, O God, and shall sing to you, shall sing to your name, O Most High! ➜ No. 2, p. 10

COLLECT   [Peace on Our Times]

Almighty ever-living God,
who govern all things,
both in heaven and on earth,
mercifully hear the pleading of your people
and bestow your peace on our times.
Through our Lord Jesus Christ, your Son,
who lives and reigns with you in the unity of the
    Holy Spirit,
one God, for ever and ever. ℟. **Amen.** ↓

FIRST READING Isa. 49.3, 5-6   [God Is My Strength]

> Through Israel the Lord will show forth glory and splendour. Israel is to be a light for all nations whereby salvation will come to all people.

A reading from the book of the Prophet Isaiah.

THE Lord said to me,
"You are my servant, Israel, in whom I will
be glorified."

And now the Lord says,
who formed me in the womb to be his servant,
to bring Jacob back to him,
and that Israel might be gathered to him,
for I am honoured in the sight of the Lord,
and my God has become my strength.

He says,
"It is too small a thing that you should be my
    servant
to raise up the tribes of Jacob
and to restore the survivors of Israel;
I will give you as a light to the nations,
that my salvation may reach to the end of the
    earth."

The word of the Lord. ℟. **Thanks be to God.** ↓

RESPONSORIAL PSALM Ps. 40   [Doing God's Will]

℟. Here I am, Lord;   I come   to   do   your   will.

I waited patiently for the Lord;
he inclined to me and heard my cry.
He put a new song in my mouth,
a song of praise to our God.—℟.

Sacrifice and offering you do not desire,
but you have given me an open ear.
Burnt offering and sin offering
you have not required.—℟.

Then I said, "Here I am;
in the scroll of the book it is written of me.
I delight to do your will, O my God;
your law is within my heart."—℟.

I have told the glad news of deliverance
in the great congregation;
see, I have not restrained my lips,
as you know, O Lord.—℟. ↓

SECOND READING 1 Cor. 1.1-3   [A Holy People]

**Paul and Sosthenes greet the people at Corinth. They are
to be a holy people, as are all who call on the name of
Jesus, acknowledging him as Lord.**

A reading from the first Letter of Saint Paul to
the Corinthians.

FROM Paul, called to be an Apostle of Christ
Jesus by the will of God, and from our brother
Sosthenes. To the Church of God that is in
Corinth, to those who are sanctified in Christ
Jesus, called to be saints, together with all those
who in every place call on the name of our Lord
Jesus Christ, both their Lord and ours: Grace to
you and peace from God our Father and the Lord
Jesus Christ.—The word of the Lord. ℟. **Thanks
be to God.** ↓

GOSPEL ACCLAMATION Jn. 1.14, 12 [Children of God]
(If the Alleluia is not sung, the acclamation is omitted.)

℣. Alleluia. ℟. **Alleluia.**

℣. The Word became flesh and lived among us. To all who received him, he gave the power to become children of God.

℟. **Alleluia.** ↓

In place of the Gospel Acclamation given for each Sunday in Ordinary Time, another may be selected.

GOSPEL Jn. 1.29-34   [Encountering Christ]

John the Baptist recognized Jesus: the Lamb of God who takes away the sins of the world. This is God's chosen one upon whom the Spirit descended and came to rest.

℣. The Lord be with you. ℟. **And with your spirit.**
✠ A reading from the holy Gospel according to John. ℟. **Glory to you, O Lord.**

JOHN the Baptist saw Jesus coming toward him and declared, "Here is the Lamb of God who takes away the sin of the world! This is he of whom I said, 'After me comes a man who ranks ahead of me because he was before me.' I myself did not know him; but I came baptizing with water for this reason, that he might be revealed to Israel."

And John testified, "I saw the Spirit descending from heaven like a dove, and remain on him. I myself did not know him, but the one who sent me to baptize with water said to me, 'He on whom you see the Spirit descend and remain is the one who baptizes with the Holy Spirit.' And I myself have seen and have testified that this is the Son of God."—The Gospel of the Lord. ℟. **Praise to you, Lord Jesus Christ.**   → No. 15, p. 18

PRAYER OVER THE OFFERINGS [Work of Redemption]

Grant us, O Lord, we pray,
that we may participate worthily in these mysteries,
for whenever the memorial of this sacrifice is
    celebrated
the work of our redemption is accomplished.
Through Christ our Lord..
℞. **Amen.**   ➜ No. 21, p. 22 (Pref. 29-36)

COMMUNION ANTIPHON Cf. Ps. 22.5

[Thirst Quenched]

**You have prepared a table before me, and how
precious is the chalice that quenches my thirst.** ↓

OR 1 Jn. 4.16   [God's Love]

**We have come to know and to believe in the love
that God has for us.** ↓

PRAYER AFTER COMMUNION   [One in Heart]

Pour on us, O Lord, the Spirit of your love,
and in your kindness
make those you have nourished
by this one heavenly Bread
one in mind and heart.
Through Christ our Lord.
℞. **Amen.**   ➜ No. 30, p. 77

Optional Solemn Blessings, p. 97, and Prayers over the People, p. 105

"Follow me, and I will make you fishers of people."

JANUARY 22
3rd SUNDAY IN ORDINARY TIME

ENTRANCE ANTIPHON Cf. Ps. 95.1, 6

[Sing to the Lord]

O sing a new song to the Lord; sing to the Lord, all the earth. In his presence are majesty and splendour, strength and honour in his holy place.

➔ No. 2, p. 10

COLLECT [Abound in Good Works]

Almighty ever-living God,
direct our actions according to your good
    pleasure,
that in the name of your beloved Son
we may abound in good works.
Through our Lord Jesus Christ, your Son,
who lives and reigns with you in the unity of the
    Holy Spirit,
one God, for ever and ever. R̰. **Amen.** ↓

FIRST READING Isa. 9.1-4   [Joy and Light]

Isaiah tells of the land in the west where there is no gloom, for the people see a great light. They are to rejoice that the yoke that bound them is to be smashed.

A reading from the book of the Prophet Isaiah.

THERE will be no gloom for those who were in anguish. In the former time the Lord brought into contempt the land of Zebulun and the land of Naphtali, but in the latter time he will make glorious the way of the sea, the land beyond the Jordan, Galilee of the nations.

The people who walked in darkness have seen a
    great light;
those who lived in a land of deep darkness—
on them light has shone.
You have multiplied the nation,
you have increased its joy;
they rejoice before you
as with joy at the harvest,
as people exult when dividing plunder.

For the yoke of their burden,
and the bar across their shoulders,
the rod of their oppressor,
you have broken as on the day of Midian.

The word of the Lord. ℟. **Thanks be to God.** ↓

RESPONSORIAL PSALM Ps. 27   [Wait with Courage]

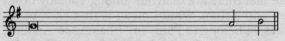

℟. The Lord is my light and my sal-va-tion.

The Lord is my light and my salvation;
whom shall I fear?
The Lord is the stronghold of my life;
of whom shall I be afraid?
R). **The Lord is my light and my salvation.**

One thing I asked of the Lord, that will I seek after:
to live in the house of the Lord all the days of my life,
to behold the beauty of the Lord,
and to inquire in his temple.—R).

I believe that I shall see the goodness of the Lord
in the land of the living.
Wait for the Lord; be strong,
and let your heart take courage; wait for the
Lord!—R). ↓

SECOND READING 1 Cor. 1.10-13, 17-18 [Need for Unity]

**Paul warns the people of Corinth that there must be
unity among the people of God. There is only one
gospel message. Jesus cannot be divided, no matter who
preaches about him.**

A reading from the first Letter of Saint Paul
to the Corinthians.

I APPEAL to you, brothers and sisters, by the
name of our Lord Jesus Christ, that all of you
be in agreement and that there be no divisions
among you, but that you be united in the same
mind and the same purpose.

For it has been reported to me by Chloe's people that there are quarrels among you, my brothers and sisters. What I mean is that each of you
says, "I belong to Paul," or "I belong to Apollos,"
or "I belong to Cephas," or "I belong to Christ."

Has Christ been divided? Was Paul crucified for you? Or were you baptized in the name of Paul?

For Christ did not send me to baptize but to proclaim the Gospel, and not with eloquent wisdom so that the Cross of Christ might not be emptied of its power.

For the message about the Cross is foolishness to those who are perishing, but to us who are being saved it is the power of God.—The word of the Lord. ℟. **Thanks be to God.** ↓

GOSPEL ACCLAMATION See Mt. 4.23   [Good News]
(If the Alleluia is not sung, the acclamation is omitted.)
℣. Alleluia. ℟. **Alleluia.**
℣. Jesus proclaimed the good news of the kingdom curing every sickness among the people.
℟. **Alleluia.** ↓

GOSPEL Mt. 4.12-23 or 4.12-17   [Reform Your Lives]

Jesus preached reform. At the Sea of Galilee he called Peter and Andrew, James and John, to become fishers of people. At once, they left their nets to follow him. Jesus taught and worked miracles.

[If the "Shorter Form" is used, the indented text in brackets is omitted.]

℣. The Lord be with you. ℟. **And with your spirit.**
✛ A reading from the holy Gospel according to Matthew. ℟. **Glory to you, O Lord.**

WHEN Jesus heard that John had been arrested, he withdrew to Galilee. He left Nazareth and made his home in Capernaum by the sea, in the territory of Zebulun and Naphtali, so that what had been spoken through the Prophet Isaiah might be fulfilled:

"Land of Zebulun, land of Naphtali,
on the road by the sea, across the Jordan,
Galilee of the Gentiles—
the people who sat in darkness
have seen a great light,
and for those who sat in the region and shadow
    of death
light has dawned."

From that time Jesus began to proclaim, "Repent, for the kingdom of heaven has come near."

[As he walked by the Sea of Galilee, he saw two brothers, Simon, who is called Peter, and Andrew his brother, casting a net into the sea, for they were fishermen. And he said to them, "Come, follow me, and I will make you fishers of people." Immediately they left their nets and followed him.

As he went from there, he saw two other brothers, James son of Zebedee and his brother John, in the boat with their father Zebedee, mending their nets, and he called them. Immediately they left the boat and their father, and followed him.

Jesus went throughout Galilee, teaching in their synagogues and proclaiming the good news of the kingdom and curing every disease and every sickness among the people.]

The Gospel of the Lord. ℟. **Praise to you, Lord Jesus Christ.**   → No. 15, p. 18

PRAYER OVER THE OFFERINGS

[Offerings for Salvation]

Accept our offerings, O Lord, we pray,
and in sanctifying them

grant that they may profit us for salvation.
Through Christ our Lord.
℞. **Amen.**   ➜ No. 21, p. 22 (Pref. 29-36)

COMMUNION ANTIPHON Cf. Ps. 33.6   [Radiance]

**Look toward the Lord and be radiant; let your
faces not be abashed.** ↓

OR Jn. 8.12   [Light of Life]

**I am the light of the world, says the Lord; who-
ever follows me will not walk in darkness, but
will have the light of life.** ↓

PRAYER AFTER COMMUNION   [New Life]

Grant, we pray, almighty God,
that, receiving the grace
by which you bring us to new life,
we may always glory in your gift.
Through Christ our Lord.
℞. **Amen.**   ➜ No. 30, p. 77

Optional Solemn Blessings, p. 97, and Prayers over the People, p. 105

"Your reward is great in heaven."

JANUARY 29
4th SUNDAY IN ORDINARY TIME

ENTRANCE ANTIPHON Ps. 105.47   [Save Us]

Save us, O Lord our God! And gather us from the nations, to give thanks to your holy name, and make it our glory to praise you.   → No. 2, p. 10

COLLECT   [Christian Love]

Grant us, Lord our God,
that we may honour you with all our mind,
and love everyone in truth of heart.
Through our Lord Jesus Christ, your Son,
who lives and reigns with you in the unity of the
   Holy Spirit,
one God, for ever and ever. ℟. **Amen.** ↓

FIRST READING Zep. 2.3; 3.12-13   [Seek the Lord]

The Lord is to be found among a people who are humble and lowly. Those who are humble seek after God. They shall find repose in God.

174

A reading from the book of the
Prophet Zephaniah.

SEEK the Lord, all you humble of the land,
who do his commands;
seek righteousness, seek humility;
perhaps you may be hidden on the day of the
Lord's wrath.

For I will leave in the midst of you
a people humble and lowly.
They shall seek refuge in the name of the Lord—
the remnant of Israel;
they shall do no wrong and utter no lies,
nor shall a deceitful tongue be found in their
mouths.
Then they will pasture and lie down,
and no one shall make them afraid.

The word of the Lord. ℟. **Thanks be to God.** ↓

RESPONSORIAL PSALM Ps. 146   [Bounty of the Lord]

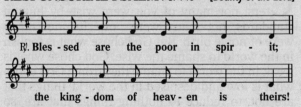

℟. Bles - sed are the poor in spir - it;
the king - dom of heav - en is theirs!

Or: ℟. **Alleluia!**

It is the Lord who keeps faith forever,
who executes justice for the oppressed;
who gives food to the hungry.
The Lord sets the prisoners free.—℟.

The Lord opens the eyes of the blind
and lifts up those who are bowed down;
the Lord loves the righteous
and watches over the strangers.
℟. **Blessed are the poor in spirit;**
    the kingdom of heaven is theirs!

The Lord upholds the orphan and the widow,
but the way of the wicked he brings to ruin.
The Lord will reign forever,
your God, O Zion, for all generations.—℟. ↓

SECOND READING 1 Cor. 1.26-31   [Boast in the Lord]

**Contrary to worldly standards, God chooses those who
are weak, small, lowborn and despised. To these God
has given the divine Son, Jesus, for sanctification and redemption.**

A reading from the first Letter of Saint Paul
to the Corinthians.

CONSIDER your own call, brothers and sisters: not many of you were wise by human
standards, not many were powerful, not many
were of noble birth. But God chose what is foolish
in the world to shame the wise; God chose what is
weak in the world to shame the strong; God chose
what is low and despised in the world, things that
are not, to reduce to nothing things that are, so
that no one might boast in the presence of God.

God is the source of your life in Christ Jesus,
who became for us wisdom from God, and righteousness and sanctification and redemption, in
order that, as it is written, "Let the one who
boasts, boast in the Lord."—The word of the
Lord. ℟. **Thanks be to God.** ↓

GOSPEL ACCLAMATION Mt. 5.12   [Rejoice]

(If the Alleluia is not sung, the acclamation is omitted.)

℣. Alleluia. ℟. **Alleluia.**

℣. Rejoice and be glad;

for your reward is great in heaven.

℟. **Alleluia ↓**

GOSPEL Mt. 5.1-12a   [A New Teaching]

Jesus says that the poor in spirit, the sorrowing, those thirsting for holiness, the merciful, the peacemakers, and those who suffer for holiness' sake are "happy"—their reward awaits them in heaven.

℣. The Lord be with you. ℟. **And with your spirit.**

✤ A reading from the holy Gospel according to Matthew. ℟. **Glory to you, O Lord.**

WHEN Jesus saw the crowds, he went up the mountain; and after he sat down, his disciples came to him. Then he began to speak, and taught them, saying:

"Blessed are the poor in spirit,

for theirs is the kingdom of heaven.

Blessed are those who mourn,

for they will be comforted.

Blessed are the meek,

for they will inherit the earth.

Blessed are those who hunger and thirst for

righteousness,

for they will be filled.

Blessed are the merciful,

for they will receive mercy.

Blessed are the pure in heart,

for they will see God.

Blessed are the peacemakers,

for they will be called children of God.
Blessed are those who are persecuted for righteousness' sake,
for theirs is the kingdom of heaven.
Blessed are you when people revile you and persecute you and utter all kinds of evil against you
falsely on my account. Rejoice and be glad, for
your reward is great in heaven, for in the same
way they persecuted the Prophets who were before you."—The Gospel of the Lord. ℟. **Praise to
you, Lord Jesus Christ.**   → No. 15, p. 18

PRAYER OVER THE OFFERINGS

[Sacrament of Redemption]

O Lord, we bring to your altar
these offerings of our service:
be pleased to receive them, we pray,
and transform them
into the Sacrament of our redemption.
Through Christ our Lord.
℟. **Amen.**   → No. 21, p. 22 (Pref. 29-36)

COMMUNION ANTIPHON Cf. Ps. 30.17-18   [Save Me]

**Let your face shine on your servant. Save me in
your merciful love. O Lord, let me never be put to
shame, for I call on you.** ↓

OR Mt 5.3-4   [Poor in Spirit]

**Blessed are the poor in spirit, for theirs is the
Kingdom of Heaven. Blessed are the meek, for
they shall possess the land.** ↓

PRAYER AFTER COMMUNION   [True Faith]

Nourished by these redeeming gifts,
we pray, O Lord,
that through this help to eternal salvation
true faith may ever increase.
Through Christ our Lord.
R̶. **Amen.**   ➙ No. 30, p. 77

Optional Solemn Blessings, p. 97, and Prayers over the People, p. 105

"You are the light of the world."

FEBRUARY 5

5th SUNDAY IN ORDINARY TIME

ENTRANCE ANTIPHON Ps. 94.6-7   [Adoration]

**O come, let us worship God and bow low before
the God who made us, for he is the Lord our God.**
          ➙ No. 2, p. 10

COLLECT   [God's Protection]

Keep your family safe, O Lord, with unfailing care,
that, relying solely on the hope of heavenly grace,

they may be defended always by your protection.
Through our Lord Jesus Christ, your Son,
who lives and reigns with you in the unity of the
    Holy Spirit,
one God, for ever and ever. ℟. **Amen.** ↓

FIRST READING Isa. 58.6-10   [Charity]

**The Lord promises that those who share their food with
the hungry and their clothing with the naked shall find
true favour with God. A light shall shine for them.**

A reading from the book of the Prophet Isaiah.

T HUS says the Lord:
    Is this not the fast that I choose:
to loose the bonds of injustice,
to undo the thongs of the yoke,
to let the oppressed go free,
and to break every yoke?
Is it not to share your bread with the hungry,
and bring the homeless poor into your house;
when you see the naked, to cover them,
and not to hide yourself from your own kin?

Then your light shall break forth like the dawn,
and your healing shall spring up quickly;
your vindicator shall go before you,
the glory of the Lord shall be your rear guard.
Then you shall call, and the Lord will answer;
you shall cry for help, and he will say, 'Here I am.'

If you remove the yoke from among you,
the pointing of the finger, the speaking of evil,
if you offer your food to the hungry
and satisfy the needs of the afflicted,

then your light shall rise in the darkness
and your gloom be like the noonday.
The word of the Lord. ℟. **Thanks be to God.** ↓

RESPONSORIAL PSALM Ps. 112   [The Upright]

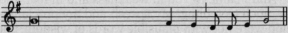

℟. **Light   rises   in   the   dark-ness for the up-right.**

Or: ℟. **Alleluia!**

Light rises in the darkness for the upright:
gracious, merciful and righteous.
It is well with the person who deals generously
    and lends,
who conducts their affairs with justice.—℟.

For the righteous person will never be moved;
they will be remembered forever.
Unafraid of evil tidings;
their heart is firm, secure in the Lord.—℟.

That person's heart is steady and will not be
    afraid.
One who has distributed freely, who has given to
    the poor,
their righteousness endures forever:
their name is exalted in honour.—℟. ↓

SECOND READING 1 Cor. 2.1-5   [Power of the Spirit]
    Paul preached to the Corinthians in weakness and fear.
    He preached Jesus crucified, but through the working of
    the Holy Spirit, these people came to be believers.

A reading from the first Letter of Saint Paul
        to the Corinthians.

WHEN I came to you, brothers and sisters, I did not come proclaiming the mystery of God to you in lofty words or wisdom. For I decided to know nothing among you except Jesus Christ, and him crucified.

And I came to you in weakness and in fear and in much trembling. My speech and my proclamation were not with plausible words of wisdom, but with a demonstration of the Spirit and of power, so that your faith might rest not on human wisdom but on the power of God.—The word of the Lord. ℟. **Thanks be to God.** ↓

GOSPEL ACCLAMATION See Jn. 8.12   [Light of Life]
(If the Alleluia is not sung, the acclamation is omitted.)

℣. Alleluia. ℟. **Alleluia.**
℣. I am the light of the world, says the Lord; whoever follows me will have the light of life.
℟. **Alleluia.** ↓

GOSPEL Mt. 5.13-16   [Light of the World]

The faithful followers of Jesus are the salt of the earth and a light to the world. Being true Christ-bearers, they become an example for others.

℣. The Lord be with you. ℟. **And with your spirit.**
✛ A reading from the holy Gospel according to Matthew. ℟. **Glory to you, O Lord.**

JESUS said to his disciples: "You are the salt of the earth; but if salt has lost its taste, how can its saltiness be restored? It is no longer good for anything, but is thrown out and trampled under foot.

You are the light of the world. A city built on a hill cannot be hidden. No one after lighting a lamp puts it under the bushel basket, but on the lampstand, and it gives light to all in the house. In the same way, let your light shine before human beings, so that they may see your good works and give glory to your Father in heaven."—The Gospel of the Lord. ℟. **Praise to you, Lord Jesus Christ.**

→ No. 15, p. 18

PRAYER OVER THE OFFERINGS   [Eternal Life]

O Lord our God,
who once established these created things
to sustain us in our frailty,
grant, we pray,
that they may become for us now
the Sacrament of eternal life.
Through Christ our Lord.
℟. **Amen.**   → No. 21, p. 22 (Pref. 29-36)

COMMUNION ANTIPHON Cf. Ps. 106.8-9   [Mercy]

Let them thank the Lord for his mercy, his wonders for the children of men, for he satisfies the thirsty soul, and the hungry he fills with good things. ↓

OR Mt. 5.5-6   [Those Who Mourn]

Blessed are those who mourn, for they shall be consoled. Blessed are those who hunger and thirst for righteousness, for they shall have their fill. ↓

PRAYER AFTER COMMUNION   [Salvation and Joy]

O God, who have willed that we be partakers
in the one Bread and the one Chalice,
grant us, we pray, so to live
that, made one in Christ,

we may joyfully bear fruit
for the salvation of the world.
Through Christ our Lord.
℟. **Amen.**

→ No. 30, p. 77

Optional Solemn Blessings, p. 97, and Prayers over the People, p. 105

"First be reconciled to your brother or sister."

FEBRUARY 12

6th SUNDAY IN ORDINARY TIME

ENTRANCE ANTIPHON Cf. Ps. 30.3-4 　　[Protector]
**Be my protector, O God, a mighty stronghold to
save me. For you are my rock, my stronghold!
Lead me, guide me, for the sake of your name.**

→ No. 2, p. 10

COLLECT 　　[Fashioned by God's Grace]
O God, who teach us that you abide
in hearts that are just and true,
grant that we may be so fashioned by your grace
as to become a dwelling pleasing to you.

Through our Lord Jesus Christ, your Son,
who lives and reigns with you in the unity of the
 Holy Spirit,
one God, for ever and ever. ℟. **Amen.** ↓

FIRST READING Sir. 15.15-20   [Freedom to Do Good]

**God is all-knowing, always aware of everything that we
do. All persons are free to choose to do God's will, for
God uses no force.**

A reading from the book of Sirach.

IF you choose, you can keep the commandments,
 and they will save you. If you trust in God, you
too shall live,
and to act faithfully is a matter of your own
 choice.

The Lord has placed before you fire and water;
stretch out your hand for whichever you choose.
Before each person are life and death, good and
 evil
and whichever one chooses, that shall be given.

For great is the wisdom of the Lord;
he is mighty in power and sees everything;
his eyes are on those who fear him,
and he knows every human action.
He has not commanded anyone to be wicked,
and he has not given anyone permission to sin.

The word of the Lord. ℟. **Thanks be to God.** ↓

RESPONSORIAL PSALM Ps. 119

[Following God's Law]

℟. **Blessed are those who walk in the law of the Lord!**

Blessed are those whose way is blameless,
who walk in the law of the Lord.
Blessed are those who keep his decrees,
who seek him with their whole heart.
℟. **Blessed are those who walk in the law of the
    Lord!**

You have commanded your precepts
to be kept diligently.
O that my ways may be steadfast
in keeping your statutes!—℟.

Deal bountifully with your servant,
so that I may live and observe your word.
Open my eyes, so that I may behold
wondrous things out of your law.—℟.

Teach me, O Lord, the way of your statutes,
and I will observe it to the end.
Give me understanding, that I may keep your law
and observe it with my whole heart.—℟. ↓

SECOND READING 1 Cor. 2.6-10   [God's Wisdom]

Out of wisdom that is beyond our imagination, God has
revealed the Divinity through the Holy Spirit. The Spirit
knows the inner workings of God.

A reading from the first Letter of Saint Paul
to the Corinthians.

BROTHERS and sisters: Among the mature we
do speak wisdom, though it is not a wisdom
of this age or of the rulers of this age, who are
doomed to perish. But we speak God's wisdom,
secret and hidden, which God decreed before the
ages for our glory. None of the rulers of this age

understood this; for if they had, they would not have crucified the Lord of glory.

As it is written,

"What no eye has seen, nor ear heard,
    nor the human heart conceived
    what God has prepared for those who love
    him."

These things God has revealed to us through the Spirit; for the Spirit searches everything, even the depths of God.—The word of the Lord. ℟. **Thanks be to God.** ↓

GOSPEL ACCLAMATION See Mt. 11.25 [The Kingdom]

(If the Alleluia is not sung, the acclamation is omitted.)

℣. Alleluia. ℟. **Alleluia.**

℣. Blessed are you, Father, Lord of heaven and
    earth;

you have revealed to little ones the mysteries of
    the kingdom.

℟. **Alleluia.** ↓

GOSPEL Mt. 5.17-37 or 5.17, 20-24, 27-28, 33-34, 37 [Holiness]

God revealed the divine law to the Israelites, and Jesus came to bring it to perfection. Those who obey God's laws will become great in the kingdom of God. Jesus explains more fully the laws of God.

[If the "Shorter Form" is used, the indented text in brackets is omitted.]

℣. The Lord be with you. ℟. **And with your spirit.**
✚ A reading from the holy Gospel according to Matthew. ℟. **Glory to you, O Lord.**

JESUS said to his disciples: "Do not think that I have come to abolish the Law or the Prophets; I have come not to abolish but to fulfill.

[For truly I tell you, until heaven and earth pass away, not one letter, not one stroke of a letter, will pass from the Law until all is accomplished. Therefore, whoever breaks one of the least of these commandments, and teaches others to do the same, will be called least in the kingdom of heaven; but whoever does them and teaches them will be called great in the kingdom of heaven.]

For I tell you, unless your righteousness exceeds that of the scribes and Pharisees, you will never enter the kingdom of heaven.

You have heard that it was said to those of ancient times, 'You shall not murder'; and 'whoever murders shall be liable to judgment.' But I say to you that the one who is angry with their brother or sister, will be liable to judgment; and whoever insults their brother or sister, will be liable to the council; and whoever says, 'You fool,' will be liable to the hell of fire.

So when you are offering your gift at the altar, if you remember that your brother or sister has something against you, leave your gift there before the altar and go; first be reconciled to your brother or sister, and then come and offer your gift.

[Come to terms quickly with your accuser while the two of you are on the way to court, or your accuser may hand you over to the judge, and the judge to the guard, and you will be thrown into prison. Truly I tell you, you will never get out until you have paid the last penny.]

You have heard that it was said, 'You shall not commit adultery.' But I say to you that everyone who looks at a woman with lust has already committed adultery with her in his heart.

[If your right eye causes you to sin, tear it out and throw it away; it is better for you to lose one of your members than for your whole body to be thrown into hell. And if your right hand causes you to sin, cut it off and throw it away; it is better for you to lose one of your members than for your whole body to go into hell.

It was also said, 'Whoever divorces his wife, let him give her a certificate of divorce.' But I say to you that anyone who divorces his wife, except on the ground of unchastity, causes her to commit adultery; and whoever marries a divorced woman commits adultery.]

Again, you have heard that it was said to those of ancient times, 'You shall not swear falsely, but carry out the vows you have made to the Lord.' But I say to you: Do not swear at all,

[either by heaven, for it is the throne of God, or by the earth, for it is his footstool, or by Jerusalem, for it is the city of the great King. And do not swear by your head, for you cannot make one hair white or black.]

Let your word be 'Yes,' if 'Yes,' or 'No,' if 'No'; anything more than this comes from the evil one."— The Gospel of the Lord. ℟. **Praise to you, Lord Jesus Christ.**   ➜ No. 15, p. 18

PRAYER OVER THE OFFERINGS   [Renewal]

May this oblation, O Lord, we pray,
cleanse and renew us
and may it become for those who do your will
the source of eternal reward.
Through Christ our Lord.
℟. **Amen.**   → No. 21, p. 22 (Pref. 29-36)

COMMUNION ANTIPHON Cf. Ps. 77.29-30

[God's Food]

**They ate and had their fill, and what they craved
the Lord gave them; they were not disappointed
in what they craved.** ↓

OR Jn. 3.16   [God's Love]

**God so loved the world that he gave his Only Begotten Son, so that all who believe in him may
not perish, but may have eternal life.** ↓

PRAYER AFTER COMMUNION   [Heavenly Delights]

Having fed upon these heavenly delights,
we pray, O Lord,
that we may always long
for that food by which we truly live.
Through Christ our Lord.
℟. **Amen.**   → No. 30, p. 77

Optional Solemn Blessings, p. 97, and Prayers over the People, p. 105

"Be perfect . . . as your heavenly Father is perfect."

FEBRUARY 19

7th SUNDAY IN ORDINARY TIME

ENTRANCE ANTIPHON Ps. 12.6   [God's Merciful Love]

O Lord, I trust in your merciful love. My heart will rejoice in your salvation. I will sing to the Lord who has been bountiful with me.   → No. 2, p. 10

COLLECT   [Word and Deed]

Grant, we pray, almighty God,
that, always pondering spiritual things,
we may carry out in both word and deed
that which is pleasing to you.
Through our Lord Jesus Christ, your Son,
who lives and reigns with you in the unity of the
    Holy Spirit,
one God, for ever and ever. ℟. **Amen.** ↓

FIRST READING Lev. 19.1-2, 17-18   [Love of Neighbour]

God's people are called to be holy. The following verses explain what is most essential for holiness. It all revolves around love, mercy, kindness and compassion.

A reading from the book of Leviticus.

THE Lord spoke to Moses: "Speak to all the congregation of the children of Israel and say to them: 'You shall be holy, for I the Lord your God am holy.

You shall not hate in your heart anyone of your kin; you shall reprove your neighbour, or you will incur guilt yourself. You shall not take vengeance or bear a grudge against any of your people, but you shall love your neighbour as yourself: I am the Lord.'"—The word of the Lord. ℟. **Thanks be to God.** ↓

RESPONSORIAL PSALM Ps. 103   [Plea for Pardon]

℟. The Lord is mer - ci - ful and gracious.

Bless the Lord, O my soul,
and all that is within me, bless his holy name.
Bless the Lord, O my soul,
and do not forget all his benefits.—℟.

It is the Lord who forgives all your iniquity,
who heals all your diseases,
who redeems your life from the Pit,
who crowns you with steadfast love and mercy.
—℟.

The Lord is merciful and gracious,
slow to anger and abounding in steadfast
  love.
He does not deal with us according to our
  sins,
nor repay us according to our iniquities.—℟.

As far as the east is from the west,
so far he removes our transgressions from us.
As a father has compassion for his children,
so the Lord has compassion for those who fear
  him.—℟. ↓

SECOND READING 1 Cor. 3.16-23   [Temple of God]

**We must be conscious of our dignity as Christians: we
are truly temples of the Holy Spirit. Let no one glory in
anything else.**

A reading from the first Letter of Saint Paul
          to the Corinthians.

BROTHERS and sisters: Do you not know that
    you are God's temple and that God's Spirit
dwells in you? If anyone destroys God's temple,
God will destroy that person. For God's temple is
holy, and you are that temple.

Do not deceive yourselves. If you think that
you are wise in this age, you should become
fools so that you may become wise. For the wisdom of this world is foolishness with God. For it
is written,
  "He catches the wise in their craftiness,"
and again,

"The Lord knows the thoughts of the wise,
that they are futile."

So let no one boast about human beings. For
all things are yours—whether Paul or Apollos or
Cephas, or the world or life or death, or the present or the future—all belong to you, and you
belong to Christ, and Christ belongs to God.—
The word of the Lord. ℟. **Thanks be to God.** ↓

GOSPEL ACCLAMATION See 1 Jn. 2.5   [Be Perfect]
(If the Alleluia is not sung, the acclamation is omitted.)

℣. Alleluia. ℟. **Alleluia.**
℣. Whoever obeys the word of Christ,
grows perfect in the love of God.
℟. **Alleluia.** ↓

GOSPEL Mt. 5.38-48   [Love of Enemies]

Christian love knows no measure. It surpasses justice
and goes so far as to show goodness to one's enemies.

℣. The Lord be with you. ℟. **And with your spirit.**
A reading from the holy Gospel according to
Matthew. ℟. **Glory to you, O Lord.**

JESUS said to his disciples, "You have heard
that it was said, 'An eye for an eye and a tooth
for a tooth.' But I say to you, Do not resist an evil-
doer. But if anyone strikes you on the right
cheek, turn the other also; and if anyone wants to
sue you and take your coat, give your cloak as
well; and if anyone forces you to go one mile, go
with them also the second mile. Give to everyone
who begs from you, and do not refuse anyone
who wants to borrow from you. You have heard
that it was said, 'You shall love your neighbour

and hate your enemy.' But I say to you, Love your enemies and pray for those who persecute you, so that you may be children of your Father in heaven; for he makes his sun rise on the evil and on the good, and sends rain on the righteous and on the unrighteous.

For if you love those who love you, what reward do you have? Do not even the tax collectors do the same? And if you greet only your brothers and sisters, what more are you doing than others? Do not even the Gentiles do the same?

Be perfect, therefore, as your heavenly Father is perfect."—The Gospel of the Lord. ℟. **Praise to you, Lord Jesus Christ.**   ➜ No. 15, p. 18

PRAYER OVER THE OFFERINGS [Celebrate Mysteries]

As we celebrate your mysteries, O Lord,
with the observance that is your due,
we humbly ask you,
that what we offer to the honour of your majesty
may profit us for salvation.
Through Christ our Lord.
℟. **Amen.**   ➜ No. 21, p. 22 (Pref. 29-36)

COMMUNION ANTIPHON Ps. 9.2-3   [Joy in God]
I will recount all your wonders, I will rejoice in you and be glad, and sing psalms to your name, O Most High. ↓

OR Jn. 11.27   [Belief in Christ]
Lord, I have come to believe that you are the Christ, the Son of the living God, who is coming into this world. ↓

PRAYER AFTER COMMUNION [Experience Salvation]

Grant, we pray, almighty God,
that we may experience the effects of the salvation
which is pledged to us by these mysteries.
Through Christ our Lord.
℟. **Amen.**   ➔ No. 30, p. 77

Optional Solemn Blessings, p. 97, and Prayers over the People, p. 105

"Consider the lilies of the field."

FEBRUARY 26
8th SUNDAY IN ORDINARY TIME

ENTRANCE ANTIPHON Cf. Ps. 17.19-20

[God Our Protector]

**The Lord became my protector. He brought me
out to a place of freedom; he saved me because
he delighted in me.**   ➔ No. 2, p. 10

COLLECT   [Peaceful Rule]

Grant us, O Lord, we pray,
that the course of our world
may be directed by your peaceful rule
and that your Church may rejoice,
untroubled in her devotion.
Through our Lord Jesus Christ, your Son,
who lives and reigns with you in the unity of the
    Holy Spirit,
one God, for ever and ever. ℞. **Amen.** ↓

FIRST READING Isa. 49.14-15   [God's Faithfulness]

The exile in Babylon was a test of the faith and patience
of the Hebrews. The unknown wandering preacher
whose sermons are preserved in Isaiah 40–55 (Second
Isaiah) encourages his fellow exiles to have faith in the
providence of God.

A reading from the book of
the Prophet Isaiah.

ZION said, "The Lord has forsaken me,
    my Lord has forgotten me."
Can a woman forget her nursing child,
or show no compassion for the child of her
    womb?
Even these may forget,
yet I will not forget you.
—The word of the Lord. ℞. **Thanks be to God.** ↓

RESPONSORIAL PSALM Ps. 62   [Trust in God]

℞. For God   a - lone   my soul waits in silence.

For God alone my soul waits in silence;
from him comes my salvation.
He alone is my rock and my salvation, my fortress;
I shall never be shaken.
℟. **For God alone my soul waits in silence.**

For God alone my soul waits in silence,
for my hope is from him.
He alone is my rock and my salvation, my fortress;
I shall not be shaken.—℟.

On God rests my deliverance and my honour;
my mighty rock, my refuge is in God.
Trust in him at all times, O people;
pour out your heart before him.—℟. ↓

SECOND READING 1 Cor. 4.1-5   [God Our Judge]

> As Christians, we must be persons of expectation and
> hope, serving others with no thought of earthly re-
> ward—but simply for the Lord.

A reading from the first Letter of Saint Paul
to the Corinthians.

BROTHERS and sisters: Think of us in this
way, as servants of Christ and stewards of
God's mysteries. Moreover, it is required of
stewards that they be found trustworthy. But
with me it is a very small thing that I should be
judged by you or by any human court. I do not
even judge myself.

I am not aware of anything against myself,
but I am not thereby acquitted. It is the Lord
who judges me. Therefore do not pronounce
judgment before the time, before the Lord
comes, who will bring to light the things now

hidden in darkness and will disclose the purposes of the heart.

Then each one will receive commendation from God.—The word of the Lord. ℟. **Thanks be to God.** ↓

GOSPEL ACCLAMATION Heb. 4.12   [Living Word]

(If the Alleluia is not sung, the acclamation is omitted.)

℣. Alleluia. ℟. **Alleluia.**
℣. The word of God is living and active;
it judges the thoughts and intentions of the heart.
℟. **Alleluia.** ↓

GOSPEL Mt. 6.24-34   [Trust in God]

We must have unlimited trust in God while at the same time working with all our might to do the things expected of us.

℣. The Lord be with you. ℟. **And with your spirit.** A reading from the holy Gospel according to Matthew. ℟. **Glory to you, O Lord.**

JESUS taught his disciples, saying, "No one can serve two masters; for a slave will either hate the one and love the other, or be devoted to the one and despise the other. You cannot serve God and wealth.

Therefore I tell you, do not worry about your life, what you will eat or what you will drink, or about your body, what you will wear. Is not life more than food, and the body more than clothing?

Look at the birds of the air; they neither sow nor reap nor gather into barns, and yet your heavenly Father feeds them. Are you not of more value than they? And can any one of you by worrying add a single hour to their span of life?

And why do you worry about clothing? Consider the lilies of the field, how they grow; they neither toil nor spin, yet I tell you, even Solomon in all his glory was not clothed like one of these. But if God so clothes the grass of the field, which is alive today and tomorrow is thrown into the oven, will he not much more clothe you—you of little faith?

Therefore do not worry, saying, 'What will we eat?' or 'What will we drink?' or 'What will we wear?' For it is the Gentiles who strive for all these things; and indeed your heavenly Father knows that you need all these things. But strive first for the kingdom of God and his righteousness, and all these things will be given to you as well.

So do not worry about tomorrow, for tomorrow will bring worries of its own. Today's trouble is enough for today."—The Gospel of the Lord. ℟. **Praise to you, Lord Jesus Christ.**

➜ No. 15, p. 18

PRAYER OVER THE OFFERING [Serve with Devotion]

O God, who provide gifts to be offered to your
   name
and count our oblations as signs
of our desire to serve you with devotion,
we ask of your mercy
that what you grant as the source of merit
may also help us to attain merit's reward.
Through Christ our Lord.
℟. **Amen.**
➜ No. 21, p. 22 (Pref. 29-36)

COMMUNION ANTIPHON Cf. Ps. 12.6   [God's Bounty]

I will sing to the Lord who has been bountiful with me, sing psalms to the name of the Lord Most High. ↓

OR Mt. 28.20   [Christ's Presence]

Behold, I am with you always, even to the end of the age, says the Lord. ↓

PRAYER AFTER COMMUNION   [Life Eternal]

Nourished by your saving gifts,
we beseech your mercy, Lord,
that by this same Sacrament
with which you feed us in the present age,
you may make us partakers of life eternal.
Through Christ our Lord.
℟. Amen.   → No. 30, p. 77

Optional Solemn Blessings, p. 97, and Prayers over the People, p. 105

"Away with you, Satan! for it is written, 'Worship the Lord your God.'"

MARCH 5

1st SUNDAY OF LENT

ENTRANCE ANTIPHON Cf. Ps. 90.15-16

[Length of Days]

When he calls on me, I will answer him; I will deliver him and give him glory, I will grant him length of days. → No. 2, p. 10 (Omit Gloria)

COLLECT [Grow in Understanding]

Grant, almighty God,
through the yearly observances of holy Lent,
that we may grow in understanding
of the riches hidden in Christ
and by worthy conduct pursue their effects.
Through our Lord Jesus Christ, your Son,
who lives and reigns with you in the unity of the
    Holy Spirit,
one God, for ever and ever. ℟. **Amen.** ↓

FIRST READING Gen. 2.7-9, 16-18, 25; 3.1-7

[Sin of Our First Parents]

God created Adam and Eve and placed them in the Garden of Eden. They could eat fruit from every tree except one. After being tempted by the devil, they disobeyed God's command. Immediately their lives changed.

A reading from the book of Genesis.

THE Lord God formed man from the dust of the ground, and breathed into his nostrils the breath of life; and the man became a living being. And the Lord God planted a garden in Eden, in the east; and there he put the man whom he had formed. Out of the ground the Lord God made to grow every tree that is pleasant to the sight and good for food, the tree of life also in the midst of the garden, and the tree of the knowledge of good and evil.

And the Lord God commanded the man, "You may freely eat of every tree of the garden; but of the tree of the knowledge of good and evil you shall not eat, for in the day that you eat of it you shall die." Then the Lord God said, "It is not good that the man should be alone; I will make him a helper as his partner." And the man and his wife were both naked, and were not ashamed.

Now the serpent was more crafty than any other wild animal that the Lord God had made. He said to the woman, "Did God say, 'You shall not eat from any tree in the garden'?" The woman said to the serpent, "We may eat of the fruit of the trees in the garden; but God said, 'You shall not eat of the fruit of the tree that is in the middle of the garden, nor shall you touch it, or you shall die.'" But the serpent said to the woman, "You will not die; for God knows that when you eat of it your eyes will be opened, and you will be like God, knowing good and evil."

So when the woman saw that the tree was good for food, and that it was a delight to the eyes, and that the tree was to be desired to make one wise, she took of its fruit and ate; and she also gave some to her husband, who was with her, and he ate.

Then the eyes of both were opened, and they knew that they were naked; and they sewed fig leaves together and made loincloths for themselves.—The word of the Lord. ℟. **Thanks be to God.** ↓

RESPONSORIAL PSALM Ps. 51   [Repentance]

℟. Have mercy, O Lord, for we have sinned.

Have mercy on me, O God,
according to your steadfast love;
according to your abundant mercy
blot out my transgressions.
Wash me thoroughly from my iniquity,
and cleanse me from my sin.—℟.

For I know my transgressions,
and my sin is ever before me.
Against you, you alone, have I sinned,
and done what is evil in your sight.—℟.

Create in me a clean heart, O God,
and put a new and right spirit within me.
Do not cast me away from your presence,
and do not take your holy spirit from me.—℟.

Restore to me the joy of your salvation,
and sustain in me a willing spirit.
O Lord, open my lips,
and my mouth will declare your praise.—℟. ↓

SECOND READING Rom. 5.12-19 or 5.12, 17-19

[Saved Through Christ]

From the fall of Adam, sin came into the world. God, however, gave the gift of his Son, Jesus. Through him justice was restored. Through the obedience of Jesus, justice comes to all.

[If the "Shorter Form" is used, the indented text in brackets is omitted.]

A reading from the Letter of Saint Paul
to the Romans.

BROTHERS and sisters: Just as sin came into the world through one man, and death came through sin, so death spread to all people, because all have sinned.

[Sin was indeed in the world before the law, but sin is not reckoned when there is no law. Yet death exercised dominion from Adam to Moses, even over those whose sins were not like the transgression of Adam, who is a type of the one who was to come.

But the free gift is not like the trespass. For if the many died through the one man's trespass, much more surely have the grace of

God and the free gift in the grace of the one man, Jesus Christ, abounded for the many. And the free gift is not like the effect of the one man's sin. For the judgment following one trespass brought condemnation, but the free gift following many trespasses brings justification.]

If, because of the one man's trespass, death exercised dominion through that one, much more surely will those who receive the abundance of grace and the free gift of righteousness exercise dominion in life through the one man, Jesus Christ.

Therefore just as one man's trespass led to condemnation for all people, so one man's act of righteousness leads to justification and life for all people. For just as by the one man's disobedience the many were made sinners, so by the one man's obedience the many will be made righteous.—The word of the Lord. ℟. **Thanks be to God.** ↓

GOSPEL ACCLAMATION Mt. 4.4   [Word of Life]

(If the acclamation is not sung, it is omitted.)

℣. Glory and praise to you, Lord Jesus Christ.*

℟. **Glory and praise to you, Lord Jesus Christ.**

℣. Man does not live by bread alone,
but by every word that comes from the mouth of God.

℟. **Glory and praise to you, Lord Jesus Christ.** ↓

GOSPEL Mt. 4.1-11   [Temptation]

The devil tempted Adam; he also tempts Jesus three times, making lavish promises. Jesus rebukes Satan, for only God is to be adored.

---

* *See p. 16 for other Gospel Acclamations.*

℣. The Lord be with you. ℟. **And with your spirit.**
✠ A reading from the holy Gospel according to
Matthew. ℟. **Glory to you, O Lord.**

JESUS was led up by the Spirit into the wilderness to be tempted by the devil. He fasted forty days and forty nights, and afterwards he was famished. The tempter came and said to him, "If you are the Son of God, command these stones to become loaves of bread." But he answered, "It is written,

'Man does not live by bread alone,
    but by every word that comes from the
        mouth of God.'"

Then the devil took him to the holy city and placed him on the pinnacle of the temple, saying to him, "If you are the Son of God, throw yourself down; for it is written,

'He will command his Angels concerning you,'

    and 'On their hands they will bear you up,
    so that you will not dash your foot against a
        stone.'"

Jesus said to him, "Again it is written, 'Do not put the Lord your God to the test.'"

Again, the devil took him to a very high mountain and showed him all the kingdoms of the world and their splendour; and he said to him, "All these I will give you, if you will fall down and worship me." Jesus said to him, "Away with you, Satan! for it is written,

'Worship the Lord your God,
    and serve only him.'"

Then the devil left him, and suddenly Angels came and waited on him.—The Gospel of the

Lord. ℟. **Praise to you, Lord Jesus Christ.**

➜ No. 15, p. 18

PRAYER OVER THE OFFERINGS   [Sacred Time]

Give us the right dispositions, O Lord, we pray,
to make these offerings,
for with them we celebrate the beginning
of this venerable and sacred time.
Through Christ our Lord. ℟. **Amen.** ↓

PREFACE (12)   [Christ's Abstinence]

℣. The Lord be with you. ℟. **And with your spirit.**
℣. Lift up your hearts. ℟. **We lift them up to the
Lord.**
℣. Let us give thanks to the Lord our God. ℟. **It is
right and just.**

It is truly right and just, our duty and our salvation,
always and everywhere to give you thanks,
Lord, holy Father, almighty and eternal God,
through Christ our Lord.

By abstaining forty long days from earthly food,
he consecrated through his fast
the pattern of our Lenten observance
and, by overturning all the snares of the ancient
    serpent,
taught us to cast out the leaven of malice,
so that, celebrating worthily the Paschal Mystery,
we might pass over at last to the eternal paschal
    feast.

And so, with the company of Angels and Saints,
we sing the hymn of your praise,
as without end we acclaim: ➜ No. 23, p. 23

COMMUNION ANTIPHON Mt. 4.4   [Life-Giving Word]

One does not live by bread alone, but by every word that comes forth from the mouth of God. ↓

OR Cf. Ps. 90.4   [Refuge in God]

The Lord will conceal you with his pinions, and under his wings you will trust. ↓

PRAYER AFTER COMMUNION   [Heavenly Bread]

Renewed now with heavenly bread,
by which faith is nourished, hope increased,
and charity strengthened,
we pray, O Lord,
that we may learn to hunger for Christ,
the true and living Bread,
and strive to live by every word
which proceeds from your mouth.
Through Christ our Lord.
℞. **Amen.** ↓

The Deacon or, in his absence, the Priest himself, says the invitation: Bow down for the blessing.

PRAYER OVER THE PEOPLE   [Bountiful Blessing]

May bountiful blessing, O Lord, we pray,
come down upon your people,
that hope may grow in tribulation,
virtue be strengthened in temptation,
and eternal redemption be assured.
Through Christ our Lord.
℞. **Amen.**   → No. 32, p. 77

"Suddenly there appeared to them Moses and Elijah, talking with him."

MARCH 12
2nd SUNDAY OF LENT

ENTRANCE ANTIPHON Cf. Ps. 26.8-9   [God's Face]

Of you my heart has spoken: Seek his face. It is your face, O Lord, that I seek; hide not your face from me.   → No. 2, p. 10 (Omit Gloria)

OR Cf. Ps. 24.6, 2, 22   [God's Merciful Love]

Remember your compassion, O Lord, and your merciful love, for they are from of old. Let not our enemies exult over us. Redeem us, O God of Israel, from all our distress.

→ No. 2, p. 10 (Omit Gloria)

COLLECT   [Nourish Us]

O God, who have commanded us
to listen to your beloved Son,
be pleased, we pray,
to nourish us inwardly by your word,

that, with spiritual sight made pure,
we may rejoice to behold your glory.
Through our Lord Jesus Christ, your Son,
who lives and reigns with you in the unity of the
   Holy Spirit,
one God, for ever and ever. R/. **Amen.** ↓

FIRST READING Gen. 12.1-4   [Mission of Abraham]

> **God calls Abraham and promises to make him a leader
> of a great nation, a person whom all will respect.**

A reading from the book of Genesis.

THE Lord said to Abram, "Go from your country and your kindred and your father's house
to the land that I will show you. I will make of you
a great nation, and I will bless you, and make
your name great, so that you will be a blessing. I
will bless those who bless you, and the one who
curses you I will curse; and in you all the families
of the earth shall be blessed."

So Abram went, as the Lord had told him.—
The word of the Lord. R/. **Thanks be to God.** ↓

RESPONSORIAL PSALM Ps. 33   [Trust in God]

R/. Let your love be upon us, Lord, ev-en as we hope in you.

The word of the Lord is upright,
and all his work is done in faithfulness.
He loves righteousness and justice;
the earth is full of the steadfast love of the
   Lord.—R/.

Truly the eye of the Lord is on those who fear him,
on those who hope in his steadfast love,
to deliver their soul from death,
and to keep them alive in famine.
℟. **Let your love be upon us, Lord,**
    even as we hope in you.

Our soul waits for the Lord;
he is our help and shield.
Let your steadfast love, O Lord, be upon us,
even as we hope in you.—℟. ↓

SECOND READING 2 Tim. 1.8b-10   [Design of God]
God has called us to a holy life and has brought life to
us through the good news of the gospel.

A reading from the second Letter of Saint Paul
to Timothy.

BROTHERS and sisters: Join with me in suffering for the Gospel, relying on the power of
God, who saved us and called us with a holy calling, not according to our works but according to
his own purpose and grace.

This grace was given to us in Christ Jesus before the ages began, but it has now been revealed
through the appearing of our Saviour Christ
Jesus, who abolished death and brought life and
immortality to light through the Gospel.—The
word of the Lord. ℟. **Thanks be to God.** ↓

GOSPEL ACCLAMATION See Lk. 9.35   [Beloved Son]
(If the acclamation is not sung, it is omitted.)

℣. Praise and honour to you, Lord Jesus Christ!*
℟. **Praise and honour to you, Lord Jesus Christ!**

---

* *See p. 16 for other Gospel Acclamations.*

℣. From the bright cloud the Father's voice is
   heard:
This is my Son, the Beloved; listen to him.
℟. **Praise and honour to you, Lord Jesus Christ!** ↓

GOSPEL Mt. 17.1-9   [Jesus Transfigured]

> Jesus is transfigured before Peter, James and John. God
> acknowledges his Son and bids the disciples to listen to
> him. Jesus asks them not to reveal this vision until after
> the resurrection.

℣. The Lord be with you. ℟. **And with your spirit.**
✚ A reading from the holy Gospel according to
Matthew. ℟. **Glory to you, O Lord.**

JESUS took with him Peter and James and his
  brother John and led them up a high mountain, by themselves. And he was transfigured before them, and his face shone like the sun, and his
clothes became dazzling white. Suddenly there
appeared to them Moses and Elijah, talking with
him.

Then Peter said to Jesus, "Lord, it is good for us
to be here; if you wish, I will make three
dwellings here, one for you, one for Moses, and
one for Elijah."

While he was still speaking, suddenly a bright
cloud overshadowed them, and from the cloud a
voice said, "This is my Son, the Beloved; with him
I am well pleased; listen to him!"

When the disciples heard this, they fell to the
ground and were overcome by fear. But Jesus
came and touched them, saying, "Get up and do
not be afraid." And when they looked up, they saw
no one except Jesus himself alone.

As they were coming down the mountain, Jesus ordered them, "Tell no one about the vision until after the Son of Man has been raised from the dead."—The Gospel of the Lord. ℟. **Praise to you, Lord Jesus Christ.**   → No. 15, p. 18

PRAYER OVER THE OFFERINGS [Cleanse Our Faults]

May this sacrifice, O Lord, we pray,
cleanse us of our faults
and sanctify your faithful in body and mind
for the celebration of the paschal festivities.
Through Christ our Lord. ℟. **Amen.** ↓

PREFACE (13)   [Jesus in Glory]

℣. The Lord be with you. ℟. **And with your spirit.**
℣. Lift up your hearts. ℟. **We lift them up to the Lord.**
℣. Let us give thanks to the Lord our God. ℟. **It is right and just.**

It is truly right and just, our duty and our salvation,
always and everywhere to give you thanks,
Lord, holy Father, almighty and eternal God,
through Christ our Lord.

For after he had told the disciples of his coming Death,
on the holy mountain he manifested to them his glory,
to show, even by the testimony of the law and the prophets,
that the Passion leads to the glory of the Resurrection.

And so, with the Powers of heaven,
we worship you constantly on earth,

and before your majesty
without end we acclaim: ➜ No. 23, p. 23

COMMUNION ANTIPHON Mt. 17.5   [Son of God]

**This is my beloved Son, with whom I am well
pleased; listen to him.** ↓

PRAYER AFTER COMMUNION   [Things of Heaven]

As we receive these glorious mysteries,
we make thanksgiving to you, O Lord,
for allowing us while still on earth
to be partakers even now of the things of heaven.
Through Christ our Lord.
℟. **Amen.** ↓

*The Deacon or, in his absence, the Priest himself, says
the invitation:* Bow down for the blessing.

PRAYER OVER THE PEOPLE   [Faithful to the Gospel]

Bless your faithful, we pray, O Lord,
with a blessing that endures for ever,
and keep them faithful
to the Gospel of your Only Begotten Son,
so that they may always desire and at last attain
that glory whose beauty he showed in his own
   Body,
to the amazement of his Apostles.
Through Christ our Lord.
℟. **Amen.**   ➜ No. 32, p. 77

"I know that the Messiah is coming." . . ."I am he."

MARCH 19

3rd SUNDAY OF LENT

The alternative prayers given below are for the Ritual Mass for the First Scrutiny assigned to this Sunday in the Rite of Christian Initiation of Adults. (The chants and readings are the same as those for the 3rd Sunday of Lent.)

ENTRANCE ANTIPHON Cf. Ps. 24.15-16

[Eyes on God]

My eyes are always on the Lord, for he rescues my feet from the snare. Turn to me and have mercy on me, for I am alone and poor.

→ No. 2, p. 10 (Omit Gloria)

OR Ez. 36.23-26 *(Also for First Scrutiny)* [A New Spirit]

When I prove my holiness among you, I will gather you from all the foreign lands; and I will pour clean water upon you and cleanse you from all your impurities, and I will give you a new spirit, says the Lord. → No. 2, p. 10 (Omit Gloria)

Or Entrance Antiphon for First Scrutiny Cf. Isa. 55.1

[Drink Joyfully]

Come to the waters, you who are thirsty, says the Lord; you who have no money, come and drink joyfully. → No. 2, p. 10 (Omit Gloria)

COLLECT   [Fasting, Prayer, Almsgiving]

O God, author of every mercy and of all goodness,
who in fasting, prayer and almsgiving
have shown us a remedy for sin,
look graciously on this confession of our
   lowliness,
that we, who are bowed down by our conscience,
may always be lifted up by your mercy.
Through our Lord Jesus Christ, your Son,
who lives and reigns with you in the unity of the
   Holy Spirit,
one God, for ever and ever. ℟. **Amen.** ↓

Collect for First Scrutiny   [Fashioned Anew]
Grant, we pray, O Lord,
that these chosen ones may come worthily and wisely
to the confession of your praise,
so that in accordance with that first dignity
which they lost by original sin
they may be fashioned anew through your glory.
Through our Lord Jesus Christ, your Son,
who lives and reigns with you in the unity of the Holy
   Spirit,
one God, for ever and ever. ℟. **Amen.** ↓

FIRST READING Ex. 17.3-7   [Water from Rock]

The Israelites murmured against God in their thirst. God directs Moses to strike a rock with his staff, and water issues forth.

A reading from the book of Exodus.

IN the wilderness the people thirsted for water; and the people complained against Moses and said, "Why did you bring us out of Egypt, to kill us and our children and livestock with thirst?" So Moses cried out to the Lord, "What shall I do with this people? They are almost ready to stone me."

The Lord said to Moses, "Go on ahead of the people, and take some of the elders of Israel with you; take in your hand the staff with which you struck the Nile, and go. I will be standing there in front of you on the rock at Horeb. Strike the rock, and water will come out of it, so that the people may drink." Moses did so, in the sight of the elders of Israel.

He called the place Massah and Meribah, because the children of Israel quarrelled and tested the Lord, saying, "Is the Lord among us or not?"— The word of the Lord. ℟. **Thanks be to God.** ↓

RESPONSORIAL PSALM Ps. 95   [The Lord Our Rock]

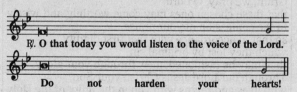

℟. O that today you would listen to the voice of the Lord.

Do   not   harden   your   hearts!

O come, let us sing to the Lord;
let us make a joyful noise to the rock of our salvation!
Let us come into his presence with thanksgiving;
let us make a joyful noise to him with songs of praise!—℟.

O come, let us worship and bow down,
let us kneel before the Lord, our Maker!
For he is our God, and we are the people of his
   pasture,
and the sheep of his hand.—℞.

O that today you would listen to his voice!
Do not harden your hearts, as at Meribah,
as on the day at Massah in the wilderness,
when your ancestors tested me,
and put me to the proof,
though they had seen my work.—℞. ↓

SECOND READING Rom. 5.1-2, 5-8   [God's Love for Us]

Through Jesus we have received the grace of faith. The love of God has been poured upon us. Jesus laid down his life for us while we were still sinners.

A reading from the Letter of Saint Paul
to the Romans.

BROTHERS and sisters: Since we are justified by faith, we have peace with God through our Lord Jesus Christ, through whom we have obtained access to this grace in which we stand; and we boast in our hope of sharing the glory of God.

And hope does not disappoint us, because God's love has been poured into our hearts through the Holy Spirit that has been given to us. For while we were still weak, at the right time Christ died for the ungodly. Indeed, rarely will anyone die for a righteous person—though perhaps for a good person someone might actually dare to die. But God proves his love for us in that while we still were sinners Christ died for us.— The word of the Lord. ℞. **Thanks be to God.** ↓

GOSPEL ACCLAMATION Jn. 4.42, 15   [Living Water]
(If the acclamation is not sung, it is omitted.)

℣. Glory to you, Word of God, Lord Jesus Christ!*
℟. **Glory to you, Word of God, Lord Jesus Christ!**
℣. Lord, you are truly the Saviour of the world;
give me living water, that I may never be thirsty.
℟. **Glory to you, Word of God, Lord Jesus Christ** ↓

GOSPEL Jn. 4.5-42 or 4.5-15, 19-26, 39a, 40-42

[Samaritan Woman]

> Jesus speaks to the Samaritan woman at the well. He searches her soul, and she recognizes him as a prophet. Jesus speaks of the water of eternal life. He also notes the fields are ready for harvest.

[If the "Shorter Form" is used, the indented text in brackets is omitted.]

℣. The Lord be with you. ℟. **And with your spirit.**
✠ A reading from the holy Gospel according to John. ℟. **Glory to you, O Lord.**

JESUS came to a Samaritan city called Sychar, near the plot of ground that Jacob had given to his son Joseph. Jacob's well was there, and Jesus, tired out by his journey, was sitting by the well. It was about noon.

A Samaritan woman came to draw water, and Jesus said to her, "Give me a drink." (His disciples had gone to the city to buy food.)

The Samaritan woman said to him, "How is it that you, a Jew, ask a drink of me, a woman of Samaria?" (Jews do not share things in common with Samaritans.) Jesus answered her, "If you knew the gift of God, and who it is that is saying

---

* *See p. 16 for other Gospel Acclamations.*

to you, 'Give me a drink,' you would have asked him, and he would have given you living water."

The woman said to him, "Sir, you have no bucket, and the well is deep. Where do you get that living water? Are you greater than our father Jacob, who gave us the well, and with his children and his flocks drank from it?" Jesus said to her, "Everyone who drinks of this water will be thirsty again, but the one who drinks of the water that I will give will never be thirsty. The water that I will give him will become in him a spring of water gushing up to eternal life." The woman said to him, "Sir, give me this water, so that I may never be thirsty or have to keep coming here to draw water."

[Jesus said to her, "Go, call your husband, and come back." The woman answered him, "I have no husband." Jesus said to her, "You are right in saying, 'I have no husband'; for you have had five husbands, and the one you have now is not your husband. What you have said is true!"]

The woman said to him, "Sir, I see that you are a Prophet. Our ancestors worshipped on this mountain, but you say that the place where people must worship is in Jerusalem."

Jesus said to her, "Woman, believe me, the hour is coming when you will worship the Father neither on this mountain nor in Jerusalem. You worship what you do not know; we worship what we know, for salvation is from the Jews. But the hour is coming, and is now here, when the true worshippers will worship the Father in spirit and truth, for the Father seeks such as these to worship him. God is spirit, and those who worship him must worship in spirit and truth."

The woman said to him, "I know that the Messiah is coming" (who is called the Christ). "When he comes, he will proclaim all things to us." Jesus said to her, "I am he, the one who is speaking to you."

[Just then his disciples came. They were astonished that he was speaking with a woman, but no one said, "What do you want?" or, "Why are you speaking with her?" Then the woman left her water jar and went back to the city. She said to the people, "Come and see a man who told me everything I have ever done! He cannot be the Messiah, can he?" They left the city and were on their way to him. Meanwhile the disciples were urging him, "Rabbi, eat something." But he said to them, "I have food to eat that you do not know about." So the disciples said to one another, "Surely no one has brought him something to eat?"

Jesus said to them, "My food is to do the will of him who sent me and to complete his work. Do you not say, 'Four months more, then comes the harvest'? But I tell you, look around you, and see how the fields are ripe for harvesting. The reaper is already receiving wages and is gathering fruit for eternal life, so that sower and reaper may rejoice together. For here the saying holds true, 'One sows and another reaps.' I sent you to reap that for which you did not labour. Others have laboured, and you have entered into their labour."]

Many Samaritans from that city believed in Jesus

[because of the woman's testimony, "He told me everything I have ever done."]

So when the Samaritans came to him, they asked him to stay with them; and he stayed there two days. And many more believed because of his word. They said to the woman, "It is no longer because of what you said that we believe, for we have heard for ourselves, and we know that this is truly the Saviour of the world."—The Gospel of the Lord. ℟. **Praise to you, Lord Jesus Christ.**

➡ No. 15, p. 18

PRAYER OVER THE OFFERINGS   [Pardon]

Be pleased, O Lord, with these sacrificial offerings,
and grant that we who beseech pardon for our own sins,
may take care to forgive our neighbour.
Through Christ our Lord.
℟. **Amen.** ↓

Prayer over the Offerings for First Scrutiny
[Merciful Grace]

May your merciful grace prepare your servants, O Lord,
for the worthy celebration of these mysteries
and lead them to it by a devout way of life.
Through Christ our Lord. ℟. **Amen.** ↓

PREFACE (14)   [Gift of Faith]

℣. The Lord be with you. ℟. **And with your spirit.**
℣. Lift up your hearts. ℟. **We lift them up to the Lord.**
℣. Let us give thanks to the Lord our God. ℟. **It is right and just.**

It is truly right and just, our duty and our salvation,
always and everywhere to give you thanks,
Lord, holy Father, almighty and eternal God,
through Christ our Lord.

For when he asked the Samaritan woman for water to drink,
he had already created the gift of faith within her
and so ardently did he thirst for her faith,
that he kindled in her the fire of divine love.

And so we, too, give you thanks
and with the Angels
praise your mighty deeds, as we acclaim:

➜ No. 23, p. 23

When the Roman Canon is used, in the section Memento, Domine *(Remember, Lord, your servants) there is a commemoration of the godparents, and the proper form of the* Hanc igitur *(Therefore, Lord, we pray), is said.*

Remember, Lord, your servants
who are to present your chosen ones
for the holy grace of your Baptism,

Here the names of the godparents are read out.

and all gathered here,
whose faith and devotion are known to you ... (p. 24)

Therefore, Lord, we pray:
graciously accept this oblation
which we make to you for your servants,
whom you have been pleased
to enrol, choose and call for eternal life
and for the blessed gift of your grace.
(Through Christ our Lord. Amen.)

The rest follows the Roman Canon, pp. 25-29.

When Eucharistic Prayer II is used, after the words and all
the clergy, *the following is added:*

Remember also, Lord, your servants
who are to present these chosen ones
at the font of rebirth.

When Eucharistic Prayer III is used, after the words the
entire people you have gained for your own, *the following is added:*

Assist your servants with your grace,
O Lord, we pray,
that they may lead these chosen ones by word and
    example
to new life in Christ, our Lord.

COMMUNION ANTIPHON Jn. 4.13-14

[Water of Eternal Life]

**For anyone who drinks it, says the Lord, the
water I shall give will become in him a spring
welling up to eternal life.** ↓

PRAYER AFTER COMMUNION

[Nourishment from Heaven]

As we receive the pledge
of things yet hidden in heaven
and are nourished while still on earth
with the Bread that comes from on high,

we humbly entreat you, O Lord,
that what is being brought about in us in mystery
may come to true completion.
Through Christ our Lord. ℟. **Amen.** ↓

Prayer after Communion for First Scrutiny

[God's Protection]

Give help, O Lord, we pray,
by the grace of your redemption
and be pleased to protect and prepare
those you are to initiate
through the Sacraments of eternal life.
Through Christ our Lord.
℟. **Amen.**   → No. 30, p. 77

Optional Solemn Blessings, p. 97, and Prayers over the People, p. 105

---

*The Deacon or, in his absence, the Priest himself, says
the invitation:* Bow down for the blessing.

PRAYER OVER THE PEOPLE

[Love of God and Neighbour]

Direct, O Lord, we pray, the hearts of your faithful,
and in your kindness grant your servants this
    grace:
that, abiding in the love of you and their neighbour,
they may fulfill the whole of your commands.
Through Christ our Lord.
℟. **Amen.**   → No. 32, p. 77

"I am the light of the world."

MARCH 26
4th SUNDAY OF LENT

The alternative chants and prayers given below are for the Ritual Mass for the Second Scrutiny assigned to this Sunday in the Rite of Christian Initiation of Adults. (The readings are the same as those for the 4th Sunday of Lent.)

ENTRANCE ANTIPHON Cf. Isa. 66.10-11   **[Rejoice]**
Rejoice, Jerusalem, and all who love her. Be joyful, all who were in mourning; exult and be satisfied at her consoling breast.

➜ No. 2, p. 10 (Omit Gloria)

Entrance Antiphon for Second Scrutiny Cf. Ps. 24.15-16
[Have Mercy]

My eyes are always on the Lord, for he rescues my feet from the snare. Turn to me and have mercy on me, for I am alone and poor.

➜ No. 2, p. 10 (Omit Gloria)

COLLECT   [Devotion and Faith]

O God, who through your Word
reconcile the human race to yourself in a
    wonderful way,
grant, we pray,
that with prompt devotion and eager faith
the Christian people may hasten
toward the solemn celebrations to come.
Through our Lord Jesus Christ, your Son,
who lives and reigns with you in the unity of the
    Holy Spirit,
one God, for ever and ever. ℟. **Amen.** ↓

Collect for Second Scrutiny   [Spiritual Joy]

Almighty ever-living God,
give to your Church an increase in spiritual joy,
so that those once born of earth
may be reborn as citizens of heaven.
Through our Lord, Jesus Christ, your Son,
who lives and reigns with you in the unity of the Holy
    Spirit,
one God, for ever and ever. ℟. **Amen.** ↓

FIRST READING 1 Sam. 16.1b, 6-7, 10-13 [God's Anointed]

**God directs Samuel to anoint David king. God looks into
the heart of each person.**

A reading from the first book of Samuel.

THE Lord said to Samuel, "Fill your horn with
oil and set out; I will send you to Jesse of
Bethlehem, for I have provided for myself a king
among his sons."

When the sons of Jesse came, Samuel looked
on Eliab and thought, "Surely the Lord's anointed
is now before the Lord." But the Lord said to

Samuel, "Do not look on his appearance or on the height of his stature, because I have rejected him; for the Lord does not see as the human sees; the human looks on the outward appearance, but the Lord looks on the heart."

Jesse made seven of his sons pass before Samuel, and Samuel said to Jesse, "The Lord has not chosen any of these." Samuel said to Jesse, "Are all your sons here?" And he said, "There remains yet the youngest, but he is keeping the sheep." And Samuel said to Jesse, "Send and bring him; for we will not sit down until he comes here." Jesse sent and brought David in. Now he was ruddy, and had beautiful eyes, and was handsome. The Lord said, "Rise and anoint him; for this is the one."

Then Samuel took the horn of oil, and anointed him in the presence of his brothers; and the spirit of the Lord came mightily upon David from that day forward.—The word of the Lord. ℟. **Thanks be to God.** ↓

RESPONSORIAL PSALM Ps. 23   [Lord's Protection]

℟. The Lord   is   my shep-herd;   I shall not want.

The Lord is my shepherd, I shall not want.
He makes me lie down in green pastures;
he leads me beside still waters;
he restores my soul.—℟.

He leads me in right paths for his name's sake.
Even though I walk through the darkest valley, I
     fear no evil;

for you are with me;
your rod and your staff—they comfort me.
℟. **The Lord is my shepherd;**
    I shall not want.

You prepare a table before me
in the presence of my enemies;
you anoint my head with oil;
my cup overflows.—℟.

Surely goodness and mercy shall follow me
all the days of my life,
and I shall dwell in the house of the Lord
my whole life long.—℟. ↓

SECOND READING Eph. 5.8-14   [Children of Light]

> **We are to walk in the light which shows goodness, justice, and truth. Evil deeds are condemned. Christ gives this light whereby we live.**

A reading from the Letter of Saint Paul
          to the Ephesians.

BROTHERS and sisters: Once you were darkness, but now in the Lord you are light. Live as children of light—for the fruit of the light is found in all that is good and right and true.

Try to find out what is pleasing to the Lord. Take no part in the unfruitful works of darkness, but instead expose them. For it is shameful even to mention what such people do secretly; but everything exposed by the light becomes visible, for everything that becomes visible is light. Therefore it is said, "Sleeper, awake! Rise from the dead, and Christ will shine on you."—The word of the Lord. ℟. **Thanks be to God.** ↓

GOSPEL ACCLAMATION Jn. 8.12   [Light of Life]
(If the acclamation is not sung, it is omitted.)

℣. Praise and honour to you, Lord Jesus Christ!*
℟. **Praise and honour to you, Lord Jesus Christ!**
℣. I am the light of the world, says the Lord;
whoever follows me will have the light of life.
℟. **Praise and honour to you, Lord Jesus Christ!** ↓

GOSPEL Jn. 9.1-41 or 9.1, 6-9, 13-17, 34-38 [Cure of Blind Man]

**Jesus is the light. He cures a man born blind by bringing
him to see. Jesus identifies himself as the Son of Man.**

*[If the "Shorter Form" is used, the indented text in brack-
ets is omitted.]*

℣. The Lord be with you. ℟. **And with your spirit.**
✚ A reading from the holy Gospel according to
John. ℟. **Glory to you, O Lord.**

AS Jesus walked along, he saw a man blind
from birth.
[His disciples asked him, "Rabbi, who sinned,
this man or his parents, that he was born
blind?"
Jesus answered, "Neither this man nor his
parents sinned; he was born blind so that
God's works might be revealed in him. We
must work the works of him who sent me
while it is day; night is coming when no one
can work. As long as I am in the world, I am
the light of the world." When he had said
this,]
he spat on the ground and made mud with the
saliva and spread the mud on the man's eyes, say-

---

* *See p. 16 for other Gospel Acclamations.*

ing to him, "Go, wash in the pool of Siloam"
(which means Sent).

Then the man who was blind went and washed,
and came back able to see. The neighbours and
those who had seen him before as a beggar began
to ask, "Is this not the man who used to sit and
beg?" Some were saying, "It is he." Others were
saying, "No, but it is someone like him." He kept
saying, "I am the man."

> [But they kept asking him, "Then how were
> your eyes opened?" He answered, "The man
> called Jesus made mud, spread it on my eyes,
> and said to me, 'Go to Siloam and wash.'
> Then I went and washed and received my
> sight." They said to him, "Where is he?" He
> said, "I do not know."]

They brought to the Pharisees the man who
had formerly been blind. Now it was a Sabbath
day when Jesus made the mud and opened his
eyes. Then the Pharisees also began to ask him
how he had received his sight. He said to them,
"He put mud on my eyes. Then I washed, and now
I see." Some of the Pharisees said, "This man is
not from God, for he does not observe the Sabbath." But others said, "How can a man who is a
sinner perform such signs?" And they were divided. So they said again to the blind man, "What
do you say about him? It was your eyes he
opened." He said, "He is a Prophet."

> [They did not believe that he had been
> blind and had received his sight until they
> called the parents of the man who had re-
> ceived his sight and asked them, "Is this your

son, who you say was born blind? How then does he now see?" His parents answered, "We know that this is our son, and that he was born blind; but we do not know how it is that now he sees, nor do we know who opened his eyes. Ask him; he is of age. He will speak for himself." His parents said this because they were afraid of the Jewish authorities, who had already agreed that anyone who confessed Jesus to be the Messiah would be put out of the synagogue. Therefore his parents said, "He is of age; ask him."

So for the second time they called the man who had been blind, and they said to him, "Give glory to God! We know that this man is a sinner." He answered, "I do not know whether he is a sinner. One thing I do know, that though I was blind, now I see." They said to him, "What did he do to you? How did he open your eyes?" He answered them, "I have told you already, and you would not listen. Why do you want to hear it again? Do you also want to become his disciples?" Then they reviled him, saying, "You are his disciple, but we are disciples of Moses. We know that God has spoken to Moses, but as for this man, we do not know where he comes from."

The man answered, "Here is an astonishing thing! You do not know where he comes from, and yet he opened my eyes. We know that God does not listen to sinners, but he does listen to one who worships him and obeys his will. Never since the world began has it been heard that anyone opened the eyes of a person born blind. If this man were not from God, he could do nothing."]

They answered him, "You were born entirely in sins, and are you trying to teach us?" And they drove him out.

Jesus heard that they had driven him out, and when he found him, he said, "Do you believe in the Son of Man?" He answered, "And who is he, sir? Tell me, so that I may believe in him." Jesus said to him, "You have seen him, and the one speaking with you is he." He said, "Lord, I believe." And he worshipped him.

[Jesus said, "I came into this world for judgment so that those who do not see may see, and those who do see may become blind." Some of the Pharisees near him heard this and said to him, "Surely we are not blind, are we?" Jesus said to them, "If you were blind, you would have no sin. But now that you say, 'We see,' your sin remains."]

The Gospel of the Lord. ℟. **Praise to you, Lord Jesus Christ.**   → No. 15, p. 18

PRAYER OVER THE OFFERINGS   [Eternal Remedy]

We place before you with joy these offerings,
which bring eternal remedy, O Lord,
praying that we may both faithfully revere them
and present them to you, as is fitting,
for the salvation of all the world.

Through Christ our Lord.
℟. **Amen.** ↓

Prayer over the Offerings for Second Scrutiny
[Seeking Salvation]

We place before you with joy these offerings,
which bring eternal remedy, O Lord,
praying that we may both faithfully revere them
and present them to you, as is fitting,
for those who seek salvation.
Through Christ our Lord. ℟. **Amen.** ↓

PREFACE (15)   [From Darkness to Light]

℣. The Lord be with you. ℟. **And with your spirit.**
℣. Lift up your hearts. ℟. **We lift them up to the Lord.**
℣. Let us give thanks to the Lord our God. ℟. **It is right and just.**

It is truly right and just, our duty and our salvation,
always and everywhere to give you thanks,
Lord, holy Father, almighty and eternal God,
through Christ our Lord.

By the mystery of the Incarnation,
he has led the human race that walked in darkness
into the radiance of the faith
and has brought those born in slavery to ancient sin
through the waters of regeneration
to make them your adopted children.

Therefore, all creatures of heaven and earth
sing a new song in adoration,

and we, with all the host of Angels,
cry out, and without end acclaim: → No. 23, p. 23

When the Roman Canon is used, in the section Memento,
Domine *(Remember, Lord, your servants) there is a com-
memoration of the godparents, and the proper form of the*
Hanc igitur *(Therefore, Lord, we pray) is said.*

Remember, Lord, your servants
who are to present your chosen ones
for the holy grace of your Baptism,

Here the names of the godparents are read out.

and all gathered here,
whose faith and devotion are known to you ... (p. 24)

Therefore, Lord, we pray:
graciously accept this oblation
which we make to you for your servants,
whom you have been pleased
to enrol, choose and call for eternal life
and for the blessed gift of your grace.
(Through Christ our Lord. Amen.)

The rest follows the Roman Canon, pp. 25-29.

*[For commemoration of the godparents in Eucharistic
Prayers II and III, see p. 225.]*

COMMUNION ANTIPHON Cf. Jn. 9.11, 38

[Spiritual Sight]

**The Lord anointed my eyes: I went, I washed, I
saw and I believed in God.** ↓

PRAYER AFTER COMMUNION [Illuminate Our Hearts]

O God, who enlighten everyone who comes into
   this world,
illuminate our hearts, we pray,
with the splendour of your grace,

that we may always ponder
what is worthy and pleasing to your majesty
and love you in all sincerity.
Through Christ our Lord. ℟. **Amen.** ↓

Prayer after Communion for Second Scrutiny
[God's Kindness]

Sustain your family always in your kindness,
O Lord, we pray,
correct them, set them in order,
graciously protect them under your rule,
and in your unfailing goodness
direct them along the way of salvation.
Through Christ our Lord.
℟. **Amen.**　　　　　　　　　　→ No. 30, p. 77

Optional Solemn Blessings, p. 97, and Prayers over the People, p. 105

---

*The Deacon or, in his absence, the Priest himself, says
the invitation:* Bow down for the blessing.

PRAYER OVER THE PEOPLE　　　[Life-Giving Light]

Look upon those who call to you, O Lord,
and sustain the weak;
give life by your unfailing light
to those who walk in the shadow of death,
and bring those rescued by your mercy from every
　evil
to reach the highest good.
Through Christ our Lord.
℟. **Amen.**　　　　　　　　　　→ No. 32, p. 77

"The dead man came out, his hands and feet bound."

APRIL 2

5th SUNDAY OF LENT

The alternative chants and prayers given below are for the Ritual Mass for the Third Scrutiny assigned to this Sunday in the Rite of Christian Initiation of Adults. (The readings are the same as those for the 5th Sunday of Lent.)

ENTRANCE ANTIPHON Cf. Ps. 42.1-2　　[Rescue Me]
Give me justice, O God, and plead my cause against a nation that is faithless. From the deceitful and cunning rescue me, for you, O God, are my strength.　　→ No. 2, p. 10 (Omit Gloria)

Entrance Antiphon for Third Scrutiny Cf. Ps. 17.5-7

[The Lord Hears Me]

The waves of death rose about me; the pains of the netherworld surrounded me. In my anguish I called to the Lord; and from his holy temple he heard my voice.　　→ No. 2, p. 10 (Omit Gloria)

COLLECT   [Walk in Charity]

By your help, we beseech you, Lord our God,
may we walk eagerly in that same charity
with which, out of love for the world,
your Son handed himself over to death.
Through our Lord Jesus Christ, your Son,
who lives and reigns with you in the unity of the
    Holy Spirit,
one God, for ever and ever. ℞. **Amen.** ↓

Collect for Third Scrutiny   [Chosen Ones]

Grant, O Lord, to these chosen ones
that, instructed in the holy mysteries,
they may receive new life at the font of Baptism
and be numbered among the members of your
    Church.
Through our Lord Jesus Christ, your Son,
who lives and reigns with you in the unity of the Holy
    Spirit,
one God, for ever and ever. ℞. **Amen.** ↓

FIRST READING Ez. 37.12-14   [The Lord's Promise]

> The Lord promises to bring God's people back to their
> homeland. He will be with them and they will know him.

A reading from the book of the Prophet Ezekiel.

THUS says the Lord God: "I am going to open
your graves, and bring you up from your
graves, O my people; and I will bring you back to
the land of Israel. And you shall know that I am
the Lord, when I open your graves, and bring you
up from your graves, O my people.

I will put my spirit within you, and you shall
live, and I will place you on your own soil; then
you shall know that I, the Lord, have spoken and

will act," says the Lord.—The word of the Lord.
℟. **Thanks be to God.** ↓

RESPONSORIAL PSALM Ps. 130

[Mercy and Redemption]

℟. **With the Lord there is stead-fast love and great power to redeem.**

Out of the depths I cry to you, O Lord.
Lord, hear my voice!
Let your ears be attentive
to the voice of my supplications!—℟.

If you, O Lord, should mark iniquities,
Lord, who could stand?
But there is forgiveness with you,
so that you may be revered.—℟.

I wait for the Lord,
my soul waits, and in his word I hope;
my soul waits for the Lord
more than watchmen for the morning.—℟.

For with the Lord there is steadfast love,
and with him is great power to redeem.
It is he who will redeem Israel
from all its iniquities.—℟. ↓

SECOND READING Rom. 8.8-11   [Indwelling Spirit]

**The followers of Jesus live in the Spirit of God. The
same Spirit who brought Jesus back to life will bring
mortal bodies to life since God's Spirit dwells in them.**

A reading from the Letter of Saint Paul
to the Romans.

Brothers and sisters: Those who are in the
flesh cannot please God. But you are not in

the flesh; you are in the Spirit, since the Spirit of God dwells in you. Anyone who does not have the Spirit of Christ does not belong to him.

But if Christ is in you, though the body is dead because of sin, the Spirit is life because of righteousness.

If the Spirit of God who raised Jesus from the dead dwells in you, he who raised Christ from the dead will give life to your mortal bodies also through his Spirit that dwells in you.—The word of the Lord. ℟. **Thanks be to God.** ↓

GOSPEL ACCLAMATION Jn. 11.25, 26   [Resurrection]
(If the acclamation is not sung, it is omitted.)

℣. Glory and praise to you, Lord Jesus Christ!*
℟. **Glory and praise to you, Lord Jesus Christ!**
℣. I am the resurrection and the life, says the Lord;
whoever believes in me will never die.
℟. **Glory and praise to you, Lord Jesus Christ!** ↓

GOSPEL Jn. 11.1-45 or 11.3-7, 17, 20-27, 33b-45   [Lazarus]

Lazarus, the brother of Martha and Mary, died and was buried. When Jesus came, he assured them that he was the resurrection and the life. Jesus gave life back to Lazarus.

[If the "Shorter Form" is used, the indented text in brackets is omitted.]

℣. The Lord be with you. ℟. **And with your spirit.**
✛ A reading from the holy Gospel according to John. ℟. **Glory to you, O Lord.**

[N]OW a certain man, Lazarus, was ill. He was from Bethany, the village of Mary

* *See p. 16 for other Gospel Acclamations.*

and her sister Martha. Mary was the one who anointed the Lord with perfume and wiped his feet with her hair; her brother Lazarus was ill.]

[So] the sisters [of Lazarus] sent a message to Jesus, "Lord, he whom you love is ill." But when Jesus heard this, he said, "This illness does not lead to death; rather it is for God's glory, so that the Son of God may be glorified through it." Accordingly, though Jesus loved Martha and her sister and Lazarus, after having heard that Lazarus was ill, he stayed two days longer in the place where he was.

Then after this he said to the disciples, "Let us go to Judea again."

[The disciples said to him, "Rabbi, the people there were just now trying to stone you, and are you going there again?" Jesus answered, "Are there not twelve hours of daylight? Those who walk during the day do not stumble, because they see the light of this world. But those who walk at night stumble, because the light is not in them."

After saying this, he told them, "Our friend Lazarus has fallen asleep, but I am going there to awaken him." The disciples said to him, "Lord, if he has fallen asleep, he will be all right." Jesus, however, had been speaking about his death, but they thought that he was referring merely to sleep. Then Jesus told them plainly, "Lazarus is dead. For your sake I am glad I was not there, so that you may

believe. But let us go to him." Thomas, who was
called the Twin, said to his fellow disciples,
"Let us also go, that we may die with him."]

When Jesus arrived, he found that Lazarus had
already been in the tomb four days.

[Now Bethany was near Jerusalem, some
two miles away, and many Jews had come to
Martha and Mary to console them about
their brother.]

When Martha heard that Jesus was coming,
she went and met him, while Mary stayed at
home. Martha said to Jesus, "Lord, if you had
been here, my brother would not have died. But
even now I know that God will give you whatever
you ask of him." Jesus said to her, "Your brother
will rise again." Martha said to him, "I know that
he will rise again in the resurrection on the last
day." Jesus said to her, "I am the resurrection and
the life. Whoever believes in me, even though they
die, will live, and everyone who lives and believes
in me will never die. Do you believe this?" She
said to him, "Yes, Lord, I believe that you are the
Christ, the Son of God, the one coming into the
world."

[When she had said this, she went back
and called her sister Mary, and told her pri-
vately, "The Teacher is here and is calling for
you." And when Mary heard it, she got up
quickly and went to him. Now Jesus had not
yet come to the village, but was still at the
place where Martha had met him. The Jews
who were with her in the house, consoling
her, saw Mary get up quickly and go out.

They followed her because they thought that she was going to the tomb to weep there.

When Mary came where Jesus was and saw him, she knelt at his feet and said to him, "Lord, if you had been here, my brother would not have died." When Jesus saw her weeping, and the Jews who came with her also weeping, he]

[Jesus] was greatly disturbed in spirit and deeply moved. He said, "Where have you laid him?" They said to him, "Lord, come and see." Jesus began to weep. So the Jews said, "See how he loved him!" But some of them said, "Could not he who opened the eyes of the blind man have kept this man from dying?"

Then Jesus, again greatly disturbed, came to the tomb. It was a cave, and a stone was lying against it. Jesus said, "Take away the stone." Martha, the sister of the dead man, said to him, "Lord, already there is a stench because he has been dead four days." Jesus said to her, "Did I not tell you that if you believed, you would see the glory of God?" So they took away the stone. And Jesus looked upward and said, "Father, I thank you for having heard me. I knew that you always hear me, but I have said this for the sake of the crowd standing here, so that they may believe that you sent me."

When he had said this, he cried with a loud voice, "Lazarus, come out!" The dead man came out, his hands and feet bound with strips of cloth, and his face wrapped in a cloth. Jesus said to them, "Unbind him, and let him go."

Many of the Jews therefore, who had come with Mary and had seen what Jesus did, believed in him.—The Gospel of the Lord. ℞. **Praise to you, Lord Jesus Christ.**   → No. 15, p. 18

PRAYER OVER THE OFFERINGS   [Hear Us]

Hear us, almighty God,
and, having instilled in your servants
the teachings of the Christian faith,
graciously purify them
by the working of this sacrifice.
Through Christ our Lord. ℞. **Amen.** ↓

Prayer over the Offerings for Third Scrutiny   [Hear Us]
Hear us, almighty God,
and, having instilled in your servants
the first fruits of the Christian faith,
graciously purify them by the working of this
    sacrifice.
Through Christ our Lord. ℞. **Amen.** ↓

PREFACE (16)   [Christ Raised Lazarus]

℣. The Lord be with you. ℞. **And with your spirit.**
℣. Lift up your hearts. ℞. **We lift them up to the Lord.**
℣. Let us give thanks to the Lord our God. ℞. **It is right and just.**

It is truly right and just, our duty and our salvation,
always and everywhere to give you thanks,
Lord, holy Father, almighty and eternal God,
through Christ our Lord.

For as true man he wept for Lazarus his friend
and as eternal God raised him from the tomb,

just as, taking pity on the human race,
he leads us by sacred mysteries to new life.

Through him the host of Angels adores your
    majesty
and rejoices in your presence for ever.
May our voices, we pray, join with theirs
in one chorus of exultant praise, as we acclaim:

➔ No. 23, p. 23

When the Roman Canon is used, in the section Memento,
Domine *(Remember, Lord, your servants) there is a com-
memoration of the godparents, and the proper form of the*
Hanc igitur *(Therefore, Lord, we pray) is said.*

Remember, Lord, your servants
who are to present your chosen ones
for the holy grace of your Baptism,

Here the names of the godparents are read out.

and all gathered here,
whose faith and devotion are known to you ... (p. 24)

Therefore, Lord, we pray:
graciously accept this oblation
which we make to you for your servants,
whom you have been pleased
to enrol, choose and call for eternal life
and for the blessed gift of your grace.
(Through Christ our Lord. Amen.)

The rest follows the Roman Canon, pp. 25-29.

*[For commemoration of the godparents in Eucharistic
Prayers II and III, see p. 225.]*

COMMUNION ANTIPHON Cf. Jn. 11.26   [Eternal Life]
**Everyone who lives and believes in me will not
die for ever, says the Lord.** ↓

PRAYER AFTER COMMUNION   [Union with Jesus]

We pray, almighty God,
that we may always be counted among the
    members of Christ,
in whose Body and Blood we have communion.
Who lives and reigns for ever and ever.
℟. **Amen.** ↓

Prayer after Communion for Third Scrutiny
                                    [God's People]

May your people be at one, O Lord, we pray,
and in wholehearted submission to you
may they obtain this grace:
that, safe from all distress,
they may readily live out their joy at being saved
and remember in loving prayer those to be reborn.
Through Christ our Lord.
℟. **Amen.**   → No. 30, p. 77

Optional Solemn Blessings, p. 97, and Prayers over the People, p. 105

---

*The Deacon or, in his absence, the Priest himself, says
the invitation:* Bow down for the blessing.

PRAYER OVER THE PEOPLE   [Gift of Mercy]

Bless, O Lord, your people,
who long for the gift of your mercy,
and grant that what, at your prompting, they
    desire
they may receive by your generous gift.
Through Christ our Lord.
℟. **Amen.**   → No. 32, p. 77

PALM SUNDAY OF THE PASSION OF THE LORD

"Blessed are you, who have come in your abundant mercy!"

The Commemoration of the Lord's Entrance into Jerusalem

FIRST FORM: THE PROCESSION

At an appropriate hour, a gathering takes place at a smaller church or other suitable place other than inside the church to which the procession will go. The faithful hold branches in their hands.

Wearing the red sacred vestments as for Mass, the Priest and the Deacon, accompanied by other ministers, approach the place where the people are gathered. Instead of the chasuble, the Priest may wear a cope, which he leaves aside when the procession is over, and puts on a chasuble.

Meanwhile, the following antiphon or another appropriate chant is sung.

ANTIPHON Mt. 21.9   [Hosanna]

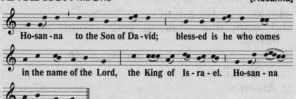

Ho-san-na to the Son of Da-vid; bless-ed is he who comes in the name of the Lord, the King of Is-ra-el. Ho-san-na in the high-est.

Or:

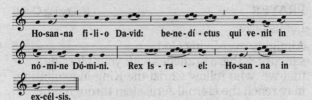

Ho-san-na fi-li-o Da-vid: be-ne-dí-ctus qui ve-nit in

nó-mi-ne Dó-mi-ni. Rex Is-ra - el: Ho-san - na in

ex-cél-sis.

After this, the Priest and people sign themselves, while the Priest says: In the name of the Father, and of the Son, and of the Holy Spirit. *Then he greets the people in the usual way. A brief address is given, in which the faithful are invited to participate actively and consciously in the celebration of this day, in these or similar words:*

Dear brethren (brothers and sisters),
since the beginning of Lent until now
we have prepared our hearts by penance and
    charitable works.
Today we gather together to herald with the
    whole Church
the beginning of the celebration
of our Lord's Paschal Mystery,
that is to say, of his Passion and Resurrection.
For it was to accomplish this mystery
that he entered his own city of Jerusalem.
Therefore, with all faith and devotion,
let us commemorate
the Lord's entry into the city for our salvation,
following in his footsteps,
so that, being made by his grace partakers of the
    Cross,
we may have a share also in his Resurrection and
    in his life.

After the address, the Priest says one of the following prayers with hands extended.

PRAYER   [Following Christ]

Let us pray.

Almighty ever-living God,
sanctify ✠ these branches with your blessing,
that we, who follow Christ the King in exultation,
may reach the eternal Jerusalem through him.
Who lives and reigns for ever and ever.
℟. **Amen.** ↓

OR   [Christ in Triumph]

Increase the faith of those who place their hope in
    you, O God,
and graciously hear the prayers of those who call
    on you,
that we, who today hold high these branches
to hail Christ in his triumph,
may bear fruit for you by good works
    accomplished in him.
Who lives and reigns for ever and ever.
℟. **Amen.** ↓

The Priest sprinkles the branches with holy water without saying anything.

Then a Deacon or, if there is no Deacon, a Priest proclaims in the usual way the Gospel concerning the Lord's entrance according to one of the four Gospels.

GOSPEL Mt. 21.1-11   [Jesus' Triumphal Entry]

**In triumphant glory Jesus comes into Jerusalem. The
people spread their cloaks on the ground for him, wave
olive branches and sing in his honour.**

℣. The Lord be with you. ℟. **And with your spirit.**
✠ A reading from the holy Gospel according to
Matthew. ℟. **Glory to you, O Lord.**

WHEN they had come near Jerusalem and had reached Bethphage, at the Mount of Olives, Jesus sent two disciples, saying to them, "Go into the village ahead of you, and immediately you will find a donkey tied, and a colt with her; untie them and bring them to me. If anyone says anything to you, just say this, 'The Lord needs them.' And he will send them immediately."

This took place to fulfill what had been spoken through the Prophet, saying,

"Tell the daughter of Zion,

Look, your king is coming to you,

humble, and mounted on a donkey,

and on a colt, the foal of a donkey."

The disciples went and did as Jesus had directed them; they brought the donkey and the colt, and put their cloaks on them, and he sat on them. A very large crowd spread their cloaks on the road, and others cut branches from the trees and spread them on the road. The crowds that went ahead of him and that followed were shouting,

"Hosanna to the Son of David!

Blessed is the one who comes in the name of the Lord!

Hosanna in the highest heaven!"

When Jesus entered Jerusalem, the whole city was in turmoil, asking, "Who is this?" The crowds were saying, "This is the Prophet Jesus from Nazareth in Galilee."—The Gospel of the Lord. ℟. **Praise to you, Lord Jesus Christ.**

After the Gospel, a brief homily may be given. Then, to begin the Procession, an invitation may be given by a

Priest or a Deacon or a lay minister, in these or similar words:

Dear brethren (brothers and sisters),
like the crowds who acclaimed Jesus in Jerusalem,
let us go forth in peace.

OR

Let us go forth in peace.
℟. **In the name of Christ. Amen.**

*The Procession to the church where Mass will be cele-
brated then sets off in the usual way. If incense is used,
the thurifer goes first, carrying a thurible with burning
incense, then an acolyte or another minister, carrying a
cross decorated with palm branches according to local
custom, between two ministers with lighted candles.
Then follow the Deacon carrying the Book of Gospels,
the Priest with the ministers, and, after them, all the
faithful carrying branches.*

*As the Procession moves forward, the following or other
suitable chants in honour of Christ the King are sung by
the choir and people.*

ANTIPHON 1   [Hosanna]

**The children of the Hebrews, carrying olive
   branches,**
went to meet the Lord, crying out and saying:
Hosanna in the highest.

*If appropriate, this antiphon is repeated between the
strophes (verses) of the following Psalm.*

PSALM 23(24)   [The King of Glory]

The Lord's is the earth and its fullness,
the world, and those who dwell in it.
It is he who set it on the seas;
on the rivers he made it firm. *(The antiphon is repeated.)*

Who shall climb the mountain of the LORD?
The clean of hands and pure of heart,
whose soul is not set on vain things,
who has not sworn deceitful words.

(The antiphon is repeated.)

Blessings from the LORD shall he receive,
and right reward from the God who saves him.
Such are the people who seek him,
who seek the face of the God of Jacob.

(The antiphon is repeated.)

O gates, lift high your heads;
grow higher, ancient doors.
Let him enter, the king of glory!
Who is this king of glory?
The LORD, the mighty, the valiant;
the LORD, the valiant in war.

(The antiphon is repeated.)

O gates, lift high your heads;
grow higher, ancient doors.
Let him enter, the king of glory!
Who is this king of glory?
He, the LORD of hosts,
he is the king of glory.   *(The antiphon is repeated.)*

ANTIPHON 2   [Hosanna]

The children of the Hebrews spread their gar-
  ments on the road,
crying out and saying: Hosanna to the Son of David;
blessed is he who comes in the name of the Lord.

*If appropriate, this antiphon is repeated between the
strophes (verses) of the following Psalm.*

PSALM 46(47)   [The Great King]

All peoples, clap your hands.
Cry to God with shouts of joy!
For the Lord, the Most High, is awesome,
the great king over all the earth.

(The antiphon is repeated.)

He humbles peoples under us
and nations under our feet.
Our heritage he chose for us,
the pride of Jacob whom he loves.
God goes up with shouts of joy.
The Lord goes up with trumpet blast.

(The antiphon is repeated.)

Sing praise for God; sing praise!
Sing praise to our king; sing praise!
God is king of all the earth.
Sing praise with all your skill.

(The antiphon is repeated.)

God reigns over the nations.
God sits upon his holy throne.
The princes of the peoples are assembled
with the people of the God of Abraham.
The rulers of the earth belong to God,
who is greatly exalted.   *(The antiphon is repeated.)*

Hymn to Christ the King

Chorus:

**Glory and honour and praise be to you, Christ,
King and Redeemer,**
to whom young children cried out loving Hosannas with joy.

All repeat: **Glory and honour . . .**

Chorus:

Israel's King are you, King David's magnificent offspring;

you are the ruler who come blest in the name of the Lord.

All repeat: **Glory and honour ...**

Chorus:

Heavenly hosts on high unite in singing your praises;

men and women on earth and all creation join in.

All repeat: **Glory and honour ...**

Chorus:

Bearing branches of palm, Hebrews came crowding to greet you;

see how with prayers and hymns we come to pay you our vows.

All repeat: **Glory and honour ...**

Chorus:

They offered gifts of praise to you, so near to your Passion;

see how we sing this song now to you reigning on high.

All repeat: **Glory and honour ...**

Chorus:

Those you were pleased to accept, now accept our gifts of devotion,

good and merciful King, lover of all that is good.

All repeat: **Glory and honour ...**

As the procession enters the church, there is sung the following responsory or another chant, which should speak of the Lord's entrance.

RESPONSORY

℞. As the Lord entered the holy city, the children of the Hebrews proclaimed the resurrection of life. Waving their branches of palm, they cried: Hosanna in the Highest.

℣. When the people had heard that Jesus was coming to Jerusalem, they went out to meet him. Waving their branches of palm, they cried: Hosanna in the Highest.

When the Priest arrives at the altar, he venerates it and, if appropriate, incenses it. Then he goes to the chair, where he puts aside the cope, if he has worn one, and puts on the chasuble. Omitting the other Introductory Rites of the Mass and, if appropriate, the Kyrie (Lord, have mercy), *he says the Collect of the Mass, and then continues the Mass in the usual way.*

SECOND FORM: THE SOLEMN ENTRANCE

When a procession outside the church cannot take place, the entrance of the Lord is celebrated inside the church by means of a Solemn Entrance before the principal Mass.

Holding branches in their hands, the faithful gather either outside, in front of the church door, or inside the church itself. The Priest and ministers and a representative group of the faithful go to a suitable place in the church outside the sanctuary, where at least the greater part of the faithful can see the rite.

While the Priest approaches the appointed place, the antiphon Hosanna *or another appropriate chant is sung. Then the blessing of branches and the proclamation of the Gospel of the Lord's entrance into Jerusalem take place as above (pp. 250-251). After the Gospel, the Priest processes solemnly with the ministers and the representative group of the faithful through the church to the sanctuary, while the responsory* As the Lord entered *(above) or another appropriate chant is sung.*

Arriving at the altar, the Priest venerates it. He then goes to the chair and, omitting the Introductory Rites of the Mass and, if appropriate, the Kyrie (Lord, have mercy), *he says the Collect of the Mass, and then continues the Mass in the usual way.*

THIRD FORM: THE SIMPLE ENTRANCE

At all other Masses of this Sunday at which the Solemn Entrance is not held, the memorial of the Lord's entrance into Jerusalem takes place by means of a Simple Entrance.

While the Priest proceeds to the altar, the Entrance Antiphon with its Psalm (below) or another chant on the same theme is sung. Arriving at the altar, the Priest venerates it and goes to the chair. After the Sign of the Cross, he greets the people and continues the Mass in the usual way.

At other Masses, in which singing at the entrance cannot take place, the Priest, as soon as he has arrived at the altar and venerated it, greets the people, reads the Entrance Antiphon, and continues the Mass in the usual way.

ENTRANCE ANTIPHON Cf. Jn. 12.1, 12-13; Ps. 23.9-10

[Hosanna in the Highest]

Six days before the Passover, when the Lord came into the city of Jerusalem, the children ran to meet him; in their hands they carried palm branches and with a loud voice cried out: Hosanna in the highest! Blessed are you, who have come in your abundant mercy!

O gates, lift high your heads; grow higher, ancient doors. Let him enter, the king of glory! Who is this king of glory? He, the Lord of hosts, he is the king of glory. Hosanna in the highest! Blessed are you, who have come in your abundant mercy!

AT THE MASS

After the Procession or Solemn Entrance the Priest begins the Mass with the Collect.

COLLECT   [Patient Suffering]

Almighty ever-living God,
who as an example of humility for the human
    race to follow
caused our Saviour to take flesh and submit to
    the Cross,
graciously grant that we may heed his lesson of
    patient suffering
and so merit a share in his Resurrection.
Who lives and reigns with you in the unity of the
    Holy Spirit,
one God, for ever and ever. ℟. **Amen.** ↓

FIRST READING Isa. 50.4-7   [Christ's Suffering]

The suffering servant was persecuted and struck by his
own people; he was spit upon and beaten. He proclaims
the true faith and suffers to atone for the sins of his people. Here we see a foreshadowing of the true servant of
God.

A reading from the book of the Prophet Isaiah.

THE servant of the Lord said: "The Lord God
    has given me the tongue of a teacher,
that I may know how to sustain the weary with
    a word.
Morning by morning he wakens—
wakens my ear to listen as those who are
    taught.
The Lord God has opened my ear,
and I was not rebellious,
I did not turn backward.

I gave my back to those who struck me,
and my cheeks to those who pulled out the
    beard;
I did not hide my face
from insult and spitting.

The Lord God helps me;
therefore I have not been disgraced;
therefore I have set my face like flint,
and I know that I shall not be put to shame."

The word of the Lord. ℟. **Thanks be to God.** ↓

RESPONSORIAL PSALM Ps. 22   [Christ's Agony]

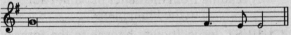

℟. **My God, my God, why have you for-sak - en me?**

All who see me mock at me;
they make mouths at me, they shake their heads;
"Commit your cause to the Lord; let him deliver;
let him rescue the one in whom he delights!"—℟.

For dogs are all around me;
a company of evildoers encircles me.
My hands and feet have shrivelled;
I can count all my bones.—℟.

They divide my clothes among themselves,
and for my clothing they cast lots.
But you, O Lord, do not be far away!
O my help, come quickly to my aid!—℟.

I will tell of your name to my brothers and sis-
    ters;

in the midst of the congregation I will praise you:
You who fear the Lord, praise him!
All you offspring of Jacob, glorify him;
stand in awe of him, all you offspring of Israel!

℟. **My God, my God; why have you forsaken
   me?** ↓

SECOND READING Phil. 2.6-11   [Humility]

**Paul urges us to humility by which we are made like
Christ our Lord. He put off the majesty of his divinity
and became man and humbled himself in obedience to
the ignominious death on the cross.**

A reading from the Letter of Saint Paul
            to the Philippians.

CHRIST Jesus, though he was in the form of
   God,
did not regard equality with God
as something to be exploited,
but emptied himself,
taking the form of a slave,
being born in human likeness.
And being found in human form,
he humbled himself
and became obedient to the point of death—
even death on a cross.

Therefore God highly exalted him
and gave him the name that is above every name,
so that at the name of Jesus every knee should
   bend,
in heaven and on earth and under the earth,
and every tongue should confess that Jesus Christ
   is Lord,

to the glory of God the Father.

The word of the Lord. ℟. **Thanks be to God.** ↓

GOSPEL ACCLAMATION Phil. 2.8-9
[Obedient to Death]

(If the acclamation is not sung, it is omitted.)

℣. Praise to you, Lord Jesus Christ, King of endless glory!*

℟. **Praise to you, Lord Jesus Christ, King of endless glory!**

℣. Christ became obedient for us to death, even death on a Cross.

Therefore God exalted him and gave him the name above every name.

℟. **Praise to you, Lord Jesus Christ, King of endless glory!** ↓

GOSPEL Mt. 26.14—27.66 or 27.11-54   [Christ's Passion]

Matthew portrays the passion and death of Jesus. Jesus gives his disciples his Body and Blood. Judas betrays him. Jesus is condemned to die on the cross.

The Passion of the Lord may also be divided into three parts in the traditional manner, the parts being read or sung by three persons. Preferably it is to be proclaimed by a priest or deacons, but in their absence, it may be proclaimed by lectors, the part of Jesus being reserved to a priest.

The Passion begins directly, without introduction.

We participate in the Passion narrative in several ways: by reading it and reflecting on it during the week ahead; by listening with faith as it is proclaimed; by singing acclamations at appropriate places in the text; by respectful posture during the narrative; by reverent silence after the passage about Christ's Death. We do not hold the palms during the reading on Palm Sunday.

---

* *See p. 16 for other Gospel Acclamations.*

Who caused the death of Jesus? In listening to God's word today, we must remember that our Lord died to save every human person. By our sins we have contributed to his suffering and Death. The authorities of his time bear responsibility for carrying out his execution; this charge must not be laid against all the Jewish people of Jesus' day or of our own. We are all responsible for sin and for our Lord's suffering.

This week we are challenged by the Passion narrative to reflect on the way we are living up to our baptismal promises of dying with Christ to sin and living with him for God.

Note: A shorter version (27.11-54) is indicated by asterisks at the beginning and the end (pp. 268-271).

N. **T**HE Passion of our Lord Jesus Christ according to Matthew.

BETRAYED BY A DISCIPLE

N. **O**NE of the twelve, who was called Judas Iscariot, went to the chief priests and said, **S.** **"What will you give me if I betray him to you?"** **N.** They paid him thirty pieces of silver. And from that moment he began to look for an opportunity to betray him.

AT THE LAST SUPPER

N. **O**N the first day of Unleavened Bread the disciples came to Jesus, saying, **S.** **"Where do you want us to make the preparations for you to eat the Passover?"** [**N.** He said,] **J.** *"Go into the city to a certain man, and say to him, 'The Teacher says, My time is near; I will keep the Passover at your house with my disciples.'"* **N.** So the disciples did as Jesus had directed them, and they prepared the Passover meal.

When it was evening, he took his place with the twelve; and while they were eating, he said,

J. *"Truly I tell you, one of you will betray me."* **N.** And they became greatly distressed and began to say to him one after another, **S. "Surely not I, Lord?"** [**N.** He answered,] **J.** *"The one who has dipped his hand into the bowl with me will betray me. The Son of Man goes as it is written of him, but woe to that man by whom the Son of Man is betrayed! It would have been better for that man not to have been born."* **N.** Judas, who betrayed him, said, **S. "Surely not I, Rabbi?"** [**N.** He replied,] **J.** *"You have said so."*

N. While they were eating, Jesus took a loaf of bread, and after blessing it he broke it, gave it to the disciples, and said, **J.** *"Take, eat; this is my Body."* **N.** Then he took a cup, and after giving thanks he gave it to them, saying, **J.** *"Drink from it, all of you; for this is my Blood of the covenant, which is poured out for many for the forgiveness of sins. I tell you, I will never again drink of this fruit of the vine until that day when I drink it new with you in my Father's kingdom."*

N. When they had sung the hymn, they went out to the Mount of Olives.

Then Jesus said to them, **J.** *"You will all become deserters because of me this night; for it is written,*

> *'I will strike the shepherd,*
>   *and the sheep of the flock will be scattered.'*

But after I am raised up, I will go ahead of you to Galilee." **N.** Peter said to him, **S. "Though all become deserters because of you, I will never desert you."** [**N.** Jesus said to him,] **J.** *"Truly I tell you, this very night, before the cock crows, you* *will deny me three times."* **N.** Peter said to him, **S. "Even though I must die with you, I will not deny you."** **N.** And so said all the disciples.

At this point all may join in singing an appropriate acclamation.

JESUS IN THE GARDEN

N. THEN Jesus went with them to a place called Gethsemane; and he said to his disciples, **J.** *"Sit here while I go over there and pray."* **N.** He took with him Peter and the two sons of Zebedee, and began to be grieved and agitated.

Then he said to them, **J.** *"I am deeply grieved, even to death; remain here, and stay awake with me."* **N.** And going a little farther, he threw himself on the ground and prayed, **J.** *"My Father, if it is possible, let this cup pass from me; yet not what I want, but what you want."*

N. Then he came to the disciples and found them sleeping; and he said to Peter, **J.** *"So, could you not stay awake with me one hour? Stay awake and pray that you may not come into temptation; for the spirit indeed is willing, but the flesh is weak."* **N.** Again he went away for the second time and prayed, **J.** *"My Father, if this cannot pass unless I drink it, your will be done."*

N. Again he came and found them sleeping, for their eyes were heavy. So leaving them again, he went away and prayed for the third time, saying the same words. Then he came to the disciples and said to them, **J.** *"Are you still sleeping and taking your rest? See, the hour is at hand, and the Son of Man is betrayed into the hands of sinners. Get up, let us be going. See, my betrayer is at hand."*

JESUS IS ARRESTED

N. WHILE he was still speaking, Judas, one of the twelve, arrived; with him was a large crowd with swords and clubs, from the chief priests and the elders of the people. Now the betrayer had given them a sign, saying, **S. "The one I will kiss is the man; arrest him."** **N.** At once he came up to Jesus and said, **S. "Greetings, Rabbi!"** **N.** and kissed him. Jesus said to him, **J.** *"Friend, do what you are here to do."* **N.** Then they came and laid hands on Jesus and arrested him.

Suddenly, one of those with Jesus put his hand on his sword, drew it, and struck the slave of the high priest, cutting off his ear. Then Jesus said to him, **J.** *"Put your sword back into its place; for all who take the sword will perish by the sword. Do you think that I cannot appeal to my Father, and he will at once send me more than twelve legions of Angels? But how then would the Scriptures be fulfilled, which say it must happen in this way?"*

N. At that hour Jesus said to the crowds, **J.** *"Have you come out with swords and clubs to arrest me as though I were a bandit? Day after day I sat in the temple teaching, and you did not arrest me. But all this has taken place so that the Scriptures of the Prophets may be fulfilled."* **N.** Then all the disciples deserted him and fled.

TRIAL IN THE HIGH PRIEST'S HOUSE

N. THOSE who had arrested Jesus took him to Caiaphas the high priest, in whose house the scribes and the elders had gathered.

But Peter was following him at a distance, as far as the courtyard of the high priest; and going inside, he sat with the guards in order to see how this would end. Now the chief priests and the whole council were looking for false testimony against Jesus so that they might put him to death, but they found none, though many false witnesses came forward.

At last two came forward and said, **S. "This fellow said, 'I am able to destroy the temple of God and to build it in three days.'"** N. The high priest stood up and said, **S. "Have you no answer? What is it that they testify against you?"** N. But Jesus was silent. Then the high priest said to him, **S. "I put you under oath before the living God, tell us if you are the Christ, the Son of God."**

N. Jesus said to him, *J. "You have said so. But I tell you, from now on you will see the Son of Man seated at the right hand of Power and coming on the clouds of heaven."* N. Then the high priest tore his clothes and said, **S. "He has blasphemed! Why do we still need witnesses? You have now heard his blasphemy. What is your verdict?"** N. They answered, **S. "He deserves death."** N. Then they spat in his face and struck him; and some slapped him, saying, **S. "Prophesy to us, Christ! Who is it that struck you?"**

PETER DENIES THE LORD JESUS

N. NOW Peter was sitting outside in the courtyard. A servant girl came to him and said, **S. "You also were with Jesus the**

Galilean." **N.** But he denied it before all of them, saying, **S.** **"I do not know what you are talking about."** **N.** When he went out to the porch, another servant girl saw him, and she said to the bystanders, **S.** **"This man was with Jesus of Nazareth."** **N.** Again he denied it with an oath, **S.** **"I do not know the man."** **N.** After a little while the bystanders came up and said to Peter, **S.** **"Certainly you are also one of them, for your accent betrays you."** **N.** Then he began to curse, and he swore an oath, **S.** **"I do not know the man!"** **N.** At that moment the cock crowed. Then Peter remembered what Jesus had said: "Before the cock crows, you will deny me three times." And he went out and wept bitterly.

At this point all may join in singing an appropriate acclamation.

TRIAL BEFORE PILATE

N. WHEN morning came, all the chief priests and the elders of the people conferred together against Jesus in order to bring about his death. They bound him, led him away, and handed him over to Pilate the governor.

When Judas, his betrayer, saw that Jesus was condemned, he repented and brought back the thirty pieces of silver to the chief priests and the elders. He said, **S.** **"I have sinned by betraying innocent blood."** **N.** But they said, **S.** **"What is that to us? See to it yourself."** **N.** Throwing down the pieces of silver in the temple, he departed; and he went and hanged himself. But the chief priests, taking the pieces of silver, said, **S.** **"It is not lawful to put them into the treasury, since they are blood money."** **N.** After conferring together, they used

them to buy the potter's field as a place to bury
foreigners. For this reason that field has been
called the Field of Blood to this day. Then was fulfilled what had been spoken through the Prophet
Jeremiah, "And they took the thirty pieces of silver, the price of the one on whom a price had been
set, on whom some of the people of Israel had set
a price, and they gave them for the potter's field,
as the Lord commanded me."

* Now Jesus stood before the governor; and the
governor asked him, **S. "Are you the King of the
Jews?"** [N. Jesus said,] **J.** *"You say so."* N. But
when he was accused by the chief priests and elders, he did not answer. Then Pilate said to him, **S.
"Do you not hear how many accusations they
make against you?"** N. But he gave him no answer, not even to a single charge, so that the governor was greatly amazed.

Now at the festival the governor was accus-
tomed to release a prisoner for the crowd, anyone
they wanted. At that time they had a notorious
prisoner, called Barabbas. So after they had gathered, Pilate said to them, **S. "Whom do you want
me to release for you, Barabbas or Jesus who is
called the Christ?"** N. For he realized that it was
out of jealousy that they had handed him over.

While he was sitting on the judgment seat, his
wife sent word to him, **S. "Have nothing to do
with that innocent man, for today I have suffered
a great deal because of a dream about him."**

N. Now the chief priests and the elders per-
suaded the crowds to ask for Barabbas and to
have Jesus killed. The governor again said to
them, **S. "Which of the two do you want me to
release for you?"** N. And they said, **S. "Barab-**

bas." **N.** Pilate said to them, **S. "Then what should I do with Jesus who is called the Christ?" N.** All of them said, **S. "Let him be crucified!" N.** Then he asked, **S. "Why, what evil has he done?" N.** But they shouted all the more, **S. "Let him be crucified!"**

N. So when Pilate saw that he could do nothing, but rather that a riot was beginning, he took some water and washed his hands before the crowd, saying, **S. "I am innocent of this man's blood; see to it yourselves." N.** Then the people as a whole answered, **S. "His blood be on us and on our children!"** So he released Barabbas for them; and after flogging Jesus, he handed him over to be crucified.

ON THE WAY TO CALVARY

N. THEN the soldiers of the governor took Jesus into the governor's headquarters, and they gathered the whole cohort around him.

They stripped him and put a scarlet robe on him, and after twisting some thorns into a crown, they put it on his head. They put a reed in his right hand and knelt before him and mocked him, saying, **S. "Hail, King of the Jews!" N.** They spat on him, and took the reed and struck him on the head. After mocking him, they stripped him of the robe and put his own clothes on him. Then they led him away to crucify him.

As they went out, they came upon a man from Cyrene named Simon; they compelled this man to carry his Cross.

At this point all may join in singing an appropriate acclamation.

JESUS IS CRUCIFIED AND DIES FOR US

N. **A**ND when they came to a place called Golgotha (which means Place of a Skull), they offered him wine to drink, mixed with gall; but when he tasted it, he would not drink it.

And when they had crucified him, they divided his clothes among themselves by casting lots; then they sat down there and kept watch over him.

Over his head they put the charge against him, which read, "This is Jesus, the King of the Jews." Then two bandits were crucified with him, one on his right and one on his left. Those who passed by derided him, shaking their heads and saying, **S.** **"You who would destroy the temple and build it in three days, save yourself! If you are the Son of God, come down from the Cross."**

N. In the same way the chief priests also, along with the scribes and elders, were mocking him, saying, **S.** **"He saved others; he cannot save himself. He is the King of Israel; let him come down from the Cross now, and we will believe in him. He trusts in God; let God deliver him now, if he wants to; for he said, 'I am God's Son.'"** **N.** The bandits who were crucified with him also taunted him in the same way.

From noon on, darkness came over the whole land until three in the afternoon. And about three o'clock Jesus cried with a loud voice, **J.** "Eli, Eli, lema sabachthani?" **N.** that is, "My God, my God, why have you forsaken me?" When some of the bystanders heard it, they said, **S.** **"This man is calling for Elijah."** **N.** At once one of them ran and got a sponge, filled it with sour wine, put it on a stick, and gave it to him to drink. But the others said, **S. "Wait, let us see whether Elijah will come to save him." N.** Then Jesus cried again with a loud voice and breathed his last.

Here all kneel and pause for a short time.

EVENTS AFTER JESUS' DEATH

N. **A**T that moment the curtain of the temple was torn in two, from top to bottom. The earth shook, and the rocks were split. The tombs also were opened, and many bodies of the saints who had fallen asleep were raised. After his resurrection they came out of the tombs and entered the holy city and appeared to many.

Now when the centurion and those with him, who were keeping watch over Jesus, saw the earthquake and what took place, they were terrified and said, **S. "Truly this man was God's Son!"***

N. Many women were also there, looking on from a distance; they had followed Jesus from Galilee and had provided for him. Among them were Mary Magdalene, and Mary the mother of James and Joseph, and the mother of the sons of Zebedee.

JESUS' BODY IS PLACED IN THE TOMB

N. **W**HEN it was evening, there came a rich man from Arimathea, named Joseph, who was also a disciple of Jesus. He went to Pilate and asked for the body of Jesus; then Pilate ordered it to be given to him. So Joseph took the body and wrapped it in a clean linen cloth and laid it in his own new tomb, which he had hewn in the rock. He then rolled a great stone to the door of the tomb and went away. Mary Magdalene and the other Mary were there, sitting opposite the tomb.

The next day, that is, after the day of Preparation, the chief priests and the Pharisees gathered before Pilate and said, **S. "Sir, we remember what that impostor said while he was still alive, 'After three days I will rise again.' Therefore command the tomb to be made secure until the third day; otherwise his disciples may go and steal him away, and tell the people, 'He has been raised from the dead,' and the last deception would be worse than the first."** N. Pilate said to them, **S. "You have a guard of soldiers; go, make it as secure as you can."** N. So they went with the guard and made the tomb secure by sealing the stone.   → No. 15, p. 18

PRAYER OVER THE OFFERINGS

[Reconciled with God]

Through the Passion of your Only Begotten Son,
  O Lord,
may our reconciliation with you be near at hand,
so that, though we do not merit it by our own
  deeds,
yet by this sacrifice made once for all,
we may feel already the effects of your mercy.
Through Christ our Lord. ℟. **Amen.** ↓

PREFACE (19)   [Purchased Our Justification]

℣. The Lord be with you. ℟. **And with your spirit.**
℣. Lift up your hearts. ℟. **We lift them up to the Lord.**

℣. Let us give thanks to the Lord our God. ℟. **It is right and just.**

It is truly right and just, our duty and our
     salvation,
always and everywhere to give you thanks,
Lord, holy Father, almighty and eternal God,
through Christ our Lord.

For, though innocent, he suffered willingly for
     sinners
and accepted unjust condemnation to save the
     guilty.
His Death has washed away our sins,
and his Resurrection has purchased our
     justification.

And so, with all the Angels,
we praise you, as in joyful celebration we acclaim:

→ No. 23, p. 23

COMMUNION ANTIPHON Mt. 26.42   [God's Will]
**Father, if this chalice cannot pass without my
drinking it, your will be done.** ↓

PRAYER AFTER COMMUNION   [Nourishing Gifts]
Nourished with these sacred gifts,
we humbly beseech you, O Lord,
that, just as through the death of your Son
you have brought us to hope for what we believe,
so by his Resurrection
you may lead us to where you call.
Through Christ our Lord.
℟. **Amen.** ↓

*The Deacon or, in his absence, the Priest himself, says
the invitation:* Bow down for the blessing.

PRAYER OVER THE PEOPLE   [God's Family]

Look, we pray, O Lord, on this your family,
for whom our Lord Jesus Christ
did not hesitate to be delivered into the hands of
   the wicked
and submit to the agony of the Cross.
Who lives and reigns for ever and ever.
R̷. **Amen.**   → No. 32, p. 77

"Do this in remembrance of me."

THE SACRED PASCHAL TRIDUUM

APRIL 13

THURSDAY OF THE LORD'S SUPPER [HOLY THURSDAY]

AT THE EVENING MASS

The Mass of the Lord's Supper is celebrated in the evening, at a convenient time, with the full participation of the whole local community and with all the Priests and ministers exercising their office.

ENTRANCE ANTIPHON Cf. Gal. 6.14   [Glory in Cross]

We should glory in the Cross of our Lord Jesus Christ, in whom is our salvation, life and resurrection, through whom we are saved and delivered.   → No. 2, p. 10

The Gloria in excelsis (Glory to God in the highest) is said. While the hymn is being sung, bells are rung, and when it is finished, they remain silent until the Gloria in excelsis of the Easter Vigil, unless, if appropriate, the

Diocesan Bishop has decided otherwise. Likewise, during this same period, the organ and other musical instruments may be used only so as to support the singing.

COLLECT   [Fullness of Charity]

O God, who have called us to participate
in this most sacred Supper,
in which your Only Begotten Son,
when about to hand himself over to death,
entrusted to the Church a sacrifice new for all
   eternity,
the banquet of his love,
grant, we pray,
that we may draw from so great a mystery,
the fullness of charity and of life.
Through our Lord Jesus Christ, your Son,
who lives and reigns with you in the unity of the
   Holy Spirit,
one God, for ever and ever. ℟. **Amen.** ↓

FIRST READING Ex. 12.1-8, 11-14   [The First Passover]

The people are instructed to prepare for the Passover meal. By the blood of the lamb they are saved from death.

A reading from the book of Exodus.

THE Lord said to Moses and Aaron in the land
   of Egypt: This month shall mark for you the
beginning of months; it shall be the first month of
the year for you. Tell the whole congregation of
Israel that on the tenth of this month they are to
take a lamb for each family, a lamb for each
household. If a household is too small for a whole
lamb, it shall join its closest neighbour in obtaining one; the lamb shall be divided in proportion to
the number of people who eat of it.

Your lamb shall be without blemish, a year-old male; you may take it from the sheep or from the goats. You shall keep it until the fourteenth day of this month; then the whole assembled congregation of Israel shall slaughter it at twilight. They shall take some of the blood and put it on the two doorposts and the lintel of the houses in which they eat it. They shall eat the lamb that same night; they shall eat it roasted over the fire with unleavened bread and bitter herbs.

This is how you shall eat it: your loins girded, your sandals on your feet, and your staff in your hand; and you shall eat it hurriedly. It is the Passover of the Lord. For I will pass through the land of Egypt that night, and I will strike down every firstborn in the land of Egypt, both human beings and animals; on all the gods of Egypt I will execute judgments: I am the Lord. The blood shall be a sign for you on the houses where you live: when I see the blood, I will pass over you, and no plague shall destroy you when I strike the land of Egypt.

This day shall be a day of remembrance for you. You shall celebrate it as a festival to the Lord; throughout your generations you shall observe it as a perpetual ordinance.—The word of the Lord. ℟. **Thanks be to God.** ↓

RESPONSORIAL PSALM Ps. 116   [Thanksgiving]

℟. The   cup   of blessing   that   we   bless

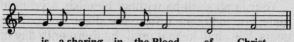

is a sharing in the Blood of Christ.

What shall I return to the Lord
for all his bounty to me?
I will lift up the cup of salvation
and call on the name of the Lord.

℟. **The cup of blessing that we bless**
    is a sharing in the Blood of Christ.

Precious in the sight of the Lord
is the death of his faithful ones.
I am your servant, the son of your serving girl.
You have loosed my bonds.—℟.

I will offer to you a thanksgiving sacrifice
and call on the name of the Lord.
I will pay my vows to the Lord
in the presence of all his people.—℟. ↓

SECOND READING 1 Cor. 11.23-26   [The Lord's Supper]

Paul recounts the events of the Last Supper which were
handed down to him. The changing of bread and wine
into the Body and Blood of the Lord proclaims again his
death. It is a sacrificial meal.

A reading from the first Letter of Saint Paul
to the Corinthians.

BROTHERS and sisters: I received from the
Lord what I also handed on to you, that the
Lord Jesus on the night when he was betrayed
took a loaf of bread, and when he had given
thanks, he broke it and said, "This is my Body
that is for you. Do this in remembrance of me."

In the same way he took the cup also, after supper, saying, "This cup is the new covenant in my

Blood. Do this, as often as you drink it, in remembrance of me." For as often as you eat this bread and drink the cup, you proclaim the Lord's death until he comes.—The word of the Lord. ℟. **Thanks be to God.** ↓

GOSPEL ACCLAMATION Jn. 13.34 [Love One Another]

(If the acclamation is not sung, it is omitted.)

℣. Praise to you, Lord Jesus Christ, King of endless glory!*

℟. **Praise to you, Lord Jesus Christ, King of endless glory!**

℣. I give you a new commandment:
love one another as I have loved you.

℟. **Praise to you, Lord Jesus Christ, King of endless glory!** ↓

GOSPEL Jn. 13.1-15 [Love and Service]

Jesus washes the feet of his disciples to prove to them his sincere love and great humility which they should imitate.

℣. The Lord be with you. ℟. **And with your spirit.**
✝ A reading from the holy Gospel according to John. ℟. **Glory to you, O Lord.**

BEFORE the festival of the Passover, Jesus knew that his hour had come to depart from this world and go to the Father. Having loved his own who were in the world, he loved them to the end.

The devil had already put it into the heart of Judas, son of Simon Iscariot, to betray him. And during supper Jesus, knowing that the Father had given all things into his hands, and that he had come from God and was going to God, got up from the table, took off his outer robe, and tied a

* See p. 16 for other Gospel Acclamations.

towel around himself. Then he poured water into a basin and began to wash the disciples' feet and to wipe them with the towel that was tied around him.

He came to Simon Peter, who said to him, "Lord, are you going to wash my feet?" Jesus answered, "You do not know now what I am doing, but later you will understand." Peter said to him, "You will never wash my feet." Jesus answered, "Unless I wash you, you have no share with me." Simon Peter said to him, "Lord, not my feet only but also my hands and my head!" Jesus said to him, "One who has bathed does not need to wash, except for the feet, but is entirely clean. And you are clean, though not all of you." For he knew who was to betray him; for this reason he said, "Not all of you are clean."

After he had washed their feet, put on his robe, and returned to the table, Jesus said to them, "Do you know what I have done to you? You call me Teacher and Lord—and you are right, for that is what I am. So if I, your Lord and Teacher, have washed your feet, you also ought to wash one another's feet. For I have set you an example, that you also should do as I have done to you."—The Gospel of the Lord. ℟. **Praise to you, Lord Jesus Christ.**

After the proclamation of the Gospel, the Priest gives a homily in which light is shed on the principal mysteries that are commemorated in this Mass, namely, the institution of the Holy Eucharist and of the priestly Order, and the commandment of the Lord concerning fraternal charity.

The Washing of Feet

After the Homily, where a pastoral reason suggests it, the Washing of Feet follows.

Those who are chosen from amongst the people of God are led by the ministers to seats prepared in a suitable place. Then the Priest (removing his chasuble if necessary) goes to each one, and, with the help of the ministers, pours water over each one's feet and then dries them.

Meanwhile some of the following antiphons or other appropriate chants are sung.

ANTIPHON 1 Cf. Jn. 13.4, 5, 15   [Jesus' Example]

**After the Lord had risen from supper,
he poured water into a basin
and began to wash the feet of his disciples:
he left them this example.**

ANTIPHON 2 Cf. Jn. 13.12, 13, 15   [Do Likewise]

**The Lord Jesus, after eating supper with his disciples,
washed their feet and said to them:
Do you know what I, your Lord and Master, have done for you?
I have given you an example, that you should do likewise.**

ANTIPHON 3 Jn. 13.6, 7, 8   [Peter's Understanding]

**Lord, are you to wash my feet? Jesus said to him in answer:
If I do not wash your feet, you will have no share with me.
℣. So he came to Simon Peter and Peter said to him:
—Lord ...
℣. What I am doing, you do not know for now,
but later you will come to know.
—Lord ...**

ANTIPHON 4 Cf. Jn. 13.14   [Service]

If I, your Lord and Master, have washed your feet, how much more should you wash each other's feet?

ANTIPHON 5 Jn. 13.35   [Identified by Love]

This is how all will know that you are my disciples:
if you have love for one another.

℣. **Jesus said to his disciples:**
—**This is how ...**

ANTIPHON 6 Jn. 13.34   [New Commandment]

I give you a new commandment,
that you love one another
as I have loved you, says the Lord.

ANTIPHON 7 1 Cor. 13.13   [Greatest Is Charity]

Let faith, hope and charity, these three, remain among you,
but the greatest of these is charity.

℣. **Now faith, hope and charity, these three, remain;**
but the greatest of these is charity.
—**Let ...**

After the Washing of Feet, the Priest washes and dries his hands, puts the chasuble back on, and returns to the chair, and from there he directs the Universal Prayer.

The Creed is not said.

The Liturgy of the Eucharist

At the beginning of the Liturgy of the Eucharist, there may be a procession of the faithful in which gifts for the poor may be presented with the bread and wine.

Meanwhile the following, or another appropriate chant, is sung.

[Christ's Love]

Ant. **Where true charity is dwelling, God is present there.**

℣. **By the love of Christ we have been brought together:**

℣. **let us find in him our gladness and our pleasure;**

℣. **may we love him and revere him, God the living,**

℣. **and in love respect each other with sincere hearts.**

Ant. **Where true charity is dwelling, God is present there.**

℣. **So when we as one are gathered all together,**

℣. **let us strive to keep our minds free of division;**

℣. **may there be an end to malice, strife and quarrels,**

℣. **and let Christ our God be dwelling here among us.**

Ant. **Where true charity is dwelling, God is present there.**

℣. **May your face thus be our vision, bright in glory,**

℣. **Christ our God, with all the blessed Saints in heaven:**

℣. **such delight is pure and faultless, joy unbounded,**

℣. **which endures through countless ages world without end. Amen.**   → No. 17, p. 20

PRAYER OVER THE OFFERINGS

[Work of Redemption]

Grant us, O Lord, we pray,
that we may participate worthily in these
   mysteries,
for whenever the memorial of this sacrifice is
   celebrated
the work of our redemption is accomplished.
Through Christ our Lord.
℟. **Amen.**   → No. 21, p. 22 (Pref. 47)

When the Roman Canon is used, this special form of it is
said, with proper formulas for the Communicantes *(In*
communion with those), Hanc igitur *(Therefore,*
Lord, we pray), *and* Qui pridie *(On the day before he*
was to suffer).

To you, therefore, most merciful Father,
we make humble prayer and petition
through Jesus Christ, your Son, our Lord:
that you accept
and bless ✠ these gifts, these offerings,
these holy and unblemished sacrifices,
which we offer you firstly
for your holy catholic Church.
Be pleased to grant her peace,
to guard, unite and govern her
throughout the whole world,
together with your servant N. our Pope
and N. our Bishop,
and all those who, holding to the truth,
hand on the catholic and apostolic faith.

Remember, Lord, your servants N. and N.
and all gathered here,
whose faith and devotion are known to you.
For them we offer you this sacrifice of praise
or they offer it for themselves

and all who are dear to them:
for the redemption of their souls,
in hope of health and well-being,
and paying their homage to you,
the eternal God, living and true.

Celebrating the most sacred day
on which our Lord Jesus Christ
was handed over for our sake,
and in communion with those whose memory we
    venerate,
especially the glorious ever-Virgin Mary,
Mother of our God and Lord, Jesus Christ,
and † blessed Joseph, her Spouse,
your blessed Apostles and Martyrs,
Peter and Paul, Andrew,
(James, John,
Thomas, James, Philip,
Bartholomew, Matthew, Simon and Jude;
Linus, Cletus, Clement, Sixtus,
Cornelius, Cyprian,
Lawrence, Chrysogonus,
John and Paul,
Cosmas and Damian)
and all your Saints;
we ask that through their merits and prayers,
in all things we may be defended
by your protecting help.
(Through Christ our Lord. Amen.)

Therefore, Lord, we pray:
graciously accept this oblation of our service,
that of your whole family,
which we make to you
as we observe the day
on which our Lord Jesus Christ
handed on the mysteries of his Body and Blood
for his disciples to celebrate;

order our days in your peace,
and command that we be delivered from eternal
  damnation
and counted among the flock of those you have chosen.
(Through Christ our Lord. Amen.)

Be pleased, O God, we pray,
to bless, acknowledge,
and approve this offering in every respect;
make it spiritual and acceptable,
so that it may become for us
the Body and Blood of your most beloved Son,
our Lord Jesus Christ.

On the day before he was to suffer
for our salvation and the salvation of all,
that is today,
he took bread in his holy and venerable hands,
and with eyes raised to heaven
to you, O God, his almighty Father,
giving you thanks, he said the blessing,
broke the bread
and gave it to his disciples, saying:

Take this, all of you, and eat of it,
for this is my Body,
which will be given up for you.

In a similar way, when supper was ended,
he took this precious chalice
in his holy and venerable hands,
and once more giving you thanks, he said the blessing
and gave the chalice to his disciples, saying:

Take this, all of you, and drink from it,
for this is the Chalice of my Blood,
the Blood of the new and eternal covenant,
which will be poured out for you and for many
for the forgiveness of sins.

Do this in memory of me.

The rest follows the Roman Canon, pp. 26-29.

COMMUNION ANTIPHON 1 Cor. 11.24-25
[In Memory of Christ]

This is the Body that will be given up for you; this is the Chalice of the new covenant in my Blood, says the Lord; do this, whenever you receive it, in memory of me. ↓

After the distribution of Communion, a ciborium with hosts for Communion on the following day is left on the altar. The Priest, standing at the chair, says the Prayer after Communion.

PRAYER AFTER COMMUNION   [Renewed]

Grant, almighty God,
that, just as we are renewed
by the Supper of your Son in this present age,
so we may enjoy his banquet for all eternity.
Who lives and reigns for ever and ever. ℟. **Amen.**

The Transfer of the Most Blessed Sacrament

After the Prayer after Communion, the Priest puts incense in the thurible while standing, blesses it and then, kneeling, incenses the Blessed Sacrament three times. Then, having put on a white humeral veil, he rises, takes the ciborium, and covers it with the ends of the veil.

A procession is formed in which the Blessed Sacrament, accompanied by torches and incense, is carried through the church to a place of repose prepared in a part of the church or in a chapel suitably decorated. A lay minister with a cross, standing between two other ministers with lighted candles leads off. Others carrying lighted candles follow. Before the Priest carrying the Blessed Sacrament comes the thurifer with a smoking thurible. Meanwhile, the hymn Pange, lingua *(exclusive of the last two stanzas) or another eucharistic chant is sung.*

When the procession reaches the place of repose, the Priest, with the help of the Deacon if necessary, places the ciborium in the tabernacle, the door of which remains open. Then he puts incense in the thurible and, kneeling, incenses the Blessed Sacrament, while Tantum ergo Sacramentum *or another eucharistic chant is sung. Then the Deacon or the Priest himself places the Sacrament in the tabernacle and closes the door.*

After a period of adoration in silence, the Priest and ministers genuflect and return to the sacristy.

At an appropriate time, the altar is stripped and, if possible, the crosses are removed from the church. It is expedient that any crosses which remain in the church be veiled.

The faithful are invited to continue adoration before the Blessed Sacrament for a suitable length of time during the night, according to local circumstances, but after midnight the adoration should take place without solemnity.

"He bowed his head and gave up his spirit."

APRIL 14

FRIDAY OF THE PASSION OF THE LORD [GOOD FRIDAY]

THE CELEBRATION OF THE PASSION OF THE LORD

This week, on Good Friday and Holy Saturday, the people of God are called to observe a solemn paschal fast. In this way, they are in union with the Christians of every century, and will be ready to receive the joys of the Lord's Resurrection with uplifted and responsive hearts.

The Priest and the Deacon, if a Deacon is present, wearing red vestments as for Mass, go to the altar in silence and, after making a reverence to the altar, prostrate themselves or, if appropriate, kneel and pray in silence for a while. All others kneel.

Then the Priest, with the ministers, goes to the chair where, facing the people, who are standing, he says, with hands extended, one of the following prayers, omitting the invitation Let us pray.

PRAYER   [Sanctify Your Servants]

Remember your mercies, O Lord,
and with your eternal protection sanctify your
   servants,

for whom Christ your Son,
by the shedding of his Blood,
established the Paschal Mystery.
Who lives and reigns for ever and ever. ℟. **Amen.**

OR   [Image of Christ]

O God, who by the Passion of Christ your Son,
    our Lord,
abolished the death inherited from ancient sin
by every succeeding generation,
grant that just as, being conformed to him,
we have borne by the law of nature
the image of the man of earth,
so by the sanctification of grace
we may bear the image of the Man of heaven.
Through Christ our Lord. ℟. **Amen.**

FIRST PART: THE LITURGY OF THE WORD

FIRST READING Isa. 52.13—53.12   [Suffering and Glory]

**The Suffering Servant shall be raised up and exalted. The
doctrine of expiatory suffering finds supreme expression
in these words.**

A reading from the book of the Prophet Isaiah.

S EE, my servant shall prosper;
    he shall be exalted and lifted up,
and shall be very high.

Just as there were many who were astonished at
    him
—so marred was his appearance, beyond human
    semblance,
and his form beyond that of the sons of man—
so he shall startle many nations;
kings shall shut their mouths because of him;

for that which had not been told them they shall
    see,
and that which they had not heard they shall con-
    template.
Who has believed what we have heard?
And to whom has the arm of the Lord been re-
    vealed?

For he grew up before the Lord like a young
    plant,
and like a root out of dry ground;
he had no form or majesty that we should look at
    him,
nothing in his appearance that we should desire
    him.
He was despised and rejected by men;
a man of suffering and acquainted with infirmity;
and as one from whom others hide their faces
he was despised,
and we held him of no account.

Surely he has borne our infirmities and carried
    our diseases;
yet we accounted him stricken,
struck down by God, and afflicted.
But he was wounded for our transgressions,
crushed for our iniquities;
upon him was the punishment that made us
    whole,
and by his bruises we are healed.
All we like sheep have gone astray;
each has turned to their own way
and the Lord has laid on him
the iniquity of us all.

He was oppressed, and he was afflicted,
yet he did not open his mouth;
like a lamb that is led to the slaughter,
and like a sheep that before its shearers is silent,
so he did not open his mouth.

By a perversion of justice he was taken away.
Who could have imagined his future?
For he was cut off from the land of the living,
stricken for the transgression of my people.
They made his grave with the wicked
and his tomb with the rich,
although he had done no violence,
and there was no deceit in his mouth.

Yet it was the will of the Lord to crush him with
pain.
When you make his life an offering for sin,
he shall see his offspring, and shall prolong his
days;
through him the will of the Lord shall prosper.
Out of his anguish he shall see light;
he shall find satisfaction through his knowledge.
The righteous one, my servant, shall make many
righteous,
and he shall bear their iniquities.

Therefore I will allot him a portion with the great,
and he shall divide the spoil with the strong;
because he poured out himself to death,
and was numbered with the transgressors;
yet he bore the sin of many,
and made intercession for the transgressors.
The word of the Lord. ℟. **Thanks be to God.** ↓

RESPONSORIAL PSALM Ps. 31   [Trust in God]

℟. Fa - ther, into your hands I com-mend my spirit.

In you, O Lord, I seek refuge;
do not let me ever be put to shame;
in your righteousness deliver me.
Into your hand I commit my spirit;
you have redeemed me,
O Lord, faithful God.—℟.

I am the scorn of all my adversaries,
a horror to my neighbours,
an object of dread to my acquaintances.
Those who see me in the street flee from me.
I have passed out of mind like one who is dead;
I have become like a broken vessel.—℟.

But I trust in you, O Lord;
I say, "You are my God."
My times are in your hand;
deliver me from the hand of my enemies and persecutors.—℟.

Let your face shine upon your servant;
save me in your steadfast love.
Be strong, and let your heart take courage,
all you who wait for the Lord.—℟. ↓

SECOND READING Heb. 4.14-16; 5.7-9
[Access to Christ]
  The theme of the compassionate high priest appears
  again in this passage. In him Christians can approach
  God confidently and without fear.

A reading from the Letter to the Hebrews.

BROTHERS and sisters: Since we have a great high priest who has passed through the heavens, Jesus, the Son of God, let us hold fast to our confession. For we do not have a high priest who is unable to sympathize with our weaknesses, but we have one who in every respect has been tested as we are, yet without sin. Let us therefore approach the throne of grace with boldness, so that we may receive mercy and find grace to help in time of need.

In the days of his flesh, Jesus offered up prayers and supplications, with loud cries and tears, to the one who was able to save him from death, and he was heard because of his reverent submission. Although he was a Son, he learned obedience through what he suffered; and having been made perfect, he became the source of eternal salvation for all who obey him.—The word of the Lord. ℟. **Thanks be to God.** ↓

GOSPEL ACCLAMATION Phil. 2.8-9   [Obedient for Us]
(*If the acclamation is not sung, it is omitted.*)

℣. Praise and honour to you, Lord Jesus Christ!*

℟. **Praise and honour to you, Lord Jesus Christ!**

℣. Christ became obedient for us to death, even death on a Cross.

Therefore God exalted him and gave him the name above every name.

℟. **Praise and honour to you, Lord Jesus Christ!** ↓

---

* *See p. 16 for other Gospel Acclamations.*

GOSPEL Jn. 18.1—19.42   [Christ's Passion]

*The Passion is read in the same way as on the preceding Sunday. The narrator is noted by **N.**, the words of Jesus by a **J.** and the words of others by **S.***

It is important for us to understand the meaning of Christ's sufferings today. See the note on pp. 261-262.

The beginning scene is Christ's agony in the garden. Our Lord knows what is to happen. The Scriptures recount the betrayal, the trial, the condemnation, and the crucifixion of Jesus.

N. THE Passion of our Lord Jesus Christ according to John.

JESUS IS ARRESTED

N. AFTER they had eaten the supper, Jesus went out with his disciples across the Kidron valley to a place where there was a garden, which he and his disciples entered. Now Judas, who betrayed him, also knew the place, because Jesus often met there with his disciples. So Judas brought a detachment of soldiers together with police from the chief priests and the Pharisees, and they came there with lanterns and torches and weapons.

Then Jesus, knowing all that was to happen to him, came forward and asked them, **J.** *"Whom are you looking for?"* **N.** They answered, **S. "Jesus of Nazareth."** [**N.** Jesus replied,] **J.** *"I am he."* **N.** Judas, who betrayed him, was standing with them. When Jesus said to them, "I am he," they stepped back and fell to the ground. Again he asked them, **J.** *"Whom are you looking for?"* [**N.** And they said,] **S. "Jesus of Nazareth."** [**N.** Jesus answered,] **J.** *"I told you that I am he. So if you are looking for me, let these men go."* **N.** This was to fulfill the word that he had spoken, "I did not lose a single one of those whom you gave me."

Then Simon Peter, who had a sword, drew it, struck the high priest's slave, and cut off his right ear. The slave's name was Malchus. Jesus said to Peter, **J.** *"Put your sword back into its sheath. Am I not to drink the cup that the Father has given me?"*

TRIAL BEFORE ANNAS

N. So the soldiers, their officer, and the Jewish police arrested Jesus and bound him. First they took him to Annas, who was the father-in-law of Caiaphas, the high priest that year. Caiaphas was the one who had advised the Jews that it was better to have one person die for the people.

Simon Peter and another disciple followed Jesus. Since that disciple was known to the high priest, he went with Jesus into the courtyard of the high priest, but Peter was standing outside at the gate. So the other disciple, who was known to the high priest, went out, spoke to the woman who guarded the gate, and brought Peter in. The woman said to Peter, **S. "You are not also one of this man's disciples, are you?" N.** Peter said, **S. "I am not." N.** Now the slaves and the police had made a charcoal fire because it was cold, and they were standing around it and warming themselves. Peter also was standing with them and warming himself.

Then the high priest questioned Jesus about his disciples and about his teaching. Jesus answered, **J.** *"I have spoken openly to the world; I* *have always taught in synagogues and in the temple, where all the Jews come together. I have said nothing in secret. Why do you ask me? Ask those who heard what I said to them; they know what I said."*

N. When he had said this, one of the police standing nearby struck Jesus on the face, saying, **S. "Is that how you answer the high priest?"** [N. Jesus answered,] **J.** *"If I have spoken wrongly, testify to the wrong. But if I have spoken rightly, why do you strike me?"* **N.** Then Annas sent him bound to Caiaphas the high priest.

PETER DENIES THE LORD JESUS

N. NOW Simon Peter was standing and warming himself. They asked him, **S. "You are not also one of his disciples, are you?"** **N.** He denied it and said, **S. "I am not."** **N.** One of the slaves of the high priest, a relative of the man whose ear Peter had cut off, asked, **S. "Did I not see you in the garden with him?"** **N.** Again Peter denied it, and at that moment the cock crowed.

At this point all may join in singing an acclamation.

TRIAL BEFORE PILATE

N. THEN they took Jesus from Caiaphas to Pilate's headquarters. It was early in the morning. They themselves did not enter the headquarters, so as to avoid ritual defilement and to be able to eat the Passover. So Pilate went out to them and said, **S. "What accusation do you bring against this man?"** **N.** They answered, **S. "If this man were not a criminal, we would**

not have handed him over to you." N. Pilate said to them, S. **"Take him yourselves and judge him according to your law."** N. They replied, S. **"We are not permitted to put anyone to death."** N. This was to fulfill what Jesus had said when he indicated the kind of death he was to die.

Then Pilate entered the headquarters again, summoned Jesus, and asked him, S. **"Are you the King of the Jews?"** [N. Jesus answered,] J. *"Do you ask this on your own, or did others tell you about me?"* [N. Pilate replied,] S. **"I am not a Jew, am I? Your own nation and the chief priests have handed you over to me. What have you done?"** [N. Jesus answered,] J. *"My kingdom is not from this world. If my kingdom were from this world, my followers would be fighting to keep me from being handed over to the Jews. But as it is, my kingdom is not from here."* [N. Pilate asked him,] S. **"So you are a king?"** [N. Jesus answered,] J. *"You say that I am a king. For this I was born, and for this I came into the world, to testify to the truth. Everyone who belongs to the truth listens to my voice."* [N. Pilate asked him,] S. **"What is truth?"**

N. After he had said this, Pilate went out to the Jews again and told them, S. **"I find no case against him. But you have a custom that I release someone for you at the Passover. Do you want me to release for you the King of the Jews?"** N. They shouted in reply, S. **"Not this man, but Barabbas!"** N. Now Barabbas was a bandit.

Then Pilate took Jesus and had him flogged. And the soldiers wove a crown of thorns and put it on his head, and they dressed him in a purple robe. They kept coming up to him, saying, **S.** **"Hail, King of the Jews!" N.** and they struck him on the face.

Pilate went out again and said to them, **S.** **"Look, I am bringing him out to you to let you know that I find no case against him." N.** So Jesus came out, wearing the crown of thorns and the purple robe. Pilate said to them, **S. "Here is the man!"**

N. When the chief priests and the police saw him, they shouted, **S. "Crucify him! Crucify him!" N.** Pilate said to them, **S. "Take him yourselves and crucify him; I find no case against him." N.** They answered him, **S. "We have a law, and according to that law he ought to die because he has claimed to be the Son of God."**

N. Now when Pilate heard this, he was more afraid than ever. He entered his headquarters again and asked Jesus, **S. "Where are you from?" N.** But Jesus gave him no answer. Pilate therefore said to him, **S. "Do you refuse to speak to me? Do you not know that I have power to release you, and power to crucify you?"** [**N.** Jesus answered him,] **J.** *"You would have no power over me unless it had been given you from above; therefore the one who handed me over to you is guilty of a greater sin." **N.** From then on Pilate tried to release him, but the Jews cried out, **S. "If you release this man, you are no friend of the emperor. Everyone who claims to be a king sets himself against the emperor." N.**

When Pilate heard these words, he brought Jesus outside and sat on the judge's bench at a place called "The Stone Pavement," or in Hebrew "Gabbatha."

Now it was the day of Preparation for the Passover; and it was about noon. Pilate said to the Jews, **S. "Here is your King!"** N. They cried out, **S. "Away with him! Away with him! Crucify him!"** N. Pilate asked them, **S. "Shall I crucify your King?"** N. The chief priests answered, **S. "We have no king but the emperor."** N. Then Pilate handed Jesus over to them to be crucified.

At this point all may join in singing an appropriate acclamation.

JESUS IS CRUCIFIED AND DIES FOR US

N. SO they took Jesus; and carrying the Cross by himself, he went out to what is called The Place of the Skull, which in Hebrew is called Golgotha. There they crucified him, and with him two others, one on either side, with Jesus between them.

Pilate also had an inscription written and put on the Cross. It read, "Jesus of Nazareth, the King of the Jews." Many of the people read this inscription, because the place where Jesus was crucified was near the city; and it was written in Hebrew, in Latin, and in Greek. Then the chief priests of the Jews said to Pilate, **S. "Do not write, 'The King of the Jews,' but, 'This man said, I am King of the Jews.'"** N. Pilate answered, **S. "What I have written I have written."**

N. When the soldiers had crucified Jesus, they took his clothes and divided them into four parts, one for each soldier. They also took his tunic; now the tunic was seamless, woven in one piece from the top. So they said to one another, **S.** **"Let us not tear it, but cast lots for it to see who will get it."** **N.** This was to fulfill what the Scripture says,

"They divided my clothes among themselves, and for my clothing they cast lots."

And that is what the soldiers did.

Meanwhile, standing near the Cross of Jesus were his mother, and his mother's sister, Mary the wife of Clopas, and Mary Magdalene. When Jesus saw his mother and the disciple whom he loved standing beside her, he said to his mother, **J.** *"Woman, here is your son."* **N.** Then he said to the disciple, **J.** *"Here is your mother."* **N.** And from that hour the disciple took her into his own home.

After this, when Jesus knew that all was now finished, in order to fulfill the Scripture, he said, **J.** *"I am thirsty."* **N.** A jar full of sour wine was standing there. So they put a sponge full of the wine on a branch of hyssop and held it to his mouth. When Jesus had received the wine, he said, **J.** *"It is finished."* **N.** Then he bowed his head and gave up his spirit.

Here all kneel and pause for a short time.

EVENTS AFTER JESUS' DEATH

N. SINCE it was the day of Preparation, the Jews did not want the bodies left on the cross during the Sabbath, especially because that Sabbath was a day of great Solemnity. So they asked Pilate to have the legs of the crucified men broken and the bodies removed.

Then the soldiers came and broke the legs of the first and of the other who had been crucified with him. But when they came to Jesus and saw that he was already dead, they did not break his legs. Instead, one of the soldiers pierced his side with a spear, and at once blood and water came out.

(He who saw this has testified so that you also may believe. His testimony is true, and he knows that he tells the truth.)

These things occurred so that the Scripture might be fulfilled, "None of his bones shall be broken." And again another passage of Scripture says, "They will look on the one whom they have pierced."

JESUS' BODY IS PLACED IN THE TOMB

N. **A**FTER these things, Joseph of Arimathea, who was a disciple of Jesus, though a secret one because of his fear of the Jews, asked Pilate to let him take away the body of Jesus. Pilate gave him permission; so he came and removed his body.

Nicodemus, who had at first come to Jesus by night, also came, bringing a mixture of myrrh and aloes, weighing about a hundredweight. They took the body of Jesus and wrapped it with the spices in linen cloths, according to the burial custom of the Jews. Now there was a garden in the place where he was crucified, and in the garden there was a new tomb in which no one had ever been laid. And so, because it was the Jewish day of Preparation, and the tomb was nearby, they laid Jesus there.

After the reading of the Lord's Passion, the Priest gives a brief homily and, at its end, the faithful may be invited to spend a short time in prayer.

THE SOLEMN INTERCESSIONS

The Liturgy of the Word concludes with the Solemn Intercessions, which take place in this way: the Deacon, if a Deacon is present, or if he is not, a lay minister, stands at the ambo, and sings or says the invitation in which the intention is expressed. Then all pray in silence for a while, and afterwards the Priest, standing at the chair or, if appropriate, at the altar, with hands extended, sings or says the prayer.

The faithful may remain either kneeling or standing throughout the entire period of the prayers.

Before the Priest's prayer, in accord with tradition, it is permissible to use the Deacon's invitations Let us kneel — Let us stand, *with all kneeling for silent prayer.*

I. For Holy Church

Let us pray, dearly beloved, for the holy Church of God,

that our God and Lord be pleased to give her peace,

to guard her and to unite her throughout the whole world

and grant that, leading our life in tranquillity and quiet,

we may glorify God the Father almighty.

Prayer in silence. Then the Priest says:

Almighty ever-living God,

who in Christ revealed your glory to all the nations,

watch over the works of your mercy,
that your Church, spread throughout all the
world,
may persevere with steadfast faith in confessing
your name.
Through Christ our Lord.
℟. **Amen.**

II. For the Pope

Let us pray also for our most Holy Father Pope
N.,
that our God and Lord,
who chose him for the Order of Bishops,
may keep him safe and unharmed for the Lord's
holy Church,
to govern the holy People of God.

Prayer in silence. Then the Priest says:

Almighty ever-living God,
by whose decree all things are founded,
look with favour on our prayers
and in your kindness protect the Pope chosen for
us,
that, under him, the Christian people,
governed by you their maker,
may grow in merit by reason of their faith.
Through Christ our Lord.
℟. **Amen.**

III. For all orders and degrees of the faithful

Let us pray also for our Bishop N.,
for all Bishops, Priests, and Deacons of the
Church
and for the whole of the faithful people.

Prayer in silence. Then the Priest says:

Almighty ever-living God,
by whose Spirit the whole body of the Church
is sanctified and governed,
hear our humble prayer for your ministers,
that, by the gift of your grace,
all may serve you faithfully.
Through Christ our Lord.
℟. **Amen.**

IV. For catechumens

Let us pray also for (our) catechumens,
that our God and Lord
may open wide the ears of their inmost hearts
and unlock the gates of his mercy,
that, having received forgiveness of all their sins
through the waters of rebirth,
they, too, may be one with Christ Jesus our Lord.

Prayer in silence. Then the Priest says:

Almighty ever-living God,
who make your Church ever fruitful with new
    offspring,
increase the faith and understanding of (our)
    catechumens,
that, reborn in the font of Baptism,
they may be added to the number of your adopted
    children.
Through Christ our Lord.
℟. **Amen.**

V. For the unity of Christians

Let us pray also for all our brothers and sisters
    who believe in Christ,

that our God and Lord may be pleased,
as they live the truth,
to gather them together and keep them in his one
  Church.

Prayer in silence. Then the Priest says:

Almighty ever-living God,
who gather what is scattered
and keep together what you have gathered,
look kindly on the flock of your Son,
that those whom one Baptism has consecrated
may be joined together by integrity of faith
and united in the bond of charity.
Through Christ our Lord.
℞. **Amen.**

VI. For the Jewish people

Let us pray also for the Jewish people,
to whom the Lord our God spoke first,
that he may grant them to advance in love of his
  name
and in faithfulness to his covenant.

Prayer in silence. Then the Priest says:

Almighty ever-living God,
who bestowed your promises on Abraham and
  his descendants,
graciously hear the prayers of your Church,
that the people you first made your own
may attain the fullness of redemption.
Through Christ our Lord.
℞. **Amen.**

VII. For those who do not believe in Christ

Let us pray also for those who do not believe in
    Christ,
that, enlightened by the Holy Spirit,
they, too, may enter on the way of salvation.

Prayer in silence. Then the Priest says:

Almighty ever-living God,
grant to those who do not confess Christ
that, by walking before you with a sincere heart,
they may find the truth
and that we ourselves, being constant in mutual
    love
and striving to understand more fully the mystery
    of your life,
may be made more perfect witnesses to your love
    in the world.
Through Christ our Lord.
℟. **Amen.**

VIII. For those who do not believe in God

Let us pray also for those who do not acknowledge
    God,
that, following what is right in sincerity of heart,
they may find the way to God himself.

Prayer in silence. Then the Priest says:

Almighty ever-living God,
who created all people
to seek you always by desiring you
and, by finding you, come to rest,
grant, we pray,
that, despite every harmful obstacle,
all may recognize the signs of your fatherly love

and the witness of the good works
done by those who believe in you,
and so in gladness confess you,
the one true God and Father of our human race.
Through Christ our Lord.
℟. **Amen.**

IX. For those in public office

Let us pray also for those in public office,
that our God and Lord
may direct their minds and hearts according to
 his will
for the true peace and freedom of all.

Prayer in silence. Then the Priest says:

Almighty ever-living God,
in whose hand lies every human heart
and the rights of peoples,
look with favour, we pray,
on those who govern with authority over us,
that throughout the whole world,
the prosperity of peoples,
the assurance of peace,
and freedom of religion
may through your gift be made secure.
Through Christ our Lord.
℟. **Amen.**

X. For those in tribulation

Let us pray, dearly beloved,
to God the Father almighty,
that he may cleanse the world of all errors,
banish disease, drive out hunger,
unlock prisons, loosen fetters,

granting to travellers safety, to pilgrims return,
health to the sick, and salvation to the dying.

Prayer in silence. Then the Priest says:

Almighty ever-living God,
comfort of mourners, strength of all who toil,
may the prayers of those who cry out in any
   tribulation
come before you,
that all may rejoice,
because in their hour of need
your mercy was at hand.
Through Christ our Lord.
℟. **Amen.**

SECOND PART: THE ADORATION OF THE HOLY CROSS

*After the Solemn Intercessions, the solemn Adoration of
the Holy Cross takes place. Of the two forms of the showing of the Cross presented here, the more appropriate
one, according to pastoral needs, should be chosen.*

The Showing of the Holy Cross

First Form

*The Deacon accompanied by ministers, or another suit-
able minister, goes to the sacristy, from which, in procession, accompanied by two ministers with lighted candles,
he carries the Cross, covered with a violet veil, through
the church to the middle of the sanctuary.*

*The Priest, standing before the altar and facing the peo-
ple, receives the Cross, uncovers a little of its upper part
and elevates it while beginning the* Ecce lignum Crucis
(Behold the wood of the Cross). *He is assisted in
singing by the Deacon or, if need be, by the choir. All respond,* Come, let us adore. *At the end of the singing, all
kneel and for a brief moment adore in silence, while the
Priest stands and holds the Cross raised.*

℣. Behold the wood of the Cross,
on which hung the salvation of the world.

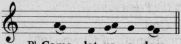

℟. **Come, let us a-dore.**

*Then the Priest uncovers the right arm of the Cross and
again, raising up the Cross, begins,* Behold the wood of
the Cross *and everything takes place as above.*

*Finally, he uncovers the Cross entirely and, raising it up,
he begins the invitation* Behold the wood of the Cross *a
third time and everything takes place like the first time.*

Second Form

*The Priest or the Deacon accompanied by ministers, or
another suitable minister, goes to the door of the church,
where he receives the unveiled Cross, and the ministers
take lighted candles; then the procession sets off through
the church to the sanctuary. Near the door, in the middle
of the church and before the entrance of the sanctuary,
the one who carries the Cross elevates it, singing,* Behold
the wood of the Cross, *to which all respond,* Come, let
us adore. *After each response all kneel and for a brief
moment adore in silence, as above.*

The Adoration of the Holy Cross

*Then, accompanied by two ministers with lighted candles,
the Priest or the Deacon carries the Cross to the entrance
of the sanctuary or to another suitable place and there
puts it down or hands it over to the ministers to hold. Candles are placed on the right and left sides of the Cross.*

*For the Adoration of the Cross, first the Priest Celebrant
alone approaches, with the chasuble and his shoes removed, if appropriate. Then the clergy, the lay ministers,
and the faithful approach, moving as if in procession, and
showing reverence to the Cross by a simple genuflection or*

by some other sign appropriate to the usage of the region, for example, by kissing the Cross.

Only one Cross should be offered for adoration. If, because of the large number of people, it is not possible for all to approach individually, the Priest, after some of the clergy and faithful have adored, takes the Cross and, standing in the middle before the altar, invites the people in a few words to adore the Holy Cross and afterwards holds the Cross elevated higher for a brief time, for the faithful to adore it in silence.

While the adoration of the Holy Cross is taking place, the antiphon Crucem tuam adoramus *(We adore your Cross, O Lord), the Reproaches, the hymn* Crux fidelis *(Faithful Cross) or other suitable chants are sung, during which all who have already adored the Cross remain seated.*

CHANTS TO BE SUNG DURING THE ADORATION OF THE HOLY CROSS

Antiphon   [Holy Cross]

**We adore your Cross, O Lord,
we praise and glorify your holy Resurrection,
for behold, because of the wood of a tree
joy has come to the whole world.**

**May God have mercy on us and bless us;
may he let his face shed its light upon us
and have mercy on us.**   Cf. Ps. 66.2

And the antiphon is repeated: **We adore . . .**

The Reproaches

Parts assigned to one of the two choirs separately are indicated by the numbers 1 (first choir) and 2 (second choir); parts sung by both choirs together are marked: 1 and 2. Some of the verses may also be sung by two cantors.

I

1 and 2: **My people, what have I done to you?**
       Or how have I grieved you? Answer me!

1: **Because I led you out of the land of Egypt,**
      you have prepared a Cross for your Saviour.

1: **Hagios o Theos,**

2: **Holy is God,**

1: **Hagios Ischyros,**

2: **Holy and Mighty,**

1: **Hagios Athanatos, eleison himas.**

2: **Holy and Immortal One, have mercy on us.**

1 and 2: **Because I led you out through the desert**
       forty years
     and fed you with manna and brought you into
       a land of plenty,
     you have prepared a Cross for your Saviour.

1: **Hagios o Theos,**

2: **Holy is God,**

1: **Hagios Ischyros,**

2: **Holy and Mighty,**

1: **Hagios Athanatos, eleison himas.**

2: **Holy and Immortal One, have mercy on us.**

1 and 2: **What more should I have done for you**
       and have not done?
     Indeed, I planted you as my most beautiful
       chosen vine
     and you have turned very bitter for me,
     for in my thirst you gave me vinegar to drink
     and with a lance you pierced your Saviour's
       side.

1: **Hagios o Theos,**
2: **Holy is God,**
1: **Hagios Ischyros,**
2: **Holy and Mighty,**
1: **Hagios Athanatos, eleison himas.**
2: **Holy and Immortal One, have mercy on us.**

II

Cantors:
I scourged Egypt for your sake with its firstborn sons,
and you scourged me and handed me over.

1 and 2 repeat:
My people, what have I done to you?
Or how have I grieved you? Answer me!

Cantors:
I led you out from Egypt as Pharaoh lay sunk in the Red Sea,
and you handed me over to the chief priests.

1 and 2 repeat:
My people . . .

Cantors:
I opened up the sea before you,
and you opened my side with a lance.

1 and 2 repeat:
My people . . .

Cantors:
I went before you in a pillar of cloud,
and you led me into Pilate's palace.

1 and 2 repeat:
My people . . .

Cantors:
I fed you with manna in the desert,
and on me you rained blows and lashes.

1 and 2 repeat:
My people . . .

Cantors:
I gave you saving water from the rock to drink,
and for drink you gave me gall and vinegar.

1 and 2 repeat:
My people . . .

Cantors:
I struck down for you the kings of the Canaanites,
and you struck my head with a reed.

1 and 2 repeat:
My people . . .

Cantors:
I put in your hand a royal sceptre,
and you put on my head a crown of thorns.

1 and 2 repeat:
My people . . .

Cantors:
I exalted you with great power,
and you hung me on the scaffold of the Cross.

1 and 2 repeat:
My people . . .

HYMN   [Faithful Cross]

All:
Faithful Cross the Saints rely on,
Noble tree beyond compare!
Never was there such a scion,

Never leaf or flower so rare.
Sweet the timber, sweet the iron,
Sweet the burden that they bear!

Cantors:

Sing, my tongue, in exultation
Of our banner and device!
Make a solemn proclamation
Of a triumph and its price:
How the Savior of creation
Conquered by his sacrifice!

All:

Faithful Cross the Saints rely
on,
Noble tree beyond compare!
Never was there such a scion,
Never leaf or flower so rare.

Cantors:

For, when Adam first offended,
Eating that forbidden fruit,
Not all hopes of glory ended
With the serpent at the root:
Broken nature would be
mended
By a second tree and shoot.

All:

Sweet the timber, sweet the
iron,
Sweet the burden that they
bear!

Cantors:

Thus the tempter was outwitted
By a wisdom deeper still:
Remedy and ailment fitted,
Means to cure and means to
kill;
That the world might be acquit-
ted,
Christ would do his Father's
will.

All:

Faithful Cross the Saints rely
on,
Noble tree beyond compare!
Never was there such a scion,
Never leaf or flower so rare.

Cantors:

So the Father, out of pity
For our self-inflicted doom,
Sent him from the heavenly city
When the holy time had come:
He, the Son and the Almighty,
Took our flesh in Mary's womb.

All:

Sweet the timber, sweet the
iron,
Sweet the burden that they
bear!

Cantors:

Hear a tiny baby crying,
Founder of the seas and
strands;
See his virgin Mother tying
Cloth around his feet and
hands;
Find him in a manger lying
Tightly wrapped in swaddling-
bands!

All:

Faithful Cross the Saints rely
on,
Noble tree beyond compare!
Never was there such a scion,
Never leaf or flower so rare.

Cantors:

So he came, the long-expected,
Not in glory, not to reign;

Only born to be rejected,
Choosing hunger, toil and pain,
Till the scaffold was erected
And the Paschal Lamb was
   slain.

All:

Sweet the timber, sweet the
   iron,
Sweet the burden that they
   bear!

Cantors:

No disgrace was too abhorrent:
Nailed and mocked and
   parched he died;
Blood and water, double war-
   rant,
Issue from his wounded side,
Washing in a mighty torrent
Earth and stars and oceantide.

All:

Faithful Cross the Saints rely
   on,
Noble tree beyond compare!
Never was there such a scion,
Never leaf or flower so rare.

Cantors:

Lofty timber, smooth your
   roughness,
Flex your boughs for blossom-
   ing;
Let your fibers lose their tough-
   ness,
Gently let your tendrils cling;

Lay aside your native gruffness,
Clasp the body of your King!

All:

Sweet the timber, sweet the
   iron,
Sweet the burden that they
   bear!

Cantors:

Noblest tree of all created,
Richly jewelled and embossed:
Post by Lamb's blood conse-
   crated;
Spar that saves the tempest-
   tossed;
Scaffold-beam which, elevated,
Carries what the world has
   cost!

All:

Faithful Cross the Saints rely
   on,
Noble tree beyond compare!
Never was there such a scion,
Never leaf or flower so rare.

*The following conclusion is
never to be omitted:*

All:

Wisdom, power, and adoration
To the blessed Trinity
For redemption and salvation
Through the Paschal Mystery,
Now, in every generation,
And for all eternity. Amen.

*In accordance with local circumstances or popular tradi-
tions and if it is pastorally appropriate, the* Stabat Mater
may be sung, as found in the Graduale Romanum, *or another suitable chant in memory of the compassion of the
Blessed Virgin Mary.*

When the adoration has been concluded, the Cross is carried by the Deacon or a minister to its place at the altar. Lighted candles are placed around or on the altar or near the Cross.

THIRD PART: HOLY COMMUNION

A cloth is spread on the altar, and a corporal and the Missal put in place. Meanwhile the Deacon or, if there is no Deacon, the Priest himself, putting on a humeral veil, brings the Blessed Sacrament back from the place of repose to the altar by a shorter route, while all stand in silence. Two ministers with lighted candles accompany the Blessed Sacrament and place their candlesticks around or upon the altar.

When the Deacon, if a Deacon is present, has placed the Blessed Sacrament upon the altar and uncovered the ciborium, the Priest goes to the altar and genuflects.

Then the Priest, with hands joined, says aloud:

At the Saviour's command
and formed by divine teaching,
we dare to say:

The Priest, with hands extended says, and all present continue:

**Our Father, who art in heaven,
hallowed be thy name;
thy kingdom come,
thy will be done
on earth as it is in heaven.
Give us this day our daily bread,
and forgive us our trespasses,
as we forgive those who trespass against us;
and lead us not into temptation,
but deliver us from evil.**

With hands extended, the Priest continues alone:

Deliver us, Lord, we pray, from every evil,
graciously grant peace in our days,

that, by the help of your mercy,
we may be always free from sin
and safe from all distress,
as we await the blessed hope
and the coming of our Saviour, Jesus Christ.

The people conclude the prayer, acclaiming:

**For the kingdom, the power and the glory are
yours now and for ever.**

Then the Priest, with hands joined, says quietly:

May the receiving of your Body and Blood,
Lord Jesus Christ,
not bring me to judgement and condemnation,
but through your loving mercy
be for me protection in mind and body
and a healing remedy.

*The Priest then genuflects, takes a particle, and, holding
it slightly raised over the ciborium, while facing the people, says aloud:*

Behold the Lamb of God,
behold him who takes away the sins of the world.
Blessed are those called to the supper of the Lamb.

And together with the people he adds once:

**Lord, I am not worthy
that you should enter under my roof,
but only say the word
and my soul shall be healed.**

*And facing the altar, he reverently consumes the Body of
Christ, saying quietly:* May the Body of Christ keep me
safe for eternal life.

*He then proceeds to distribute Communion to the faith-
ful. During Communion, Psalm 21 or another appropriate chant may be sung.*

When the distribution of Communion has been completed, the ciborium is taken by the Deacon or another suitable minister to a place prepared outside the church or, if circumstances so require, it is placed in the tabernacle.

Then the Priest says: Let us pray, *and, after a period of sacred silence, if circumstances so suggest, has been observed, he says the Prayer after Communion.*

Almighty ever-living God,   [Devoted to God]
who have restored us to life
by the blessed Death and Resurrection of your
    Christ,
preserve in us the work of your mercy,
that, by partaking of this mystery,
we may have a life unceasingly devoted to you.
Through Christ our Lord. ℟. **Amen.** ↓

For the Dismissal the Deacon or, if there is no Deacon, the Priest himself, may say the invitation Bow down for the blessing.

Then the Priest, standing facing the people and extending his hands over them, says this:

PRAYER OVER THE PEOPLE   [Redemption Secured]

May abundant blessing, O Lord, we pray,
descend upon your people,
who have honoured the Death of your Son
in the hope of their resurrection:
may pardon come,
comfort be given,
holy faith increase,
and everlasting redemption be made secure.
Through Christ our Lord. ℟. **Amen.**

And all, after genuflecting to the Cross, depart in silence.

After the celebration, the altar is stripped, but the Cross remains on the altar with two or four candlesticks.

———————

APRIL 15

HOLY SATURDAY

On Holy Saturday the Church waits at the Lord's tomb in prayer and fasting, meditating on his Passion and Death and on his Descent into Hell, and awaiting his Resurrection.

The Church abstains from the Sacrifice of the Mass, with the sacred table left bare, until after the solemn Vigil, that is, the anticipation by night of the Resurrection, when the time comes for paschal joys, the abundance of which overflows to occupy fifty days.

"He is not here; for he has been raised."

APRIL 15

THE EASTER VIGIL IN THE HOLY NIGHT

By most ancient tradition, this is the night of keeping vigil for the Lord (Ex. 12.42), in which, following the Gospel admonition (Lk. 12.35-37), the faithful, carrying lighted lamps in their hands, should be like those looking for the Lord when he returns, so that at his coming he may find them awake and have them sit at his table.

Of this night's Vigil, which is the greatest and most noble of all solemnities, there is to be only one celebration in each church. It is arranged, moreover, in such a way that after the Lucernarium and Easter Proclamation (which constitutes the first part of this Vigil), Holy Church meditates on the wonders the Lord God has done for his people from the beginning, trusting in his word and promise (the second part, that is, the Liturgy of the Word) until, as day approaches, with new members reborn in Baptism (the third part), the Church is called to the table the Lord has prepared for his people, the memorial of his Death and Resurrection until he comes again (the fourth part).

Candles should be prepared for all who participate in the Vigil. The lights of the church are extinguished.

FIRST PART:
THE SOLEMN BEGINNING OF THE VIGIL OR LUCERNARIUM

THE BLESSING OF THE FIRE AND PREPARATION OF THE CANDLE

A blazing fire is prepared in a suitable place outside the church. When the people are gathered there, the Priest approaches with the ministers, one of whom carries the paschal candle. The processional cross and candles are not carried.

Where, however, a fire cannot be lit outside the church, the rite is carried out as below, p. 324.

The Priest and faithful sign themselves while the Priest says: In the name of the Father, and of the Son, and of the Holy Spirit, *and then he greets the assembled people in the usual way and briefly instructs them about the night vigil in these or similar words:*

[Keeping the Lord's Paschal Solemnity]

Dear brethren (brothers and sisters),
on this most sacred night,
in which our Lord Jesus Christ
passed over from death to life,
the Church calls upon her sons and daughters,
scattered throughout the world,
to come together to watch and pray.
If we keep the memorial
of the Lord's paschal solemnity in this way,
listening to his word and celebrating his mysteries,
then we shall have the sure hope
of sharing his triumph over death
and living with him in God.

Then the Priest blesses the fire, saying with hands extended:

Let us pray.   [Fire of God's Glory]

O God, who through your Son
bestowed upon the faithful the fire of your glory,
sanctify ✠ this new fire, we pray,
and grant that,
by these paschal celebrations,
we may be so inflamed with heavenly desires,
that with minds made pure
we may attain festivities of unending splendour.
Through Christ our Lord.
℞. **Amen.** ↓

*After the blessing of the new fire, one of the ministers
brings the paschal candle to the Priest, who cuts a cross
into the candle with a stylus. Then he makes the Greek
letter Alpha above the cross, the letter Omega below, and
the four numerals of the current year between the arms
of the cross, saying meanwhile:*

1. Christ yesterday and today *(he cuts a vertical line);*
2. the Beginning and the End *(he cuts a hori-
   zontal line);*
3. the Alpha *(he cuts the letter Alpha above
   the vertical line);*
4. and the Omega *(he cuts the letter Omega
   below the vertical line).*
5. All time belongs to him *(he cuts the first numeral of the current year in the upper left
   corner of the cross);*
6. and all the ages *(he cuts the second numeral
   of the current year in the upper right corner of the cross).*

7. To him be glory and power *(he cuts the third numeral of the current year in the lower left corner of the cross);*

8. through every age forever. Amen *(he cuts the fourth numeral of the current year in the lower right corner of the cross).*

```
        A
   2  |  0
  ----+----
   1  |  7
        Ω
```

When the cutting of the cross and of the other signs has been completed, the Priest may insert five grains of incense into the candle in the form of a cross, meanwhile saying:

1. By his holy
2. and glorious wounds,
3. may Christ the Lord
4. guard us
5. and protect us. Amen.

```
        1
   4    2    5
        3
```

Where, because of difficulties that may occur, a fire is not lit, the blessing of fire is adapted to the circumstances. When the people are gathered in the church as on other occasions, the Priest comes to the door of the church, along with the ministers carrying the paschal candle. The people, insofar as it is possible, turn to face the Priest.

The greeting and address take place as above, p. 322; then the fire is blessed and the candle is prepared, as above, pp. 323-324.

The Priest lights the paschal candle from the new fire, saying:

May the light of Christ rising in glory
dispel the darkness of our hearts and minds.

PROCESSION

When the candle has been lit, one of the ministers takes burning coals from the fire and places them in the thuri-

ble, and the Priest puts incense into it in the usual way. The Deacon or, if there is no Deacon, another suitable minister takes the paschal candle and a procession forms. The thurifer with the smoking thurible precedes the Deacon or other minister who carries the paschal candle. After them follows the Priest with the ministers and the people, all holding in their hands unlit candles.

At the door of the church the Deacon, standing and raising up the candle, sings:

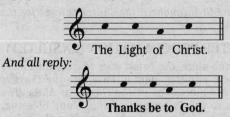

The Light of Christ.

And all reply:

Thanks be to God.

The Priest lights his candle from the flame of the paschal candle.

Then the Deacon moves forward to the middle of the church and, standing and raising up the candle, sings a second time:

The Light of Christ.

And all reply:

Thanks be to God.

All light their candles from the flame of the paschal candle and continue in procession.

When the Deacon arrives before the altar, he stands facing the people, raises up the candle and sings a third time:

The Light of Christ.

And all reply:

Thanks be to God.

And lights are lit throughout the church, except for the altar candles.

THE EASTER PROCLAMATION (EXSULTET)

Arriving at the altar, the Priest goes to his chair, gives his candle to a minister, puts incense into the thurible and blesses the incense as at the Gospel at Mass. The Deacon goes to the Priest and saying, Your blessing, Father, *asks for and receives a blessing from the Priest, who says in a low voice:*

May the Lord be in your heart and on your lips,
that you may proclaim his paschal praise
   worthily and well,
in the name of the Father and of the Son, ✝ and
   of the Holy Spirit.

The Deacon replies: Amen. ↓

This blessing is omitted if the Proclamation is made by someone who is not a Deacon.

The Deacon, after incensing the book and the candle, proclaims the Easter Proclamation (Exsultet) at the ambo or at a lectern, with all standing and holding lighted candles in their hands.

The Easter Proclamation may be made, in the absence of a Deacon, by the Priest himself or by another concelebrating Priest. If, however, because of necessity, a lay cantor sings the Proclamation, the words Therefore, dearest friends *up to the end of the invitation are omitted, along with the greeting* The Lord be with you.

[When the Shorter Form is used, omit the italicized parts.]

Exult, let them exult, the hosts of heaven,
exult, let Angel ministers of God exult,
let the trumpet of salvation
sound aloud our mighty King's triumph!
Be glad, let earth be glad, as glory floods her,
ablaze with light from her eternal King,
let all corners of the earth be glad,
knowing an end to gloom and darkness.
Rejoice, let Mother Church also rejoice,
arrayed with the lightning of his glory,
let this holy building shake with joy,
filled with the mighty voices of the peoples.
(Therefore, dearest friends,
standing in the awesome glory of this holy light,
invoke with me, I ask you,
the mercy of God almighty,
that he, who has been pleased to number me,
though unworthy, among the Levites,
may pour into me his light unshadowed,
that I may sing this candle's perfect praises).

(℣. The Lord be with you. ℟. **And with your spirit.)**
℣. Lift up your hearts. ℟. **We lift them up to the
Lord.**
℣. Let us give thanks to the Lord our God. ℟. **It is
right and just.**

It is truly right and just,
with ardent love of mind and heart

and with devoted service of our voice,
to acclaim our God invisible, the almighty Father,
and Jesus Christ, our Lord, his Son, his Only
   Begotten.

Who for our sake paid Adam's debt to the eternal
   Father,
and, pouring out his own dear Blood,
wiped clean the record of our ancient sinfulness.

These, then, are the feasts of Passover,
in which is slain the Lamb, the one true Lamb,
whose Blood anoints the doorposts of believers.

This is the night,
when once you led our forebears, Israel's children,
from slavery in Egypt
and made them pass dry-shod through the Red
   Sea.

This is the night
that with a pillar of fire
banished the darkness of sin.

This is the night
that even now, throughout the world,
sets Christian believers apart from worldly vices
and from the gloom of sin,
leading them to grace
and joining them to his holy ones.

This is the night,
when Christ broke the prison-bars of death
and rose victorious from the underworld.

Our birth would have been no gain,
had we not been redeemed.
O wonder of your humble care for us!

O love, O charity beyond all telling,
to ransom a slave you gave away your Son!

O truly necessary sin of Adam,
destroyed completely by the Death of Christ!

O happy fault
that earned so great, so glorious a Redeemer!

O truly blessed night,
worthy alone to know the time and hour
when Christ rose from the underworld!

This is the night
of which it is written:
The night shall be as bright as day,
dazzling is the night for me,
and full of gladness.

The sanctifying power of this night
dispels wickedness, washes faults away,
restores innocence to the fallen, and joy to
    mourners,
drives out hatred, fosters concord, and brings
    down the mighty.

On this, your night of grace, O holy Father,
accept this candle, a solemn offering,
the work of bees and of your servants' hands,
an evening sacrifice of praise,
this gift from your most holy Church.

But now we know the praises of this pillar,
which glowing fire ignites for God's honour,
a fire into many flames divided,
yet never dimmed by sharing of its light,
for it is fed by melting wax,
drawn out by mother bees
to build a torch so precious.

O truly blessed night,
when things of heaven are wed to those of earth,
and divine to the human.

Short Form only:

On this, your night of grace, O holy Father,
accept this candle, a solemn offering,
the work of bees and of your servants' hands,
an evening sacrifice of praise,
this gift from your most holy Church.

Therefore, O Lord,
we pray you that this candle,
hallowed to the honour of your name,
may persevere undimmed,
to overcome the darkness of this night.
Receive it as a pleasing fragrance,
and let it mingle with the lights of heaven.
May this flame be found still burning
by the Morning Star:
the one Morning Star who never sets,
Christ your Son,
who, coming back from death's domain,
has shed his peaceful light on humanity,
and lives and reigns for ever and ever.

℟. A - men.

SECOND PART:
THE LITURGY OF THE WORD

*In this Vigil, the mother of all Vigils, nine readings are
provided, namely seven from the Old Testament and two*

from the New (the Epistle and Gospel), all of which should be read whenever this can be done, so that the character of the Vigil, which demands an extended period of time, may be preserved.

Nevertheless, where more serious pastoral circumstances demand it, the number of readings from the Old Testament may be reduced, always bearing in mind that the reading of the Word of God is a fundamental part of this Easter Vigil. At least three readings should be read from the Old Testament, both from the Law and from the Prophets, and their respective Responsorial Psalms should be sung. Never, moreover, should the reading of chapter 14 of Exodus with its canticle be omitted.

After setting aside their candles, all sit. Before the readings begin, the Priest instructs the people in these or similar words:

[Listen with Quiet Hearts]

Dear brethren (brothers and sisters),
now that we have begun our solemn Vigil,
let us listen with quiet hearts to the Word of God.
Let us meditate on how God in times past saved
  his people
and in these, the last days, has sent us his Son as
  our Redeemer.
Let us pray that our God may complete this
  paschal work of salvation
by the fullness of redemption.

Then the readings follow. A reader goes to the ambo and proclaims the reading. Afterwards a psalmist or a cantor sings or says the Psalm with the people making the response. Then all rise, the Priest says, Let us pray and, after all have prayed for a while in silence, he says the prayer corresponding to the reading. In place of the Responsorial Psalm a period of sacred silence may be observed, in which case the pause after Let us pray is omitted.

FIRST READING Gen. 1.1—2.2 or 1.1, 26-31a **[Our Creator]**

God created the world and all that is in it, and saw that it was good. This reading from the first book of the Bible shows that God made and loves all that exists.

[If the "Shorter Form" is used, the indented text in brackets is omitted.]

A reading from the book of Genesis.

IN the beginning when God created the heavens and the earth,

[the earth was a formless void and darkness covered the face of the deep, while the spirit of God swept over the face of the waters. Then God said, "Let there be light"; and there was light. And God saw that the light was good; and God separated the light from the darkness. God called the light "Day," and the darkness he called "Night." And there was evening and there was morning, the first day.

And God said, "Let there be a dome in the midst of the waters, and let it separate the waters from the waters." So God made the dome and separated the waters that were under the dome from the waters that were above the dome. And it was so. God called the dome "Sky." And there was evening and there was morning, the second day.

And God said, "Let the waters under the sky be gathered together into one place, and let the dry land appear." And it was so. God called the dry land "Earth," and the waters that were gathered together he called "Seas." And God saw that it was good.

Then God said, "Let the earth put forth vegetation: plants yielding seed, and fruit trees of every kind on earth that bear fruit with the seed in it." And it was so. The earth brought forth vegetation: plants yielding seed of every kind, and trees of every kind bearing fruit with the seed in it. And God saw that it was good. And there was evening and there was morning, the third day.

And God said, "Let there be lights in the dome of the sky to separate the day from the night; and let them be for signs and for seasons and for days and years, and let them be lights in the dome of the sky to give light upon the earth." And it was so.

God made the two great lights—the greater light to rule the day and the lesser light to rule the night—and the stars. God set them in the dome of the sky to give light upon the earth, to rule over the day and over the night, and to separate the light from the darkness. And God saw that it was good. And there was evening and there was morning, the fourth day.

And God said, "Let the waters bring forth swarms of living creatures, and let birds fly above the earth across the dome of the sky." So God created the great sea monsters and every living creature that moves, of every kind, with which the waters swarm, and every winged bird of every kind. And God saw that it was good. God blessed them, saying, "Be fruitful and multiply and fill the waters in the seas, and let birds multiply on the earth." And there was evening and there was morning, the fifth day.

And God said, "Let the earth bring forth living creatures of every kind: cattle and creeping things and wild animals of the earth of every kind." And it was so. God made the wild animals of the earth of every kind, and the cattle of every kind, and everything that creeps upon the ground of every kind. And God saw that it was good.]

[Then] God said, "Let us make man in our image, according to our likeness; and let them have dominion over the fish of the sea, and over the birds of the air, and over the cattle, and over all the wild animals of the earth, and over every creeping thing that creeps upon the earth."

So God created man in his image,
    in the image of God he created him;
    male and female he created them.

God blessed them, and God said to them, "Be fruitful and multiply, and fill the earth and subdue it; and have dominion over the fish of the sea and over the birds of the air and over every living thing that moves upon the earth."

God said, "See, I have given you every plant yielding seed that is upon the face of all the earth, and every tree with seed in its fruit; you shall have them for food. And to every beast of the earth, and to every bird of the air, and to everything that creeps on the earth, everything that has the breath of life, I have given every green plant for food." And it was so.

God saw everything that he had made, and indeed, it was very good. And there was evening and there was morning, the sixth day.

[Thus the heavens and the earth were finished, and all their multitude. And on the seventh day God finished the work that he had done, and he rested on the seventh day from all the work that he had done.]

The word of the Lord. ℟. **Thanks be to God.** ↓

RESPONSORIAL PSALM Ps. 104   [Creator Spirit]

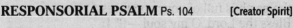

℟. **Lord, send forth   your Spir   -   it,**

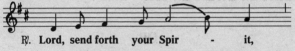

and re - new   the face of   the earth.

Bless the Lord, O my soul.
O Lord my God, you are very great.
You are clothed with honour and majesty,
wrapped in light as with a garment.—℟.

You set the earth on its foundations,
so that it shall never be shaken.
You cover it with the deep as with a garment;
the waters stood above the moun-tains.—℟.

You make springs gush forth in the valleys;
they flow between the hills.
By the streams the birds of the air have their
    habitation;
they sing among the branches.—℟.

From your lofty abode you water the mountains;
the earth is satisfied with the fruit of your work.
You cause the grass to grow for the cattle,
and plants for people to use, to bring forth food
    from the earth.
℟. **Lord, send forth your Spirit,**
    and renew the face of the earth.

O Lord, how manifold are your works!
In wisdom you have made them all;
the earth is full of your creatures.
Bless the Lord, O my soul.—℟. ↓

OR

RESPONSORIAL PSALM Ps. 33   [God's Goodness]

℟. The earth is full of the stead-fast love of the Lord.

The word of the Lord is upright,
and all his work is done in faithfulness.
He loves righteousness and justice;
the earth is full of the steadfast love of the
    Lord.—℟.

By the word of the Lord the heavens were made,
and all their host by the breath of his mouth.

He gathered the waters of the sea as in a bottle;
he put the deeps in storehouses.—℟.

Blessed is the nation whose God is the Lord,
the people whom he has chosen as his heritage.
The Lord looks down from heaven;
he sees all human beings.—℟.

Our soul waits for the Lord;
he is our help and shield.
Let your steadfast love, O Lord, be upon us,
even as we hope in you.—℟. ↓

PRAYER   [Creation in the Beginning]

Let us pray.

Almighty ever-living God,
who are wonderful in the ordering of all your
   works,
may those you have redeemed understand
that there exists nothing more marvellous
than the world's creation in the beginning
except that, at the end of the ages,
Christ our Passover has been sacrificed.
Who lives and reigns for ever and ever.
℟. **Amen.** ↓

OR

PRAYER (On the creation of man)   [Eternal Joys]
O God, who wonderfully created human nature
and still more wonderfully redeemed it,
grant us, we pray,
to set our minds against the enticements of sin,
that we may merit to attain eternal joys.

Through Christ our Lord.
℞. **Amen.** ↓

SECOND READING Gen. 22.1-18 or 22.1-2, 9-13, 15-18

[Obedience to God]

Abraham is obedient to the will of God. Because God asks him, without hesitation he prepares to sacrifice his son Isaac. In the new order, God sends the only Son to redeem us by his death on the cross.

[If the "Shorter Form" is used, the indented text in brackets is omitted.]

A reading from the book of Genesis.

GOD tested Abraham. He said to him, "Abraham!" And Abraham said, "Here I am." God said, "Take your son, your only son Isaac, whom you love, and go to the land of Moriah, and offer him there as a burnt offering on one of the mountains that I shall show you."

[So Abraham rose early in the morning, saddled his donkey, and took two of his young men with him, and his son Isaac; he cut the wood for the burnt offering, and set out and went to the place in the distance that God had shown him.

On the third day Abraham looked up and saw the place far away. Then Abraham said to his young men, "Stay here with the donkey; the boy and I will go over there; we will worship, and then we will come back to you." Abraham took the wood of the burnt offering and laid it on his son Isaac, and he himself carried the fire and the knife. So the two of them walked on together.

Isaac said to his father Abraham, "Father!" And Abraham said, "Here I am, my son." Isaac said, "The fire and the wood are here, but where is the lamb for a burnt offering?" Abraham said, "God himself will provide the lamb for a burnt offering, my son." So the two of them walked on together.]

When Abraham and Isaac came to the place that God had shown him, Abraham built an altar there and laid the wood in order. He bound his son Isaac, and laid him on the altar, on top of the wood. Then Abraham reached out his hand and took the knife to kill his son.

But the Angel of the Lord called to him from heaven, and said, "Abraham, Abraham!" And he said, "Here I am." The Angel said, "Do not lay your hand on the boy or do anything to him; for now I know that you fear God, since you have not withheld your son, your only son, from me." And Abraham looked up and saw a ram, caught in a thicket by its horns. Abraham went and took the ram and offered it up as a burnt offering instead of his son.

[So Abraham called that place "The Lord will provide"; as it is said to this day, "On the mount of the Lord it shall be provided."]

The Angel of the Lord called to Abraham a second time from heaven, and said, "By myself I have sworn, says the Lord: Because you have done this, and have not withheld your son, your only son, I will indeed bless you, and I will make your offspring as numerous as the stars of heaven and as the sand that is on the seashore. And your offspring shall possess the gate of their enemies, and by your offspring shall all the nations of the earth gain blessing for themselves, because you have obeyed my voice."—The word of the Lord. ℟. **Thanks be to God.** ↓

RESPONSORIAL PSALM Ps. 16   [God Our Hope]

℟. **Pro - tect me, O God, for in you I take refuge.**

The Lord is my chosen portion and my cup;
you hold my lot.
I keep the Lord always before me;
because he is at my right hand, I shall not be
    moved.—℟.

Therefore my heart is glad, and my soul rejoices;
my body also rests secure.
For you do not give me up to Sheol,
or let your faithful one see the Pit.—℟.

You show me the path of life.
In your presence there is fullness of joy;
in your right hand are pleasures
forevermore.—℟. ↓

PRAYER   [Entering into Grace]
Let us pray.

O God, supreme Father of the faithful,
who increase the children of your promise
by pouring out the grace of adoption
throughout the whole world

and who through the Paschal Mystery
make your servant Abraham father of nations,
as once you swore,
grant, we pray,
that your peoples may enter worthily
into the grace to which you call them.
Through Christ our Lord. ℟. **Amen.** ↓

THIRD READING Ex. 14.15-31; 15.20, 1   [Exodus]

God saved the chosen people from slavery and death by leading them through the waters of the sea; now our God saves us by leading us through the waters of baptism, by which we come to share in the death and rising of Jesus.

A reading from the book of Exodus.

THE Lord said to Moses, "Why do you cry out to me? Tell the children of Israel to go forward. But you, lift up your staff, and stretch out your hand over the sea and divide it, that the children of Israel may go into the sea on dry ground. Then I will harden the hearts of the Egyptians so that they will go in after them; and so I will gain glory for myself over Pharaoh and all his army, his chariots, and his chariot drivers. And the Egyptians shall know that I am the Lord, when I have gained glory for myself over Pharaoh, his chariots, and his chariot drivers."

The Angel of God who was going before the Israelite army moved and went behind them; and the pillar of cloud moved from in front of them and took its place behind them. It came between the army of Egypt and the army of Israel. And so the cloud was there with the darkness, and it lit up the night; one did not come near the other all night.

Then Moses stretched out his hand over the sea. The Lord drove the sea back by a strong east wind all night, and turned the sea into dry land; and the waters were divided. The children of Israel went into the sea on dry ground, the waters forming a wall for them on their right and on their left.

The Egyptians pursued, and went into the sea after them, all of Pharaoh's horses, chariots, and chariot drivers. At the morning watch, the Lord in the pillar of fire and cloud looked down upon the Egyptian army, and threw the Egyptian army into panic. He clogged their chariot wheels so that they turned with difficulty. The Egyptians said, "Let us flee from the children of Israel, for the Lord is fighting for them against Egypt."

Then the Lord said to Moses, "Stretch out your hand over the sea, so that the water may come back upon the Egyptians, upon their chariots and chariot drivers." So Moses stretched out his hand over the sea, and at dawn the sea returned to its normal depth. As the Egyptians fled before it, the Lord tossed the Egyptians into the sea. The waters returned and covered the chariots and the chariot drivers, the entire army of Pharaoh that had followed them into the sea; not one of them remained.

But the children of Israel walked on dry ground through the sea, the waters forming a wall for them on their right and on their left. Thus the Lord saved Israel that day from the Egyptians; and Israel saw the Egyptians dead on the seashore. Israel saw the great work that the Lord did against the Egyptians. So the people feared the Lord and believed in the Lord and in his servant Moses.

The Prophet Miriam, Aaron's sister, took a tambourine in her hand; and all the women went out after her with tambourines and with dancing. Moses and the children of Israel sang this song to the Lord: ↓

RESPONSORIAL PSALM Ex. 15   [God the Saviour]

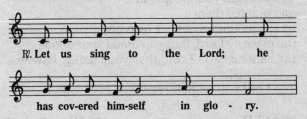

℟. Let us sing to the Lord; he has cov-ered him-self in glo - ry.

I will sing to the Lord, for he has triumphed gloriously;
horse and rider he has thrown into the sea.
The Lord is my strength and my might,
and he has become my salvation;
this is my God, and I will praise him,
my father's God, and I will exalt him.—℟.

The Lord is a warrior;
the Lord is his name.
Pharaoh's chariots and his army he cast into the
   sea;
his picked officers were sunk in the Red Sea.
The floods covered them;
they went down into the depths like a stone.—℟.

Your right hand, O Lord, glorious in power;
your right hand, O Lord, shattered the enemy.
In the greatness of your majesty
you overthrew your adversaries;
you sent out your fury,
it consumed them like stubble.

℟. **Let us sing to the Lord;**
    he has covered himself in glory.

You brought your people in
and planted them
on the mountain of your own possession,
the place, O Lord, that you made your abode,
the sanctuary, O Lord, that your hands have established.
The Lord will reign forever and ever.—℟. ↓

PRAYER   [Children of Abraham]

Let us pray.

O God, whose ancient wonders
remain undimmed in splendour even in our day,
for what you once bestowed on a single people,
freeing them from Pharaoh's persecution
by the power of your right hand,
now you bring about as the salvation of the
    nations
through the waters of rebirth,
grant, we pray, that the whole world
may become children of Abraham
and inherit the dignity of Israel's birthright.
Through Christ our Lord.

℟. **Amen.** ↓

OR

PRAYER   [Reborn]

O God, who by the light of the New Testament
have unlocked the meaning
of wonders worked in former times,
so that the Red Sea prefigures the sacred font
and the nation delivered from slavery
foreshadows the Christian people,
grant, we pray, that all nations,
obtaining the privilege of Israel by merit of faith,
may be reborn by partaking of your Spirit.
Through Christ our Lord.
℟. **Amen.** ↓

FOURTH READING Isa. 54.5-14   [God's Love]

For a time, God hid from the chosen people, but God's
love for this people is everlasting. God takes pity on
them and promises them prosperity.

A reading from the book of the Prophet Isaiah.

THUS says the Lord, the God of hosts.
Your Maker is your husband,
the Lord of hosts is his name;
the Holy One of Israel is your Redeemer,
the God of the whole earth he is called.
For the Lord has called you
like a wife forsaken and grieved in spirit,
like the wife of a man's youth when she is cast
    off,
says your God.

For a brief moment I abandoned you,
but with great compassion I will gather you.

In overflowing wrath for a moment
I hid my face from you,
but with everlasting love I will have compassion
    on you,
says the Lord, your Redeemer.

This is like the days of Noah to me:
Just as I swore that the waters of Noah
would never again go over the earth,
so I have sworn that I will not be angry with you
and will not rebuke you.
For the mountains may depart
and the hills be removed,
but my steadfast love shall not depart from you,
and my covenant of peace shall not be removed,
says the Lord, who has compassion on you.

O afflicted one, storm-tossed, and not comforted,
I am about to set your stones in antimony,
and lay your foundations with sapphires.
I will make your pinnacles of rubies,
your gates of jewels,
and all your walls of precious stones.

All your children shall be taught by the Lord,
and great shall be the prosperity of your chil-
    dren.
In righteousness you shall be established;
you shall be far from oppression, for you shall
    not fear;
and from terror, for it shall not come near you.

The word of the Lord.
℞. **Thanks be to God.** ↓

RESPONSORIAL PSALM Ps. 30   [God Our Help]

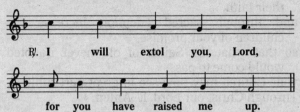

℟. I will extol you, Lord, for you have raised me up.

I will extol you, O Lord, for you have drawn me
   up,
and did not let my foes rejoice over me.
O Lord, you brought up my soul from Sheol,
restored me to life from among those gone down
   to the Pit.—℟.

Sing praises to the Lord, O you his faithful ones,
and give thanks to his holy name.
For his anger is but for a moment;
his favour is for a lifetime.
Weeping may linger for the night,
but joy comes with the morning.—℟.

Hear, O Lord, and be gracious to me!
O Lord, be my helper!
You have turned my mourning into dancing.
O Lord my God, I will give thanks to you for-
   ever.—℟. ↓

PRAYER   [Fulfillment of God's Promise]
Let us pray.

Almighty ever-living God,
surpass, for the honour of your name,

what you pledged to the Patriarchs by reason of
their faith,
and through sacred adoption increase the
children of your promise,
so that what the Saints of old never doubted
would come to pass
your Church may now see in great part fulfilled.
Through Christ our Lord. ℟. **Amen.** ↓

*Alternatively, other prayers may be used from among
those which follow the readings that have been omitted.*

FIFTH READING Isa. 55.1-11   [God of Forgiveness]

**God is a loving Father, calling all people to come back.
Our God promises an everlasting covenant with them.
God is merciful, generous, and forgiving.**

A reading from the book of the Prophet Isaiah.

THUS says the Lord:
  "Everyone who thirsts,
come to the waters;
and you that have no money,
come, buy and eat!
Come, buy wine and milk
without money and without price.
Why do you spend your money for that which is
not bread,
and your labour for that which does not satisfy?
Listen carefully to me, and eat what is good,
and delight yourselves in rich food.
Incline your ear, and come to me;
listen, so that you may live.
I will make with you an everlasting covenant,
my steadfast, sure love for David.

See, I made him a witness to the peoples,
a leader and commander for the peoples.
See, you shall call nations that you do not know,
and nations that do not know you shall run to you,
because of the Lord your God, the Holy One of
    Israel,
for he has glorified you.

Seek the Lord while he may be found,
call upon him while he is near;
let the wicked person forsake their way,
and the unrighteous person their thoughts;
let that person return to the Lord that he may have
    mercy on them,
and to our God, for he will abundantly pardon.

For my thoughts are not your thoughts,
nor are your ways my ways, says the Lord.
For as the heavens are higher than the earth,
so are my ways higher than your ways
and my thoughts than your thoughts.

For as the rain and the snow come down from
    heaven,
and do not return there until they have watered
    the earth,
making it bring forth and sprout,
giving seed to the sower and bread to the one
    who eats,
so shall my word be that goes out from my mouth;
it shall not return to me empty,
but it shall accomplish that which I purpose,
and succeed in the thing for which I sent it."

The word of the Lord. ℟. **Thanks be to God.** ↓

RESPONSORIAL PSALM Isa. 12   [God's Deeds]

℟. With joy you will draw wa - ter

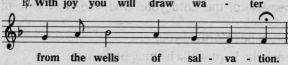

from the wells of sal - va - tion.

Surely God is my salvation;
I will trust, and will not be afraid,
for the Lord God is my strength and my might;
he has become my salvation.
With joy you will draw water
from the wells of salvation.—℟.

Give thanks to the Lord,
call on his name;
make known his deeds among the nations;
proclaim that his name is exalted.—℟.

Sing praises to the Lord,
for he has done gloriously;
let this be known in all the earth.
Shout aloud and sing for joy, O royal Zion,
for great in your midst
is the Holy One of Israel.—℟. ↓

PRAYER   [Progress in Virtue]

Let us pray.

Almighty ever-living God,
sole hope of the world,
who by the preaching of your Prophets
unveiled the mysteries of this present age,

graciously increase the longing of your people,
for only at the prompting of your grace
do the faithful progress in any kind of virtue.
Through Christ our Lord.
℟. **Amen.** ↓

SIXTH READING Bar. 3.9-15, 32—4.4   [God's Ways]

Baruch tells the people of Israel to walk in the ways of
God. They have to learn prudence, wisdom, understanding. Then they will have peace forever.

A reading from the book of the Prophet Baruch.

HEAR the commandments of life, O Israel;
give ear, and learn wisdom!
Why is it, O Israel,
why is it that you are in the land of your enemies,
that you are growing old in a foreign country,
that you are defiled with the dead,
that you are counted among those in Hades?
You have forsaken the fountain of wisdom.
If you had walked in the way of God,
you would be living in peace forever.

Learn where there is wisdom,
where there is strength,
where there is understanding,
so that you may at the same time discern
where there is length of days, and life,
where there is light for the eyes, and peace.
Who has found her place?
And who has entered her storehouses?

But the one who knows all things knows her,
he found her by his understanding.
The one who prepared the earth for all time
filled it with four-footed creatures;

the one who sends forth the light, and it goes;
he called it, and it obeyed him, trembling;
the stars shone in their watches, and were glad;
he called them, and they said, "Here we are!"
They shone with gladness for him who made
   them.

This is our God;
no other can be compared to him.
He found the whole way to knowledge,
and gave her to his servant Jacob
and to Israel, whom he loved.
Afterward she appeared on earth
and lived with humanity.

She is the book of the commandments of God,
the law that endures forever.
All who hold her fast will live,
and those who forsake her will die.

Turn, O Jacob, and take her;
walk toward the shining of her light.
Do not give your glory to another,
or your advantages to an alien people.
Happy are we, O Israel,
for we know what is pleasing to God.

The word of the Lord. ℟. **Thanks be to God.** ↓

RESPONSORIAL PSALM Ps. 19   [Words of Life]

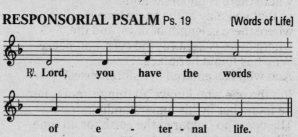

℟. Lord, you have the words of e-ter-nal life.

The law of the Lord is perfect,
reviving the soul;
the decrees of the Lord are sure,
making wise the simple.—R̸.

The precepts of the Lord are right,
rejoicing the heart;
the commandment of the Lord is clear,
enlightening the eyes.—R̸.

The fear of the Lord is pure,
enduring forever;
the ordinances of the Lord are true
and righteous altogether.—R̸.

More to be desired are they than gold,
even much fine gold;
sweeter also than honey,
and drippings of the honeycomb.—R̸. ↓

PRAYER   [Unfailing Protection]

Let us pray.

O God, who constantly increase your Church
by your call to the nations,
graciously grant
to those you wash clean in the waters of Baptism
the assurance of your unfailing protection.
Through Christ our Lord.
R̸. **Amen.** ↓

SEVENTH READING Ez. 36.16-17a, 18-28
                                                    [God's Name]

God wants the chosen people to respect God's holy
name. All shall know the holiness of God, who will
cleanse this people from idol worship and bring them
home again.

A reading from the book of the Prophet Ezekiel.

THE word of the Lord came to me: Son of man, when the house of Israel lived on their own soil, they defiled it with their ways and their deeds; their conduct in my sight was unclean. So I poured out my wrath upon them for the blood that they had shed upon the land, and for the idols with which they had defiled it. I scattered them among the nations, and they were dispersed through the countries; in accordance with their conduct and their deeds I judged them.

But when they came to the nations, wherever they came, they profaned my holy name, in that it was said of them, "These are the people of the Lord, and yet they had to go out of his land."

But I had concern for my holy name, which the house of Israel had profaned among the nations to which they came. Therefore say to the house of Israel, Thus says the Lord God: It is not for your sake, O house of Israel, that I am about to act, but for the sake of my holy name, which you have profaned among the nations to which you came.

I will sanctify my great name, which has been profaned among the nations, and which you have profaned among them; and the nations shall know that I am the Lord, says the Lord God, when through you I display my holiness before their eyes.

I will take you from the nations, and gather you from all the countries, and bring you into your own land.

I will sprinkle clean water upon you, and you shall be clean from all your uncleanness, and from all your idols I will cleanse you. A new heart I will give you, and a new spirit I will put within you; and I will remove from your body the heart of stone and give you a heart of flesh.

I will put my spirit within you, and make you follow my statutes and be careful to observe my ordinances. Then you shall live in the land that I gave to your ancestors; and you shall be my people, and I will be your God.—The word of the Lord. ℟. **Thanks be to God.** ↓

When Baptism is celebrated, the following Responsorial Psalm is used.

RESPONSORIAL PSALM Ps. 42   [Longing]

℟. As a deer longs for flowing streams, my soul longs for you, O God.

My soul thirsts for God, for the living God.
When shall I come and behold the face of God?
    —℟.

I went with the throng,
and led them in procession to the house of God,
with glad shouts and songs of thanksgiving,
a multitude keeping festival.—℟.

O send out your light and your truth;
let them lead me;

let them bring me to your holy mountain
and to your dwelling.

℟. **As a deer longs for flowing streams,**
   my soul longs for you, O God.

Then I will go to the altar of God,
to God my exceeding joy;
and I will praise you with the harp,
O God, my God. —℟. ↓

OR

*When Baptism is not celebrated, the Responsorial Psalm
after the Fifth Reading (Isa. 12) as above, p. 350, may be
used; or the following:*

OR

RESPONSORIAL PSALM Ps. 51   [A Clean Heart]

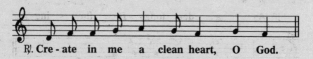

℟. Cre-ate in me a clean heart, O God.

Create in me a clean heart, O God,
and put a new and right spirit within me.
Do not cast me away from your presence,
and do not take your holy spirit from me.—℟.

Restore to me the joy of your salvation,
and sustain in me a willing spirit.
Then I will teach transgressors your ways,
and sinners will return to you.—℟.

For you have no delight in sacrifice;
if I were to give a burnt offering, you would not
   be pleased.

The sacrifice acceptable to God
is a broken spirit;
a broken and contrite heart, O God,
you will not despise.—℟. ↓

PRAYER   [Human Salvation]

Let us pray.

O God of unchanging power and eternal light,
look with favour on the wondrous mystery of the
    whole Church
and serenely accomplish the work of human
    salvation,
which you planned from all eternity;
may the whole world know and see
that what was cast down is raised up,
what had become old is made new,
and all things are restored to integrity through
    Christ,
just as by him they came into being.
Who lives and reigns for ever and ever.
℟. **Amen.** ↓

OR

PRAYER   [Confirm Our Hope]

O God, who by the pages of both Testaments
instruct and prepare us to celebrate the Paschal
    Mystery,
grant that we may comprehend your mercy,
so that the gifts we receive from you this night
may confirm our hope of the gifts to come.
Through Christ our Lord.
℟. **Amen.** ↓

After the last reading from the Old Testament with its Responsorial Psalm and its prayer, the altar candles are lit, and the Priest intones the hymn Gloria in excelsis Deo *(Glory to God in the highest), which is taken up by all, while bells are rung, according to local custom.*

COLLECT [Renewed in Body and Mind]

Let us pray.

O God, who make this most sacred night radiant
with the glory of the Lord's Resurrection,
stir up in your Church a spirit of adoption,
so that, renewed in body and mind,
we may render you undivided service.
Through our Lord Jesus Christ, your Son,
who lives and reigns with you in the unity of the
    Holy Spirit,
one God, for ever and ever. ℟. **Amen.** ↓

Then the reader proclaims the reading from the Apostle.

EPISTLE Rom. 6.3-11 [Alive in Christ]

In baptism we are united to Christ, and we begin to be formed in him. Christ has died; we will die. Christ is risen; we will rise.

A reading from the Letter of Saint Paul
to the Romans.

BROTHERS and sisters: Do you not know that all of us who have been baptized into Christ Jesus were baptized into his death? Therefore we have been buried with him by baptism into death, so that, just as Christ was raised from the dead by the glory of the Father, so we too might walk in newness of life. For if we have been united with him in a death like his, we will certainly be united with him in a resurrection like his.

We know that our old self was crucified with him so that the body of sin might be destroyed, and we might no longer be enslaved to sin. For whoever has died is freed from sin. But if we have died with Christ, we believe that we will also live with him.

We know that Christ, being raised from the dead, will never die again; death no longer has dominion over him. The death he died, he died to sin, once for all; but the life he lives, he lives to God. So you also must consider yourselves dead to sin and alive to God in Christ Jesus.—The word of the Lord. ℟. **Thanks be to God.** ↓

After the Epistle has been read, all rise, then the Priest solemnly intones the Alleluia *three times, rasing his voice by a step each time, with all repeating it. If necessary, the psalmist intones the* Alleluia.

RESPONSORIAL PSALM Ps. 118   [God's Mercy]

℟. Al - le lu - ia!   Al-le - lu - ia!   Al-le - lu - ia!

O give thanks to the Lord, for he is good;
his steadfast love endures forever.
Let Israel say,
"His steadfast love endures forever."—℟.

"The right hand of the Lord is exalted;
the right hand of the Lord does valiantly."
I shall not die, but I shall live,
and recount the deeds of the Lord.—℟.

The stone that the builders rejected
has become the chief cornerstone.
This is the Lord's doing;
it is marvellous in our eyes.
℟. **Alleluia! Alleluia! Alleluia!** ↓

GOSPEL Mt. 28.1-10   [The Resurrection]

Jesus has risen; he is not here. Death has yielded to life. The Easter message is first announced to the faithful, devoted women who followed Jesus.

℣. The Lord be with you. ℟. **And with your spirit.**
✠ A reading from the holy Gospel according to Matthew. ℟. **Glory to you, O Lord.**

AFTER the Sabbath, as the first day of the week was dawning, Mary Magdalene and the other Mary went to see the tomb. And suddenly there was a great earthquake; for an Angel of the Lord, descending from heaven, came and rolled back the stone and sat on it. His appearance was like lightning, and his clothing white as snow. For fear of him the guards shook and became like dead men.

But the Angel said to the women, "Do not be afraid; I know that you are looking for Jesus who was crucified. He is not here; for he has been raised, as he said. Come, see the place where he lay. Then go quickly and tell his disciples, 'He has been raised from the dead, and indeed he is going ahead of you to Galilee; there you will see him.' This is my message for you."

So they left the tomb quickly with fear and great joy, and ran to tell his disciples. Suddenly Jesus met them and said, "Greetings!" And they came to him, took hold of his feet, and worshipped him. Then Jesus said to them, "Do not be afraid; go and tell my brothers to go to Galilee; there they will see me."—The Gospel of the Lord. ℞. **Praise to you, Lord Jesus Christ.**

After the Gospel, the Homily, even if brief, is not to be omitted.

Then the Liturgy of the Sacraments of Initiation begins.

THIRD PART:
THE LITURGY OF THE SACRAMENTS OF INITIATION

The following is adapted from the Rite of Christian Initiation of Adults.

Celebration of Baptism

PRESENTATION OF THE CANDIDATES

An assisting Deacon or other minister calls the candidates for Baptism forward and their godparents present them. The Invitation to Prayer and the Litany of the Saints follow.

INVITATION TO PRAYER   [Supportive Prayer]

The Priest addresses the following or a similar invitation for the assembly to join in prayer for the candidates for Baptism.

Dearly beloved,
with one heart and one soul, let us by our prayers
come to the aid of these our brothers and sisters
    in their blessed hope,
so that, as they approach the font of rebirth,
the almighty Father may bestow on them
all his merciful help.

LITANY OF THE SAINTS   [Petitioning the Saints]

The singing of the Litany of the Saints is led by cantors and may include, at the proper place, names of other Saints (for example, the Titular Saint of the church, the Patron Saints of the place or of those to be baptized) or petitions suitable to the occasion.

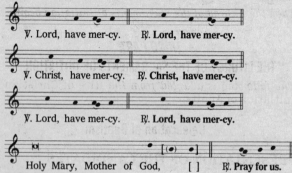

℣. Lord, have mer-cy.   ℟. **Lord, have mer-cy.**

℣. Christ, have mer-cy.   ℟. **Christ, have mer-cy.**

℣. Lord, have mer-cy.   ℟. **Lord, have mer-cy.**

Holy Mary, Mother of God,   [ ]   ℟. **Pray for us.**

Saint Michael,*
Holy Angels of God,
Saint John the Baptist,
Saint Joseph,
Saint Peter and Saint Paul,
Saint Andrew,
Saint John,
Saint Mary Magdalene,
Saint Stephen,
Saint Ignatius of Antioch,
Saint Lawrence,
Saint Perpetua and Saint Felicity,
Saint Agnes,
Saint Gregory,
Saint Augustine,

---

* *Repeat* Pray for us *after each invocation.*

Saint Athanasius,
Saint Basil,
Saint Martin,
Saint Benedict,
Saint Francis and Saint Dominic,
Saint Francis Xavier,
Saint John Vianney,
Saint Catherine of Siena,
Saint Teresa of Jesus,
All holy men and women, Saints of God,

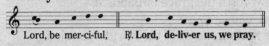

Lord, be mer-ci-ful,   ℟. **Lord, de-liv-er us, we pray.**

From all evil,*
From every sin,
From everlasting death,
By your Incarnation,
By your Death and Resurrection,
By the outpouring of the Holy Spirit,

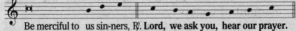

Be merciful to us sin-ners, ℟. **Lord, we ask you, hear our prayer.**

Bring these chosen ones to new birth through the
   grace of Baptism, **Lord, we ask you, hear our
   prayer.**
Jesus, Son of the living God, **Lord, we ask you,
   hear our prayer.**

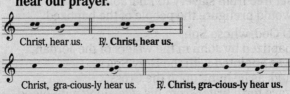

Christ, hear us.   ℟. **Christ, hear us.**

Christ, gra-cious-ly hear us.   ℟. **Christ, gra-cious-ly hear us.**

* *Repeat* Lord, deliver us, we pray *after each invocation.*

BLESSING OF BAPTISMAL WATER
[Grace-Filled Water]

The Priest then blesses the baptismal water, saying the following prayer with hands extended:

O God, who by invisible power
accomplish a wondrous effect
through sacramental signs
and who in many ways have prepared water, your creation,
to show forth the grace of Baptism;

O God, whose Spirit
in the first moments of the world's creation
hovered over the waters,
so that the very substance of water
would even then take to itself the power to sanctify;

O God, who by the outpouring of the flood
foreshadowed regeneration,
so that from the mystery of one and the same element of water
would come an end to vice and a beginning of virtue;

O God, who caused the children of Abraham
to pass dry-shod through the Red Sea,
so that the chosen people,
set free from slavery to Pharaoh,
would prefigure the people of the baptized;

O God, whose Son,
baptized by John in the waters of the Jordan,
was anointed with the Holy Spirit,
and, as he hung upon the Cross,
gave forth water from his side along with blood,

and after his Resurrection, commanded his
  disciples:
"Go forth, teach all nations, baptizing them
in the name of the Father and of the Son and of
  the Holy Spirit,"
look now, we pray, upon the face of your Church
and graciously unseal for her the fountain of
  Baptism.

May this water receive by the Holy Spirit
the grace of your Only Begotten Son,
so that human nature, created in your image
and washed clean through the Sacrament of
  Baptism
from all the squalor of the life of old,
may be found worthy to rise to the life of
  newborn children
through water and the Holy Spirit.

*And, if appropriate, lowering the paschal candle into the
water either once or three times, he continues:*

May the power of the Holy Spirit,
O Lord, we pray,
come down through your Son
into the fullness of this font,

and, holding the candle in the water, he continues:

so that all who have been buried with Christ
by Baptism into death
may rise again to life with him.
Who lives and reigns with you in the unity of the
  Holy Spirit,
one God, for ever and ever.

℟. **A-men.**

Then the candle is lifted out of the water, as the people acclaim:

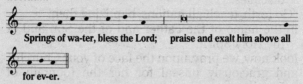

Springs of wa-ter, bless the Lord;   praise and exalt him above all

for ev-er.

THE BLESSING OF WATER [Memorial of Baptism]

If no one present is to be baptized and the font is not to be blessed, the Priest introduces the faithful to the blessing of water, saying:

Dear brothers and sisters,
let us humbly beseech the Lord our God
to bless this water he has created,
which will be sprinkled upon us
as a memorial of our Baptism.
May he graciously renew us,
that we may remain faithful to the Spirit
whom we have received.

And after a brief pause in silence, he proclaims the following prayer, with hands extended:

Lord our God,
in your mercy be present to your people
who keep vigil on this most sacred night,
and, for us who recall the wondrous work of our
    creation
and the still greater work of our redemption,
graciously bless this water.
For you created water to make the fields fruitful
and to refresh and cleanse our bodies.
You also made water the instrument of your
    mercy:

for through water you freed your people from slavery
and quenched their thirst in the desert;
through water the Prophets proclaimed the new covenant
you were to enter upon with the human race;
and last of all,
through water, which Christ made holy in the Jordan,
you have renewed our corrupted nature
in the bath of regeneration.

Therefore, may this water be for us
a memorial of the Baptism we have received,
and grant that we may share
in the gladness of our brothers and sisters,
who at Easter have received their Baptism.
Through Christ our Lord. ℟. **Amen.**

RENUNCIATION OF SIN AND PROFESSION OF FAITH   [Witnessing to Our Faith]

*If there are baptismal candidates, the Priest, in a series of questions to which the candidates reply, **I do**, asks the candidates to renounce sin and profess their faith.*

BAPTISM   [Children of God]

The Priest baptizes each candidate either by immersion or by the pouring of water.

N., I baptize you in the name of the Father, and of the Son, and of the Holy Spirit.

EXPLANATORY RITES

The celebration of Baptism continues with the explanatory rites, after which the celebration of Confirmation normally follows.

ANOINTING AFTER BAPTISM   [Chrism of Salvation]

If the Confirmation of those baptized is separated from their Baptism, the Priest anoints them with chrism immediately after Baptism.

The God of power and Father of our Lord Jesus
   Christ
has freed you from sin
and brought you to new life
through water and the Holy Spirit.

He now anoints you with the chrism of salvation,
so that, united with his people,
you may remain for ever a member of Christ
who is Priest, Prophet, and King.

Newly baptized: **Amen.**

In silence each of the newly baptized is anointed with chrism on the crown of the head.

CLOTHING WITH A BAPTISMAL GARMENT
[Clothed in Christ]

The garment used in this Rite may be white or of a colour that conforms to local custom. If circumstances suggest, this Rite may be omitted.

N. and N., you have become a new creation
and have clothed yourselves in Christ.
Receive this baptismal garment
and bring it unstained to the judgment seat of
   our Lord Jesus Christ,
so that you may have everlasting life.

Newly baptized: **Amen.**

PRESENTATION OF A LIGHTED CANDLE
[Light of Christ]

The Priest takes the Easter candle in his hands or touches it, saying:

Godparents, please come forward to give to the newly baptized the light of Christ.

A godparent of each of the newly baptized goes to the Priest, lights a candle from the Easter candle, then presents it to the newly baptized.

You have been enlightened by Christ.
Walk always as children of the light
and keep the flame of faith alive in your hearts.
When the Lord comes, may you go out to meet him
with all the saints in the heavenly kingdom.

Newly baptized: **Amen.**

The Renewal of Baptismal Promises

INVITATION   **[Call to Renewal]**

After the celebration of Baptism, the Priest addresses the community, in order to invite those present to the renewal of their baptismal promises; the candidates for reception into full communion join the rest of the community in this renunciation of sin and profession of faith. All stand and hold lighted candles.

The Priest addresses the faithful in these or similar words.

Dear brethren (brothers and sisters), through the Paschal Mystery
we have been buried with Christ in Baptism,
so that we may walk with him in newness of life.
And so, now that our Lenten observance is concluded,
let us renew the promises of Holy Baptism,
by which we once renounced Satan and his works
and promised to serve God in the holy Catholic Church.
And so I ask you:

A   [Reject Evil]

Priest: Do you renounce Satan?
All: **I do.**

Priest: And all his works?
All: **I do.**

Priest: And all his empty show?
All: **I do.**

B

Priest: Do you renounce sin,
   so as to live in the freedom of the children of
   God?
All: **I do.**

Priest: Do you renounce the lure of evil,
   so that sin may have no mastery over you?
All: **I do.**

Priest: Do you renounce Satan,
   the author and prince of sin?
All: **I do.**

PROFESSION OF FAITH   [I Believe]

Then the Priest continues:

Priest: Do you believe in God,
   the Father almighty,
   Creator of heaven and earth?
All: **I do.**

Priest: Do you believe in Jesus Christ, his only
   Son, our Lord,
   who was born of the Virgin Mary,
   suffered death and was buried,
   rose again from the dead
   and is seated at the right hand of the Father?

All: **I do.**

Priest: Do you believe in the Holy Spirit,
   the holy Catholic Church,
   the communion of saints,
   the forgiveness of sins,
   the resurrection of the body,
   and life everlasting?

All: **I do.**

And the Priest concludes:

And may almighty God, the Father of our Lord
   Jesus Christ,
who has given us new birth by water and the
   Holy Spirit
and bestowed on us forgiveness of our sins,
keep us by his grace,
in Christ Jesus our Lord,
for eternal life.

All: **Amen.**

SPRINKLING WITH BAPTISMAL WATER
[Water of Life]

*The Priest sprinkles all the people with the blessed bap-
tismal water, while all sing the following song or any
other that is baptismal in character.*

ANTIPHON

I saw water flowing from the Temple,
from its right-hand side, alleluia;
and all to whom this water came were saved
and shall say: Alleluia, alleluia.

Celebration of Reception

INVITATION [Call to Come Forward]

If Baptism has been celebrated at the font, the Priest, the assisting ministers, and the newly baptized with their godparents proceed to the sanctuary. As they do so the assembly may sing a suitable song.

Then in the following or similar words the Priest invites the candidates for reception, along with their sponsors, to come into the sanctuary and before the community to make a profession of faith.

N. and N., of your own free will you have asked to be received into the full communion of the Catholic Church. You have made your decision after careful thought under the guidance of the Holy Spirit. I now invite you to come forward with your sponsors and in the presence of this community to profess the Catholic faith. In this faith you will be one with us for the first time at the eucharistic table of the Lord Jesus, the sign of the Church's unity.

PROFESSION BY THE CANDIDATES
[Belief in Church]

When the candidates for reception and their sponsors have taken their places in the sanctuary, the Priest asks the candidates to make the following profession of faith. The candidates say:

I believe and profess all that the holy Catholic Church believes, teaches, and proclaims to be revealed by God.

ACT OF RECEPTION [Full Communion]

Then the candidates with their sponsors go individually to the Priest, who says to each candidate (laying his

*right hand on the head of any candidate who is not to re-
ceive Confirmation):*

N., the Lord receives you into the Catholic Church.
His loving kindness has led you here,
so that in the unity of the Holy Spirit
you may have full communion with us
in the faith that you have professed in the
   presence of his family.

Celebration of Confirmation

INVITATION   [Strength in the Spirit]

*The newly baptized with their godparents and, if they
have not received the Sacrament of Confirmation, the
newly received with their sponsors, stand before the
Priest. He first speaks briefly to the newly baptized and
the newly received in these or similar words.*

My dear candidates for Confirmation, by your
Baptism you have been born again in Christ and
you have become members of Christ and of his
priestly people. Now you are to share in the outpouring of the Holy Spirit among us, the Spirit
sent by the Lord upon his apostles at Pentecost
and given by them and their successors to the
baptized.

The promised strength of the Holy Spirit, which
you are to receive, will make you more like Christ
and help you to be witnesses to his suffering,
death, and resurrection. It will strengthen you to
be active members of the Church and to build up
the Body of Christ in faith and love.

My dear friends, let us pray to God our Father,
that he will pour out the Holy Spirit on these can-

didates for Confirmation to strengthen them with his gifts and anoint them to be more like Christ, the Son of God.

All pray briefly in silence.

LAYING ON OF HANDS   [Gifts of the Spirit]

The Priest holds his hands outstretched over the entire group of those to be confirmed and says the following prayer.

Almighty God, Father of our Lord Jesus Christ,
Who brought these your servants to new birth
by water and the Holy Spirit,
freeing them from sin:
send upon them, O Lord, the Holy Spirit, the Paraclete;
give them the spirit of wisdom and understanding,
the spirit of counsel and fortitude,
the spirit of knowledge and piety;
fill them with the spirit of the fear of the Lord.
Through Christ our Lord.
℟. **Amen.**

ANOINTING WITH CHRISM   [Sealed in the Spirit]

Either or both godparents and sponsors place the right hand on the shoulder of the candidate; and a godparent or a sponsor of the candidate gives the candidate's name to the minister of the sacrament. During the conferral of the sacrament an appropriate song may be sung.

The minister of the sacrament dips his right thumb in the chrism and makes the Sign of the Cross on the forehead of the one to be confirmed as he says:

N., be sealed with the Gift of the Holy Spirit.
Newly confirmed: **Amen.**

Minister: Peace be with you.
Newly confirmed: **And with your spirit.**

After all have received the sacrament, the newly confirmed as well as the godparents and sponsors are led to their places in the assembly.

[Since the Profession of Faith is not said, the Universal Prayer (no. 16, p. 19) begins immediately and for the first time the neophytes take part in it.]

FOURTH PART:
THE LITURGY OF THE EUCHARIST

The Priest goes to the altar and begins the Liturgy of the Eucharist in the usual way.

It is desirable that the bread and wine be brought forward by the newly baptized or, if they are children, by their parents or godparents.

PRAYER OVER THE OFFERINGS [God's Saving Work]

Accept, we ask, O Lord,
the prayers of your people
with the sacrificial offerings,
that what has begun in the paschal mysteries
may, by the working of your power,
bring us to the healing of eternity.
Through Christ our Lord.
℟. **Amen.**

➙ No. 21, p. 22 (Pref. 21: on this night above all)

In the Eucharistic Prayer, a commemoration is made of the baptized and their godparents in accord with the formulas which are found in the Roman Missal and Roman Ritual for each of the Eucharistic Prayers.

COMMUNION ANTIPHON 1 Cor. 5.7-8 [Purity and Truth]

Christ our Passover has been sacrificed; therefore let us keep the feast with the unleavened bread of purity and truth, alleluia. ↓

Psalm 117 may appropriately be sung.

PRAYER AFTER COMMUNION

[One in Mind and Heart]

Pour out on us, O Lord, the Spirit of your love,
and in your kindness make those you have
   nourished
by this paschal Sacrament
one in mind and heart.
Through Christ our Lord. ℟. **Amen.** ↓

SOLEMN BLESSING

[God's Blessings]

May almighty God bless you
through today's Easter Solemnity
and, in his compassion,
defend you from every assault of sin.
℟. **Amen.**

And may he, who restores you to eternal life
in the Resurrection of his Only Begotten,
endow you with the prize of immortality.
℟. **Amen.**

Now that the days of the Lord's Passion have
   drawn to a close,
may you who celebrate the gladness of the
   Paschal Feast
come with Christ's help, and exulting in spirit,
to those feasts that are celebrated in eternal joy.
℟. **Amen.**

And may the blessing of almighty God,
the Father, and the Son, ✠ and the Holy Spirit,
come down on you and remain with you for ever.
℟. **Amen.**

*The final blessing formula from the Rite of Baptism of
Adults or of Children may also be used, according to circumstances.*

*To dismiss the people the Deacon or, if there is no Dea-
con, the Priest himself sings or says:*

Go forth, the Mass is ended, alleluia, alleluia.

OR

Go in peace, alleluia, alleluia.

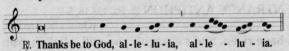

℟. **Thanks be to God, al - le - lu - ia,   al - le - lu - ia.**

*This practice is observed throughout the Octave of
Easter.*

"I have risen, and I am with you still."

APRIL 16

THE RESURRECTION OF THE LORD: EASTER SUNDAY

ENTRANCE ANTIPHON Cf. Ps. 138.18, 5-6

[Christ's Resurrection]

I have risen, and I am with you still, alleluia. You have laid your hand upon me, alleluia. Too wonderful for me, this knowledge, alleluia, alleluia.

→ No. 2, p. 10

OR Lk. 24.34; cf. Rev. 1.6

[Glory and Power]

The Lord is truly risen, alleluia. To him be glory and power for all the ages of eternity, alleluia, alleluia.

→ No. 2, p. 10

COLLECT

[Renewal]

O God, who on this day,
through your Only Begotten Son,
have conquered death
and unlocked for us the path to eternity,
grant, we pray, that we who keep
the solemnity of the Lord's Resurrection

may, through the renewal brought by your Spirit,
rise up in the light of life.
Through our Lord Jesus Christ, your Son,
who lives and reigns with you in the unity of the
  Holy Spirit,
one God, for ever and ever. ℟. **Amen.** ↓

FIRST READING Acts 10.34a, 37-43   [Salvation in Christ]

**In his sermon Peter sums up the good news, the Gospel.
Salvation comes through Christ, the beloved Son of the
Father, and the anointed of the Holy Spirit.**

A reading from the Acts of the Apostles.

PETER began to speak: "You know the message that spread throughout Judea, beginning
in Galilee after the baptism that John announced:
how God anointed Jesus of Nazareth with the
Holy Spirit and with power; how he went about
doing good and healing all who were oppressed
by the devil, for God was with him.

We are witnesses to all that he did both in
Judea and in Jerusalem. They put him to death by
hanging him on a tree; but God raised him on the
third day and allowed him to appear, not to all the
people but to us who were chosen by God as witnesses, and who ate and drank with him after he
rose from the dead.

He commanded us to preach to the people and
to testify that he is the one ordained by God as
judge of the living and the dead. All the Prophets
testify about him that everyone who believes in
him receives forgiveness of sins through his
name."—The word of the Lord. ℟. **Thanks be to
God.** ↓

RESPONSORIAL PSALM Ps. 118   [Day of the Lord]

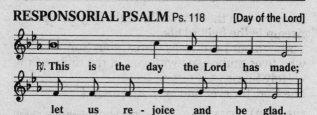

℞. This is the day the Lord has made;
let us re-joice and be glad.

Or: ℞. **Alleluia! Alleluia! Alleluia!**

O give thanks to the Lord, for he is good;
his steadfast love endures forever.
Let Israel say,
"His steadfast love endures forever."—℞.

"The right hand of the Lord is exalted;
the right hand of the Lord does valiantly."
I shall not die, but I shall live,
and recount the deeds of the Lord.—℞.

The stone that the builders rejected
has become the chief cornerstone.
This is the Lord's doing;
it is marvellous in our eyes.—℞. ↓

*One of the following texts may be chosen as the Second
Reading.*

SECOND READING Col. 3.1-4   [Seek Heavenly Things]

Look to the glory of Christ in which we share because
our lives are hidden in him through baptism, and we are
destined to share in his glory.

A reading from the Letter of Saint Paul
to the Colossians.

BROTHERS and sisters: If you have been
raised with Christ, seek the things that are

above, where Christ is, seated at the right hand of God. Set your minds on things that are above, not on things that are on earth, for you have died, and your life is hidden with Christ in God. When Christ who is your life is revealed, then you also will be revealed with him in glory.—The word of the Lord. ℟. **Thanks be to God.** ↓

OR

SECOND READING 1 Cor. 5.6b-8   [Change of Heart]

Turn away from your old ways, from sin. Have a change of heart; be virtuous.

A reading from the first Letter of Saint Paul to the Corinthians.

DO you not know that a little yeast leavens the whole batch of dough? Clean out the old yeast so that you may be a new batch, as you really are unleavened. For our paschal lamb, Christ, has been sacrificed. Therefore, let us celebrate the festival, not with the old yeast, the yeast of malice and evil, but with the unleavened bread of sincerity and truth.—The word of the Lord. ℟. **Thanks be to God.** ↓

SEQUENCE (*Victimae paschali laudes*) [Hymn to the Victor]

1. **Christians, praise the paschal victim!**
   Offer thankful sacrifice!

2. **Christ the Lamb has saved the sheep,**
   Christ the just one paid the price,
   Reconciling sinners to the Father.

3. **Death and life fought bitterly**
   For this wondrous victory;
   The Lord of life who died reigns glorified!

4. "O Mary, come and say
   what you saw at break of day."

5. "The empty tomb of my living Lord!
   I saw Christ Jesus risen and adored!

6. "Bright Angels testified,
   Shroud and grave clothes side by side!

7. "Yes, Christ my hope rose gloriously.
   He goes before you into Galilee."

8. Share the Good News, sing joyfully:
   His death is victory!
   Lord Jesus, Victor King, show us mercy. ↓

GOSPEL ACCLAMATION 1 Cor. 5.7-8   **[Joy in the Lord]**
(If the Alleluia is not sung, the acclamation is omitted.)

℣. Alleluia. ℟. **Alleluia.**

℣. Christ, our Paschal Lamb, has been sacrificed;
let us feast with joy in the Lord.

℟. **Alleluia.** ↓

(FOR MORNING MASS)

GOSPEL Jn. 20.1-18 or 20.1-9   **[Renewed Faith]**

Let us ponder this mystery of Christ's rising, and like
Christ's first followers be strengthened in our faith.

*[If the "Shorter Form" is used, the indented text in brack-
ets is omitted.]*

℣. The Lord be with you. ℟. **And with your spirit.**
✙ A reading from the holy Gospel according to
John. ℟. **Glory to you, O Lord.**

EARLY on the first day of the week, while it
was still dark, Mary Magdalene came to the
tomb and saw that the stone had been removed
from the tomb. So she ran and went to Simon

Peter and the other disciple, the one whom Jesus loved, and said to them, "They have taken the Lord out of the tomb, and we do not know where they have laid him."

Then Peter and the other disciple set out and went toward the tomb. The two were running together, but the other disciple outran Peter and reached the tomb first. He bent down to look in and saw the linen wrappings lying there, but he did not go in.

Then Simon Peter came, following him, and went into the tomb. He saw the linen wrappings lying there, and the cloth that had been on Jesus' head, not lying with the linen wrappings but rolled up in a place by itself. Then the other disciple, who reached the tomb first, also went in, and he saw and believed; for as yet they did not understand the Scripture, that he must rise from the dead.

[Then the disciples returned to their homes. But Mary Magdalene stood weeping outside the tomb. As she wept, she bent over to look into the tomb; and she saw two Angels in white, sitting where the body of Jesus had been lying, one at the head and the other at the feet. They said to her, "Woman, why are you weeping?" She said to them, "They have taken away my Lord, and I do not know where they have laid him."

When she had said this, she turned around and saw Jesus standing there, but she did not know that it was Jesus. Jesus said to her, "Woman, why are you weeping? Whom are you looking for?" Supposing him to be the gardener, she said to him, "Sir, if you have carried him away, tell me where you have laid him, and I will take him away."

Jesus said to her, "Mary!" She turned and said to him in Hebrew, "Rabbouni!" which means Teacher. Jesus said to her, "Do not hold on to me, because I have not yet ascended to the Father. But go to my brothers and say to them, 'I am ascending to my Father and your Father, to my God and your God.'"

Mary Magdalene went and announced to the disciples, "I have seen the Lord," and she told them that he had said these things to her.]

The Gospel of the Lord. ℟. **Praise to you, Lord Jesus Christ.**   → No. 15, p. 18

However, in Easter Sunday Masses which are celebrated with a congregation, the rite of the renewal of baptismal promises may take place after the Homily, according to the text used at the Easter Vigil (p. 369). In that case the Creed is omitted.

OR

GOSPEL Mt. 28.1-10   [The Resurrection]
See p. 360.

(FOR AN AFTERNOON OR EVENING MASS)

GOSPEL Lk. 24.13-35   [The Messiah's Need To Suffer]

Let us accept the testimony of these two witnesses that our hearts may burn with the fire of faith.

℣. The Lord be with you. ℟. **And with your spirit.**
✤ A reading from the holy Gospel according to Luke. ℟. **Glory to you, O Lord.**

O N the first day of the week, two of the disciples were going to a village called Emmaus, about eleven kilometres from Jerusalem, and talking with each other about all these things that had happened. While they were talking and discussing, Jesus himself came near and went with them, but their eyes were kept from recognizing him.

And he said to them, "What are you discussing with each other while you walk along?" They stood still, looking sad. Then one of them, whose name was Cleopas, answered him, "Are you the only stranger in Jerusalem who does not know the things that have taken place there in these days?"

He asked them, "What things?" They replied, "The things about Jesus of Nazareth, who was a Prophet mighty in deed and word before God and all the people, and how our chief priests and leaders handed him over to be condemned to death and crucified him. But we had hoped that he was the one to redeem Israel. Yes, and besides all this, it is now the third day since these things took place. Moreover, some women of our group astounded us. They were at the tomb early this morning, and when they did not find his body there, they came back and told us that they had indeed seen a vision of Angels who said that he was alive. Some of those who were with us went to the tomb and found it just as the women had said; but they did not see him."

Then he said to them, "Oh, how foolish you are, and how slow of heart to believe all that the Prophets have declared! Was it not necessary that the Christ should suffer these things and then enter into his glory?"

Then beginning with Moses and all the Prophets, he interpreted to them the things about himself in all the Scriptures. As they came near the village to which they were going, he walked ahead as if he were going on. But they urged him strongly, saying, "Stay with us, because it is almost evening and the day is now nearly over." So he went in to stay with them.

When he was at the table with them, he took bread, blessed and broke it, and gave it to them. Then their eyes were opened, and they recognized him; and he vanished from their sight.

They said to each other, "Were not our hearts burning within us while he was talking to us on the road, while he was opening the Scriptures to us?"

That same hour they got up and returned to Jerusalem; and they found the eleven and their companions gathered together. These were saying, "The Lord has risen indeed, and he has appeared to Simon!"

Then they told what had happened on the road, and how he had been made known to them in the breaking of the bread.—The Gospel of the Lord. ℟. **Praise to you, Lord Jesus Christ.**

➜ No. 15, p. 18

However, in Easter Sunday Masses which are celebrated with a congregation, the rite of the renewal of baptismal promises may take place after the Homily, according to the text used at the Easter Vigil (p. 369). In that case the Creed is omitted.

PRAYER OVER THE OFFERINGS
[Reborn and Nourished]

Exultant with paschal gladness, O Lord,
we offer the sacrifice
by which your Church
is wondrously reborn and nourished.
Through Christ our Lord.
℟. **Amen.**

➡ No. 21, p. 22 (Pref. 21: on this day above all)

When the Roman Canon is used, the proper forms of the
Communicantes (In communion with those) *and*
Hanc igitur (Therefore, Lord, we pray) *are said.*

COMMUNION ANTIPHON 1 Cor. 5.7-8
[Purity and Truth]

**Christ our Passover has been sacrificed, alleluia;
therefore let us keep the feast with the unleavened bread of purity and truth, alleluia, alleluia.** ↓

PRAYER AFTER COMMUNION
[Glory of Resurrection]

Look upon your Church, O God,
with unfailing love and favour,
so that, renewed by the paschal mysteries,
she may come to the glory of the resurrection.
Through Christ our Lord. ℟. **Amen.** ➡ No. 30, p. 77

*To impart the blessing at the end of Mass, the Priest may
appropriately use the formula of Solemn Blessing for the
Mass of the Easter Vigil, p. 376.*

Dismissal: see p. 377.

"Thomas answered him, 'My Lord and my God!'"

APRIL 23

2nd SUNDAY OF EASTER
(or of DIVINE MERCY)

ENTRANCE ANTIPHON 1 Pet. 2.2   [Spiritual Milk]

Like newborn infants, you must long for the pure, spiritual milk, that in him you may grow to salvation, alleluia.   → No. 2, p. 10

OR 4 Esdr. 2.36-37   [Give Thanks]

Receive the joy of your glory, giving thanks to God, who has called you into the heavenly Kingdom, alleluia.   → No. 2, p. 10

COLLECT   [Kindle Faith]

God of everlasting mercy,
who in the very recurrence of the paschal feast
kindle the faith of the people you have made your
   own,
increase, we pray, the grace you have bestowed,

that all may grasp and rightly understand
in what font they have been washed,
by whose Spirit they have been reborn,
by whose Blood they have been redeemed.
Through our Lord Jesus Christ, your Son,
who lives and reigns with you in the unity of the
    Holy Spirit,
one God, for ever and ever.
℟. **Amen.** ↓

FIRST READING Acts 2.42-47   [True Christian Fellowship]

**The faithful lived a common life, sharing all their goods.
The apostles worked many miracles. They prayed together and broke bread. Daily their numbers increased.**

A reading from the Acts of the Apostles.

THEY devoted themselves to the Apostles'
teaching and fellowship, to the breaking of
bread and the prayers.

Awe came upon everyone, because many wonders and signs were being done by the Apostles.

All who believed were together and had all
things in common; they would sell their possessions and goods and distribute the proceeds to all,
as any had need. Day by day, as they spent much
time together in the temple, they broke bread in
various houses and ate their food with glad and
generous hearts, praising God and having the
goodwill of all the people. And day by day the
Lord added to their number those who were
being saved.—The word of the Lord. ℟. **Thanks
be to God.** ↓

RESPONSORIAL PSALM Ps. 118   [God's Goodness]

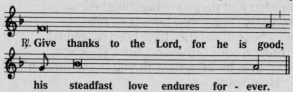

℟. Give thanks to the Lord, for he is good;

his steadfast love endures for - ever.

Or: ℟. **Alleluia!**

Let Israel say,
"His steadfast love endures forever."
Let the house of Aaron say,
"His steadfast love endures forever."
Let those who fear the Lord say,
"His steadfast love endures forever."—℟.

I was pushed hard, so that I was falling,
but the Lord helped me.
The Lord is my strength and my might;
he has become my salvation.
There are glad songs of victory
in the tents of the righteous.—℟.

The stone that the builders rejected
has become the chief cornerstone.
This is the Lord's doing;
it is marvellous in our eyes.
This is the day that the Lord has made;
let us rejoice and be glad in it.—℟. ↓

SECOND READING 1 Pet. 1.3-9   [Love in Practice]

God, our Father, has given us a new hope in Jesus, a
birthright kept in heaven. Although there may be suffering,
this is at the same time a cause for rejoicing. Faith in Jesus
will bring salvation.

A reading from the first Letter of Saint Peter.

BLESSED be the God and Father of our Lord Jesus Christ! By his great mercy he has given us a new birth into a living hope through the resurrection of Jesus Christ from the dead: a birth into an inheritance that is imperishable, undefiled, and unfading, kept in heaven for you, who are being protected by the power of God through faith for a salvation ready to be revealed in the last time.

In this you rejoice, even if now for a little while you have had to suffer various trials, so that the genuineness of your faith—being more precious than gold that, though perishable, is tested by fire—may be found to result in praise and glory and honour when Jesus Christ is revealed.

Although you have not seen him, you love him; and even though you do not see him now, you believe in him and rejoice with an indescribable and glorious joy, for you are receiving the outcome of your faith, the salvation of your souls.—The word of the Lord. ℟. **Thanks be to God.** ↓

GOSPEL ACCLAMATION See Jn. 20.29   [Blind Faith]

(If the Alleluia is not sung, the acclamation is omitted.)

℣. Alleluia. ℟. **Alleluia.**

℣. You believed, Thomas, because you have seen me;

blessed are those who have not seen, and yet believe.

℟. **Alleluia.** ↓

GOSPEL Jn. 20.19-31   [Living Faith]

Jesus appears to the disciples, coming through locked doors. He shows them his hands and side. He greets them in peace and gives them the power to forgive sin. A week later Jesus appears again directly to Thomas who now professes his belief.

℣. The Lord be with you. ℟. **And with your spirit.** ✜ A reading from the holy Gospel according to John. ℟. **Glory to you, O Lord.**

IT was evening on the day Jesus rose from the dead, the first day of the week, and the doors of the house where the disciples had met were locked for fear of the Jews. Jesus came and stood among them and said, "Peace be with you." After he said this, he showed them his hands and his side. Then the disciples rejoiced when they saw the Lord.

Jesus said to them again, "Peace be with you. As the Father has sent me, so I send you."

When he had said this, he breathed on them and said to them, "Receive the Holy Spirit. If you forgive the sins of any, they are forgiven them; if you retain the sins of any, they are retained."

But Thomas, who was called the Twin, one of the twelve, was not with them when Jesus came. So the other disciples told him, "We have seen the Lord." But he said to them, "Unless I see the mark of the nails in his hands, and put my finger in the mark of the nails and my hand in his side, I will not believe."

After eight days his disciples were again in the house, and Thomas was with them. Although the doors were shut, Jesus came and stood among them and said, "Peace be with you." Then he said to Thomas, "Put your finger here and see my hands. Reach out your hand and put it in my side. Do not doubt but believe." Thomas answered him, "My Lord and my God!"

Jesus said to him, "Have you believed because you have seen me? Blessed are those who have not seen and yet have come to believe."

Now Jesus did many other signs in the presence of his disciples, which are not written in this book. But these are written so that you may come to believe that Jesus is the Christ, the Son of God, and that through believing you may have life in his name.—The Gospel of the Lord. R̶/. **Praise to you, Lord Jesus Christ.**   ➜ No. 15, p. 18

PRAYER OVER THE OFFERINGS
[Unending Happiness]

Accept, O Lord, we pray,
the oblations of your people
(and of those you have brought to new birth),
that, renewed by confession of your name and by
   Baptism,
they may attain unending happiness.
Through Christ our Lord.
R̶/. **Amen.**
   ➜ No. 21, p. 22 (Pref. 21: on this day above all)

When the Roman Canon is used, the proper forms of the Communicantes *(In communion with those)* and Hanc igitur *(Therefore, Lord, we pray) are said.*

COMMUNION ANTIPHON Cf. Jn. 20.27   [Believe]
Bring your hand and feel the place of the nails, and do not be unbelieving but believing, alleluia. ↓

PRAYER AFTER COMMUNION   [Devout Reception]

Grant, we pray, almighty God,
that our reception of this paschal Sacrament
may have a continuing effect
in our minds and hearts.
Through Christ our Lord.
R⫽. **Amen.**   → No. 30, p. 77

Optional Solemn Blessings, p. 97, and Prayers over the People, p. 105

Dismissal: see p. 377.

"Their eyes were opened, and they recognized [Jesus]."

APRIL 30
3rd SUNDAY OF EASTER

ENTRANCE ANTIPHON Cf. Ps. 65.1-2

[Praise the Lord]

Cry out with joy to God, all the earth; O sing to the glory of his name. O render him glorious praise, alleluia.   → No. 2, p. 10

COLLECT   [Hope of Resurrection]

May your people exult for ever, O God,
in renewed youthfulness of spirit,
so that, rejoicing now in the restored glory of our
    adoption,
we may look forward in confident hope
to the rejoicing of the day of resurrection.
Through our Lord Jesus Christ, your Son,
who lives and reigns with you in the unity of the
    Holy Spirit,
one God, for ever and ever. ℟. **Amen.** ↓

FIRST READING Acts 2.14, 22b-28   [Reform Your Lives]

> This address of St. Peter is the first of the missionary dis-
> courses. Peter proposes in short summary the name,
> work, death, and resurrection of our Lord. The statement
> has one main clause: "You killed [our Lord]. . . . But God
> raised him [to life.]"

A reading from the Acts of the Apostles.

WHEN the day of Pentecost had come, Peter,
standing with the eleven, raised his voice
and addressed the crowd, "Men of Judea and all
who live in Jerusalem, let this be known to you,
and listen to what I say. Jesus of Nazareth, a man
attested to you by God with deeds of power, wonders, and signs that God did through him among
you, as you yourselves know—this man, handed
over to you according to the definite plan and
foreknowledge of God, you crucified and killed by
the hands of those outside the law.

But God raised him up, having freed him from
death, because it was impossible for him to be
held in its power. For David says concerning him,

'I saw the Lord always before me,
  for he is at my right hand so that I will not
    be shaken;
  therefore my heart was glad, and my tongue
    rejoiced;
  moreover my flesh will live in hope.
For you will not abandon my soul to Hades,
  or let your Holy One experience corruption.
You have made known to me the ways of life;
  you will make me full of gladness with your
    presence.'"

The word of the Lord. ℟. **Thanks be to God.** ↓

RESPONSORIAL PSALM Ps. 16 [Divine Security]

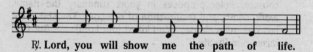

℟. **Lord, you will show me the path of life.**

Or: ℟. **Alleluia!**

Protect me, O God, for in you I take refuge.
I say to the Lord, "You are my Lord;
I have no good apart from you."
The Lord is my chosen portion and my cup; you
  hold my lot.—℟.

I bless the Lord who gives me counsel;
in the night also my heart instructs me.
I keep the Lord always before me;
because he is at my right hand, I shall not be
  moved.—℟.

Therefore my heart is glad, and my soul rejoices;
my body also rests secure.

For you do not give me up to Sheol,
or let your faithful one see the Pit.—℟.

You show me the path of life.
In your presence there is fullness of joy;
in your right hand are pleasures forevermore.—
 ℟. ↓

SECOND READING 1 Pet. 1.17-21

[Conduct Yourselves Reverently]

As followers of Jesus we have been ransomed by his
blood. Through him we are believers in God who raised
Jesus from the dead. Our faith and hope are in him.

A reading from the first Letter of Saint Peter.

BELOVED: If you invoke as Father the one
who judges each person impartially according to each one's deeds, live in reverent fear during the time of your exile.

You know that you were ransomed from the futile ways inherited from your ancestors, not with
perishable things like silver or gold, but with the
precious blood of Christ, like that of a lamb without defect or blemish.

Christ was destined before the foundation of the
world, but was revealed at the end of the ages for
your sake. Through him you have come to trust in
God, who raised him from the dead and gave him
glory, so that your faith and hope are set on God.—
The word of the Lord. ℟. **Thanks be to God.** ↓

GOSPEL ACCLAMATION See Lk. 24.32   [Ardent Word]
(If the Alleluia is not sung, the acclamation is omitted.)

℣. Alleluia. ℟. **Alleluia.**
℣. Lord Jesus, open the Scriptures to us;

make our hearts burn with love when you speak.
℞. **Alleluia.** ↓

GOSPEL Lk. 24.13-35   [Christ Is Lord]

Two disciples who do not recognize Jesus walk with
him. Cleopas tells about Jesus—his miracles, passion,
death and resurrection, and the hope Israel had in him.
Finally, in the breaking of bread they see that Jesus is
with them, truly risen.

℣. The Lord be with you. ℞. **And with your spirit.**
✛ A reading from the holy Gospel according to
Luke. ℞. **Glory to you, O Lord.**

ON the first day of the week, two of the disciples were going to a village called Emmaus,
about eleven kilometres from Jerusalem, and talking with each other about all these things that had
happened. While they were talking and discussing,
Jesus himself came near and went with them, but
their eyes were kept from recognizing him.

And he said to them, "What are you discussing
with each other while you walk along?" They
stood still, looking sad. Then one of them, whose
name was Cleopas, answered him, "Are you the
only stranger in Jerusalem who does not know the
things that have taken place there in these days?"

He asked them, "What things?" They replied,
"The things about Jesus of Nazareth, who was a
Prophet mighty in deed and word before God and
all the people, and how our chief priests and leaders handed him over to be condemned to death
and crucified him. But we had hoped that he was
the one to redeem Israel. Yes, and besides all this,
it is now the third day since these things took
place. Moreover, some women of our group as-

tounded us. They were at the tomb early this
morning, and when they did not find his body
there, they came back and told us that they had
indeed seen a vision of Angels who said that he
was alive. Some of those who were with us went
to the tomb and found it just as the women had
said; but they did not see him."

Then he said to them, "Oh, how foolish you are,
and how slow of heart to believe all that the
Prophets have declared! Was it not necessary that
the Christ should suffer these things and then
enter into his glory?"

Then beginning with Moses and all the
Prophets, he interpreted to them the things about
himself in all the Scriptures. As they came near
the village to which they were going, he walked
ahead as if he were going on. But they urged him
strongly, saying, "Stay with us, because it is almost evening and the day is now nearly over." So
he went in to stay with them.

When he was at the table with them, he took
bread, blessed and broke it, and gave it to them.
Then their eyes were opened, and they recognized him; and he vanished from their sight.

They said to each other, "Were not our hearts
burning within us while he was talking to us on the
road, while he was opening the Scriptures to us?"

That same hour they got up and returned to
Jerusalem; and they found the eleven and their
companions gathered together. These were saying, "The Lord has risen indeed, and he has appeared to Simon!"

Then they told what had happened on the road,
and how he had been made known to them in the

breaking of the bread.—The Gospel of the Lord.
℟. **Praise to you, Lord Jesus Christ.** → No. 15, p. 18

PRAYER OVER THE OFFERINGS   [Exultant Church]

Receive, O Lord, we pray,
these offerings of your exultant Church,
and, as you have given her cause for such great
   gladness,
grant also that the gifts we bring
may bear fruit in perpetual happiness.
Through Christ our Lord.
℟. **Amen.**   → No. 21, p. 22 (Pref. 21-25)

COMMUNION ANTIPHON Cf. Lk. 24.35

[Christ's Presence]

**The disciples recognized the Lord Jesus in the
breaking of the bread, alleluia.** ↓

PRAYER AFTER COMMUNION   [The Lord's Kindness]

Look with kindness upon your people, O Lord,
and grant, we pray,
that those you were pleased to renew by eternal
   mysteries
may attain in their flesh
the incorruptible glory of the resurrection.
Through Christ our Lord.
℟. **Amen.**   → No. 30, p. 77

Optional Solemn Blessings, p. 97, and Prayers over the People, p. 105

"The sheep follow him because they know his voice."

MAY 7

4th SUNDAY OF EASTER

ENTRANCE ANTIPHON Cf. Ps. 32.5-6

[God the Creator]

The merciful love of the Lord fills the earth; by the word of the Lord the heavens were made, alleluia.

→ No. 2, p. 10

COLLECT [Joys of Heaven]

Almighty ever-living God,
lead us to a share in the joys of heaven,
so that the humble flock may reach
where the brave Shepherd has gone before.
Who lives and reigns with you in the unity of the
    Holy Spirit,
one God, for ever and ever. ℟. **Amen.** ↓

FIRST READING Acts 2.14a, 36b-41 [Salvation in Jesus]

In this first missionary discourse Peter states that Jesus is the Messiah whom the Jews crucified. Peter admonishes them to reform and be baptized to receive the Holy Spirit. Three thousand were received that day into the Church.

A reading from the Acts of the Apostles.

WHEN the day of Pentecost had come, Peter, standing with the eleven, raised his voice and addressed the crowd. "Let the entire house of Israel know with certainty that God has made him both Lord and Christ, this Jesus whom you crucified."

Now when the people heard this, they were cut to the heart and said to Peter and to the other Apostles, "Brothers, what should we do?" Peter said to them, "Repent, and be baptized every one of you in the name of Jesus Christ so that your sins may be forgiven; and you will receive the gift of the Holy Spirit. For the promise is for you, for your children, and for all who are far away, everyone whom the Lord our God calls to him."

And he testified with many other arguments and exhorted them, saying, "Save yourselves from this corrupt generation." So those who welcomed his message were baptized, and that day were added about three thousand souls.—The word of the Lord. ℟. **Thanks be to God.** ↓

RESPONSORIAL PSALM Ps. 23   [Refuge in God]

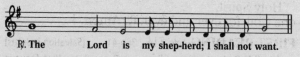

℟. The   Lord   is   my shep-herd; I shall not want.

Or: ℟. **Alleluia!**

The Lord is my shepherd, I shall not want.
He makes me lie down in green pastures;

he leads me beside still waters;
he restores my soul.—℞.

He leads me in right paths for his name's sake.
Even though I walk through the darkest valley, I
    fear no evil;
for you are with me;
your rod and your staff—they comfort me.—℞.

You prepare a table before me
in the presence of my enemies;
you anoint my head with oil;
my cup overflows.—℞.

Surely goodness and mercy shall follow me
all the days of my life,
and I shall dwell in the house of the Lord
my whole life long.—℞. ↓

SECOND READING 1 Pet. 2.20b-25   [Christ Our Saviour]
**Jesus gave an example. He suffered for us. He did no
wrong; he did not answer with insults or threats. He
died for our sins. By his wounds we are healed.**

A reading from the first Letter of Saint Peter.

BELOVED: If you endure when you do right
and suffer for it, you have God's approval. For
to this you have been called, because Christ also
suffered for you, leaving you an example, so that
you should follow in his steps.
    "He committed no sin,
        and no deceit was found in his mouth."
When he was abused, he did not return abuse;
when he suffered, he did not threaten; but he entrusted himself to the one who judges justly.
    Christ himself bore our sins in his body on the
Cross, so that, free from sins, we might live for

righteousness; by his wounds you have been healed. For you were going astray like sheep, but now you have returned to the shepherd and guardian of your souls.—The word of the Lord. ℟. **Thanks be to God.** ↓

GOSPEL ACCLAMATION Jn. 10.14   [God's Sheep]
(If the Alleluia is not sung, the acclamation is omitted.)

℣. Alleluia. ℟. **Alleluia.**

℣. I am the good shepherd, says the Lord;
I know my sheep, and my own know me.
℟. **Alleluia.** ↓

GOSPEL Jn. 10.1-10   [The Good Shepherd]

> **Jesus is the "Good Shepherd." He knows his sheep and they know him. Whoever enters his sheepfold will be safe.**

℣. The Lord be with you. ℟. **And with your spirit.**
✠ A reading from the holy Gospel according to John. ℟. **Glory to you, O Lord.**

JESUS said: "Very truly, I tell you, anyone who does not enter the sheepfold by the gate but climbs in by another way is a thief and a bandit. The one who enters by the gate is the shepherd of the sheep. The gatekeeper opens the gate for him, and the sheep hear his voice. He calls his own sheep by name and leads them out. When he has brought out all his own, he goes ahead of them, and the sheep follow him because they know his voice. They will not follow a stranger, but they will run from him because they do not know the voice of strangers."

Jesus used this figure of speech with them, but they did not understand what he was saying to them. So again Jesus said to them, "Very truly, I tell you, I am the gate for the sheep. All who came before me are thieves and bandits; but the sheep did not listen to them. I am the gate. Whoever enters by me will be saved, and will come in and go out and find pasture. The thief comes only to steal and kill and destroy. I came that they may have life, and have it abundantly."—The Gospel of the Lord. ℟. **Praise to you, Lord Jesus Christ.**

➔ No. 15, p. 18

PRAYER OVER THE OFFERINGS   [Unending Joy]

Grant, we pray, O Lord,
that we may always find delight in these paschal
    mysteries,
so that the renewal constantly at work within us
may be the cause of our unending joy.
Through Christ our Lord.
℟. **Amen.**   ➔ No. 21, p. 22 (Pref. 21-25)

COMMUNION ANTIPHON   [The Risen Shepherd]

The Good Shepherd has risen, who laid down his life for his sheep and willingly died for his flock, alleluia. ↓

PRAYER AFTER COMMUNION   [Kind Shepherd]

Look upon your flock, kind Shepherd,
and be pleased to settle in eternal pastures
the sheep you have redeemed
by the Precious Blood of your Son.
Who lives and reigns for ever and ever.
℟. **Amen.**   ➔ No. 30, p. 77

Optional Solemn Blessings, p. 97, and Prayers over the People, p. 105

"In my Father's house there are many dwelling places."

MAY 14

5th SUNDAY OF EASTER

ENTRANCE ANTIPHON Cf. Ps. 97.1-2

[Wonders of the Lord]

O sing a new song to the Lord, for he has worked wonders; in the sight of the nations he has shown his deliverance, alleluia. ➜ No. 2, p. 10

COLLECT [Much Fruit]

Almighty ever-living God,
constantly accomplish the Paschal Mystery
    within us,
that those you were pleased to make new in Holy
    Baptism
may, under your protective care, bear much fruit
and come to the joys of life eternal.
Through our Lord Jesus Christ, your Son,
who lives and reigns with you in the unity of the
    Holy Spirit,
one God, for ever and ever. ℟. **Amen.** ↓

FIRST READING Acts 6.1-7   [Spiritual and Material Tasks]

Since the number of faithful was growing, seven men were proposed as ministers to help in the work of the Church. The apostles prayed over them and imposed hands on them.

A reading from the Acts of the Apostles.

NOW during those days, when the disciples were increasing in number, the Hellenists complained against the Hebrews because their widows were being neglected in the daily distribution of food. And the twelve called together the whole community of the disciples and said, "It is not right that we should neglect the word of God in order to wait on tables. Therefore, brothers, select from among yourselves seven men of good standing, full of the Spirit and of wisdom, whom we may appoint to this task, while we, for our part, will devote ourselves to prayer and to serving the word."

What they said pleased the whole community, and they chose Stephen, a man full of faith and the Holy Spirit, together with Philip, Prochorus, Nicanor, Timon, Parmenas, and Nicolaus, a convert of Antioch. They had these men stand before the Apostles, who prayed and laid their hands on them.

The word of God continued to spread; the number of the disciples increased greatly in Jerusalem, and a great many of the priests became obedient to the faith.—The word of the Lord. ℟. **Thanks be to God.** ↓

RESPONSORIAL PSALM Ps. 33   [Exult in the Lord]

℟. Let your love be upon us, Lord, ev-en as we hope in you.

Or: ℟. **Alleluia!**

Rejoice in the Lord, O you righteous.
Praise befits the upright.
Praise the Lord with the lyre;
make melody to him with the harp of ten
   strings.—℟.

For the word of the Lord is upright,
and all his work is done in faithfulness.
He loves righteousness and justice;
the earth is full of the steadfast love of the
   Lord.—℟.

Truly the eye of the Lord is on those who fear him,
on those who hope in his steadfast love,
to deliver their soul from death,
and to keep them alive in famine.—℟. ↓

SECOND READING 1 Pet. 2.4-9   [A Royal Priesthood]

Jesus is the cornerstone of the Church. The people of God
are living stones. We are a royal priesthood, a consecrated
nation, a people set apart to proclaim Jesus' good works.

A reading from the first Letter of Saint Peter.

BELOVED: Come to the Lord, a living stone,
though rejected by human beings yet chosen
and precious in God's sight. Like living stones, let
yourselves be built into a spiritual house, to be a
holy priesthood, to offer spiritual sacrifices acceptable to God through Jesus Christ.

For it stands in Scripture:

"See, I am laying in Zion a stone,
    a cornerstone chosen and precious;
and whoever believes in him will not be put to
    shame."

To you then who believe, he is precious; but for
those who do not believe,

"The stone that the builders rejected
    has become the very head of the corner,"

and

"A stone that makes them stumble,
    and a rock that makes them fall."

They stumble because they disobey the word, as
they were destined to do.

But you are a chosen race, a royal priesthood, a
holy nation, God's own people, in order that you
may proclaim the mighty acts of him who called
you out of darkness into his marvellous light.—
The word of the Lord. ℟. **Thanks be to God.** ↓

GOSPEL ACCLAMATION Jn. 14.6   [Christ the Way]
(If the Alleluia is not sung, the acclamation is omitted.)
℣. Alleluia. ℟. **Alleluia.**
℣. I am the way, the truth, and the life, says the
    Lord;
no one comes to the Father, except through me.
℟. **Alleluia.** ↓

GOSPEL Jn. 14.1-12   [Faith in God]

Jesus assures his apostles that he is the way, the truth,
and the life. The Father lives in him and he in the Father.
Whoever has faith in Jesus will do the works of God.

℣. The Lord be with you. ℟. **And with your spirit.**
✤ A reading from the holy Gospel according to
John. ℟. **Glory to you, O Lord.**

JESUS said to his disciples: "Do not let your hearts be troubled. Believe in God, believe also in me. In my Father's house there are many dwelling places. If it were not so, would I have told you that I go to prepare a place for you? And if I go and prepare a place for you, I will come again and will take you to myself, so that where I am, there you may be also. And you know the way to the place where I am going."

Thomas said to him, "Lord, we do not know where you are going. How can we know the way?"

Jesus said to him, "I am the way, and the truth, and the life. No one comes to the Father except through me. If you know me, you will know my Father also. From now on you do know him and have seen him."

Philip said to him, "Lord, show us the Father, and we will be satisfied."

Jesus said to him, "Have I been with you all this time, Philip, and you still do not know me? Whoever has seen me has seen the Father. How can you say, 'Show us the Father'? Do you not believe that I am in the Father and the Father is in me? The words that I say to you I do not speak on my own; but the Father who dwells in me does his works. Believe me that I am in the Father and the Father is in me; but if you do not, then believe me because of the works themselves. Very truly, I tell you, the one who believes in me will also do the works that I do and, in fact, will do greater works than these, because I am going to the Father."— The Gospel of the Lord. ℟. **Praise to you, Lord Jesus Christ.**

➡ No. 15, p. 18

PRAYER OVER THE OFFERINGS
[Guided by God's Truth]

O God, who by the wonderful exchange effected
   in this sacrifice
have made us partakers of the one supreme
   Godhead,
grant, we pray,
that, as we have come to know your truth,
we may make it ours by a worthy way of life.
Through Christ our Lord.
R̺. **Amen.**   → No. 21, p. 22 (Pref. 21-25)

COMMUNION ANTIPHON Cf. Jn. 15.1, 5
[Union with Christ]

**I am the true vine and you are the branches, says
the Lord. Whoever remains in me, and I in him,
bears fruit in plenty, alleluia.** ↓

PRAYER AFTER COMMUNION   [New Life]

Graciously be present to your people, we pray, O
   Lord,
and lead those you have imbued with heavenly
   mysteries
to pass from former ways to newness of life.
Through Christ our Lord.
R̺. **Amen.**   → No. 30, p. 77

Optional Solemn Blessings, p. 97, and Prayers over the People, p. 105

"I will ask the Father, and he will give you
another Advocate."

MAY 21

6th SUNDAY OF EASTER

ENTRANCE ANTIPHON Cf. Isa. 48.20   **[Freedom]**

**Proclaim a joyful sound and let it be heard; pro-
claim to the ends of the earth: The Lord has
freed his people, alleluia.**   → No. 2, p. 10

COLLECT   [Heartfelt Devotion]

Grant, almighty God,
that we may celebrate with heartfelt devotion
   these days of joy,
which we keep in honour of the risen Lord,
and that what we relive in remembrance
we may always hold to in what we do.
Through our Lord Jesus Christ, your Son,
who lives and reigns with you in the unity of the
   Holy Spirit,
one God, for ever and ever. ℟. **Amen.** ↓

FIRST READING Acts 8.5-8, 14-17 [Reception of Holy Spirit]

Philip carried the Good News to Samaria. He performed many miracles. Peter and John laid hands on these people in Samaria and they received the Holy Spirit.

A reading from the Acts of the Apostles.

IN those days: Philip went down to the city of Samaria and proclaimed the Christ to them. The crowds with one accord listened eagerly to what was said by Philip, hearing and seeing the signs that he did, for unclean spirits, crying with loud shrieks, came out of many who were possessed; and many others who were paralysed or lame were cured. So there was great joy in that city.

Now when the Apostles at Jerusalem heard that Samaria had accepted the word of God, they sent Peter and John to them. The two went down and prayed for them that they might receive the Holy Spirit; (for as yet the Spirit had not come upon any of them; they had only been baptized in the name of the Lord Jesus). Then Peter and John laid their hands on them, and they received the Holy Spirit. —The word of the Lord. ℟. **Thanks be to God.** ↓

RESPONSORIAL PSALM Ps. 66   [Glorious Deeds]

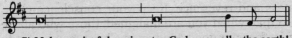

℟. **Make a joyful noise to God,   all the earth!**
Or: ℟. **Alleluia!**

Make a joyful noise to God, all the earth!
sing the glory of his name;
give to him glorious praise.
Say to God, "How awesome are your deeds!"—℟.

"All the earth worships you;
they sing praises to you, sing praises to your name."
Come and see what God has done:
he is awesome in his deeds among the children of
    Adam.
℟. **Make a joyful noise to God, all the earth!**
Or: ℟. **Alleluia!**

He turned the sea into dry land;
they passed through the river on foot.
There we rejoiced in him,
who rules by his might forever.—℟.

Come and hear, all you who fear God,
and I will tell what he has done for me.
Blessed be God, because he has not rejected my
    prayer
or removed his steadfast love from me.—℟. ↓

SECOND READING 1 Pet. 3.15-18   [Life in the Spirit]
    Always worship God in your hearts. Jesus died for sins
    for all who are sinners, to lead us to God.

A reading from the first Letter of Saint Peter.

BELOVED: In your hearts sanctify Christ as
Lord. Always be ready to make your defence
to anyone who demands from you an accounting
for the hope that is in you; yet do it with gentleness and reverence. Keep your conscience clear,
so that, when you are maligned, those who abuse
you for your good conduct in Christ may be put to
shame. For it is better to suffer for doing good, if
suffering should be God's will, than to suffer for
doing evil.
    For Christ also suffered for sins once for all, the
righteous for the unrighteous, in order to bring

you to God. He was put to death in the flesh, but made alive in the spirit.—The word of the Lord. ℟. **Thanks be to God.** ↓

GOSPEL ACCLAMATION Jn. 14.23   [Divine Love]

(If the Alleluia is not sung, the acclamation is omitted.)

℣. Alleluia. ℟. **Alleluia.**

℣. All who love me will keep my word,
and my Father will love them, and we will come
  to them.

℟. **Alleluia.** ↓

GOSPEL Jn. 14.15-21   [Eternal Presence]

Jesus promises to ask for an Advocate for those who love him. The world will not accept or understand the Advocate. All who obey the commandments show their love for God and will be loved in return.

℣. The Lord be with you. ℟. **And with your spirit.**
✟ A reading from the holy Gospel according to John. ℟. **Glory to you, O Lord.**

JESUS said to his disciples: "If you love me, you will keep my commandments. And I will ask the Father, and he will give you another Advocate, to be with you forever. This is the Spirit of truth, whom the world cannot receive, because it neither sees him nor knows him. You know him, because he abides with you, and he will be in you.

I will not leave you orphaned; I am coming to you. In a little while the world will no longer see me, but you will see me; because I live, you also will live. On that day you will know that I am in my Father, and you in me, and I in you.

The one who has my commandments and keeps them is the one who loves me; and the one who loves me will be loved by my Father, and I will love them and reveal myself to them."— The Gospel of the Lord. ℟. **Praise to you, Lord Jesus Christ.**   → No. 15, p. 18

PRAYER OVER THE OFFERINGS [God's Mighty Love]

May our prayers rise up to you, O Lord,
together with the sacrificial offerings,
so that, purified by your graciousness,
we may be conformed to the mysteries of your
    mighty love.
Through Christ our Lord.
℟. **Amen.**   → No. 21, p. 22 (Pref. 21-25)

COMMUNION ANTIPHON Jn. 14.15-16
[Role of the Paraclete]

If you love me, keep my commandments, says the Lord, and I will ask the Father and he will send you another Paraclete, to abide with you for ever, alleluia. ↓

PRAYER AFTER COMMUNION [Eucharistic Strength]

Almighty ever-living God,
who restore us to eternal life in the Resurrection
    of Christ,
increase in us, we pray, the fruits of this paschal
    Sacrament
and pour into our hearts the strength of this
    saving food.
Through Christ our Lord.
℟. **Amen.**   → No. 30, p. 77

Optional Solemn Blessings, p. 97, and Prayers over the People, p. 105

"Go therefore and make disciples of all nations."

MAY 28

THE ASCENSION OF THE LORD

Solemnity

AT THE VIGIL MASS (May 27)

ENTRANCE ANTIPHON Ps. 67.33, 35

[Praise the Lord]

You kingdoms of the earth, sing to God; praise the Lord, who ascends above the highest heavens; his majesty and might are in the skies, alleluia.

➔ No. 2, p. 10

COLLECT [Jesus' Promise]

O God, whose Son today ascended to the heavens
as the Apostles looked on,

grant, we pray, that, in accordance with his
    promise,

we may be worthy for him to live with us always
    on earth,

and we with him in heaven.

417

Who lives and reigns with you in the unity of the
  Holy Spirit,
one God, for ever and ever. ℟. **Amen.** ↓

The readings for this Mass can be found beginning on p. 419.

PRAYER OVER THE OFFERINGS   [Obtain Mercy]

O God, whose Only Begotten Son, our High Priest,
is seated ever-living at your right hand to
  intercede for us,
grant that we may approach with confidence the
  throne of grace
and there obtain your mercy.
Through Christ our Lord.
℟. **Amen.**   → No. 21, p. 22 (Pref. 26-27)

When the Roman Canon is used, the proper form of the
Communicantes (In communion with those) *is said.*

COMMUNION ANTIPHON Cf. Heb. 10.12

[Christ at God's Right Hand]

**Christ, offering a single sacrifice for sins, is seated
for ever at God's right hand, alleluia.** ↓

PRAYER AFTER COMMUNION   [Longing for Heaven]

May the gifts we have received from your altar,
  Lord,
kindle in our hearts a longing for the heavenly
  homeland
and cause us to press forward, following in the
  Saviour's footsteps,
to the place where for our sake he entered
  before us.
Who lives and reigns for ever and ever.
℟. **Amen.**   → No. 30, p. 77

Optional Solemn Blessings, p. 97, and Prayers over the People, p. 105

AT THE MASS DURING THE DAY

ENTRANCE ANTIPHON Acts 1.11 [The Lord Will Return]

Men of Galilee, why gaze in wonder at the heavens? This Jesus whom you saw ascending into heaven will return as you saw him go, alleluia.

→ No. 2, p. 10

COLLECT   [Thankful for the Ascension]

Gladden us with holy joys, almighty God,
and make us rejoice with devout thanksgiving,
for the Ascension of Christ your Son
is our exaltation,
and, where the Head has gone before in glory,
the Body is called to follow in hope.
Through our Lord Jesus Christ, your Son,
who lives and reigns with you in the unity of the
    Holy Spirit,
one God, for ever and ever. ℟. **Amen.** ↓

OR   [Belief in the Ascension]

Grant, we pray, almighty God,
that we, who believe that your Only Begotten
    Son, our Redeemer,
ascended this day to the heavens,
may in spirit dwell already in heavenly realms.
Who lives and reigns with you in the unity of the
    Holy Spirit,
one God, for ever and ever. ℟. **Amen.** ↓

FIRST READING Acts 1.1-11   [Christ's Ascension]

Christ is divine! He will come again! Our faith affirms
this for us. We live in the era of the Holy Spirit.

A reading from the Acts of the Apostles.

IN the first book, Theophilus, I wrote about all that Jesus did and taught from the beginning until the day when he was taken up to heaven, after giving instructions through the Holy Spirit to the Apostles whom he had chosen. After his suffering he presented himself alive to them by many convincing proofs, appearing to them during forty days and speaking about the kingdom of God.

While staying with them, he ordered them not to leave Jerusalem, but to wait there for the promise of the Father. "This," he said, "is what you have heard from me; for John baptized with water, but you will be baptized with the Holy Spirit not many days from now."

So when they had come together, they asked him, "Lord, is this the time when you will restore the kingdom to Israel?" He replied, "It is not for you to know the times or periods that the Father has set by his own authority. But you will receive power when the Holy Spirit has come upon you; and you will be my witnesses in Jerusalem, in all Judea and Samaria, and to the ends of the earth."

When he had said this, as they were watching, he was lifted up, and a cloud took him out of their sight. While he was going and they were gazing up toward heaven, suddenly two men in white robes stood by them.

They said, "Men of Galilee, why do you stand looking up toward heaven? This Jesus, who has been taken up from you into heaven, will come in the same way as you saw him go into heaven."— The word of the Lord. ℟. **Thanks be to God.** ↓

RESPONSORIAL PSALM Ps. 47   [Praise to the Lord]

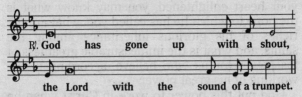

R̸. God has gone up with a shout, the Lord with the sound of a trumpet.

Or: R̸. **Alleluia!**

Clap your hands, all you peoples;
shout to God with loud songs of joy.
For the Lord, the Most High, is awesome,
a great king over all the earth.—R̸.

God has gone up with a shout,
the Lord with the sound of a trumpet.
Sing praises to God, sing praises;
sing praises to our King, sing praises.—R̸.

For God is the king of all the earth;
sing praises with a Psalm.
God is king over the nations;
God sits on his holy throne.—R̸. ↓

SECOND READING Eph. 1.17-23   [Glorification of Jesus]

Our hope is in God, our strength. With Christ our head,
we his people will receive the gift of wisdom and insight.

A reading from the Letter of Saint Paul
to the Ephesians.

BROTHERS and sisters: I pray that the God of
our Lord Jesus Christ, the Father of glory,
may give you a spirit of wisdom and revelation as

you come to know him, so that, with the eyes of your heart enlightened, you may know what is the hope to which he has called you, what are the riches of his glorious inheritance among the saints, and what is the immeasurable greatness of his power for us who believe, according to the working of his great power.

God put this power to work in Christ when he raised him from the dead and seated him at his right hand in the heavenly places, far above all rule and authority and power and dominion, and above every name that is named, not only in this age but also in the age to come.

And he has put all things under his feet and has made him the head over all things for the Church, which is his body, the fullness of him who fills all in all.—The word of the Lord. ℞. **Thanks be to God.** ↓

GOSPEL ACCLAMATION Mt. 28.19, 20
[Christ's Abiding Presence]

(If the Alleluia is not sung, the acclamation is omitted.)

℣. Alleluia. ℞. **Alleluia.**
℣. Go make disciples of all nations;
I am with you always, to the end of the age.
℞. **Alleluia.** ↓

GOSPEL Mt. 28.16-20   [Commission of the Apostles]
Jesus speaks to the eleven admitting his full authority. He commissions them to make disciples of all people, to baptize them. Jesus also promises to be with them to the end of the world.

℣. The Lord be with you. ℟. **And with your spirit.**
✣ A reading from the holy Gospel according to Matthew. ℟. **Glory to you, O Lord.**

THE eleven disciples went to Galilee, to the mountain to which Jesus had directed them. When they saw him, they worshipped him; but some doubted.

And Jesus came and said to them, "All authority in heaven and on earth has been given to me. Go therefore and make disciples of all nations, baptizing them in the name of the Father and of the Son and of the Holy Spirit, and teaching them to obey everything that I have commanded you.

And remember, I am with you always, to the end of the age."—The Gospel of the Lord. ℟. **Praise to you, Lord Jesus Christ.**   → No. 15, p. 18

PRAYER OVER THE OFFERINGS
[Rise to Heavenly Realms]

We offer sacrifice now in supplication, O Lord,
to honour the wondrous Ascension of your Son:
grant, we pray,
that through this most holy exchange
we, too, may rise up to the heavenly realms.
Through Christ our Lord.
℟. **Amen.**   → No. 21, p. 22 (Pref. 26-27)

When the Roman Canon is used, the proper form of the
Communicantes (In communion with those) *is said.*

COMMUNION ANTIPHON Mt. 28.20 [Christ's Presence]
Behold, I am with you always, even to the end of the age, alleluia. ↓

PRAYER AFTER COMMUNION   [United with Christ]

Almighty ever-living God,
who allow those on earth to celebrate divine
  mysteries,
grant, we pray,
that Christian hope may draw us onward
to where our nature is united with you.
Through Christ our Lord.
℞. **Amen.**   → No. 30, p. 77

Optional Solemn Blessings, p. 97, and Prayers over the People, p. 105

"All of them were filled with the Holy Spirit."

JUNE 4

PENTECOST SUNDAY

Solemnity

AT THE VIGIL MASS (Simple Form) (June 3)

ENTRANCE ANTIPHON Rom. 5.5; cf. 8.11

[Love-Imparting Spirit]

The love of God has been poured into our hearts through the Spirit of God dwelling within us, alleluia. ➔ No. 2, p. 10

COLLECT [Heavenly Grace]

Almighty ever-living God,
who willed the Paschal Mystery
to be encompassed as a sign in fifty days,
grant that from out of the scattered nations
the confusion of many tongues
may be gathered by heavenly grace
into one great confession of your name.
Through our Lord Jesus Christ, your Son,

425

who lives and reigns with you in the unity of the
  Holy Spirit,
one God, for ever and ever. ℞. **Amen.** ↓

OR   [New Birth in the Spirit]

Grant, we pray, almighty God,
that the splendour of your glory
may shine forth upon us
and that, by the bright rays of the Holy Spirit,
the light of your light may confirm the hearts
of those born again by your grace.
Through our Lord Jesus Christ, your Son,
who lives and reigns with you in the unity of the
  Holy Spirit,
one God, for ever and ever. ℞. **Amen.** ↓

FIRST READING

A Gen. 11.1-9   [Dangers of Human Pride]

**Those who put their trust in pride, and human ability, are
bound to fail.**

A reading from the book of Genesis.

NOW the whole earth had one language and
the same words. And as people migrated
from the east, they came upon a plain in the land
of Shinar and settled there. And they said to one
another, "Come, let us make bricks, and burn
them thoroughly." And they had brick for stone,
and bitumen for mortar. Then they said, "Come,
let us build ourselves a city, and a tower with its
top in the heavens, and let us make a name for
ourselves; otherwise we shall be scattered abroad
upon the face of the whole earth." The Lord came

down to see the city and the tower, which the children of Adam had built. And the Lord said, "Look, they are one people, and they have all one language; and this is only the beginning of what they will do; nothing that they propose to do will now be impossible for them. Come, let us go down, and confuse their language there, so that they will not understand one another's speech." So the Lord scattered them abroad from there over the face of all the earth, and they left off building the city. Therefore it was called Babel, because there the Lord confused the language of all the earth; and from there the Lord scattered them abroad over the face of all the earth.—The word of the Lord. ℟. **Thanks be to God.** ↓

OR

B Ex. 19.3-8a, 16-20   [The Lord on Mount Sinai]

The Lord God covenants with the Israelites—they are to be a holy nation, a princely Kingdom.

A reading from the book of Exodus.

MOSES went up to God; the Lord called to him from the mountain, saying, "Thus you shall say to the house of Jacob, and tell the children of Israel: 'You have seen what I did to the Egyptians, and how I bore you on eagles' wings and brought you to myself. Now therefore, if you obey my voice and keep my covenant, you shall be my treasured possession out of all the peoples. Indeed, the whole earth is mine, but you shall be for me a priestly kingdom and a holy nation.' These are the words that you shall speak to the children of Israel." So Moses came, summoned the elders of the people, and set before them all these words that the Lord had commanded him. The people all answered as one: "Everything that the Lord has spoken we will do."

On the morning of the third day there was thunder and lightning, as well as a thick cloud on the mountain, and a blast of a trumpet so loud that all the people who were in the camp trembled. Moses brought the people out of the camp to meet God. They took their stand at the foot of the mountain. Now Mount Sinai was wrapped in smoke, because the Lord had descended upon it in fire; the smoke went up like the smoke of a kiln, while the whole mountain shook violently. As the blast of the trumpet grew louder and louder, Moses would speak and God would answer him in thunder. When the Lord descended upon Mount Sinai, to the top of the mountain, the Lord summoned Moses to the top of the mountain, and Moses went up.—The word of the Lord. ℟. **Thanks be to God.** ↓

OR

C Ez. 37.1-14   [Life-Giving Spirit]

The prophet, in a vision, sees the power of God—the band of the living and the dead, as he describes the resurrection of the dead.

A reading from the book of the Prophet Ezekiel.

THE hand of the Lord came upon me, and he brought me out by the spirit of the Lord and set me down in the middle of a valley; it was full of bones. He led me all around them; there were very many lying in the valley, and they were very dry. He said to me, "Son of man, can these bones live?" I answered, "O Lord God, you know." Then he said to me, "Prophesy to these bones, and say to them: O dry bones, hear the word of the Lord. Thus says the Lord God to these bones: I will cause breath to enter you, and you shall live. I will lay sinews on you, and will cause flesh to come upon you, and cover you with skin, and put breath in you, and you shall live; and you shall know that I am the Lord." So I prophesied as I had been commanded; and as I prophesied, suddenly there was a noise, a rattling, and the bones came together, bone to its bone. I looked, and there were sinews on them, and flesh had come upon them, and skin had covered them; but there was no breath in them. Then he said to me, "Prophesy to the breath, prophesy, son of man, and say to the breath: Thus says the Lord God: Come from the four winds, and breathe upon these slain, that they may live." I prophesied as he commanded me, and the breath came into them, and they lived, and stood on their feet, a vast multitude. Then he said to me, "Son of man, these bones are the whole house of Israel. They say, 'Our bones are dried up, and our hope is lost; we are cut off completely.' Therefore prophesy, and say to them, Thus says the Lord God: I am going to open your graves, and bring you up from your graves, O my people; and I will bring you back to the land of Israel. And you shall know that I am the Lord, when I open your graves, and bring you up from your graves, O my people. I will put my spirit within you, and you shall live, and I will place you on your own soil; then you shall know that I, the

Lord, have spoken and will act," says the Lord.—
The word of the Lord. ℟. **Thanks be to God.** ↓

OR

D Joel 2.28-32   [Signs of the Spirit]

**At the end of time, the Day of the Lord, Judgment Day,
those who persevere in faith will be saved.**

A reading from the book of the Prophet Joel.

THUS says the Lord:
I will pour out my spirit on all flesh;
your sons and your daughters shall prophesy,
    your elders shall dream dreams,
    and your young people shall see visions.
Even on the male and female slaves,
    in those days, I will pour out my spirit.
I will show portents in the heavens and on the
        earth,
    blood and fire and columns of smoke.
The sun shall be turned to darkness,
    and the moon to blood,
    before the great and terrible day of the
        Lord comes.
Then everyone who calls on the name of the
        Lord
    shall be saved;
for in Mount Zion and in Jerusalem
    there shall be those who escape, as the
        Lord has said,
and among the survivors shall be those whom
    the Lord calls.

The word of the Lord. ℟. **Thanks be to God.** ↓

RESPONSORIAL PSALM Ps. 104

[Send Forth Your Spirit]

℟. Lord, send forth your Spir - it, and re-new the face of the earth.

Or: ℟. Alleluia!

Bless the Lord, O my soul.
O Lord my God, you are very great.
You are clothed with honour and majesty,
wrapped in light as with a garment.—℟.

O Lord, how manifold are your works!
In wisdom you have made them all;
the earth is full of your creatures,
living things both small and great.—℟.

These all look to you
to give them their food in due season;
when you give to them, they gather it up;
when you open your hand, they are filled with
    good things.—℟.

When you take away their breath,
they die and return to their dust.
When you send forth your spirit, they are created;
and you renew the face of the earth.—℟. ↓

SECOND READING Rom. 8.22-27   [The Spirit Our Helper]

Be patient and have hope. The Spirit intercedes for us.

A reading from the Letter of Saint Paul
to the Romans.

BROTHERS and sisters: we know that the
whole creation has been groaning in labour

pains until now; and not only the creation, but we ourselves, who have the first fruits of the Spirit, groan inwardly while we wait for adoption to sonship, the redemption of our bodies. For in hope we were saved. Now hope that is seen is not hope. For who hopes for what is seen? But if we hope for what we do not see, we wait for it with patience. Likewise the Spirit helps us in our weakness; for we do not know how to pray as we ought, but that very Spirit intercedes with sighs too deep for words. And God, who searches the heart, knows what is the mind of the Spirit, because the Spirit intercedes for the saints according to the will of God.—The word of the Lord. ℟. **Thanks be to God.** ↓

GOSPEL ACCLAMATION   [Fire of God's Love]

(If the Alleluia is not sung, the acclamation is omitted.)

℣. Alleluia. ℟. **Alleluia.**

℣. Come, Holy Spirit, fill the hearts of your faithful and kindle in them the fire of your love.

℟. **Alleluia.** ↓

GOSPEL Jn. 7.37-39   [Prediction of the Spirit]

Jesus indicates that the Holy Spirit will bear witness to the good news. He will guide Christians to the truth and teach about things to come.

℣. The Lord be with you. ℟. **And with your spirit.**
✠ A reading from the holy Gospel according to John. ℟. **Glory to you, O Lord.**

ON the last day of the festival, the great day, while Jesus was standing in the temple, he cried out, "Let anyone who is thirsty come to me and drink. As the Scripture has said, 'Out of the heart of the one who believes in me shall flow rivers of living water.'" Now he said this about the Spirit, which believers in him were to receive; for as yet there was no Spirit, because Jesus was not yet glorified.—The Gospel of the Lord. ℟. **Praise to you, Lord Jesus Christ.**

➜ No. 15, p. 18

PRAYER OVER THE OFFERINGS

[Manifestation of Salvation]

Pour out upon these gifts the blessing of your Spirit,
we pray, O Lord,
so that through them your Church may be imbued with such love
that the truth of your saving mystery
may shine forth for the whole world.
Through Christ our Lord.
℟. **Amen.**   ➜ Pref. 28, p. 439

When the Roman Canon is used, the proper form of the Communicantes (In communion with those) *is said.*

COMMUNION ANTIPHON Jn. 7.37 [Thirst for the Spirit]

On the last day of the festival, Jesus stood and cried out: If anyone is thirsty, let him come to me and drink, alleluia. ↓

PRAYER AFTER COMMUNION [Aflame with the Spirit]

May these gifts we have consumed
benefit us, O Lord,
that we may always be aflame with the same Spirit,

whom you wondrously poured out on your
  Apostles.
Through Christ our Lord.
℟. **Amen.**   → No. 30, p. 77

Optional Solemn Blessings, p. 97, and Prayers over the People, p. 105

(At the end of the Dismissal the people respond: **"Thanks be
to God, alleluia, alleluia.")**

AT THE MASS DURING THE DAY

ENTRANCE ANTIPHON Wis. 1.7 [The Spirit in the World]
**The Spirit of the Lord has filled the whole world
and that which contains all things understands
what is said, alleluia.**   → No. 2, p. 10

OR Rom. 5.5; cf. 8.11   [God's Love for Us]
**The love of God has been poured into our hearts
through the Spirit of God dwelling within us, alleluia.**   → No. 2, p. 10

COLLECT   [Gifts of the Spirit]
O God, who by the mystery of today's great feast
sanctify your whole Church in every people and
  nation,
pour out, we pray, the gifts of the Holy Spirit
across the face of the earth
and, with the divine grace that was at work
when the Gospel was first proclaimed,
fill now once more the hearts of believers.
Through our Lord Jesus Christ, your Son,
who lives and reigns with you in the unity of the
  Holy Spirit,
one God, for ever and ever. ℟. **Amen.** ↓

FIRST READING Acts 2.1-11   [Coming of the Spirit]

As promised by Jesus, the Holy Spirit fills the faithful, and, inspired, they proclaim the good news.

A reading from the Acts of the Apostles.

WHEN the day of Pentecost had come, they were all together in one place. And suddenly from heaven there came a sound like the rush of a violent wind, and it filled the entire house where they were sitting. Divided tongues, as of fire, appeared among them, and a tongue rested on each of them. All of them were filled with the Holy Spirit and began to speak in other languages, as the Spirit gave them ability.

Now there were devout Jews from every nation under heaven living in Jerusalem. And at this sound the crowd gathered and was bewildered, because each one heard them speaking in their own language. Amazed and astonished, they asked, "Are not all these who are speaking Galileans? And how is it that we hear, each of us, in our own language? Parthians, Medes, Elamites, and residents of Mesopotamia, Judea and Cappadocia, Pontus and Asia, Phrygia and Pamphylia, Egypt and the parts of Libya belonging to Cyrene, and visitors from Rome, both Jews and converts, Cretans and Arabs—in our own languages we hear them speaking about God's deeds of power." —The word of the Lord. ℟. **Thanks be to God.** ↓

RESPONSORIAL PSALM Ps. 104   [Renewal]

℟. Lord, send forth your Spir - it, and re-new the face of the earth.

Or: ℟. **Alleluia!**

Bless the Lord, O my soul.
O Lord my God, you are very great.
O Lord, how manifold are your works!
The earth is full of your creatures.
℟. **Lord, send forth your Spirit,**
   and renew the face of the earth.

Or: ℟. **Alleluia!**

When you take away their breath,
they die and return to their dust.
When you send forth your spirit, they are created;
and you renew the face of the earth.—℟.

May the glory of the Lord endure forever;
may the Lord rejoice in his works.
May my meditation be pleasing to him,
for I rejoice in the Lord.—℟. ↓

SECOND READING 1 Cor. 12.3b-7, 12-13

[Grace of the Spirit]

**The gifts of the Spirit are not exclusive but for all. The
Spirit brings a radical unity to the body of Christ.**

A reading from the first Letter of Saint Paul
to the Corinthians.

BROTHERS and sisters: No one can say "Jesus
is Lord" except by the Holy Spirit.

Now there are varieties of gifts, but the same
Spirit; and there are varieties of services, but the
same Lord; and there are varieties of activities,
but it is the same God who activates all of them in
everyone. To each is given the manifestation of
the Spirit for the common good.

For just as the body is one and has many members, and all the members of the body, though many, are one body, so it is with Christ. For in the one Spirit we were all baptized into one body—Jews or Greeks, slaves or free—and we were all made to drink of one Spirit.—The word of the Lord. ℟. **Thanks be to God.** ↓

SEQUENCE *(Veni, Sancte Spiritus)*   [Come, Holy Spirit]

1. Holy Spirit, Lord divine,
   Come, from heights of heav'n and shine,
   Come with blessed radiance bright!

2. Come, O Father of the poor,
   Come, whose treasured gifts ensure,
   Come, our heart's unfailing light!

3. Of consolers, wisest, best,
   And our soul's most welcome guest,
   Sweet refreshment, sweet repose.

4. In our labour rest most sweet,
   Pleasant coolness in the heat,
   Consolation in our woes.

5. Light most blessed, shine with grace
   In our heart's most secret place,
   Fill your faithful through and through.

6. Left without your presence here,
   Life itself would disappear,
   Nothing thrives apart from you!

7. Cleanse our soiled hearts of sin,
   Arid souls refresh within,
   Wounded lives to health restore.

8. **Bend the stubborn heart and will,**
   Melt the frozen, warm the chill,
   Guide the wayward home once more!

9. **On the faithful who are true**
   And profess their faith in you,
   In your sev'nfold gift descend!

10. **Give us virtue's sure reward,**
    Give us your salvation, Lord,
    Give us joys that never end! ↓

GOSPEL ACCLAMATION   [Fire of God's Love]

(If the Alleluia is not sung, the acclamation is omitted.)

℣. Alleluia. ℟. **Alleluia.**
℣. Come, Holy Spirit, fill the hearts of your
   faithful
and kindle in them the fire of your love.
℟. **Alleluia.** ↓

GOSPEL Jn. 20.19-23   [Christ Imparts the Spirit]

Jesus gives the blessing of peace, and bestows his authority on the disciples as he confers on them the Holy Spirit.

℣. The Lord be with you. ℟. **And with your spirit.**
✛ A reading from the holy Gospel according to
John. ℟. **Glory to you, O Lord.**

IT was evening on the day Jesus rose from the
dead, the first day of the week, and the doors of
the house where the disciples had met were
locked for fear of the Jews. Jesus came and stood
among them and said, "Peace be with you." After
he said this, he showed them his hands and his
side. Then the disciples rejoiced when they saw
the Lord.

Jesus said to them again, "Peace be with you. As the Father has sent me, so I send you."

When he had said this, he breathed on them and said to them, "Receive the Holy Spirit. If you forgive the sins of any, they are forgiven them; if you retain the sins of any, they are retained."— The Gospel of the Lord. ℟. **Praise to you, Lord Jesus Christ.**   → No. 15, p. 18

PRAYER OVER THE OFFERINGS   [All Truth]

Grant, we pray, O Lord,
that, as promised by your Son,
the Holy Spirit may reveal to us more abundantly
the hidden mystery of this sacrifice
and graciously lead us into all truth.
Through Christ our Lord. ℟. **Amen.** ↓

PREFACE (28)   [Coming of the Spirit]

℣. The Lord be with you. ℟. **And with your spirit.**
℣. Lift up your hearts. ℟. **We lift them up to the Lord.**
℣. Let us give thanks to the Lord our God. ℟. **It is right and just.**

It is truly right and just, our duty and our salvation,
always and everywhere to give you thanks,
Lord, holy Father, almighty and eternal God.

For, bringing your Paschal Mystery to completion,
you bestowed the Holy Spirit today
on those you made your adopted children
by uniting them to your Only Begotten Son.
This same Spirit, as the Church came to birth,
opened to all peoples the knowledge of God
and brought together the many languages of the
    earth
in profession of the one faith.

Therefore, overcome with paschal joy,
every land, every people exults in your praise
and even the heavenly Powers, with the angelic
   hosts,
sing together the unending hymn of your glory,
as they acclaim: ➜ No. 23, p. 23

When the Roman Canon is used, the proper form of the
Communicantes *(In communion with those) is said.*

COMMUNION ANTIPHON Acts 2.4, 11   [Spirit-Filled]

**They were all filled with the Holy Spirit and
spoke of the marvels of God, alleluia.** ↓

PRAYER AFTER COMMUNION   [Safeguard Grace]

O God, who bestow heavenly gifts upon your
   Church,
safeguard, we pray, the grace you have given,
that the gift of the Holy Spirit poured out upon
   her
may retain all its force
and that this spiritual food
may gain her abundance of eternal redemption.
Through Christ our Lord.
R). **Amen.** ➜ No. 30, p. 77

Optional Solemn Blessings, p. 97, and Prayers over the People, p. 105

(At the end of the Dismissal, the people respond: **"Thanks
be to God, alleluia, alleluia."***)*

*With Easter Time now concluded, the paschal candle is ex-
tinguished. It is desirable to keep the paschal candle in the
baptistery with due honour so that it is lit at the celebration of Baptism and the candles of those baptized are lit
from it.*

"Glory to the Father, the Son, and the Holy Spirit."

JUNE 11

THE MOST HOLY TRINITY

Solemnity

ENTRANCE ANTIPHON [Blessed Trinity]

Blest be God the Father, and the Only Begotten Son of God, and also the Holy Spirit, for he has shown us his merciful love. → No. 2, p. 10

COLLECT [Witnessing to the Trinity]

God our Father, who by sending into the world
the Word of truth and the Spirit of sanctification
made known to the human race your wondrous
    mystery,
grant us, we pray, that in professing the true faith,
we may acknowledge the Trinity of eternal glory
and adore your Unity, powerful in majesty.
Through our Lord Jesus Christ, your Son,
who lives and reigns with you in the unity of the
    Holy Spirit,
one God, for ever and ever. ℟. **Amen.** ↓

FIRST READING Ex. 34.4b-6, 8-9   [The One God]

Moses takes two stone tablets up on Mount Sinai.
Moses bows down in worship, asking the Lord to be
with his people and pardon their sins and offenses.

A reading from the book of Exodus.

MOSES rose early in the morning and went
up on Mount Sinai, as the Lord had commanded him, and took in his hand the two
tablets of stone. The Lord descended in the
cloud and stood with him there, and proclaimed
the name, "The Lord."

The Lord passed before Moses, and proclaimed, "The Lord, the Lord, a God merciful
and gracious, slow to anger, and abounding in
steadfast love and faithfulness."

And Moses quickly bowed his head toward
the earth, and worshipped. He said, "If now I
have found favour in your sight, O Lord, I pray,
let the Lord go with us. Although this is a stiff-
necked people, pardon our iniquity and our sin,
and take us for your inheritance."—The word of
the Lord. ℟. **Thanks be to God.** ↓

RESPONSORIAL PSALM Dan. 3   [Praise the Lord]

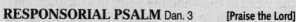

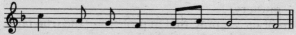

℟. **Glo - ry and praise for - ev - er!**

Blessed are you, O Lord, God of our fathers
and blessed is your glorious and holy name.—℟.

Blessed are you in the temple of your holy
    glory,
and to be extolled and highly glorified forever.—℟.

Blessed are you on the throne of your kingdom,
and to be extolled and highly exalted forever.—℞.

Blessed are you who look into the depths
from your throne on the cherubim.—℞.

Blessed are you in the firmament of heaven,
to be sung and glorified forever.—℞. ↓

SECOND READING 2 Cor. 13.11-13   [God's Fidelity]

Paul encourages the Corinthians to live showing the love of God among them—to live in harmony, peace, and love in the fellowship of the Holy Spirit.

A reading from the second Letter of Saint Paul
to the Corinthians.

BROTHERS and sisters, put things in order,
listen to my appeal, agree with one another,
live in peace; and the God of love and peace will
be with you. Greet one another with a holy kiss.
All the saints greet you.
   The grace of the Lord Jesus Christ, the love of
God, and the communion of the Holy Spirit be
with all of you.—The word of the Lord.
℞. **Thanks be to God.** ↓

GOSPEL ACCLAMATION See Rev. 1.8   [Triune God]
(If the Alleluia is not sung, the acclamation is omitted.)
℣. Alleluia. ℞. **Alleluia.**
℣. Glory to the Father, the Son, and the Holy Spirit:
to God who is, who was, and who is to come.
℞. **Alleluia.** ↓

GOSPEL Jn. 3.16-18   [God's Love]

God sent his Son into the world that whoever would believe would therefore have eternal life. Whoever does not believe, however, will be condemned.

℣. The Lord be with you. ℟. **And with your spirit.**
✞ A reading from the holy Gospel according to John. ℟. **Glory to you, O Lord.**

JESUS said to Nicodemus: "God so loved the world that he gave his only-begotten Son, so that everyone who believes in him may not perish but may have eternal life.

Indeed, God did not send the Son into the world to condemn the world, but in order that the world might be saved through him. The one who believes in him is not condemned; but the one who does not believe is condemned already, for not having believed in the name of the only-begotten Son of God."—The Gospel of the Lord. ℟. **Praise to you, Lord Jesus Christ.** → No. 15, p. 18

PRAYER OVER THE OFFERINGS   [Eternal Offering]
Sanctify by the invocation of your name,
we pray, O Lord our God,
this oblation of our service,
and by it make of us an eternal offering to you.
Through Christ our Lord. ℟. **Amen.** ↓

PREFACE (43)   [Mystery of the One Godhead]
℣. The Lord be with you. ℟. **And with your spirit.**
℣. Lift up your hearts. ℟. **We lift them up to the Lord.**
℣. Let us give thanks to the Lord our God. ℟. **It is right and just.**

It is truly right and just, our duty and our
    salvation,
always and everywhere to give you thanks,
Lord, holy Father, almighty and eternal God.

For with your Only Begotten Son and the Holy
    Spirit
you are one God, one Lord:
not in the unity of a single person,
but in a Trinity of one substance.

For what you have revealed to us of your glory
we believe equally of your Son
and of the Holy Spirit,
so that, in the confessing of the true and eternal
    Godhead,
you might be adored in what is proper to each
    Person,
their unity in substance,
and their equality in majesty.

For this is praised by Angels and Archangels,
Cherubim, too, and Seraphim,
who never cease to cry out each day,
as with one voice they acclaim: → No. 23, p. 23

COMMUNION ANTIPHON Gal. 4.6   [Abba, Father]
**Since you are children of God, God has sent into
your hearts the Spirit of his Son, the Spirit who
cries out: Abba, Father.** ↓

PRAYER AFTER COMMUNION   [Eternal Trinity]
May receiving this Sacrament, O Lord our God,
bring us health of body and soul,

as we confess your eternal holy Trinity and
    undivided Unity.
Through Christ our Lord.
℟. **Amen.**   → No. 30, p. 77

Optional Solemn Blessings, p. 97, and Prayers over the People, p. 105

"Behold the bread of angels. . . ."

JUNE 18

THE MOST HOLY BODY AND BLOOD OF CHRIST
(CORPUS CHRISTI)
Solemnity

ENTRANCE ANTIPHON Cf. Ps. 80.17   [Finest Wheat]

He fed them with the finest wheat and satisfied them with honey from the rock.   → No. 2, p. 10

COLLECT   [Memorial of Christ's Passion]

O God, who in this wonderful Sacrament
have left us a memorial of your Passion,
grant us, we pray,
so to revere the sacred mysteries of your Body
    and Blood
that we may always experience in ourselves
the fruits of your redemption.
Who live and reign with God the Father
in the unity of the Holy Spirit,
one God, for ever and ever. ℟. **Amen.** ↓

FIRST READING Deut. 8.2-3, 14-16 [Manna in the Desert]

Moses reminds the Israelites that although God let them hunger, still he fed them with manna, a food unknown. He brought them out of the slavery of Egypt and cared for them.

A reading from the book of Deuteronomy.

MOSES spoke to the people: "Remember the long way that the Lord your God has led you these forty years in the wilderness, in order to humble you, testing you to know what was in your heart, whether or not you would keep his commandments.

He humbled you by letting you hunger, then by feeding you with manna, with which neither you nor your ancestors were acquainted, in order to make you understand that man does not live by bread alone, but by every word that comes from the mouth of the Lord.

Do not exalt yourself, forgetting the Lord your God, who brought you out of the land of Egypt, out of the house of slavery, who led you through the great and terrible wilderness, an arid wasteland with poisonous snakes and scorpions. He made water flow for you from flint rock, and fed you in the wilderness with manna that your ancestors did not know, to humble you and to test you, and in the end to do you good."—The word of the Lord. ℟. **Thanks be to God.** ↓

RESPONSORIAL PSALM Ps. 147 [Finest of Wheat]

℟. Praise   the Lord,   Je - ru - sa-lem.

Or: ℟. **Alleluia!**

Praise the Lord, O Jerusalem!
Praise your God, O Zion!
For he strengthens the bars of your gates;
he blesses your children within you.—℞.

He grants peace within your borders;
he fills you with the finest of wheat.
He sends out his command to the earth;
his word runs swiftly.—℞.

He declares his word to Jacob,
his statutes and ordinances to Israel.
He has not dealt thus with any other nation;
they do not know his ordinances.—℞. ↓

SECOND READING 1 Cor. 10.16-17   **[Body and Blood]**

In the one bread and sharing the one cup, we are united in the Body and Blood of Jesus. We, though many, are still one body in Jesus.

A reading from the first Letter of Saint Paul
to the Corinthians.

BROTHERS and sisters: The cup of blessing that we bless, is it not a sharing in the Blood of Christ? The bread that we break, is it not a sharing in the Body of Christ?

Because there is one bread, we who are many are one body, for we all partake of the one bread.—The word of the Lord. ℞. **Thanks be to God.** ↓

SEQUENCE *(Lauda Sion)*   **[Praise of the Eucharist]**

The optional sequence (Lauda Sion) *is intended to be sung. The shorter version* (Ecce Panis) *begins at the asterisk.*

1. Laud, O Sion, your salvation,
laud with hymns of exultation
Christ, your King and Shepherd
true:
Bring him all the praise you know,
He is more than you bestow;
never can you reach his due.
2. Wondrous theme for glad
thanksgiving
is the living and life-giving
Bread today before you set,
from his hands of old partaken,
As we know, by faith unshaken,
where the Twelve at supper met.
3. Full and clear ring out your
chanting,
let not joy nor grace be wanting,
From your heart let praises burst.
For this day the Feast is holden,
When the institution olden
of that Supper was rehearsed.
4. Here the new law's new oblation,
by the new King's revelation,
Ends the forms of ancient rite.
Now the new the old effaces,
Substance now the shadow
chases,
light of day dispels the night.
5. What he did at supper seated,
Christ ordained to be repeated,
His remembrance not to cease.
And his rule for guidance taking,
Bread and wine we hallow, making,
thus, our sacrifice of peace.
6. This the truth each Christian
learns:
bread into his own flesh Christ
turns,
To his precious Blood the wine.
Sight must fail, no thought con-
ceives,
But a steadfast faith believes,
resting on a power divine.
7. Here beneath these signs are
hidden
priceless things to sense forbidden.
Signs alone, not things, we see:

Blood and flesh as wine, bread
broken;
Yet beneath each wondrous token,
Christ entire we know to be.
8. All who of this great food partake,
they sever not the Lord, nor break:
Christ is whole to all that taste.
Be one or be a thousand fed
They eat alike that living Bread,
eat of him who cannot waste.
9. Good and guilty likewise sharing,
though their different ends prepar-
ing:
timeless death, or blessed life.
Life to these, to those damnation,
Even like participation
is with unlike outcomes rife.
10. When the sacrament is broken,
doubt not, but believe as spoken,
That each severed outward token
does the very whole contain.
None that precious gift divides,
breaking but the sign betides.
Jesus still the same abides,
still unbroken he remains.
*11. Hail, the food of Angels given
to the pilgrim who has striven,
to the child as bread from heaven,
food alone for spirit meant:
Now the former types fulfilling—
Isaac bound, a victim willing,
Paschal Lamb, its life-blood
spilling,
manna to the ancients sent.
12. Bread yourself, good Shepherd, tend us;
Jesus, with your love befriend us.
You refresh us and defend us;
to your lasting goodness send us
That the land of life we see.
Lord, who all things both rule and
know,
who on this earth such food bestow,
Grant that with your saints we follow
to that banquet ever hallow,
With them heirs and guests to be. ↓

GOSPEL ACCLAMATION Jn. 6.51-52   [Living Bread]

(If the Alleluia is not sung, the acclamation is omitted.)

℣. Alleluia. ℟. **Alleluia.**
℣. I am the living bread that came down from
    heaven, says the Lord;
whoever eats of this bread will live forever.
℟. **Alleluia.** ↓

GOSPEL Jn. 6.51-59   [True Food, True Drink]

> **Jesus speaks of his Body and Blood in the holy eu-
> charist. Whoever receives the holy eucharist will be
> raised up on the last day; whoever eats this bread will
> live forever.**

℣. The Lord be with you. ℟. **And with your spirit.**
✤ A reading from the holy Gospel according to
John. ℟. **Glory to you, O Lord.**

JESUS said to the people: "I am the living
    bread that came down from heaven. Whoever
eats of this bread will live forever; and the
bread that I will give for the life of the world is
my flesh."

The people then disputed among themselves,
saying, "How can this man give us his flesh to
eat?"

So Jesus said to them, "Very truly, I tell you,
unless you eat the flesh of the Son of Man and
drink his blood, you have no life in you. Whoever eats my flesh and drinks my blood has
eternal life, and I will raise them up on the last
day; for my flesh is true food and my blood is
true drink. Whoever eats my flesh and drinks
my blood abides in me, and I in them.

Just as the living Father sent me, and I live because of the Father, so whoever eats me will live because of me. This is the bread that came down from heaven, not like that which your ancestors ate, and they died. But the one who eats this bread will live forever."

Jesus said these things while he was teaching in the synagogue at Capernaum.—The Gospel of the Lord. ℟. **Praise to you, Lord Jesus Christ.**

→ No. 15, p. 18

PRAYER OVER THE OFFERINGS   [Unity and Peace]

Grant your Church, O Lord, we pray,
the gifts of unity and peace,
whose signs are to be seen in mystery
in the offerings we here present.
Through Christ our Lord.
℟. **Amen.**   → No. 21, p. 22 (Pref. 47-48)

COMMUNION ANTIPHON Jn. 6.57   [Eucharistic Life]

Whoever eats my flesh and drinks my blood remains in me and I in him, says the Lord. ↓

PRAYER AFTER COMMUNION   [Divine Life]

Grant, O Lord, we pray,
that we may delight for all eternity
in that share in your divine life,
which is foreshadowed in the present age
by our reception of your precious Body and
    Blood.
Who live and reign for ever and ever.
℟. **Amen.**   → No. 30, p. 77

Optional Solemn Blessings, p. 97, and Prayers over the People, p. 105

"What I say to you in the dark, tell in the light."

JUNE 25

12th SUNDAY IN ORDINARY TIME

ENTRANCE ANTIPHON Cf. Ps. 27.8-9   [Saving Refuge]

The Lord is the strength of his people, a saving refuge for the one he has anointed. Save your people, Lord, and bless your heritage, and govern them for ever.   ➜ No. 2, p. 10

COLLECT   [Foundation of God's Love]

Grant, O Lord,
that we may always revere and love your holy
    name,
for you never deprive of your guidance
those you set firm on the foundation of your
    love.
Through our Lord Jesus Christ, your Son,
who lives and reigns with you in the unity of the
    Holy Spirit,
one God, for ever and ever.
℟. **Amen.** ↓

453

FIRST READING Jer. 20.10-13   [The Lord Our Champion]

Jeremiah, a man chosen by God, tells how threatened his life is. His enemies lurk on every side, anxious to take vengeance on him. The Lord will protect him and confound the evildoers.

A reading from the book of the
Prophet Jeremiah.

JEREMIAH cried out:
I hear many whispering:
"Terror is all around!
Denounce him! Let us denounce him!"
All my close friends
are watching for me to stumble.
"Perhaps he can be enticed,
and we can prevail against him,
and take our revenge on him."

But the Lord is with me like a dread warrior;
therefore my persecutors will stumble,
and they will not prevail.
They will be greatly shamed,
for they will not succeed.
Their eternal dishonour
will never be forgotten.

O Lord of hosts, you test the righteous,
you see the heart and the mind;
let me see your retribution upon them,
for to you I have committed my cause.

Sing to the Lord;
praise the Lord!
For he has delivered the life of the needy
from the hands of evildoers.

The word of the Lord. ℟. **Thanks be to God.** ↓

RESPONSORIAL PSALM Ps. 69   [The Lord's Kindness]

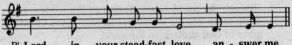

℞. Lord,   in   your stead-fast love,   an - swer me.

It is for your sake that I have borne reproach,
that shame has covered my face.
I have become a stranger to my kindred,
an alien to my mother's children.
It is zeal for your house that has consumed me;
the insults of those who insult you have fallen
    on me.—℞.

But as for me, my prayer is to you, O Lord.
At an acceptable time, O God,
in the abundance of your steadfast love, answer
    me.
With your steadfast help, rescue me.
Answer me, O Lord, for your steadfast love is
    good;
according to your abundant mercy, turn to me.
    —℞.

Let the oppressed see it and be glad;
you who seek God, let your hearts revive.
For the Lord hears the needy,
and does not despise his own that are in bonds.
Let heaven and earth praise him,
the seas and everything that moves in them.
    —℞. ↓

SECOND READING Rom. 5.12-15   [The Grace of God]

**Through the sin of Adam, death and the consequences
of sin came into the world. But through Jesus Christ the
grace of God abounds in the world.**

A reading from the Letter of Saint Paul
to the Romans.

BROTHERS and sisters: Just as sin came into
the world through one man, and death came
through sin, so death spread to all people because all have sinned.

Sin was indeed in the world before the law,
but sin is not reckoned when there is no law. Yet
death exercised dominion from Adam to Moses,
even over those whose sins were not like the
transgression of Adam, who is a type of the one
who was to come.

But the free gift is not like the trespass. For if
the many died through the one man's trespass,
much more surely have the grace of God and the
free gift in the grace of the one man, Jesus
Christ, abounded for the many.—The word of the
Lord. ℟. **Thanks be to God.** ↓

GOSPEL ACCLAMATION See Jn. 15.26, 27 [God's Truth]

(If the Alleluia is not sung, the acclamation is omitted.)

℣. Alleluia. ℟. **Alleluia.**

℣. The Spirit of truth will testify on my behalf,
says the Lord,
and you also are to testify.

℟. **Alleluia.** ↓

GOSPEL Mt. 10.26-33   [Witnesses for Christ]

**Jesus directs his apostles to fear no humans. All truth
will become known. He describes the worth of human**

beings in the eyes of God who knows all things. Whoever confesses Jesus before others will be saved.

℣. The Lord be with you. ℟. **And with your spirit.**
✛ A reading from the holy Gospel according to
Matthew. ℟. **Glory to you, O Lord.**

JESUS said to his Apostles: "Fear no one; for nothing is covered up that will not be uncovered, and nothing secret that will not become known. What I say to you in the dark, tell in the light; and what you hear whispered, proclaim from the housetops.

Do not fear those who kill the body but cannot kill the soul; rather fear him who can destroy both soul and body in hell. Are not two sparrows sold for a penny? Yet not one of them will fall to the ground apart from your Father. And even the hairs of your head are all counted. So do not be afraid; you are of more value than many sparrows.

Everyone therefore who acknowledges me before humans, I also will acknowledge before my Father in heaven; but whoever denies me before humans, I also will deny before my Father in heaven."—The Gospel of the Lord. ℟. **Praise to you, Lord Jesus Christ.** → No. 15, p. 18

PRAYER OVER THE OFFERINGS   [Pleasing Offering]

Receive, O Lord, the sacrifice of conciliation and
    praise
and grant that, cleansed by its action,
we may make offering of a heart pleasing to you.
Through Christ our Lord.
℟. **Amen.**   → No. 21, p. 22 (Pref. 29-36)

COMMUNION ANTIPHON Ps. 144.15

[Divine Food]

The eyes of all look to you, Lord, and you give them their food in due season. ↓

OR Jn. 10.11, 15   [The Good Shepherd]

I am the Good Shepherd, and I lay down my life for my sheep, says the Lord. ↓

PRAYER AFTER COMMUNION

[Pledge of Redemption]

Renewed and nourished
by the Sacred Body and Precious Blood of your
    Son,
we ask of your mercy, O Lord,
that what we celebrate with constant devotion
may be our sure pledge of redemption.
Through Christ our Lord.
℟. **Amen.**   ➜ No. 30, p. 77

Optional Solemn Blessings, p. 97, and Prayers over the People, p. 105

"Whoever does not take up their cross and follow me is not worthy of me."

JULY 2

13th SUNDAY IN ORDINARY TIME

ENTRANCE ANTIPHON Ps. 46.2   [Shouts of Joy]

All peoples, clap your hands. Cry to God with shouts of joy! <section>→ No. 2, p. 10</section>

COLLECT   [Children of Light]

O God, who through the grace of adoption
chose us to be children of light,
grant, we pray,
that we may not be wrapped in the darkness of
   error
but always be seen to stand in the bright light of
   truth.
Through our Lord Jesus Christ, your Son,
who lives and reigns with you in the unity of the
   Holy Spirit,
one God, for ever and ever. ℟. **Amen.** ↓

459

FIRST READING 2 Kgs. 4.8-12a, 14-16

[Rewards of Hospitality]

The woman received Elisha into her home because she knew he was "a holy man of God," a preacher, which means in the Bible "a bearer of God's word." We should accept our priests as such, especially when listening to the homily.

A reading from the second book of Kings.

ONE day Elisha was passing through Shunem, where a wealthy woman lived, who urged him to have a meal. So whenever he passed that way, he would stop there for a meal. She said to her husband, "Look, I am sure that this man who regularly passes our way is a holy man of God. Let us make a small roof chamber with walls, and put there for him a bed, a table, a chair, and a lamp, so that he can stay there whenever he comes to us."

One day when Elisha came there, he went up to the chamber and lay down there. He said to his servant Gehazi, "What then may be done for the woman?" Gehazi answered, "Well, she has no son, and her husband is old." Elisha said, "Call her." When the servant had called her, she stood at the door. Elisha said, "At this season, in due time, you shall embrace a son."—The word of the Lord. ℟. **Thanks be to God.** ↓

RESPONSORIAL PSALM Ps. 89   [Eternal Gratitude]

℟. For - ev - er   I will sing of your stead-fast love, O Lord.

I will sing of your steadfast love, O Lord, for-
    ever;
with my mouth I will proclaim your faithfulness
    to all generations.
I declare that your steadfast love is established
    forever;
your faithfulness is as firm as the heavens.—℟.

Blessed are the people who know the festal
    shout,
who walk, O Lord, in the light of your counte-
    nance;
they exult in your name all day long,
and extol your righteousness.—℟.

For you are the glory of their strength;
by your favour our horn is exalted.
For our shield belongs to the Lord,
our king to the Holy One of Israel.—℟. ↓

SECOND READING Rom. 6.3-4, 8-11 [Baptized into Christ]

**Through the waters of baptism we rise to a new life of
grace in Jesus who was buried and came back to life. In
the same way we who were dead to sin become alive
for God in Jesus.**

A reading from the Letter of Saint Paul to the
Romans.

BROTHERS and sisters: All of us who have
been baptized into Christ Jesus were baptized into his death. Therefore we have been
buried with him by baptism into death, so that,
just as Christ was raised from the dead by the

glory of the Father, so we too might walk in newness of life.

But if we have died with Christ, we believe that we will also live with him. We know that Christ, being raised from the dead, will never die again; death no longer has dominion over him. The death he died, he died to sin, once for all; but the life he lives, he lives to God.

So you also must consider yourselves dead to sin and alive to God in Christ Jesus.—The word of the Lord. ℟. **Thanks be to God.** ↓

GOSPEL ACCLAMATION See 1 Pet. 2.9   [Praise God]
(If the Alleluia is not sung, the acclamation is omitted.)

℣. Alleluia. ℟. **Alleluia.**

℣. You are a chosen race, a royal priesthood, a holy nation.

Praise God who called you out of darkness into his marvellous light.

℟. **Alleluia.** ↓

GOSPEL Mt. 10.37-42   [Welcoming Christ's Workers]

Jesus speaks of the supreme commandment of God. Those who do not carry their cross for Jesus are not worthy of him. Jesus also describes the tremendous rewards for those who show love for him and for others.

℣. The Lord be with you. ℟. **And with your spirit.**
✚ A reading from the holy Gospel according to Matthew. ℟. **Glory to you, O Lord.**

JESUS said to his Apostles: "Whoever loves father or mother more than me is not worthy of me; and whoever loves son or daughter more than me is not worthy of me; and whoever does not take up their cross and follow me is not worthy of me. Whoever finds their life will lose it, and whoever loses their life for my sake will find it.

Whoever welcomes you welcomes me, and whoever welcomes me welcomes the one who sent me. Whoever welcomes a prophet in the name of a prophet will receive a prophet's reward; and whoever welcomes a righteous person in the name of a righteous person will receive the reward of the righteous; and whoever gives even a cup of cold water to one of these little ones in the name of a disciple—truly I tell you—that person will not lose their reward."—The Gospel of the Lord.
℟. **Praise to you, Lord Jesus Christ.**   → No. 15, p. 18

PRAYER OVER THE OFFERINGS   [Serving God]

O God, who graciously accomplish
the effects of your mysteries,
grant, we pray,
that the deeds by which we serve you
may be worthy of these sacred gifts.
Through Christ our Lord.
℟. **Amen.**   → No. 21, p. 22 (Pref. 29-36)

COMMUNION ANTIPHON Cf. Ps. 102.1
[Bless the Lord]

Bless the Lord, O my soul, and all within me, his holy name. ↓

OR Jn. 17.20-21   [One in God]

O Father, I pray for them, that they may be one in us, that the world may believe that you have sent me, says the Lord. ↓

PRAYER AFTER COMMUNION   [Lasting Charity]

May this divine sacrifice we have offered and
  received
fill us with life, O Lord, we pray,
so that, bound to you in lasting charity,
we may bear fruit that lasts for ever.
Through Christ our Lord.

℟. **Amen.**

→ No. 30, p. 77

Optional Solemn Blessings, p. 97, and Prayers over the People, p. 105

"Come to me, all you that are weary and are carrying
heavy burdens, and I will give you rest."

JULY 9

14th SUNDAY IN ORDINARY TIME

ENTRANCE ANTIPHON Cf. Ps. 47.10-11   [God's Love]

**Your merciful love, O God, we have received in
the midst of your temple. Your praise, O God, like
your name, reaches the ends of the earth; your
right hand is filled with saving justice.**

→ No. 2, p. 10

COLLECT [Holy Joy]

O God, who in the abasement of your Son
have raised up a fallen world,
fill your faithful with holy joy,
for on those you have rescued from slavery to sin
you bestow eternal gladness.
Through our Lord Jesus Christ, your Son,
who lives and reigns with you in the unity of the
    Holy Spirit,
one God, for ever and ever. ℟. **Amen.** ↓

FIRST READING Zech. 9.9-10 [Portrait of the Messiah]

**Zechariah foretells the coming of the Messiah. Rejoic-
ing shall come to Jerusalem. He shall bring peace to all
nations and he shall rule over them.**

A reading from the book of the Prophet Zechariah.

THUS says the Lord:
Rejoice greatly, O daughter Zion!
Shout aloud, O daughter Jerusalem!
Lo, your king comes to you;
triumphant and victorious is he,
humble and riding on a donkey,
on a colt, the foal of a donkey.

He will cut off the chariot from Ephraim
and the war horse from Jerusalem;
and the warrior's bow shall be cut off,
and he shall command peace to the nations;
his dominion shall be from sea to sea,
and from the River to the ends of the earth.

The word of the Lord. ℟. **Thanks be to God.** ↓

RESPONSORIAL PSALM Ps. 145   [God's Mercy]

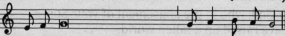

R̸. **I will bless your name for ever,   my King and my God.**
Or: R̸. **Alleluia!**

I will extol you, my God and King,
and bless your name forever and ever.
Every day I will bless you,
and praise your name forever and ever.—R̸.

The Lord is gracious and merciful,
slow to anger and abounding in steadfast love.
The Lord is good to all,
and his compassion is over all that he has
   made.—R̸.

All your works shall give thanks to you, O Lord,
and all your faithful shall bless you.
They shall speak of the glory of your kingdom,
and tell of your power.—R̸.

The Lord is faithful in all his words,
and gracious in all his deeds.
The Lord upholds all who are falling,
and raises up all who are bowed down.—R̸. ↓

SECOND READING Rom. 8.9, 11-13 [The Spirit of Christ]

Although we are both flesh and spirit, we must live according to the Spirit of God who dwells in us. This is a pledge for life if we die to sin and live by the Spirit.

A reading from the Letter of Saint Paul
         to the Romans.

BROTHERS and sisters: You are not in the flesh; you are in the Spirit, since the Spirit of God dwells in you. Anyone who does not have the Spirit of Christ does not belong to him.

If the Spirit of God who raised Jesus from the dead dwells in you, he who raised Christ from the dead will give life to your mortal bodies also through his Spirit that dwells in you.

So then, brothers and sisters, we are debtors, not to the flesh, to live according to the flesh—for if you live according to the flesh, you will die; but if by the Spirit you put to death the deeds of the body, you will live.—The word of the Lord. ℟. **Thanks be to God.** ↓

GOSPEL ACCLAMATION See Mt. 11.25   [Little Ones]

(If the Alleluia is not sung, the acclamation is omitted.)

℣. Alleluia. ℟. **Alleluia.**

℣. Blessed are you, Father, Lord of heaven and earth;

you have revealed to little ones the mysteries of the kingdom.

℟. **Alleluia.** ↓

GOSPEL Mt. 11.25-30   [Solace in Christ]

Jesus gives praise to his Father. No one knows the Son but the Father and those to whom the Father reveals this truth. Jesus calls to himself those who are troubled and weary that they may find refreshment.

℣. The Lord be with you. ℟. **And with your spirit.**
✛ A reading from the holy Gospel according to Matthew. ℟. **Glory to you, O Lord.**

A T that time Jesus said, "I thank you, Father, Lord of heaven and earth, because you have hidden these things from the wise and the intelligent and have revealed them to infants; yes, Father, for such was your gracious will."

He continued: "All things have been handed over to me by my Father; and no one knows the Son except the Father, and no one knows the Father except the Son and anyone to whom the Son chooses to reveal him.

Come to me, all you that are weary and are carrying heavy burdens, and I will give you rest. Take my yoke upon you, and learn from me; for I am gentle and humble in heart, and you will find rest for your souls. For my yoke is easy, and my burden is light."—The Gospel of the Lord. ℟. **Praise to you, Lord Jesus Christ.** ➤ No. 15, p. 18

PRAYER OVER THE OFFERINGS   [Purify Us]

May this oblation dedicated to your name
purify us, O Lord,
and day by day bring our conduct
closer to the life of heaven
℟. **Amen.**   ➤ No. 21, p. 22 (Pref. 29-36)

COMMUNION ANTIPHON Ps. 33.9
[The Lord's Goodness]

Taste and see that the Lord is good; blessed the man who seeks refuge in him. ↓

OR Mt. 11.28   [Refuge in God]

Come to me, all who labour and are burdened, and I will refresh you, says the Lord. ↓

PRAYER AFTER COMMUNION [Salvation and Praise]

Grant, we pray, O Lord,
that, having been replenished by such great gifts,
we may gain the prize of salvation
and never cease to praise you.
Through Christ our Lord.
℟. **Amen.**   → No. 30, p. 77

Optional Solemn Blessings, p. 97, and Prayers over the People, p. 105

"A sower went out to sow. . . ."

JULY 16

15th SUNDAY IN ORDINARY TIME

ENTRANCE ANTIPHON Cf. Ps. 16.15   [God's Face]

As for me, in justice I shall behold your face; I shall be filled with the vision of your glory.

→ No. 2, p. 10

COLLECT   [Right Path]

O God, who show the light of your truth
to those who go astray,
so that they may return to the right path,
give all who for the faith they profess
are accounted Christians
the grace to reject whatever is contrary to the
    name of Christ
and to strive after all that does it honour.
Through our Lord Jesus Christ, your Son,
who lives and reigns with you in the unity of the
    Holy Spirit,
one God, for ever and ever. ℟. **Amen.** ↓

FIRST READING Isa. 55.10-11   [God's Fruitful Word]

> Isaiah uses the example of rain and snow seeping into
> the ground to make it fertile to show how the word of
> God filters into the hearts of humans.

A reading from the book of the Prophet Isaiah.

THUS says the Lord:
  "As the rain and the snow come down from
  heaven,
and do not return there until they have watered
  the earth,
making it bring forth and sprout,
giving seed to the sower and bread to the one who
  eats,
so shall my word be that goes out from my mouth;
it shall not return to me empty,
but it shall accomplish that which I purpose,
and succeed in the thing for which I sent it."

The word of the Lord. ℟. **Thanks be to God.** ↓

RESPONSORIAL PSALM Ps. 65   [Fruitful Harvest]

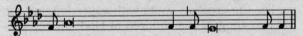

℟. The seed that fell on good soil pro-duced a   hun - dredfold.

You visit the earth and water it,
you greatly enrich it;
the river of God is full of water;
you provide the people with grain.—℟.

For so you have prepared the earth:
you water its furrows abundantly,
settling its ridges, softening it with showers,
and blessing its growth.—℟.

You crown the year with your bounty;
your pathways overflow with richness.
The pastures of the wilderness overflow,
the hills gird themselves with joy.

R/. **The seed that fell on good soil produced a
     hundredfold.**

The meadows clothe themselves with flocks,
the valleys deck themselves with grain,
they shout and sing together for joy.—R/. ↓

SECOND READING Rom. 8.18-23   [Future Redemption]

**The sufferings and trials of the present are destined to
be only a prelude to the glorious future of the children
of God. During this life we await the redemption of our
bodies.**

A reading from the Letter of Saint Paul
to the Romans.

BROTHERS and sisters: I consider that the sufferings of this present time are not worth
comparing with the glory about to be revealed to
us. For the creation waits with eager longing for
the revealing of the children of God; for the creation was subjected to futility, not of its own will
but by the will of the one who subjected it, in
hope that the creation itself will be set free from
its bondage to decay and will obtain the freedom
of the glory of the children of God.

We know that the whole creation has been
groaning in labour pains until now; and not only
the creation, but we ourselves, who have the first
fruits of the Spirit, groan inwardly while we wait
for adoption to sonship, the redemption of our bodies.—The word of the Lord. R/. **Thanks be to God.** ↓

GOSPEL ACCLAMATION See Lk. 8.11

[Christ the Sower]

(If the Alleluia is not sung, the acclamation is omitted.)

℣. Alleluia. ℟. **Alleluia.**

℣. The seed is the word of God, Christ is the sower;

all who come to him will live for ever.

℟. **Alleluia.** ↓

GOSPEL Mt. 13.1-23 or 13.1-9   [Parable of the Sower]

Jesus teaches in parables that can be easily understood. He speaks of sowing the message of salvation which by some is heeded for a while, or ignored. Others, however, listen intently and try to live according to the will of God. Jesus explains this parable in detail.

[If the "Shorter Form" is used, the indented text in brackets is omitted.]

℣. The Lord be with you. ℟. **And with your spirit.**

✝ A reading from the holy Gospel according to Matthew. ℟. **Glory to you, O Lord.**

JESUS went out of the house and sat beside the sea. Such great crowds gathered around him that he got into a boat and sat there, while the whole crowd stood on the beach. And he told them many things in parables.

"Listen! A sower went out to sow. And as he sowed, some seeds fell on the path, and the birds came and ate them up. Other seeds fell on rocky ground, where they did not have much soil, and they sprang up quickly, since they had no depth of soil. But when the sun rose, they were scorched; and since they had no root, they withered away. Other seeds fell among thorns, and the thorns grew up and choked them. Other seeds fell on good soil and brought forth grain, some a hundredfold, some sixty, some thirty.

Let anyone with ears listen!"

[Then the disciples came and asked Jesus, "Why do you speak to them in parables?" He answered, "To you it has been given to know the secrets of the kingdom of heaven, but to them it has not been given. For to those who have, more will be given, and they will have an abundance; but from those who have nothing, even what they have will be taken away.

The reason I speak to them in parables is that 'seeing they do not perceive, and hearing they do not listen, nor do they understand.' With them indeed is fulfilled the prophecy of Isaiah that says:

'You will indeed listen, but never understand,

and you will indeed look, but never perceive.

For this people's heart has grown dull,

and their ears are hard of hearing,

and they have shut their eyes;

so that they might not look with their eyes,

and listen with their ears,

and understand with their heart and turn—

and I would heal them.'

But blessed are your eyes, for they see, and your ears, for they hear. Truly I tell you, many Prophets and righteous people longed to see what you see, but did not see it, and to hear what you hear, but did not hear it.

Hear then the parable of the sower. When anyone hears the word of the kingdom and does not understand it, the evil one comes and snatches away what is sown in the heart; this is what was sown on the path. As for what was sown on rocky ground, this is the one who hears the word and immediately receives it with joy; yet such a person has no root, but endures only for a while, and when trouble or persecution arises on account of the word, that person immediately falls away. As for what was sown among thorns, this is the one who hears the word, but the cares of the world and the lure of wealth choke the word, and it yields nothing.

But as for what was sown on good soil, this is the one who hears the word and understands it, who indeed bears fruit and yields, in one case a hundredfold, in another sixty, and in another thirty."]

The Gospel of the Lord. ℟. **Praise to you, Lord Jesus Christ.**   ➤ No. 15, p. 18

PRAYER OVER THE OFFERINGS   [Greater Holiness]

Look upon the offerings of the Church, O Lord,
as she makes her prayer to you,
and grant that, when consumed by those who
    believe,
they may bring ever greater holiness.

Through Christ our Lord.
R/. **Amen.** → No. 21, p. 22 (Pref. 29-36)

COMMUNION ANTIPHON Cf. Ps. 83.4-5

[The Lord's House]

The sparrow finds a home, and the swallow a nest for her young: by your altars, O Lord of hosts, my King and my God. Blessed are they who dwell in your house, for ever singing your praise. ↓

OR Jn. 6.57 [Remain in Jesus]

Whoever eats my flesh and drinks my blood remains in me and I in him, says the Lord. ↓

PRAYER AFTER COMMUNION [Saving Effects]

Having consumed these gifts, we pray, O Lord,
that, by our participation in this mystery,
its saving effects upon us may grow.
Through Christ our Lord.
R/. **Amen.** → No. 30, p. 77

Optional Solemn Blessings, p. 97, and Prayers over the People, p. 105

"An enemy came and sowed weeds among the wheat."

JULY 23

16th SUNDAY IN ORDINARY TIME

ENTRANCE ANTIPHON Ps. 53.6, 8   [God Our Help]

See, I have God for my help. The Lord sustains
my soul. I will sacrifice to you with willing heart,
and praise your name, O Lord, for it is good.

→ No. 2, p. 10

COLLECT   [Keeping God's Commands]

Show favour, O Lord, to your servants
and mercifully increase the gifts of your grace,
that, made fervent in hope, faith and charity,
they may be ever watchful in keeping your
    commands.
Through our Lord Jesus Christ, your Son,
who lives and reigns with you in the unity of the
    Holy Spirit,
one God, for ever and ever.
℟. **Amen.** ↓

FIRST READING Wis. 12.13, 16-19   [God's Mercy]

The real source of might and power is justice. Through justice we become masters of our power. We can become lenient and kind and encourage repentance for sin.

A reading from the book of Wisdom.

THERE is no god besides you, Lord,
  whose care is for all people,
to whom you should prove that you have not judged unjustly.

For your strength is the source of righteousness,
and your sovereignty over all causes you to spare all.
For you show your strength
when people doubt the completeness of your power,
and you rebuke any insolence among those who know it.

Although you are sovereign in strength,
you judge with mildness,
and with great forbearance you govern us;
for you have power to act whenever you choose.

Through such works you have taught your people
that the righteous must be kind,
and you have filled your children with good hope,
because you give repentance for sins.

The word of the Lord. ℟. **Thanks be to God.** ↓

RESPONSORIAL PSALM Ps. 86 [Kindness and Fidelity]

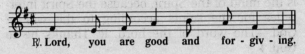

℟. Lord, you are good and for-giv-ing.

You, O Lord, are good and forgiving,
abounding in steadfast love to all who call on
    you.
Give ear, O Lord, to my prayer;
listen to my cry of supplication.—℟.

All the nations you have made shall come
and bow down before you, O Lord,
and shall glorify your name.
For you are great and do wondrous things;
you alone are God.—℟.

But you, O Lord, are a God merciful and gra-
    cious,
slow to anger and abounding in steadfast love
    and faithfulness.
Turn to me and be gracious to me.
Give your strength to your servant.—℟. ↓

SECOND READING Rom. 8.26-27 [Intercession of Spirit]

Through the Spirit our weakness in prayer is overcome.
He searches our hearts and intercedes on our behalf.

A reading from the Letter of Saint Paul
to the Romans.

BROTHERS and sisters: The Spirit helps us in
our weakness; for we do not know how to
pray as we ought, but that very Spirit intercedes
with sighs too deep for words.

And God, who searches the heart, knows what is the mind of the Spirit, because the Spirit intercedes for the saints according to the will of God.—The word of the Lord. ℟. **Thanks be to God.** ↓

GOSPEL ACCLAMATION See Mt. 11.25   **[Little Ones]**
(If the Alleluia is not sung, the acclamation is omitted.)

℣. Alleluia. ℟. **Alleluia.**

℣. Blessed are you, Father, Lord of heaven and earth;

you have revealed to little ones the mysteries of the kingdom.

℟. **Alleluia.** ↓

GOSPEL Mt. 13.24-43 or 13.24-33   **[Parable of the Weeds]**

Jesus teaches about God's reign in parables. His kingdom is like a field in which good grain and weeds grow. At harvest time the good will be sorted from the bad. God's kingdom is also like a mustard plant reaching out to embrace all as it grows.

[If the "Shorter Form" is used, the indented text in brackets is omitted.]

℣. The Lord be with you. ℟. **And with your spirit.**
✣ A reading from the holy Gospel according to Matthew. ℟. **Glory to you, O Lord.**

JESUS put before the crowds a parable: "The kingdom of heaven may be compared to someone who sowed good seed in his field; but while everybody was asleep, an enemy came and sowed weeds among the wheat, and then went away.

So when the plants came up and bore grain, then the weeds appeared as well. And the slaves of the householder came and said to him, 'Master, did you not sow good seed in your field? Where, then, did these weeds come from?' He answered, 'An enemy has done this.' The slaves said to him, 'Then do you want us to go and gather them?' But he replied, 'No; for in gathering the weeds you would uproot the wheat along with them. Let both of them grow together until the harvest; and at harvest time I will tell the reapers, Collect the weeds first and bind them in bundles to be burned, but gather the wheat into my barn.'"

Jesus put before them another parable: "The kingdom of heaven is like a mustard seed that someone took and sowed in his field; it is the smallest of all the seeds, but when it has grown it is the greatest of shrubs and becomes a tree, so that the birds of the air come and make nests in its branches."

He told them another parable: "The kingdom of heaven is like yeast that a woman took and mixed in with three measures of flour until all of it was leavened."

[Jesus told the crowds all these things in parables; without a parable he told them nothing. This was to fulfill what had been spoken through the Prophet:

"I will open my mouth to speak in parables;
  I will proclaim what has been hidden from
    the foundation of the world."

Then Jesus left the crowds and went into the house. And his disciples approached him, saying, "Explain to us the parable of the weeds of the field." He answered, "The one who sows the good seed is the Son of Man; the field is the world, and the good seed are the children of the kingdom; the weeds are the children of the evil one, and the enemy who sowed them is the devil; the harvest is the end of the age, and the reapers are Angels.

Just as the weeds are collected and burned up with fire, so will it be at the end of the age. The Son of Man will send his Angels, and they will collect out of his kingdom all causes of sin and all evildoers, and they will throw them into the furnace of fire, where there will be weeping and gnashing of teeth. Then the righteous will shine like the sun in the kingdom of their Father. Let anyone with ears listen!"]

The Gospel of the Lord. ℟. **Praise to you, Lord Jesus Christ.** ➜ No. 15, p. 18

PRAYER OVER THE OFFERINGS [Saving Offerings]

O God, who in the one perfect sacrifice
brought to completion varied offerings of the law,
accept, we pray, this sacrifice from your faithful
  servants
and make it holy, as you blessed the gifts of Abel,
so that what each has offered to the honour of
  your majesty
may benefit the salvation of all.
Through Christ our Lord.
℟. **Amen.** ➜ No. 21, p. 22 (Pref. 29-36)

COMMUNION ANTIPHON Ps. 110.4-5

[Jesus Gives]

The Lord, the gracious, the merciful, has made a memorial of his wonders; he gives food to those who fear him. ↓

OR Rev. 3.20   [Jesus Knocks]

Behold, I stand at the door and knock, says the Lord. If anyone hears my voice and opens the door to me, I will enter his house and dine with him, and he with me. ↓

PRAYER AFTER COMMUNION   [New Life]

Graciously be present to your people, we pray, O Lord,
and lead those you have imbued with heavenly mysteries
to pass from former ways to newness of life.
Through Christ our Lord.
℟. **Amen.**   → No. 30, p. 77

Optional Solemn Blessings, p. 97, and Prayers over the People, p. 105

"The kingdom of heaven is like treasure . . .
a merchant in search of fine pearls . . . a net."

JULY 30

17th SUNDAY IN ORDINARY TIME

ENTRANCE ANTIPHON Cf. Ps. 67.6-7, 36

[God Our Strength]

**God is in his holy place, God who unites those
who dwell in his house; he himself gives might
and strength to his people.** ➙ No. 2, p. 10

COLLECT [Enduring Things]

O God, protector of those who hope in you,
without whom nothing has firm foundation,
　　nothing is holy,
bestow in abundance your mercy upon us
and grant that, with you as our ruler and guide,
we may use the good things that pass
in such a way as to hold fast even now
to those that ever endure.
Through our Lord Jesus Christ, your Son,

484

who lives and reigns with you in the unity of the
   Holy Spirit,
one God, for ever and ever. ℟. **Amen.** ↓

FIRST READING 1 Kgs. 3.5-12   [Gift of Understanding]

Solomon prays for wisdom to lead the people of God.
God is pleased that Solomon asked above all else to
know right from wrong. God promises him wisdom and
understanding that will be unequalled either in times
past or in the future.

A reading from the first book of Kings.

AT Gibeon the Lord appeared to Solomon in a
   dream by night; and God said, "Ask what I
should give you." And Solomon said, "You have
shown great and steadfast love to your servant
my father David, because he walked before you in
faithfulness, in righteousness, and in uprightness
of heart toward you; and you have kept for him
this great and steadfast love, and have given him
a son to sit on his throne today.

And now, O Lord my God, you have made your
servant king in place of my father David, although I am only a little child; I do not know how
to go out or come in. And your servant is in the
midst of the people whom you have chosen, a
great people, so numerous they cannot be numbered or counted.

Give your servant therefore an understanding
mind to govern your people, able to discern between good and evil; for who can govern this,
your great people?"

It pleased the Lord that Solomon had asked
this. God said to him, "Because you have asked

this, and have not asked for yourself long life or riches, or for the life of your enemies, but have asked for yourself understanding to discern what is right, I now do according to your word. Indeed I give you a wise and discerning mind; no one like you has been before you and no one like you shall arise after you."—The word of the Lord. ℟. **Thanks be to God.** ↓

RESPONSORIAL PSALM Ps. 119   [The Lord's Decrees]

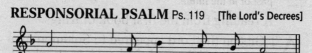

℟. **Lord,   how I   love your law!**

The Lord is my portion;
I promise to keep your words.
The law of your mouth is better to me
than thousands of gold and silver pieces.—℟.

Let your steadfast love become my comfort
according to your promise to your servant.
Let your mercy come to me, that I may live;
for your law is my delight.—℟.

Truly I love your commandments more than
    gold,
more than fine gold.
Truly I direct my steps by all your precepts;
I hate every false way.—℟.

Your decrees are wonderful;
therefore my soul keeps them.

The unfolding of your words gives light;
it imparts understanding to the simple.—℟. ↓

SECOND READING Rom. 8.28-30

[All Things Work for Good]

God makes all his works of creation fit into his divine plan. He planned to share the image of his Son with us so that we might be justified and thereby enter into eternal glory.

A reading from the Letter of Saint Paul
to the Romans.

BROTHERS and sisters: We know that all things work together for good for those who love God, who are called according to his purpose.

For those whom God foreknew he also predestined to be conformed to the image of his Son, in order that he might be the firstborn among many brothers and sisters.

And those whom God predestined he also called; and those whom he called he also justified; and those whom he justified he also glorified.—The word of the Lord. ℟. **Thanks be to God.** ↓

GOSPEL ACCLAMATION See Mt. 11.25   [Little Ones]

(If the Alleluia is not sung, the acclamation is omitted.)

℣. Alleluia. ℟. **Alleluia.**

℣. Blessed are you, Father, Lord of heaven and earth;

you have revealed to little ones the mysteries of the kingdom.

℟. **Alleluia.** ↓

GOSPEL Mt. 13.44-52 or 13.44-48   [The Reign of God]

Jesus compares the value of the kingdom of God to a hidden treasure, to a most valuable pearl, to a dragnet. It is beyond human comprehension but in the end God's angels will sort out those who have lived good lives from the unrepentant sinners.

[If the "Shorter Form" is used, the indented text in brackets is omitted.]

℣. The Lord be with you. ℟. **And with your spirit.**
✚ A reading from the holy Gospel according to Matthew. ℟. **Glory to you, O Lord.**

JESUS spoke to the crowds: "The kingdom of heaven is like treasure hidden in a field, which someone found and hid; then in his joy he goes and sells all that he has and buys that field.

Again, the kingdom of heaven is like a merchant in search of fine pearls; on finding one pearl of great value, he went and sold all that he had and bought it.

Again, the kingdom of heaven is like a net that was thrown into the sea and caught fish of every kind; when it was full, they drew it ashore, sat down, and put the good into baskets but threw out the bad.

[So it will be at the end of the age. The Angels will come out and separate the evil from the righteous and throw them into the furnace of fire, where there will be weeping and gnashing of teeth.

Have you understood all this?" They answered, "Yes." And he said to them, "Therefore every scribe who has been trained for the kingdom of heaven is like the master of a household who brings out of his treasure what is new and what is old."]

The Gospel of the Lord. ℟. **Praise to you, Lord Jesus Christ.**   ➔ No. 15, p. 18

PRAYER OVER THE OFFERINGS
[Sanctifying Mysteries]

Accept, O Lord, we pray, the offerings
which we bring from the abundance of your gifts,
that through the powerful working of your grace
these most sacred mysteries may sanctify our
   present way of life
and lead us to eternal gladness.
Through Christ our Lord.
℟. **Amen.**   ➔ No. 21, p. 22 (Pref. 29-36)

COMMUNION ANTIPHON Ps. 102.2
[Bless the Lord]

Bless the Lord, O my soul, and never forget all his benefits. ↓

OR Mt. 5.7-8   [Blessed the Clean of Heart]

Blessed are the merciful, for they shall receive mercy. Blessed are the clean of heart, for they shall see God. ↓

PRAYER AFTER COMMUNION   [Memorial of Christ]

We have consumed, O Lord, this divine Sacrament,
the perpetual memorial of the Passion of your Son;
grant, we pray, that this gift,
which he himself gave us with love beyond all
   telling,
may profit us for salvation.

Through Christ our Lord.
R̸. **Amen.**   → No. 30, p. 77

Optional Solemn Blessings, p. 97, and Prayers over the People, p. 105

"He was transfigured before them. . . ."

AUGUST 6
THE TRANSFIGURATION OF THE LORD
Feast

ENTRANCE ANTIPHON Cf. Mt. 17.5 [Father, Son, and Spirit]

In a resplendent cloud the Holy Spirit appeared. The Father's voice was heard: This is my beloved Son, with whom I am well pleased. Listen to him.   → No. 2, p. 10

COLLECT   [Listening to Christ]

O God, who in the glorious Transfiguration
of your Only Begotten Son
confirmed the mysteries of faith by the witness of
    the Fathers
and wonderfully prefigured our full adoption to
    sonship,

grant, we pray, to your servants,
that, listening to the voice of your beloved Son,
we may merit to become co-heirs with him.
Who lives and reigns with you in the unity of the
   Holy Spirit,
one God, for ever and ever. ℞. **Amen.** ↓

FIRST READING Dan. 7.9-10, 13-14

[Clothing White as Snow]

Daniel's vision portrays the son of man who has power,
glory and dominion. Thousands minister to him. His dominion is everlasting.

A reading from the book of the Prophet Daniel.

A S I watched,
   thrones were set in place,
and the One who is Ancient of Days took his
   throne.
His clothing was white as snow,
and the hair of his head like pure wool.
His throne was fiery flames,
and its wheels were burning fire.
A stream of fire issued
and flowed out from his presence.
A thousand thousands served him,
and ten thousand times ten thousand stood at-
   tending him.
The court sat in judgment,
and the books were opened.

As I watched in the night visions,
I saw one like a son of man coming with the
   clouds of heaven.
And he came to the One who is Ancient of Days
and was presented before him.

To him was given dominion and glory and kingship,
that all peoples, nations, and languages should
 serve him.
His dominion is an everlasting dominion
that shall not pass away,
and his kingship is one that shall never be destroyed.
The word of the Lord. ℟. **Thanks be to God.** ↓

RESPONSORIAL PSALM Ps. 97   [Lord Is King]

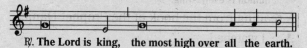

℟. **The Lord is king,   the most high over all   the earth.**

The Lord is king! Let the earth rejoice;
let the many coastlands be glad!
Clouds and thick darkness are all around him;
righteousness and justice are the foundation of
 his throne.—℟.

The mountains melt like wax before the Lord,
before the Lord of all the earth.
The heavens proclaim his righteousness;
and all the peoples behold his glory. —℟.

For you, O Lord, are most high over all the
 earth;
you are exalted far above all gods.—℟. ↓

SECOND READING 2 Pet. 1.16-19   [Peter, an Eyewitness]

Peter was an eyewitness of the Transfiguration of the Lord
Jesus in power and glory. He proclaims Jesus' message
with authority; his teaching is trustworthy and reliable.

A reading from the second Letter of Saint Peter.

WE did not follow cleverly devised myths when we made known to you the power and coming of our Lord Jesus Christ, but we had been eyewitnesses of his majesty. For he received honour and glory from God the Father when that voice was conveyed to him by the Majestic Glory, saying, "This is my Son, the Beloved. With him I am well pleased."

We ourselves heard this voice come from heaven, while we were with him on the holy mountain. So we have the prophetic message more fully confirmed. You will do well to be attentive to this as to a lamp shining in a dark place, until the day dawns and the morning star rises in your hearts.—The word of the Lord. ℟. **Thanks be to God.** ↓

GOSPEL ACCLAMATION Mt. 17.5c   [Listen to Him]

(If the Alleluia is not sung, the acclamation is omitted.)

℣. Alleluia. ℟. **Alleluia.**
℣. This is my Son, the Beloved;
with him I am well pleased; listen to him!
℟. **Alleluia.** ↓

GOSPEL Mt. 17.1-9   [Face Like the Sun]

Jesus is transfigured before Peter, James, and John. God acknowledges his Son and bids the disciples to listen to him. Jesus asks them not to reveal this vision until after the resurrection.

℣. The Lord be with you. ℟. **And with your spirit.**
✠ A reading from the holy Gospel according to Matthew. ℟. **Glory to you, O Lord.**

JESUS took with him Peter and James and his brother John and led them up a high mountain, by themselves. And he was transfigured before them, and his face shone like the sun, and his clothes became dazzling white. Suddenly there appeared to them Moses and Elijah, talking with him.

Then Peter said to Jesus, "Lord, it is good for us to be here; if you wish, I will make dwellings here, one for you, one for Moses, and one for Elijah."

While he was still speaking, suddenly a bright cloud overshadowed them, and from the cloud a voice said, "This is my Son, the Beloved; with him I am well pleased; listen to him!"

When the disciples heard this, they fell to the ground and were overcome by fear. But Jesus came and touched them, saying, "Get up and do not be afraid."

And when they looked up, they saw no one except Jesus himself alone. As they were coming down the mountain, Jesus ordered them, "Tell no one about the vision until after the Son of Man has been raised from the dead."—The Gospel of the Lord. ℟. **Praise to you, Lord Jesus Christ.**

→ No. 15, p. 18

When this Feast falls on a Sunday, the Creed is said.

PRAYER OVER THE OFFERINGS

[Cleanse Us from Sin]

Sanctify, O Lord, we pray,
these offerings here made to celebrate
the glorious Transfiguration of your Only
   Begotten Son,

and by his radiant splendour
cleanse us from the stains of sin.
Through Christ our Lord. ℟. **Amen.** ↓

PREFACE (50)   [Sharing Christ's Glory]

℣. The Lord be with you. ℟. **And with your spirit.**
℣. Lift up your hearts. ℟. **We lift them up to the Lord.**
℣. Let us give thanks to the Lord our God.
℟. **It is right and just.**

It is truly right and just, our duty and our
    salvation,
always and everywhere to give you thanks,
Lord, holy Father, almighty and eternal God,
through Christ our Lord.

For he revealed his glory in the presence of chosen
    witnesses
and filled with the greatest splendour that bodily
    form
which he shares with all humanity,
that the scandal of the Cross
might be removed from the hearts of his disciples
and that he might show
how in the Body of the whole Church is to be
    fulfilled
what so wonderfully shone forth first in its Head.

And so, with the Powers of heaven,
we worship you constantly on earth,
and before your majesty
without end we acclaim: → No. 23, p. 23

COMMUNION ANTIPHON Cf. 1 Jn. 3.2 [Vision of Christ]

**When Christ appears, we shall be like him, for
we shall see him as he is.** ↓

PRAYER AFTER COMMUNION [In Christ's Likeness]

May the heavenly nourishment we have received,
O Lord, we pray,
transform us into the likeness of your Son,
whose radiant splendour you willed to make
    manifest
in his glorious Transfiguration.
Who lives and reigns for ever and ever.
℟. **Amen.**   → No. 30, p. 77

Optional Solemn Blessings, p. 97, and Prayers over the People, p. 105

"It is I; do not be afraid."

AUGUST 13

19th SUNDAY IN ORDINARY TIME

ENTRANCE ANTIPHON Cf. Ps. 73.20, 19, 22, 23

[Arise, O God]

**Look to your covenant, O Lord, and forget not
the life of your poor ones for ever. Arise, O God,
and defend your cause, and forget not the cries of
those who seek you.**   → No. 2, p. 10

COLLECT   [Spirit of Adoption]

Almighty ever-living God,
whom, taught by the Holy Spirit,
we dare to call our Father,
bring, we pray, to perfection in our hearts
the spirit of adoption as your sons and daughters,
that we may merit to enter into the inheritance
which you have promised.
Through our Lord Jesus Christ, your Son,
who lives and reigns with you in the unity of the
   Holy Spirit,
one God, for ever and ever. ℟. **Amen.** ↓

FIRST READING 1 Kgs. 19.9, 11-13   [Coming of the Lord]

The Lord tells Elijah to await him on the mountain. Elijah's faith is tried as he witnesses a devastating wind, an earthquake, and a fire. After these the Lord speaks to Elijah in the sound of silence.

A reading from the first book of Kings.

WHEN Elijah reached Horeb, the mountain of God, he came to a cave, and spent the night there. Then the word of the Lord came to him, saying, "Go out and stand on the mountain before the Lord, for the Lord is about to pass by."

Now there was a great wind, so strong that it was splitting mountains and breaking rocks in pieces before the Lord, but the Lord was not in the wind; and after the wind an earthquake, but the Lord was not in the earthquake; and after the earthquake a fire, but the Lord was not in the fire; and after the fire a sound of sheer silence.

When Elijah heard it, he wrapped his face in his mantle and went out and stood at the entrance of the cave.—The word of the Lord. ℟. **Thanks be to God.** ↓

RESPONSORIAL PSALM Ps. 85   [Truth and Justice]

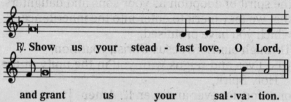

℟. Show us your stead - fast love, O Lord, and grant us your sal - va - tion.

Let me hear what God the Lord will speak,
for he will speak peace to his people.
Surely his salvation is at hand for those who fear him,
that his glory may dwell in our land.—℟.

Steadfast love and faithfulness will meet;
righteousness and peace will kiss each other.
Faithfulness will spring up from the ground,
and righteousness will look down from the sky.
—℟.

The Lord will give what is good,
and our land will yield its increase.
Righteousness will go before him,
and will make a path for his steps.—℟. ↓

SECOND READING Rom. 9.1-5   [Blessed Be God]

Paul admits that grief is in his heart. He would even accept separation from Jesus if it would help his brothers and sisters who have been privileged to know the revelation of God through the ages. Blessed be God forever.

A reading from the Letter of Saint Paul
to the Romans.

BROTHERS and sisters: I am speaking the truth in Christ. I am not lying; my conscience confirms it by the Holy Spirit. I have great sorrow and unceasing anguish in my heart.

For I could wish that I myself were accursed and cut off from Christ for the sake of my own people, my kindred according to the flesh. They are children of Israel, and to them belong the adoption, the glory, the covenants, the giving of the law, the worship, and the promises; to them belong the patriarchs, and from them, according to the flesh, comes the Christ, who is over all, God be blessed forever. Amen.—The word of the Lord. ℟. **Thanks be to God.** ↓

GOSPEL ACCLAMATION Ps. 129.5   [Hope and Trust]

(If the Alleluia is not sung, the acclamation is omitted.)

℣. Alleluia. ℟. **Alleluia.**
℣. I wait for the Lord;
I hope in his word.
℟. **Alleluia.** ↓

GOSPEL Mt.14.22-33   [Jesus Walks on Water]

Jesus feeds the crowds and then withdraws to pray. His disciples want to cross the lake but a threatening storm arises. Jesus appears, and Peter gets out of the boat to walk to Jesus, but because Peter doubts, he begins to sink. Jesus saves him and admonishes him for his little faith. Jesus calms the storm.

℣. The Lord be with you. ℟. **And with your spirit.**
✠ A reading from the holy Gospel according to
Matthew. ℟. **Glory to you, O Lord.**

IMMEDIATELY after feeding the crowd with
the five loaves and two fish, Jesus made the
disciples get into the boat and go on ahead to the
other side, while he dismissed the crowds. And
after he had dismissed the crowds, he went up the
mountain by himself to pray.

When evening came, he was there alone, but by
this time the boat, battered by the waves, was far
from the land, for the wind was against them.

And early in the morning Jesus came walking
toward them on the sea. But when the disciples
saw him walking on the sea, they were terrified,
saying, "It is a ghost!" And they cried out in fear.
But immediately Jesus spoke to them and said,
"Take heart, it is I; do not be afraid."

Peter answered him, "Lord, if it is you, command me to come to you on the water." Jesus said,
"Come." So Peter got out of the boat, started walking on the water, and came toward Jesus. But
when he noticed the strong wind, he became
frightened, and beginning to sink, he cried out,
"Lord, save me!"

Jesus immediately reached out his hand and
caught him, saying to him, "You of little faith, why
did you doubt?" When they got into the boat, the
wind ceased. And those in the boat worshiped
him, saying, "Truly you are the Son of God."—The
Gospel of the Lord. ℟. **Praise to you, Lord Jesus
Christ.**   → No. 15, p. 18

PRAYER OVER THE OFFERINGS
[Mystery of Salvation]

Be pleased, O Lord, to accept the offerings of your
    Church,
for in your mercy you have given them to be
    offered
and by your power you transform them
into the mystery of our salvation.
Through Christ our Lord.
℟. **Amen.**   → No. 21, p. 22 (Pref. 29-36)

COMMUNION ANTIPHON Ps 147.12, 14
[Glorify the Lord]

**O Jerusalem, glorify the Lord, who gives you
your fill of finest wheat. ↓**

OR Cf. Jn. 6.51   [The Flesh of Jesus]
**The bread that I will give, says the Lord, is my
flesh for the life of the world. ↓**

PRAYER AFTER COMMUNION
[Confirm Us in God's Truth]

May the communion in your Sacrament
that we have consumed, save us, O Lord,
and confirm us in the light of your truth.
Through Christ our Lord.
℟. **Amen.**   → No. 30, p. 77

Optional Solemn Blessings, p. 97, and Prayers over the People, p. 105

"Woman, great is your faith! Let it be done
for you as you wish."

AUGUST 20

20th SUNDAY IN ORDINARY TIME

ENTRANCE ANTIPHON Ps. 83.10-11

[God Our Shield]

**Turn your eyes, O God, our shield; and look on
the face of your anointed one; one day within
your courts is better than a thousand elsewhere.**

➥ No. 2, p. 10

COLLECT [Attaining God's Promises]

O God, who have prepared for those who love you
good things which no eye can see,
fill our hearts, we pray, with the warmth of your
love,
so that, loving you in all things and above all
things,
we may attain your promises,
which surpass every human desire.
Through our Lord Jesus Christ, your Son,

502

who lives and reigns with you in the unity of the
 Holy Spirit,
one God, for ever and ever. ℟. **Amen.** ↓

FIRST READING Isa. 56.1, 6-7   [Salvation for All]

Isaiah warns his people that for salvation they must do
what is just, love the Lord, and keep the sabbath. God
will then lead them to his mountain and accept their
sacrifices.

A reading from the book of the Prophet Isaiah.

THUS says the Lord:
 "Maintain justice, and do what is right,
for soon my salvation will come,
and my deliverance be revealed.

And the foreigners who join themselves to the
 Lord,
to minister to him, to love the name of the Lord,
and to be his servants,
all who keep the Sabbath, and do not profane it,
and hold fast my covenant—
these I will bring to my holy mountain,
and make them joyful in my house of prayer;
their burnt offerings and their sacrifices
will be accepted on my altar;
for my house shall be called a house of prayer
for all peoples."

The word of the Lord. ℟. **Thanks be to God.** ↓

RESPONSORIAL PSALM Ps. 67   [Praise for the Lord]

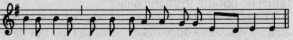

℟. Let the peo-ples praise you, O God, let all the peo-ples praise you!

May God be gracious to us and bless us
and make his face to shine upon us,
that your way may be known upon earth,
your saving power among all nations.
℟. **Let the peoples praise you, O God,**
   let all the peoples praise you!

Let the nations be glad and sing for joy,
for you judge the peoples with equity
and guide the nations upon earth.
Let the peoples praise you, O God;
let all the peoples praise you.—℟.

The earth has yielded its increase;
God, our God, has blessed us.
May God continue to bless us;
let all the ends of the earth revere him.—℟. ↓

SECOND READING Rom. 11.13-15, 29-32 [Gifts and Call]

> Paul is proud of his ministry and he is anxious to lead
> his Jewish brothers and sisters to reconciliation with
> God. In spite of their disobedience, God has been mer-
> ciful toward them.

A reading from the Letter of Saint Paul
to the Romans.

BROTHERS and sisters: Now I am speaking to
you Gentiles. Inasmuch then as I am an Apostle to the Gentiles, I glorify my ministry in order
to make my own flesh and blood jealous, and thus
save some of them. For if their rejection is the reconciliation of the world, what will their acceptance be but life from the dead!
   The gifts and the calling of God are irrevocable.
Just as you were once disobedient to God but have
now received mercy because of their disobedi-

ence, so they have now been disobedient in order
that, by the mercy shown to you, they too may
now receive mercy. For God has imprisoned all in
disobedience so that he may be merciful to all.—
The word of the Lord. ℟. **Thanks be to God.** ↓

GOSPEL ACCLAMATION See Mt. 4.23   [Jesus Heals]
(If the alleluia is not sung, the acclamation is omitted.)

℣. Alleluia. ℟. **Alleluia.**

℣. Jesus proclaimed the good news of the kingdom

and cured every sickness.

℟. **Alleluia.** ↓

GOSPEL Mt. 15.21-28   [Reward of Faith]

A Canaanite woman whose daughter is possessed
comes to Jesus and asks for a favour with perseverance.
Jesus commends her great faith and cures her daughter.

℣. The Lord be with you. ℟. **And with your spirit.**
✠ A reading from the holy Gospel according to
Matthew. ℟. **Glory to you, O Lord.**

JESUS went away to the district of Tyre and
Sidon. A Canaanite woman from that region
came out, and started shouting, "Have mercy on
me, Lord, Son of David; my daughter is tormented
by a demon." But he did not answer her at all.

And his disciples came and urged him, saying,
"Send her away, for she keeps shouting after us."
He answered, "I was sent only to the lost sheep of
the house of Israel."

But the woman came and knelt before him,
saying, "Lord, help me." He answered, "It is not
fair to take the children's food and throw it to the

dogs." She said, "Yes, Lord, yet even the dogs eat the crumbs that fall from their masters' table."

Then Jesus answered her, "Woman, great is your faith! Let it be done for you as you wish." And her daughter was healed instantly.—The Gospel of the Lord. ℟. **Praise to you, Lord Jesus Christ.**   ➜ No. 15, p. 18

PRAYER OVER THE OFFERINGS [Glorious Exchange]

Receive our oblation, O Lord,
by which is brought about a glorious exchange,
that, by offering what you have given,
we may merit to receive your very self.
Through Christ our Lord.
℟. **Amen.**   ➜ No. 21, p. 22 (Pref. 29-36)

COMMUNION ANTIPHON Ps. 129.7

[Plentiful Redemption]

With the Lord there is mercy; in him is plentiful redemption. ↓

OR Jn. 6.51   [Eternal Life]

I am the living bread that came down from heaven, says the Lord. Whoever eats of this bread will live for ever. ↓

PRAYER AFTER COMMUNION [Co-heirs in Heaven]

Made partakers of Christ through these Sacraments,
we humbly implore your mercy, Lord,
that, conformed to his image on earth,
we may merit also to be his co-heirs in heaven.
Who lives and reigns for ever and ever.
℟. **Amen.**   ➜ No. 30, p. 77

Optional Solemn Blessings, p. 97, and Prayers over the People, p. 105

"You are Peter, and on this rock
I will build my Church."

AUGUST 27

21st SUNDAY IN ORDINARY TIME

ENTRANCE ANTIPHON Cf. Ps. 85.1-3   [Save Us]

Turn your ear, O Lord, and answer me; save the
servant who trusts in you, my God. Have mercy
on me, O Lord, for I cry to you all the day long.

→ No. 2, p. 10

COLLECT   [One in Mind and Heart]

O God, who cause the minds of the faithful
to unite in a single purpose,
grant your people to love what you command
and to desire what you promise,
that, amid the uncertainties of this world,
our hearts may be fixed on that place
where true gladness is found.
Through our Lord Jesus Christ, your Son,

who lives and reigns with you in the unity of the
  Holy Spirit,
one God, for ever and ever. ℟. **Amen.**↓

FIRST READING Isa. 22.15, 19-23   [The Gift of Authority]
      **Eliakim is given the leadership of the Israelites. He is to
      become the father of the Jewish people. He shall have
      the key of the house of David. He is to have a place of
      honour for his family.**

A reading from the book of the Prophet Isaiah.

THUS says the Lord God of hosts: Go to the
  steward, to Shebna, who is master of the
household, and say to him:

"I will thrust you from your office, and you
will be pulled down from your post. On that day
I will call my servant Eliakim son of Hilkiah,
and will clothe him with your robe and bind
your sash on him. I will commit your authority
to his hand, and he shall be a father to the inhabitants of Jerusalem and to the house of
Judah.

I will place on his shoulder the key of the
house of David; he shall open, and no one shall
shut; he shall shut, and no one shall open. I will
fasten him like a peg in a secure place, and he
will become a throne of honour to the house of
his ancestors."—The word of the Lord. ℟. **Thanks
be to God.** ↓

RESPONSORIAL PSALM Ps. 138   [God's Eternal Love]

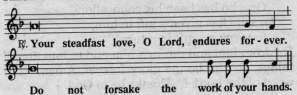

℟. Your steadfast love, O Lord, endures for - ever.

Do not forsake the work of your hands.

I give you thanks, O Lord, with my whole heart;
before the Angels I sing your praise;
I bow down toward your holy temple, and give
    thanks to your name
for your steadfast love and your faithfulness.—℟.

For you have exalted your name
and your word above everything.
On the day I called, you answered me,
you increased my strength of soul.—℟.

For though the Lord is high, he regards the lowly;
but the haughty he perceives from far away.
Your steadfast love, O Lord, endures forever.
Do not forsake the work of your hands.—℟. ↓

SECOND READING Rom. 11.33-36   [Eternal Glory]

**Paul offers a description of God, stressing God's infinite
wisdom. God's ways are unsearchable and no one can
really measure the mind of God. But in God all things
have their being.**

A reading from the Letter of Saint Paul
to the Romans.

O THE depth of the riches and wisdom and
knowledge of God! How unsearchable are his
judgments and how inscrutable his ways!

"For who has known the mind of the Lord?
   Or who has been his counsellor?"
"Or who has given a gift to him,
   to receive a gift in return?"
For from him and through him and to him are all
things. To him be the glory forever. Amen.—The
word of the Lord. ℟. **Thanks be to God.** ↓

GOSPEL ACCLAMATION Mt. 16.18   [Christ's Church]
(If the Alleluia is not sung, the acclamation is omitted.)
℣. Alleluia. ℟. **Alleluia.**
℣. You are Peter, and on this rock I will build my
   Church;
the gates of Hades will not prevail against it.
℟. **Alleluia.** ↓

GOSPEL Mt. 16.13-20   [The First Pope]

Peter acknowledges that Jesus is the Messiah. Jesus in
turn declares Peter the rock upon which his Church is to
be built. He also gives Peter the power of the keys.

℣. The Lord be with you. ℟. **And with your spirit.**
✚ A reading from the holy Gospel according to
Matthew. ℟. **Glory to you, O Lord.**

WHEN Jesus came into the district of Caes-
area Philippi, he asked his disciples, "Who
do people say that the Son of Man is?" And they
said, "Some say John the Baptist, but others Elijah, and still others Jeremiah or one of the
Prophets."
   He said to them, "But who do you say that I
am?" Simon Peter answered, "You are the Christ,
the Son of the living God."

And Jesus answered him, "Blessed are you, Simon son of Jonah! For flesh and blood has not revealed this to you, but my Father in heaven.

And I tell you, you are Peter, and on this rock I will build my Church, and the gates of Hades will not prevail against it. I will give you the keys of the kingdom of heaven, and whatever you bind on earth will be bound in heaven, and whatever you loose on earth will be loosed in heaven."

Then Jesus sternly ordered the disciples not to tell anyone that he was the Christ.—The Gospel of the Lord. ℟. **Praise to you, Lord Jesus Christ.**
→ No. 15, p. 18

PRAYER OVER THE OFFERINGS   [Unity and Peace]

O Lord, who gained for yourself a people by
    adoption
through the one sacrifice offered once for all,
bestow graciously on us, we pray,
the gifts of unity and peace in your Church.
Through Christ our Lord.
℟. **Amen.**
→ No. 21, p. 22 (Pref. 29-36)

COMMUNION ANTIPHON Cf. Ps. 103.13-15

[Sacred Bread and Wine]

The earth is replete with the fruits of your work, O Lord; you bring forth bread from the earth and wine to cheer the heart. ↓

OR Cf. Jn. 6.54
[Eternal Life]

Whoever eats my flesh and drinks my blood has eternal life, says the Lord, and I will raise him up on the last day. ↓

PRAYER AFTER COMMUNION   [Pleasing God]

Complete within us, O Lord, we pray,
the healing work of your mercy
and graciously perfect and sustain us,
so that in all things we may please you.
Through Christ our Lord.
℟. **Amen.**

→ No. 30, p. 77

Optional Solemn Blessings, p. 97, and Prayers over the People, p. 105

"Jesus began to show his disciples that he must . . .
be killed, and on the third day be raised."

SEPTEMBER 3

22nd SUNDAY IN ORDINARY TIME

ENTRANCE ANTIPHON Cf. Ps. 85.3, 5

[Call upon God]

Have mercy on me, O Lord, for I cry to you all
the day long. O Lord, you are good and forgiving,
full of mercy to all who call to you.   → No. 2, p. 10

COLLECT   [God's Watchful Care]

God of might, giver of every good gift,
put into our hearts the love of your name,
so that, by deepening our sense of reverence,
you may nurture in us what is good
and, by your watchful care,
keep safe what you have nurtured.
Through our Lord Jesus Christ, your Son,
who lives and reigns with you in the unity of the
    Holy Spirit,
one God, for ever and ever. R̷. **Amen.** ↓

FIRST READING Jer. 20.7-9   [Power of God's Word]

Jeremiah admits that he has become a mockery for the
Lord. He is derided and reproached, but he cannot help
speaking out the word of the Lord.

A reading from the book of the Prophet Jeremiah.

O LORD, you have enticed me,
    and I was enticed;
you have overpowered me,
and you have prevailed.
I have become a laughingstock all day long;
everyone mocks me.
For whenever I speak, I must cry out,
I must shout, "Violence and destruction!"
For the word of the Lord has become for me
a reproach and derision all day long.

If I say, "I will not mention him,
or speak any more in his name,"
then within me there is something like a burning
    fire
shut up in my bones;

I am weary with holding it in,
and I cannot.

The word of the Lord. ℟. **Thanks be to God.** ↓

RESPONSORIAL PSALM Ps. 63   [Longing for God]

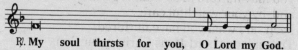

℟. My soul thirsts for you, O Lord my God.

O God, you are my God, I seek you,
my soul thirsts for you;
my flesh faints for you,
as in a dry and weary land where there is no
  water.—℟.

So I have looked upon you in the sanctuary,
beholding your power and glory.
Because your steadfast love is better than life,
my lips will praise you.—℟.

So I will bless you as long as I live;
I will lift up my hands and call on your name.
My soul is satisfied as with a rich feast,
and my mouth praises you with joyful lips.—℟.

For you have been my help,
and in the shadow of your wings I sing for joy.
My soul clings to you;
your right hand upholds me.—℟. ↓

SECOND READING Rom. 12.1-2   [A Living Sacrifice]

Paul recommends sacrifice, to offer our bodies as a sacrifice to the Lord. We must ignore the standards of the
world and become renewed in spirit to be pleasing to God.

A reading from the Letter of Saint Paul
to the Romans.

I APPEAL to you, brothers and sisters, by the mercies of God, to present your bodies as a living sacrifice, holy and acceptable to God, which is your spiritual worship. Do not be conformed to this world, but be transformed by the renewing of your minds, so that you may discern what is the will of God—what is good and acceptable and perfect.—The word of the Lord. ℟. **Thanks be to God.** ↓

GOSPEL ACCLAMATION See Eph. 1.17-18   [Hope]
(If the Alleluia is not sung, the acclamation is omitted.)
℣. Alleluia. ℟. **Alleluia.**
℣. May the Father of our Lord Jesus Christ enlighten the eyes of our heart,
that we might know the hope to which we are called.
℟. **Alleluia.** ↓

GOSPEL Mt. 16.21-27   [Taking up the Cross]
Jesus foretells his suffering, passion, and death. All those who wish to follow Jesus must take up their cross and lose their life in order to find it. What good would the world be if we would gain it all and lose our soul?

℣. The Lord be with you. ℟. **And with your spirit.**
✝ A reading from the holy Gospel according to Matthew. ℟. **Glory to you, O Lord.**

J ESUS began to show his disciples that he must go to Jerusalem and undergo great suffering at the hands of the elders and chief priests and scribes, and be killed, and on the third day be raised.

And Peter took Jesus aside and began to rebuke him, saying, "God forbid it, Lord! This must never happen to you." But he turned and said to Peter, "Get behind me, Satan! You are a stumbling block to me; for you are thinking not as God does, but as humans do."

Then Jesus told his disciples, "If anyone wants to become my follower, let him deny himself and take up his cross and follow me. For whoever wants to save their life will lose it, and whoever loses their life for my sake will find it. For what will it profit anyone to gain the whole world but forfeit their life? Or what will anyone give in return for their life?

For the Son of Man is to come with his Angels in the glory of his Father, and then he will repay each according to their work."—The Gospel of the Lord. ℟. **Praise to you, Lord Jesus Christ.**

→ No. 15, p. 18

PRAYER OVER THE OFFERINGS

[Blessing of Salvation]

May this sacred offering, O Lord,
confer on us always the blessing of salvation,
that what it celebrates in mystery
it may accomplish in power.
Through Christ our Lord.
℟. **Amen.**   → No. 21, p. 22 (Pref. 29-36)

COMMUNION ANTIPHON Ps. 30.20

[God's Goodness]

How great is the goodness, Lord, that you keep for those who fear you. ↓

OR Mt. 5.9-10   [Blessed Are the Peacemakers]

Blessed are the peacemakers, for they shall be called children of God. Blessed are they who are persecuted for the sake of righteousness, for theirs is the Kingdom of Heaven. ↓

PRAYER AFTER COMMUNION
[Serving God in Neighbour]

Renewed by this bread from the heavenly table,
we beseech you, Lord,
that, being the food of charity,
it may confirm our hearts
and stir us to serve you in our neighbour.
Through Christ our Lord.
℟. **Amen.**   → No. 30, p. 77

Optional Solemn Blessings, p. 97, and Prayers over the People, p. 105

"If he or she listens to you,
you have regained your brother or sister."

SEPTEMBER 10
23rd SUNDAY IN ORDINARY TIME

ENTRANCE ANTIPHON Ps. 118.137, 124

[Plea for Mercy]

**You are just, O Lord, and your judgement is right;
treat your servant in accord with your merciful
love.**

➙ No. 2, p. 10

COLLECT [Christian Freedom]

O God, by whom we are redeemed and receive
    adoption,
look graciously upon your beloved sons and
    daughters,
that those who believe in Christ
may receive true freedom
and an everlasting inheritance.
Through our Lord Jesus Christ, your Son,
who lives and reigns with you in the unity of the
    Holy Spirit,
one God, for ever and ever. ℟. **Amen.** ↓

FIRST READING Ez. 33.7-9   [Warning the Wicked]

Ezekiel is charged to dissuade evildoers from their faults.
If evildoers do not heed this warning, they will die.

A reading from the book of the Prophet Ezekiel.

THUS says the Lord: "So you, O son of man, I
have made a watchman for the house of Israel; whenever you hear a word from my mouth,
you shall give them warning from me.

"If I say to the wicked, 'O wicked one, you shall
surely die,' and you do not speak to warn the
wicked to turn from their ways, the wicked person shall die in their iniquity, but their blood I will
require at your hand.

But if you warn the wicked person to turn from
their ways, and they do not turn from their ways,
they shall die in their iniquity, but you will have
saved your life."—The word of the Lord. ℞. **Thanks
be to God.** ↓

RESPONSORIAL PSALM Ps. 95 [Answering God's Call]

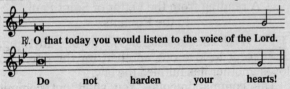

℞. **O that today you would listen to the voice of the Lord.**

Do   not   harden   your   hearts!

O come, let us sing to the Lord;
let us make a joyful noise to the rock of our sal-
    vation!
Let us come into his presence with thanksgiving;
let us make a joyful noise to him with songs of
    praise!—℞.

O come, let us worship and bow down,
let us kneel before the Lord, our Maker!
For he is our God, and we are the people of his
     pasture,
and the sheep of his hand.

℟. **O that today you would listen to the voice of
     the Lord.
     Do not harden your hearts!**

O that today you would listen to his voice!
Do not harden your hearts, as at Meribah,
as on the day at Massah in the wilderness,
when your ancestors tested me,
and put me to the proof,
though they had seen my work.—℟. ↓

SECOND READING Rom. 13.8-10   [Love of Neighbour]

All who love their neighbours truly fulfill the law. The
commandments forbidding adultery, stealing, murder,
and coveting are all summed up in this law of laws.

A reading from the Letter of Saint Paul
to the Romans.

BROTHERS and sisters: Owe no one anything,
except to love one another; for the one who
loves another has fulfilled the law.

The commandments, "You shall not commit
adultery; You shall not murder; You shall not
steal; You shall not covet"; and any other commandment, are summed up in this word, "Love
your neighbour as yourself."

Love does no wrong to a neighbour; therefore,
love is the fulfilling of the law.—The word of the
Lord. ℟. **Thanks be to God.** ↓

GOSPEL ACCLAMATION See 2 Cor. 5.19

[Reconciliation]

(If the Alleluia is not sung, the acclamation is omitted.)

℣. Alleluia. ℟. **Alleluia.**

℣. In Christ, God was reconciling the world to himself,

and entrusting the message of reconciliation to us.

℟. **Alleluia.** ↓

GOSPEL Mt. 18.15-20   [Communal Correction and Prayer]

> To correct another person's fault, first speak to him or her. If this fails, invite a witness or two. But if the person continues in this fault, note it before the church assembly. Pray together and make your petitions in the name of Jesus.

℣. The Lord be with you. ℟. **And with your spirit.**

✟ A reading from the holy Gospel according to Matthew. ℟. **Glory to you, O Lord.**

JESUS spoke to his disciples. "If your brother or sister sins against you, go and point out the fault when the two of you are alone. If he or she listens to you, you have regained your brother or sister. But if the person does not listen, take one or two others along with you, so that every word may be confirmed by the evidence of two or three witnesses. If the person refuses to listen to them, tell it to the Church; and if that person refuses to listen even to the Church, let such a one be to you as a Gentile and a tax collector.

Truly I tell you, whatever you bind on earth will be bound in heaven, and whatever you loose on earth will be loosed in heaven. Again, truly I tell you, if two of you agree on earth about anything you ask, it will be done for you by my Father in heaven. For where two or three are gathered in my name, I am there among them."—The Gospel of the Lord. ℟. **Praise to you, Lord Jesus Christ.**

→ No. 15, p. 18

PRAYER OVER THE OFFERINGS [Prayer and Peace]

O God, who give us the gift of true prayer and of
    peace,
graciously grant that, through this offering,
we may do fitting homage to your divine majesty
and, by partaking of the sacred mystery,
we may be faithfully united in mind and heart.
Through Christ our Lord.
℟. **Amen.**   → No. 21, p. 22 (Pref. 29-36)

COMMUNION ANTIPHON Cf. Ps. 41.2-3

[Yearning for God]

Like the deer that yearns for running streams, so my soul is yearning for you, my God; my soul is thirsting for God, the living God. ↓

OR Jn. 8.12   [The Light of Life]

I am the light of the world, says the Lord; whoever follows me will not walk in darkness, but will have the light of life. ↓

PRAYER AFTER COMMUNION [Word and Sacrament]

Grant that your faithful, O Lord,
whom you nourish and endow with life
through the food of your Word and heavenly
    Sacrament,
may so benefit from your beloved Son's great
    gifts

that we may merit an eternal share in his life.
Who lives and reigns for ever and ever.
℞. **Amen.**   ➔ No. 30, p. 77

Optional Solemn Blessings, p. 97, and Prayers over the People, p. 105

"His lord handed him over to be tortured."

SEPTEMBER 17

24th SUNDAY IN ORDINARY TIME

ENTRANCE ANTIPHON Cf. Sir. 36.18   [God's Peace]
**Give peace, O Lord, to those who wait for you,
that your prophets be found true. Hear the
prayers of your servant, and of your people
Israel.**   ➔ No. 2, p. 10

COLLECT   [Serving God]
Look upon us, O God,
Creator and ruler of all things,
and, that we may feel the working of your mercy,
grant that we may serve you with all our heart.
Through our Lord Jesus Christ, your Son,

who lives and reigns with you in the unity of the
  Holy Spirit,
one God, for ever and ever. ℞. **Amen.** ↓

FIRST READING Sir. 27.30—28.7   [Need for Forgiveness]

**The sinner abounds in wrath. It is the Lord who pun-
ishes, and we are to forgive injustice and be merciful.
We should think of our last days.**

A reading from the book of Sirach.

ANGER and wrath, these are abominations,
  yet a sinner holds on to them.
The vengeful person will face the Lord's vengeance,
for he keeps a strict account of their sins.
Forgive your neighbour the wrong that is done,
and then your sins will be pardoned when you
  pray.
Does anyone harbour anger against another,
and expect healing from the Lord?
If one has no mercy toward another like oneself,
can one then seek pardon for one's own sins?
If one who is but flesh harbours wrath,
who will make an atoning sacrifice for that person's sins?
Remember the end of your life,
and set enmity aside;
remember corruption and death,
and be true to the commandments.
Remember the commandments,
and do not be angry with your neighbour;
remember the covenant of the Most High,
and overlook faults.

The word of the Lord. ℞. **Thanks be to God.** ↓

RESPONSORIAL PSALM Ps. 103   [God's Mercy]

℟. The Lord is merciful and gra-cious;
slow to anger and abounding in steadfast love.

Bless the Lord, O my soul,
and all that is within me, bless his holy name.
Bless the Lord, O my soul,
and do not forget all his benefits.—℟.

It is the Lord who forgives all your iniquity,
who heals all your diseases,
who redeems your life from the Pit,
who crowns you with steadfast love and mercy.
—℟.

He will not always accuse,
nor will he keep his anger forever.
He does not deal with us according to our sins,
nor repay us according to our iniquities.—℟.

For as the heavens are high above the earth,
so great is his steadfast love toward those who
    fear him;
as far as the east is from the west,
so far he removes our transgressions from us.
—℟. ↓

SECOND READING Rom. 14.7-9   [God's Partners]

After the example of Christ, who died for sinners, we
must strive to live for God and for others.

A reading from the Letter of Saint Paul
to the Romans.

BROTHERS and sisters: We do not live to ourselves, and we do not die to ourselves. If we
live, we live to the Lord, and if we die, we die to
the Lord; so then, whether we live or whether we
die, we are the Lord's. For to this end Christ died
and lived again, so that he might be Lord of both
the dead and the living.—The word of the Lord.
℟. **Thanks be to God.** ↓

GOSPEL ACCLAMATION Jn. 13.34 [Love One Another]
(If the Alleluia is not sung, the acclamation is omitted.)
℣. Alleluia. ℟. **Alleluia.** ↓
I give you a new commandment:
love one another just as I have loved you.
℟. **Alleluia.** ↓

GOSPEL Mt. 18.21-35   [Forgiving Our Neighbour]

Jesus answers Peter that we are to forgive our neighbour's faults without any limit. Jesus uses the parable
of the unjust steward who was forgiven a large debt by
his master but refused to forgive a small debt owed to
himself. The master then dealt severely with his official.

℣. The Lord be with you. ℟. **And with your spirit.**
✝ A reading from the holy Gospel according to
Matthew. ℟. **Glory to you, O Lord.**

PETER came and said to Jesus, "Lord, how
often should I forgive my brother or sister if
they sin against me? As many as seven times?"

Jesus said to him, "Not seven times, but, I tell
you, seventy-seven times.

For this reason the kingdom of heaven may be
compared to a king who wished to settle accounts

with his slaves. When he began the reckoning, one who owed him ten thousand talents was brought to him; and, as he could not pay, his lord ordered him to be sold, together with his wife and children and all his possessions, and payment to be made. So the slave fell on his knees before him, saying, 'Have patience with me, and I will pay you everything.' The lord of that slave released him and forgave him the debt.

But that same slave, as he went out, came upon one of his fellow slaves who owed him a hundred denarii; and seizing him by the throat, he said, 'Pay what you owe.' Then his fellow slave fell down and pleaded with him, 'Have patience with me, and I will pay you.' But he refused; then he went and threw him into prison until he would pay the debt.

When his fellow slaves saw what had happened, they were greatly distressed, and they went and reported to their lord all that had taken place. Then his lord summoned him and said to him, 'You wicked slave! I forgave you all that debt because you pleaded with me. Should you not have had mercy on your fellow slave, as I had mercy on you?' And in anger his lord handed him over to be tortured until he would pay his entire debt.

So my heavenly Father will also do to every one of you, if you do not forgive your brother or sister from your heart."—The Gospel of the Lord. ℟. **Praise to you, Lord Jesus Christ.**

→ No. 15, p. 18

PRAYER OVER THE OFFERINGS

[Accept Our Offerings]

Look with favour on our supplications, O Lord,
and in your kindness accept these, your servants'
   offerings,
that what each has offered to the honour of your
   name
may serve the salvation of all.
Through Christ our Lord.
℞. **Amen.**   → No. 21, p. 22 (Pref. 29-36)

COMMUNION ANTIPHON Cf. Ps. 35.8

[God's Mercy]

**How precious is your mercy, O God! The children
of men seek shelter in the shadow of your wings.** ↓

OR Cf. 1 Cor. 10.16   [Share of Christ]

**The chalice of blessing that we bless is a commu-
nion in the Blood of Christ; and the bread that we
break is a sharing in the Body of the Lord.** ↓

PRAYER AFTER COMMUNION   [Heavenly Gift]

May the working of this heavenly gift, O Lord, we
   pray,
take possession of our minds and bodies,
so that its effects, and not our own desires,
may always prevail in us.
Through Christ our Lord.
℞. **Amen.**   → No. 30, p. 77

Optional Solemn Blessings, p. 97, and Prayers over the People, p. 105

"The last will be first, and the first will be last."

SEPTEMBER 24

25th SUNDAY IN ORDINARY TIME

ENTRANCE ANTIPHON   [Salvation of People]

I am the salvation of the people, says the Lord.
Should they cry to me in any distress, I will hear
them, and I will be their Lord for ever.

→ No. 2, p. 10

COLLECT   [Attaining Eternal Life]

O God, who founded all the commands of your
  sacred Law
upon love of you and of our neighbour,
grant that, by keeping your precepts,
we may merit to attain eternal life.
Through our Lord Jesus Christ, your Son,
who lives and reigns with you in the unity of the
  Holy Spirit,
one God, for ever and ever. ℟. **Amen.** ↓

FIRST READING Isa. 55.6-9   [Seek the Lord]

> Seek the Lord. His ways are far above human ways. The thoughts of God are not the thoughts of human beings. God is rich in forgiving.

A reading from the book of the Prophet Isaiah.

SEEK the Lord while he may be found,
call upon him while he is near;
let the wicked person forsake their way,
and the unrighteous person their thoughts;
let that person return to the Lord that he may
  have mercy on them,
and to our God, for he will abundantly pardon.
For my thoughts are not your thoughts,
nor are your ways my ways, says the Lord.
For as the heavens are higher than the earth,
so are my ways higher than your ways
and my thoughts than your thoughts.

The word of the Lord. ℟. **Thanks be to God.** ↓

RESPONSORIAL PSALM Ps. 145 [The Nearness of God]

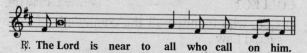

℟. **The Lord is near to all who call on him.**

Every day I will bless you,
and praise your name forever and ever.
Great is the Lord, and greatly to be praised;
his greatness is unsearchable.—℟.

The Lord is gracious and merciful,
slow to anger and abounding in steadfast love.

The Lord is good to all,
and his compassion is over all that he has
  made.—℞.

The Lord is just in all his ways,
and kind in all his doings.
The Lord is near to all who call on him,
to all who call on him in truth.—℞. ↓

SECOND READING Phil. 1.20-24, 27   [Life in Christ]

Paul notes that whether he lives or dies, his life belongs
to Christ. It would be more beneficial for the Philippians for Paul to continue living in the flesh to bring them
the message of Jesus.

A reading from the Letter of Saint Paul
          to the Philippians.

BROTHERS and sisters: Christ will be exalted
now as always in my body, whether by life or
by death.
  For to me, living is Christ and dying is gain. If I
am to live in the flesh, that means fruitful labour
for me; and I do not know which I prefer. I am
hard pressed between the two: my desire is to depart and be with Christ, for that is far better; but to
remain in the flesh is more necessary for you.
  Live your life in a manner worthy of the Gospel
of Christ.—The word of the Lord. ℞. **Thanks be to
God.** ↓

GOSPEL ACCLAMATION See Acts 16.14

[Listen to Jesus]

(If the Alleluia is not sung, the acclamation is omitted.)
℣. Alleluia. ℞. **Alleluia.**
℣. Open our hearts, O Lord,

to listen to the words of your Son.

℟. **Alleluia.** ↓

GOSPEL Mt. 20.1-16   [The Workers in the Vineyard]

> Jesus teaches that the kingdom of God is like the landowner who hires early in the morning, again at midmorning, at noon and midafternoon. At payment time, all the workers receive the same wage. How just and generous God is!

℣. The Lord be with you. ℟. **And with your spirit.**
✠ A reading from the holy Gospel according to Matthew. ℟. **Glory to you, O Lord.**

JESUS spoke this parable to his disciples. "The kingdom of heaven is like a landowner who went out early in the morning to hire labourers for his vineyard. After agreeing with the labourers for the usual daily wage, he sent them into his vineyard.

When he went out about nine o'clock, he saw others standing idle in the marketplace; and he said to them, 'You also go into the vineyard, and I will pay you whatever is right.' So they went.

When he went out again about noon and about three o'clock, he did the same. And about five o'clock he went out and found others standing around; and he said to them, 'Why are you standing here idle all day?' They said to him, 'Because no one has hired us.' He said to them, 'You also go into the vineyard.'

When evening came, the owner of the vineyard said to his manager, 'Call the labourers and give them their pay, beginning with the last and then going to the first.' When those hired about five o'clock came, each of them received the usual daily wage. Now when the first came, they thought they would receive more; but each of them also received the usual daily wage. And when they received it, they grumbled against the landowner, saying, 'These last worked only one hour, and you have made them equal to us who have borne the burden of the day and the scorching heat.' But he replied to one of them, 'Friend, I am doing you no wrong; did you not agree with me for the usual daily wage? Take what belongs to you and go; I choose to give to this last the same as I give to you. Am I not allowed to do what I choose with what belongs to me? Or are you envious because I am generous?'

So the last will be first, and the first will be last."—The Gospel of the Lord. ℟. **Praise to you, Lord Jesus Christ.**   → No. 15, p. 18

PRAYER OVER THE OFFERINGS

[Devotion and Faith]

Receive with favour, O Lord, we pray,
the offerings of your people,
that what they profess with devotion and faith
may be theirs through these heavenly mysteries.
Through Christ our Lord.
℟. **Amen.**   → No. 21, p. 22 (Pref. 29-36)

COMMUNION ANTIPHON Ps. 118.4-5

[Keeping God's Statutes]

You have laid down your precepts to be carefully kept; may my ways be firm in keeping your statutes. ↓

OR Jn. 10.14   [The Good Shepherd]

I am the Good Shepherd, says the Lord; I know my sheep, and mine know me. ↓

PRAYER AFTER COMMUNION

[Possessing Redemption]

Graciously raise up, O Lord,
those you renew with this Sacrament,
that we may come to possess your redemption
both in mystery and in the manner of our life.
Through Christ our Lord.
R̸. **Amen.**   → No. 30, p. 77

Optional Solemn Blessings, p. 97, and Prayers over the People, p. 105

"The tax collectors and the prostitutes are going
into the kingdom of God ahead of you."

OCTOBER 1
26th SUNDAY IN ORDINARY TIME

ENTRANCE ANTIPHON Dan. 3.31, 29, 30, 43, 42

[God's Mercy]

All that you have done to us, O Lord, you have done with true judgement, for we have sinned against you and not obeyed your command-

ments. But give glory to your name and deal with
us according to the bounty of your mercy.

→ No. 2, p. 10

COLLECT   [God's Pardon]

O God, who manifest your almighty power
above all by pardoning and showing mercy,
bestow, we pray, your grace abundantly upon us
and make those hastening to attain your promises
heirs to the treasures of heaven.
Through our Lord Jesus Christ, your Son,
who lives and reigns with you in the unity of the
   Holy Spirit,
one God, for ever and ever. R̸. **Amen.** ↓

FIRST READING Ez. 18.25-28   [Virtuous Man Shall Live]

The Lord's way is fair and just. It is when sinners repent
from their faults and do what is right that they are to
live. Because of this reform, they deserve to live.

A reading from the book of
the Prophet Ezekiel.

THUS says the Lord: "You object, O House of
Israel! You say, 'The way of the Lord is unfair.'
Hear now, O house of Israel: Is my way unfair? Is
it not your ways that are unfair?

When the righteous person turns away from
their righteousness and commits iniquity, they
shall die for it; for the iniquity that they have
committed they shall die.

Again, when the wicked person turns away
from the wickedness they have committed and
does what is lawful and right, they shall save their
life. Because that person considered and turned
away from all the transgressions that they had

committed, they shall surely live; they shall not die."—The word of the Lord. ℟. **Thanks be to God.** ↓

RESPONSORIAL PSALM Ps. 25 [God's Compassion]

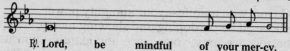

℟. **Lord, be mindful of your mer-cy.**

Make me to know your ways, O Lord;
teach me your paths.
Lead me in your truth, and teach me,
for you are the God of my salvation. —℟.

Be mindful of your mercy, O Lord, and of your steadfast love,
for they have been from of old.
According to your steadfast love remember me,
for the sake of your goodness, O Lord!—℟.

Good and upright is the Lord;
therefore he instructs sinners in the way.
He leads the humble in what is right,
and teaches the humble his way.—℟. ↓

SECOND READING Phil. 2.1-11 or 2.1-5 [Jesus Is Lord]

Paul urges us to be of one heart and mind, to possess a single love for one another. We should adopt the attitude of Jesus. At his name every knee should bend.

[If the "Shorter Form" is used, the indented text in brackets is omitted.]

A reading from the Letter of Saint Paul
to the Philippians.

BROTHERS and sisters: If there is any encouragement in Christ, any consolation from love, any sharing in the Spirit, any compassion and sympathy, then make my joy complete: be of the same mind, having the same love, being in full accord and of one mind. Do nothing from selfish ambition or conceit, but in humility regard others as better than yourselves. Let each of you look not to your own interests, but to the interests of others.

Let the same mind be in you that was in Christ Jesus,

[who, though he was in the form of God,
did not regard equality with God
as something to be exploited,
but emptied himself,
taking the form of a slave,
being born in human likeness.
And being found in human form,
he humbled himself
and became obedient to the point of death—
even death on a cross.

Therefore God highly exalted him
and gave him the name
that is above every name,
so that at the name of Jesus
every knee should bend,
in heaven and on earth and under the earth,
and every tongue should confess
that Jesus Christ is Lord,
to the glory of God the Father.]

The word of the Lord. ℟. **Thanks be to God.** ↓

GOSPEL ACCLAMATION See Jn. 10.27   [Listen]

(If the Alleluia is not sung, the acclamation is omitted.)

℣. Alleluia. ℟. **Alleluia.**

℣. My sheep hear my voice, says the Lord;
I know them, and they follow me.

℟. **Alleluia.** ↓

GOSPEL Mt. 21.28-32   [Obeying God's Will]

Jesus cites an example of a son who after having second thoughts obeyed his father. Even sinners, once they repent and sincerely search after God, will be saved and enter the kingdom of God.

℣. The Lord be with you. ℟. **And with your spirit.**
✤ A reading from the holy Gospel according to Matthew. ℟. **Glory to you, O Lord.**

JESUS said to the chief priests and the elders of the people: "What do you think? A man had two sons; he went to the first and said, 'Son, go and work in the vineyard today.' He answered, 'I will not'; but later he changed his mind and went. The father went to the second and said the same; and he answered, 'I am going, sir'; but he did not go. Which of the two did the will of his father?" They said, "The first."

Jesus said to them, "Truly I tell you, the tax collectors and the prostitutes are going into the kingdom of God ahead of you. For John came to you in the way of righteousness and you did not believe him, but the tax collectors and the prostitutes believed him; and even after you saw it, you did not change your minds and believe him."— The Gospel of the Lord. ℟. **Praise to you, Lord Jesus Christ.**
➜ No. 15, p. 18

PRAYER OVER THE OFFERINGS

[Offering as a Blessing]

Grant us, O merciful God,
that this our offering may find acceptance with
    you
and that through it the wellspring of all blessing
may be laid open before us.
Through Christ our Lord.
℟. **Amen.**   ➜ No. 21, p. 22 (Pref. 29-36)

COMMUNION ANTIPHON Cf. Ps. 118.49-50   [Hope]

**Remember your word to your servant, O Lord, by
which you have given me hope. This is my comfort when I am brought low.** ↓

OR 1 Jn. 3.16   [Offering of Self]

**By this we came to know the love of God: that
Christ laid down his life for us; so we ought to lay
down our lives for one another.** ↓

PRAYER AFTER COMMUNION [Co-heirs with Christ]

May this heavenly mystery, O Lord,
restore us in mind and body,
that we may be co-heirs in glory with Christ,
to whose suffering we are united
whenever we proclaim his Death.
Who lives and reigns for ever and ever.
℟. **Amen.**   ➜ No. 30, p. 77

Optional Solemn Blessings, p. 97, and Prayers over the People, p. 105

"The kingdom of God will be . . . given to a people
that produces the fruits of the kingdom."

OCTOBER 8

27th SUNDAY IN ORDINARY TIME

ENTRANCE ANTIPHON Cf. Est. 4.17   **[Lord of All]**

Within your will, O Lord, all things are established, and there is none that can resist your will. For you have made all things, the heaven and the earth, and all that is held within the circle of heaven; you are the Lord of all. → No. 2, p. 10

COLLECT   **[Mercy and Pardon]**

Almighty ever-living God,
who in the abundance of your kindness
surpass the merits and the desires of those who
   entreat you,
pour out your mercy upon us
to pardon what conscience dreads
and to give what prayer does not dare to ask.
Through our Lord Jesus Christ, your Son,

who lives and reigns with you in the unity of the
  Holy Spirit,
one God, for ever and ever. ℟. **Amen.** ↓

FIRST READING Isa. 5.1-7   [The Lord's Vineyard]

Isaiah uses the story of a vineyard to show how the
Lord respects his people. The vineyard is well culti-
vated, but it does not produce. The vineyard of the Lord
is the house of Israel and the people of Judah his cher-
ished plants.

A reading from the book of the Prophet Isaiah.

L ET me sing for my beloved
  my love song concerning his vineyard:

"My beloved had a vineyard on a very fertile
  hill.
He dug it and cleared it of stones,
and planted it with choice vines;
he built a watchtower in the midst of it,
and hewed out a wine vat in it;
he expected it to yield grapes,
but it yielded wild grapes.

And now, inhabitants of Jerusalem and people
  of Judah,
judge between me and my vineyard.
What more was there to do for my vineyard
that I have not done in it?
When I expected it to yield grapes,
why did it yield wild grapes?

And now I will tell you what I will do to my
  vineyard.
I will remove its hedge, and it shall be devoured;
I will break down its wall, and it shall be trampled down.

I will make it a waste;
it shall not be pruned or hoed,
and it shall be overgrown with briers and thorns;
I will also command the clouds
that they rain no rain upon it.
For the vineyard of the Lord of hosts is the
    house of Israel,
and the people of Judah are his pleasant plant-
    ing;
he expected justice, but saw bloodshed;
righteousness, but heard a cry!"

The word of the Lord. ℟. **Thanks be to God.** ↓

RESPONSORIAL PSALM Ps. 80   [Safety in the Lord]

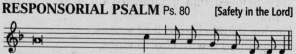

℟. The vineyard of the Lord is the house of Is - ra-el.

You brought a vine out of Egypt;
you drove out the nations and planted it.
It sent out its branches to the sea,
and its shoots to the River.—℟.

Why then have you broken down its walls,
so that all who pass along the way pluck its fruit?
The boar from the forest ravages it,
and all that move in the field feed on it.—℟.

Turn again, O God of hosts;
look down from heaven, and see;
have regard for this vine,
the stock that your right hand planted.—℟.

Then we will never turn back from you;
give us life, and we will call on your name.
Restore us, O Lord God of hosts;
let your face shine, that we may be saved.—℟. ↓

SECOND READING Phil. 4.6-9   [Wholesome Thoughts]

> Pray to God for your needs. God will guard over you. Discern what is true, honourable, just, pure, pleasing, commendable, excellent, and worthy of praise. The peace of God will then be with you.

A reading from the Letter of Saint Paul
to the Philippians.

BROTHERS and sisters: Do not worry about anything, but in everything by prayer and supplication with thanksgiving let your requests be made known to God. And the peace of God, which surpasses all understanding, will guard your hearts and your minds in Christ Jesus.

Finally, brothers and sisters, whatever is true, whatever is honourable, whatever is just, whatever is pure, whatever is pleasing, whatever is commendable, if there is any excellence and if there is anything worthy of praise, think about these things. Keep on doing the things that you have learned and received and heard and seen in me, and the God of peace will be with you.—The word of the Lord. ℟. **Thanks be to God.** ↓

GOSPEL ACCLAMATION See Jn. 15.16   [Bear Fruit]

(If the Alleluia is not sung, the acclamation is omitted.)

℣. Alleluia. ℟. **Alleluia.**

℣. I have chosen you from the world, says the Lord,

to go and bear fruit that will last.
℟. **Alleluia.** ↓

GOSPEL Mt. 21.33-43   [The Tenant Farmers]

> Jesus uses the parable of a landowner. Salvation is of-
> fered to all. The chosen who reject Christ are really
> turning him over to the whole world. The vineyard will
> be leased to others. The kingdom of God will produce
> fruit.

℣. The Lord be with you. ℟. **And with your spirit.**
✢ A reading from the holy Gospel according to
Matthew. ℟. **Glory to you, O Lord.**

JESUS said to the chief priests and the elders of
the people: "Listen to another parable. There
was a landowner who planted a vineyard, put a
fence around it, dug a wine press in it, and built a
watchtower. Then he leased it to tenants and went
to another country.

When the harvest time had come, he sent his
slaves to the tenants to collect his produce. But
the tenants seized his slaves and beat one, killed
another, and stoned another. Again he sent other
slaves, more than the first; and they treated them
in the same way.

Finally he sent his son to them, saying, 'They
will respect my son.' But when the tenants saw the
son, they said to themselves, 'This is the heir;
come, let us kill him and get his inheritance.' So
they seized him, threw him out of the vineyard,
and killed him.

Now when the owner of the vineyard comes,
what will he do to those tenants?" They said to
him, "He will put those wretches to a miserable
death, and lease the vineyard to other tenants

who will give him the produce at the harvest time."

Jesus said to them,

"Have you never read in the Scriptures:

'The stone that the builders rejected
   has become the cornerstone;

this was the Lord's doing,
   and it is amazing in our eyes'?

Therefore I tell you, the kingdom of God will be taken away from you and given to a people that produces the fruits of the kingdom."—The Gospel of the Lord. ℟. **Praise to you, Lord Jesus Christ.**   ➔ No. 15, p. 18

PRAYER OVER THE OFFERINGS [Sanctifying Work]

Accept, O Lord, we pray,
the sacrifices instituted by your commands
and, through the sacred mysteries,
which we celebrate with dutiful service,
graciously complete the sanctifying work
by which you are pleased to redeem us.
Through Christ our Lord.
℟. **Amen.**   ➔ No. 21, p. 22 (Pref. 29-36)

COMMUNION ANTIPHON Lam. 3.25 [Hope in the Lord]

The Lord is good to those who hope in him, to the soul that seeks him. ↓

OR Cf. 1 Cor. 10.17   [One Bread, One Body]

Though many, we are one bread, one body, for we all partake of the one Bread and one Chalice. ↓

PRAYER AFTER COMMUNION

[Nourished by Sacrament]

Grant us, almighty God,
that we may be refreshed and nourished
by the Sacrament which we have received,
so as to be transformed into what we consume.
Through Christ our Lord.
℞. **Amen.**   → No. 30, p. 77

Optional Solemn Blessings, p. 97, and Prayers over the People, p. 105

"Many are called, but few are chosen."

OCTOBER 15
28th SUNDAY IN ORDINARY TIME

ENTRANCE ANTIPHON Ps. 129.3-4

[A Forgiving God]

If you, O Lord, should mark iniquities, Lord, who
could stand? But with you is found forgiveness, O
God of Israel.   → No. 2, p. 10

COLLECT [Good Works]

May your grace, O Lord, we pray,
at all times go before us and follow after
and make us always determined
to carry out good works.
Through our Lord Jesus Christ, your Son,
who lives and reigns with you in the unity of the
    Holy Spirit,
one God, for ever and ever. ℟. **Amen.** ↓

FIRST READING Isa. 25.6-10a   [God as Saviour]

The Lord will set up a sumptuous feast for all peoples
and wipe away their tears. Then all will recognize the
Lord as their God.

A reading from the book of the Prophet Isaiah.

ON this mountain the Lord of hosts will make
    for all peoples
a feast of rich food, a feast of well-aged wines,
of rich food filled with marrow,
of well-aged wines strained clear.

And he will destroy on this mountain
the shroud that is cast over all peoples,
the sheet that is spread over all nations;
he will swallow up death forever.
Then the Lord God will wipe away the tears
    from all faces,
and the disgrace of his people
he will take away from all the earth,
for the Lord has spoken.

It will be said on that day,
"Lo, this is our God;
we have waited for him, so that he might save us.

This is the Lord for whom we have waited;
let us be glad and rejoice in his salvation.
For the hand of the Lord will rest on this mountain."
The word of the Lord. ℟. **Thanks be to God.** ↓

RESPONSORIAL PSALM Ps. 23 [Dwelling with the Lord]

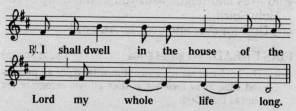

℟. I shall dwell in the house of the Lord my whole life long.

The Lord is my shepherd, I shall not want.
He makes me lie down in green pastures;
he leads me beside still waters;
he restores my soul.—℟.

He leads me in right paths for his name's sake.
Even though I walk through the darkest valley, I
   fear no evil;
for you are with me;
your rod and your staff—they comfort me.—℟.

You prepare a table before me
in the presence of my enemies;
you anoint my head with oil;
my cup overflows.—℟.

Surely goodness and mercy shall follow me
all the days of my life,
and I shall dwell in the house of the Lord
my whole life long.—℟. ↓

SECOND READING Phil. 4.12-14, 19-20

[Sharing in Hardships]

Paul admits that he has learned how to live and accept joy and sorrows, pleasure and pain. This lesson he has learned in Jesus.

A reading from the Letter of Saint Paul
      to the Philippians.

Brothers and sisters: I know what it is to have little, and I know what it is to have plenty. In any and all circumstances I have learned the secret of being well-fed and of going hungry, of having plenty and of being in need.

I can do all things through him who strengthens me. In any case, it was kind of you to share my distress.

My God will fully satisfy every need of yours according to his riches in glory in Christ Jesus. To our God and Father be glory forever and ever. Amen.—The word of the Lord. ℟. **Thanks be to God.** ↓

GOSPEL ACCLAMATION See Eph. 1.17-18   [Hope]

(If the Alleluia is not sung, the acclamation is omitted.)

℣. Alleluia. ℟. **Alleluia.**
℣. May the Father of our Lord Jesus Christ enlighten the eyes of our heart,
that we might know the hope to which we are called.
℟. **Alleluia.** ↓

GOSPEL Mt. 22.1-14 or 22.1-10   [The Wedding Banquet]

Jesus uses a parable to teach that many are called but few are chosen.

[If the "Shorter Form" is used, the indented text in brackets is omitted.]

℣. The Lord be with you. ℟. **And with your spirit.**
✛ A reading from the holy Gospel according to
Matthew. ℟. **Glory to you, O Lord.**

O NCE more Jesus spoke to the chief priests
and Pharisees in parables: "The kingdom of
heaven may be compared to a king who gave a
wedding banquet for his son. He sent his slaves
to call those who had been invited to the wedding banquet, but they would not come. Again
he sent other slaves, saying, 'Tell those who
have been invited: "Look, I have prepared my
dinner, my oxen and my fat calves have been
slaughtered, and everything is ready; come to
the wedding banquet."'

But they made light of it and went away, one
to his farm, another to his business, while the
rest seized his slaves, mistreated them, and
killed them. The king was enraged. He sent his
troops, destroyed those murderers, and burned
their city.

Then he said to his slaves, 'The wedding is
ready, but those invited were not worthy. Go
therefore into the main streets, and invite everyone you find to the wedding banquet.' Those
slaves went out into the streets and gathered all
whom they found, both good and bad; so the
wedding hall was filled with guests.

But when the king came in to see the
guests, he noticed a man there who was not
wearing a wedding robe, and he said to

him, 'Friend, how did you get in here without a wedding robe?' And he was speechless. Then the king said to the attendants, 'Bind him hand and foot, and throw him into the outer darkness, where there will be weeping and gnashing of teeth.' For many are called, but few are chosen."]

The Gospel of the Lord. ℟. **Praise to you, Lord Jesus Christ.**
➙ No. 15, p. 18

PRAYER OVER THE OFFERINGS   [Devotedness]

Accept, O Lord, the prayers of your faithful
with the sacrificial offerings,
that, through these acts of devotedness,
we may pass over to the glory of heaven.
Through Christ our Lord.
℟. **Amen.**
➙ No. 21, p. 22 (Pref. 29-36)

COMMUNION ANTIPHON Cf. Ps. 33.11
[God's Providence]

The rich suffer want and go hungry, but those who seek the Lord lack no blessing. ↓

OR 1 Jn. 3.2   [Vision of God]

When the Lord appears, we shall be like him, for we shall see him as he is. ↓

PRAYER AFTER COMMUNION   [Christ's Divine Nature]

We entreat your majesty most humbly, O Lord,
that, as you feed us with the nourishment
which comes from the most holy Body and Blood
    of your Son,
so you may make us sharers of his divine nature.

Who lives and reigns for ever and ever.
℟. **Amen.**   ➙ No. 30, p. 77

Optional Solemn Blessings, p. 97, and Prayers over the People, p. 105

"Give . . . to God the things that are God's."

OCTOBER 22

29th SUNDAY IN ORDINARY TIME

ENTRANCE ANTIPHON Cf. Ps. 16.6, 8

[Refuge in God]

To you I call; for you will surely heed me, O God;
turn your ear to me; hear my words. Guard me as
the apple of your eye; in the shadow of your
wings protect me.   ➙ No. 2, p. 10

COLLECT   [Sincerity of Heart]

Almighty ever-living God,
grant that we may always conform our will to
   yours
and serve your majesty in sincerity of heart.
Through our Lord Jesus Christ, your Son,

who lives and reigns with you in the unity of the
   Holy Spirit,
one God, for ever and ever. ℟. **Amen.** ↓

FIRST READING Isa. 45.1, 4-6   [One God]

For the sake of the Israelites, the Lord calls Cyrus and
gives him a title. It is the Lord who arms him, and through
him all people will know that there is only one Lord.

A reading from the book of the Prophet Isaiah.

THUS says the Lord to his anointed,
   to Cyrus, whose right hand I have grasped
to subdue nations before him
and strip kings of their robes,
to open doors before him—
and the gates shall not be closed:

"For the sake of my servant Jacob,
and Israel my chosen,
I call you by your name,
I surname you, though you do not know me.
I am the Lord, and there is no other;
besides me there is no god.
I arm you, though you do not know me,
so that all may know,
from the rising of the sun and from the west,
that there is no one besides me;
I am the Lord, and there is no other."

The word of the Lord. ℟. **Thanks be to God.** ↓

RESPONSORIAL PSALM Ps. 96   [The Lord Is King]

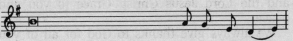

℟. Ascribe   to   the   Lord   glo-ry   and strength.

O sing to the Lord a new song;
sing to the Lord, all the earth.
Declare his glory among the nations,
his marvellous works among all the peoples.
℟. **Ascribe to the Lord glory and strength.**

For great is the Lord, and greatly to be praised;
he is to be revered above all gods.
For all the gods of the peoples are idols,
but the Lord made the heavens.—℟.

Ascribe to the Lord, O families of the peoples,
ascribe to the Lord glory and strength.
Ascribe to the Lord the glory due his name;
bring an offering, and come into his courts.—℟.

Worship the Lord in holy splendour;
tremble before him, all the earth.
Say among the nations, "The Lord is king!
He will judge the peoples with equity."—℟. ↓

SECOND READING 1 Thess. 1.1-5ab [Preaching the Gospel]

Paul writes to encourage the Thessalonians. He prays
for them constantly as they prove their faith through
works of love, for God has chosen them.

A reading from the first Letter of Saint Paul
to the Thessalonians.

FROM Paul, Silvanus, and Timothy, to the
Church of the Thessalonians in God the Father
and the Lord Jesus Christ: Grace to you and
peace.

We always give thanks to God for all of you
and mention you in our prayers, constantly re-

membering before our God and Father your work of faith and labour of love and steadfastness of hope in our Lord Jesus Christ. For we · know, brothers and sisters beloved by God, that he has chosen you, because our message of the Gospel came to you not in word only, but also in power and in the Holy Spirit and with full conviction.— The word of the Lord. ℟. **Thanks be to God.** ↓

GOSPEL ACCLAMATION See Phil. 2.15-16

[Word of Life]

(If the Alleluia is not sung, the acclamation is omitted.)

℣. Alleluia. ℟. **Alleluia.**
℣. Shine like stars in the world,
holding fast to the word of life.
℟. **Alleluia.** ↓

GOSPEL Mt. 22.15-21   [Lawful Taxes]

Jesus tells us: Give to the emperor what belongs to him and to God what belongs to God.

℣. The Lord be with you. ℟. **And with your spirit.**
✠ A reading from the holy Gospel according to Matthew. ℟. **Glory to you, O Lord.**

THE Pharisees went and plotted to entrap Jesus in what he said. So they sent their disciples to him, along with the Herodians, saying, "Teacher, we know that you are sincere, and teach the way of God in accordance with truth, and show deference to no one; for you do not regard people with partiality. Tell us, then, what you think. Is it lawful to pay taxes to the emperor, or not?"

But Jesus, aware of their malice, said, "Why are you putting me to the test, you hypocrites? Show

me the coin used for the tax." And they brought
him a denarius.

Then he said to them, "Whose head is this, and
whose title?" They answered, "Caesar's." Then he
said to them, "Give therefore to Caesar the things
that are Caesar's, and to God the things that are
God's."—The Gospel of the Lord. ℟. **Praise to you,
Lord Jesus Christ.**   ➔ No. 15, p. 18

PRAYER OVER THE OFFERINGS   [Respect Gifts]

Grant us, Lord, we pray,
a sincere respect for your gifts,
that, through the purifying action of your grace,
we may be cleansed by the very mysteries we
  serve.
Through Christ our Lord.
℟. **Amen.**   ➔ No. 21, p. 22 (Pref. 29-36)

COMMUNION ANTIPHON Cf. Ps. 32.18-19
[Divine Protection]

**Behold, the eyes of the Lord are on those who
fear him, who hope in his merciful love, to rescue
their souls from death, to keep them alive in
famine.** ↓

OR Mk. 10.45   [Christ Our Ransom]
**The Son of Man has come to give his life as a ran-
som for many.** ↓

PRAYER AFTER COMMUNION   [Eternal Gifts]

Grant, O Lord, we pray,
that, benefiting from participation in heavenly
  things,

we may be helped by what you give in this present
 age
and prepared for the gifts that are eternal.
Through Christ our Lord.
R⫰. **Amen.**   ➜ No. 30, p. 77

Optional Solemn Blessings, p. 97, and Prayers over the People, p. 105

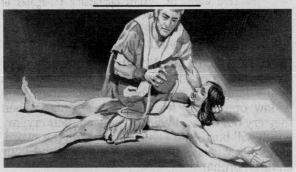

"'You shall love your neighbour as yourself.'"

OCTOBER 29

30th SUNDAY IN ORDINARY TIME

ENTRANCE ANTIPHON Cf. Ps. 104.3-4

[Seek the Lord]

**Let the hearts that seek the Lord rejoice; turn to
the Lord and his strength; constantly seek his
face.**   ➜ No. 2, p. 10

COLLECT   [Increase Virtues]

Almighty ever-living God,
increase our faith, hope and charity,
and make us love what you command,
so that we may merit what you promise.

Through our Lord Jesus Christ, your Son,
who lives and reigns with you in the unity of the
    Holy Spirit,
one God, for ever and ever. ℟. **Amen.** ↓

FIRST READING Ex. 22.21-27   [Kindness to Others]

> The Lord warns us against oppressing foreigners or
> harming widows or orphans. Consideration for the poor
> and needy should be a prime concern.

A reading from the book of Exodus.

THUS says the Lord: "You shall not wrong or
oppress a resident alien, for you were aliens
in the land of Egypt. You shall not abuse any
widow or orphan. If you do abuse them, when
they cry out to me, I will surely heed their cry; my
wrath will burn, and I will kill you with the sword,
and your wives shall become widows and your
children orphans.

If you lend money to my people, to the poor
one among you, you shall not deal with them as
a creditor; you shall not exact interest from
them. If you take your neighbour's cloak in
pawn, you shall restore it to that person before
the sun goes down; for it may be their only
clothing to use as cover; in what else shall that
person sleep? And if that person cries out to me,
I will listen, for I am compassionate."—The word
of the Lord. ℟. **Thanks be to God.** ↓

RESPONSORIAL PSALM Ps. 18   [God Our Rock]

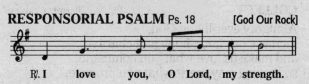

℟. I   love   you,   O   Lord,   my strength.

I love you, O Lord, my strength.
The Lord is my rock, my fortress, and my deliv-
    erer.
My God, my rock in whom I take refuge,
my shield, and the source of my salvation, my
    stronghold.—R̸.

I call upon the Lord, who is worthy to be praised,
so I shall be saved from my enemies.
From his temple he heard my voice,
and my cry to him reached his ears.—R̸.

The Lord lives! Blessed be my rock,
and exalted be the God of my salvation.
Great triumphs he gives to his king,
and shows steadfast love to his anointed.—R̸. ↓

SECOND READING 1 Thess. 1.5c-10   [Imitating Christ]

**The Thessalonians received the word of the Lord in
spite of great hardships. They then became model
Christians for their neighbours. They turned from idols
to worship the true God.**

A reading from the first Letter of Saint Paul
            to the Thessalonians.

BROTHERS and sisters: You know what kind
of persons we proved to be among you for
your sake. And you became imitators of us and of
the Lord, for in spite of persecution you received
the word with joy inspired by the Holy Spirit, so
that you became an example to all the believers in
Macedonia and in Achaia. For the word of the
Lord has sounded forth from you not only in

Macedonia and Achaia, but in every place your faith in God has become known, so that we have no need to speak about it. For the people of those regions report about us what kind of welcome we had among you, and how you turned to God from idols, to serve a living and true God, and to wait for his Son from heaven, whom he raised from the dead—Jesus, who rescues us from the wrath that is coming.—The word of the Lord. ℟. **Thanks be to God.** ↓

GOSPEL ACCLAMATION Jn. 14.23   [Keep My Word]

(If the Alleluia is not sung, the acclamation is omitted.)

℣. Alleluia. ℟. **Alleluia.**
℣. The one who loves me will keep my word
and my Father will love him
and we will come to him.
℟. **Alleluia.** ↓

GOSPEL Mt. 22.34-40   [The Greatest Commandments]

Jesus tells the lawyer that the greatest of all the commandments is love—to love God above all else and one's neighbour as oneself. This sums up the whole law.

℣. The Lord be with you. ℟. **And with your spirit.**
✠ A reading from the holy Gospel according to Matthew. ℟. **Glory to you, O Lord.**

WHEN the Pharisees heard that Jesus had silenced the Sadducees, they gathered together, and one of them, a lawyer, asked him a question to test him. "Teacher, which commandment in the Law is the greatest?"

Jesus said to him, "'You shall love the Lord your God with all your heart, and with all your

soul, and with all your mind.' This is the greatest
and first commandment.

And a second is like it: 'You shall love your
neighbour as yourself.' On these two commandments hang all the Law and the Prophets."—The
Gospel of the Lord. ℟. **Praise to you, Lord Jesus
Christ.**   ➜ No. 15, p. 18

PRAYER OVER THE OFFERINGS   [Glorifying God]

Look, we pray, O Lord,
on the offerings we make to your majesty,
that whatever is done by us in your service
may be directed above all to your glory.
Through Christ our Lord.
℟. **Amen.**   ➜ No. 21, p. 22 (Pref. 29-36)

COMMUNION ANTIPHON Cf. Ps. 19.6   [Saving Help]

**We will ring out our joy at your saving help and
exult in the name of our God.** ↓

OR Eph. 5.2   [Christ's Offering for Us]

**Christ loved us and gave himself up for us, as a
fragrant offering to God.** ↓

PRAYER AFTER COMMUNION   [Celebrate in Signs]

May your Sacraments, O Lord, we pray,
perfect in us what lies within them,
that what we now celebrate in signs
we may one day possess in truth.
Through Christ our Lord.
℟. **Amen.**   ➜ No. 30, p. 77

Optional Solemn Blessings, p. 97, and Prayers over the People, p. 105

"Whoever exalts himself will be humbled,
and whoever humbles himself will be exalted."

NOVEMBER 5

31st SUNDAY IN ORDINARY TIME

ENTRANCE ANTIPHON Cf. Ps. 37.22-23

[Call for God's Help]

Forsake me not, O Lord, my God; be not far from
me! Make haste and come to my help, O Lord,
my strong salvation! ➔ No. 2, p. 10

COLLECT [Praiseworthy Service]

Almighty and merciful God,
by whose gift your faithful offer you
right and praiseworthy service,
grant, we pray,
that we may hasten without stumbling
to receive the things you have promised.
Through our Lord Jesus Christ, your Son,

who lives and reigns with you in the unity of the
   Holy Spirit,
one God, for ever and ever. ℟. **Amen.** ↓

FIRST READING Mal. 1.14—2.2, 8-10
[Violating the Covenant]

I have sent a curse upon you, says the Lord, since you
have turned from me. You have not kept my ways. Only
one God has created us. Why do we break faith with
one another?

A reading from the book of the
Prophet Malachi.

"I AM a great King," says the Lord of hosts,
   "and my name is reverenced among the nations.

And now, O priests, this command is for you.
If you will not listen, if you will not lay it to
heart to give glory to my name," says the Lord of
hosts, "then I will send the curse on you and I
will curse your blessings; indeed I have already
cursed them, because you do not lay it to heart.

You have turned aside from the way; you have
caused many to stumble by your instruction;
you have corrupted the covenant of Levi," says
the Lord of hosts, "and so I make you despised
and abased before all the people, inasmuch as
you have not kept my ways but have shown partiality in your instruction."

Have we not all one father? Has not one God
created us? Why then are we faithless to one another, profaning the covenant of our ancestors?—The word of the Lord. ℟. **Thanks be to
God.** ↓

RESPONSORIAL PSALM Ps. 131　　[Peace in the Lord]

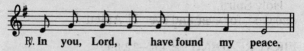

℟. In you, Lord, I have found my peace.

O Lord, my heart is not lifted up,
my eyes are not raised too high;
I do not occupy myself with things
too great and too marvellous for me.—℟.

But I have calmed and quieted my soul,
like a weaned child with its mother;
my soul is like the weaned child
that is with me.—℟.

O Israel, hope in the Lord
from this time on and forevermore.—℟. ↓

SECOND READING 1 Thess. 2.7-9, 13

[God's Good Tidings]

**Paul tells the Thessalonians how he wanted to share the
teachings of Jesus with them as well as his very life. He
works day and night for them. The word of God works
in those who believe.**

A reading from the first Letter of Saint Paul
to the Thessalonians.

BROTHERS and sisters: Though we might
have made demands as Apostles of Christ, we
were gentle among you, like a nurse tenderly car-
ing for her own children. So deeply do we care
for you that we are determined to share with you
not only the Gospel of God but also our own
selves, because you have become very dear to us.

You remember our labour and toil, brothers and sisters; we worked night and day, so that we might not burden any of you while we proclaimed to you the Gospel of God.

We also constantly give thanks to God for this, that when you received the word of God that you heard from us, you accepted it not as a human word but as what it really is, the word of God, which is also at work in you believers.—The word of the Lord. ℟. **Thanks be to God.** ↓

GOSPEL ACCLAMATION See Mt. 23.9, 10 [One Father]
(If the Alleluia is not sung, the acclamation is omitted.)
℣. Alleluia. ℟. **Alleluia.**
℣. You have one Father, your Father in heaven;
You have one teacher; the Lord Jesus Christ!
℟. **Alleluia.** ↓

GOSPEL Mt. 23.1-12   [The Virtue of Humility]

Jesus warns that the Pharisees speak many words boldly, admonishing others to observe the Law, but themselves fail in deeds fulfilling the Law. They act only to be seen. Only the humble will be exalted.

℣. The Lord be with you. ℟. **And with your spirit.**
✛ A reading from the holy Gospel according to Matthew. ℟. **Glory to you, O Lord.**

THEN Jesus said to the crowds and to his disciples, "The scribes and the Pharisees sit in Moses' chair; therefore, do whatever they teach you and follow it; but do not do as they do, for they do not practise what they teach. They tie up heavy burdens, hard to bear, and lay them on the shoulders of others; but they themselves are unwilling to lift a finger to move them. They do all their deeds to be seen by others; for they make their phylacteries broad and their fringes long. They love to have the place of honour at banquets and the best seats in the synagogues, and to be greeted with respect in the marketplaces, and to have people call them rabbi.

But you are not to be called rabbi, for you have one teacher, and you are all brothers and sisters. And call no one your father on earth, for you have one Father—the one in heaven. Nor are you to be called instructors, for you have one instructor, the Christ. The greatest among you will be your servant. Whoever exalts himself will be humbled, and whoever humbles himself will be exalted."— The Gospel of the Lord. ℟. **Praise to you, Lord Jesus Christ.** → No. 15, p. 18

PRAYER OVER THE OFFERINGS [God's Mercy]

May these sacrificial offerings, O Lord,
become for you a pure oblation,
and for us a holy outpouring of your mercy.
Through Christ our Lord.
℟. **Amen.** → No. 21, p. 22 (Pref. 29-36)

COMMUNION ANTIPHON Cf. Ps. 15.11 [Joy]

You will show me the path of life, the fullness of joy in your presence, O Lord. ↓

OR Jn. 6.58 [Life]

Just as the living Father sent me and I have life because of the Father, so whoever feeds on me shall have life because of me, says the Lord. ↓

PRAYER AFTER COMMUNION   [Renewal]

May the working of your power, O Lord,
increase in us, we pray,
so that, renewed by these heavenly Sacraments,
we may be prepared by your gift
for receiving what they promise.
Through Christ our Lord.
R̹. **Amen.**   → No. 30, p. 77

Optional Solemn Blessings, p. 97, and Prayers over the People, p. 105

"The bridegroom came, and those who were ready went
with him into the wedding banquet."

NOVEMBER 12

32nd SUNDAY IN ORDINARY TIME

ENTRANCE ANTIPHON Cf. Ps. 87.3

[Answer to Prayer]

Let my prayer come into your presence. Incline
your ear to my cry for help, O Lord. → No. 2, p. 10

COLLECT   [Freedom of Heart]

Almighty and merciful God,
graciously keep from us all adversity,
so that, unhindered in mind and body alike,
we may pursue in freedom of heart
the things that are yours.
Through our Lord Jesus Christ, your Son,
who lives and reigns with you in the unity of the
    Holy Spirit,
one God, for ever and ever.
R/. **Amen.** ↓

FIRST READING Wis. 6.12-16   [Love of Wisdom]

> Wisdom is found by those who seek after it. All who
> watch for wisdom shall find it. Wisdom graciously ap-
> pears.

A reading from the book of Wisdom.

WISDOM is radiant and unfading,
    and she is easily discerned by those who
  love her,
and is found by those who seek her.
She hastens to make herself known to those who
    desire her.
One who rises early to seek her will have no diffi-
    culty,
for she will be found sitting at the gate.
To fix one's thought on her is perfect understand-
    ing,
and one who is vigilant on her account will soon
    be free from care,
because she goes about seeking those worthy of
  her,

and she graciously appears to them in their paths,
and meets them in every thought.

The word of the Lord. ℟. **Thanks be to God.** ↓

RESPONSORIAL PSALM Ps. 63   [Seeking the Lord]

℟. My   soul   thirsts   for   you,   O Lord my   God.

O God, you are my God, I seek you,
my soul thirsts for you;
my flesh faints for you,
as in a dry and weary land where there is no
    water.—℟.

So I have looked upon you in the sanctuary,
beholding your power and glory.
Because your steadfast love is better than life,
my lips will praise you.—℟.

So I will bless you as long as I live;
I will lift up my hands and call on your name.
My soul is satisfied as with a rich feast,
and my mouth praises you with joyful lips.—℟.

I think of you on my bed,
and meditate on you in the watches of the night;
for you have been my help,
and in the shadow of your wings I sing for joy.
    —℟. ↓

SECOND READING 1 Thess. 4.13-18

[Rising from the Dead]

Those who die believing in Jesus will rise with him. They will in the final judgment rise first to enjoy God's life with Jesus.

A reading from the first Letter of Saint Paul to the Thessalonians.

WE do not want you to be uninformed, brothers and sisters, about those who have died, so that you may not grieve as others do who have no hope. For since we believe that Jesus died and rose again, even so, through Jesus, God will bring with him those who have died. For this we declare to you by the word of the Lord, that we who are alive, who are left until the coming of the Lord, will by no means precede those who have died.

For the Lord himself, with a cry of command, with the Archangel's call and with the sound of God's trumpet, will descend from heaven, and the dead in Christ will rise first. Then we who are alive, who are left, will be caught up in the clouds together with them to meet the Lord in the air; and so we will be with the Lord forever. Therefore encourage one another with these words.—The word of the Lord. ℟. **Thanks be to God. ↓**

GOSPEL ACCLAMATION See Mt. 24.42, 44 [Be Ready]

(If the Alleluia is not sung, the acclamation is omitted.)

℣. Alleluia. ℟. **Alleluia.**
℣. Keep awake and be ready:
you do not know when the Son of Man is coming.
℟. **Alleluia. ↓**

GOSPEL Mt. 25.1-13   [The Need for Watchfulness]

Jesus compares heaven to the five wise and five foolish
bridesmaids, waiting for the master. Only those who
are ever watchful will be ready to meet him. We know
neither the time nor the hour when he will come.

℣. The Lord be with you. ℟. **And with your spirit.**
✛ A reading from the holy Gospel according to
Matthew. ℟. **Glory to you, O Lord.**

JESUS spoke this parable to the disciples: "The
kingdom of heaven will be like this. Ten bridesmaids took their lamps and went to meet the
bridegroom. Five of them were foolish, and five
were wise. When the foolish took their lamps, they
took no oil with them; but the wise took flasks of
oil with their lamps. As the bridegroom was de-
layed, all of them became drowsy and slept.

But at midnight there was a shout, 'Look! Here
is the bridegroom! Come out to meet him.' Then all
those bridesmaids got up and trimmed their
lamps. The foolish said to the wise, 'Give us some
of your oil, for our lamps are going out.' But the
wise replied, 'No! There will not be enough for
you and for us; you had better go to the dealers
and buy some for yourselves.' And while they
went to buy it, the bridegroom came, and those
who were ready went with him into the wedding
banquet; and the door was shut.

Later the other bridesmaids came also, saying,
'Lord, lord, open to us.' But he replied, 'Truly I tell
you, I do not know you.' Keep awake therefore, for
you know neither the day nor the hour."—The
Gospel of the Lord. ℟. **Praise to you, Lord Jesus
Christ.**   ➔ No. 15, p. 18

PRAYER OVER THE OFFERINGS
[Celebrating the Passion]

Look with favour, we pray, O Lord,
upon the sacrificial gifts offered here,
that, celebrating in mystery the Passion of your
    Son,
we may honour it with loving devotion.
Through Christ our Lord.
℟. **Amen.**   ➔ No. 21, p. 22 (Pref. 29-36)

COMMUNION ANTIPHON Cf. Ps. 22.1-2
[The Lord Our Shepherd]

**The Lord is my shepherd; there is nothing I shall
want. Fresh and green are the pastures where
he gives me repose, near restful waters he leads
me.** ↓

OR Cf. Lk 24.35 [Jesus in the Eucharist]

**The disciples recognized the Lord Jesus in the
breaking of bread.** ↓

PRAYER AFTER COMMUNION
[Outpouring of the Spirit]

Nourished by this sacred gift, O Lord,
we give you thanks and beseech your mercy,
that, by the pouring forth of your Spirit,
the grace of integrity may endure
in those your heavenly power has entered.
Through Christ our Lord.
℟. **Amen.**   ➔ No. 30, p. 77

Optional Solemn Blessings, p. 97, and Prayers over the People, p. 105

"To all those who have, more will be given."

NOVEMBER 19

33rd SUNDAY IN ORDINARY TIME

ENTRANCE ANTIPHON Jer. 29.11, 12, 14 **[God Hears Us]**
The Lord said: I think thoughts of peace and not of affliction. You will call upon me, and I will answer you, and I will lead back your captives from every place. ➔ No. 2, p. 10

COLLECT [Glad Devotion]
Grant us, we pray, O Lord our God,
the constant gladness of being devoted to you,
for it is full and lasting happiness
to serve with constancy
the author of all that is good.
Through our Lord Jesus Christ, your Son,
who lives and reigns with you in the unity of the
    Holy Spirit,
one God, for ever and ever.
℟. **Amen.** ↓

FIRST READING Prov. 31.10-13, 16-18, 20, 26, 28-31

[A Worthy Wife]

A true wife is valued beyond all pearls. She brings good to her husband. She works for the household. She helps the poor. She deserves her reward.

A reading from the book of Proverbs.

A CAPABLE wife, who can find her?
   She is far more precious than jewels.
The heart of her husband trusts in her,
and he will have no lack of gain.
She does him good, and not harm,
all the days of her life.
She seeks wool and flax,
and works with willing hands.

She considers a field and buys it;
with the fruit of her hands she plants a vineyard.
She girds herself with strength,
and makes her arms strong.
She perceives that her merchandise is profitable.
Her lamp does not go out at night.

She opens her hand to the poor,
and reaches out her hands to the needy.
She opens her mouth with wisdom,
and the teaching of kindness is on her tongue.

Her children rise up and call her happy;
her husband too, and he praises her:
"Many women have done excellently,
but you surpass them all."

Charm is deceitful, and beauty is vain,
but a woman who fears the Lord is to be
   praised.

Give her a share in the fruit of her hands,
and let her works praise her in the city gates.

The word of the Lord. ℟. **Thanks be to God.** ↓

RESPONSORIAL PSALM Ps. 128   [Fear of the Lord]

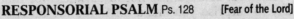
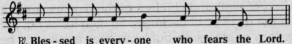

℟. Bles - sed is every - one who fears the Lord.

Blessed is everyone who fears the Lord,
who walks in his ways.
You shall eat the fruit of the labour of your hands;
you shall be happy, and it shall go well with you.—℟.

Your wife will be like a fruitful vine
within your house;
your children will be like olive shoots
around your table.—℟.

Thus shall the man be blessed who fears the Lord.
The Lord bless you from Zion.
May you see the prosperity of Jerusalem
all the days of your life.—℟. ↓

SECOND READING 1 Thess. 5.1-6   [The Day of the Lord]

**The day of the Lord will come like a thief in the night. It
will be sudden. There will be no escape.**

A reading from the first Letter of Saint Paul
to the Thessalonians.

NOW concerning the times and the seasons,
brothers and sisters, you do not need to have
anything written to you. For you yourselves know
very well that the day of the Lord will come like a
thief in the night. When they say, "There is peace

and security," then sudden destruction will come upon them, as labour pains come upon a pregnant woman, and there will be no escape!

But you, beloved, are not in darkness for that day to surprise you like a thief. You are all children of light and children of the day; we are not of the night or of darkness. So then let us not fall asleep as others do, but let us keep awake and be sober.—The word of the Lord. ℟. **Thanks be to God.** ↓

GOSPEL ACCLAMATION See Jn. 15.4, 5 [Live in Christ]

(If the Alleluia is not sung, the acclamation is omitted.)

℣. Alleluia. ℟. **Alleluia.**
℣. Abide in me as I in you, says the Lord;
my branches bear much fruit.
℟. **Alleluia.** ↓

GOSPEL Mt. 25.14-30 or 25.14-15, 19-21

[Faithful Servant]

Jesus speaks of the master who is going on a journey. He entrusts his property to three servants. Upon his return the first two are rewarded for their work. But the third who did not increase his wealth is chastised and punished.

[If the "Shorter Form" is used, the indented text in brackets is omitted.]

℣. The Lord be with you. ℟. **And with your spirit.**
✛ A reading from the holy Gospel according to Matthew. ℟. **Glory to you, O Lord.**

JESUS spoke this parable to his disciples: "For it is as if a man, going on a journey, summoned his slaves and entrusted his property to them; to one he gave five talents, to another two, to another one, to each according to his ability. Then he went away.

[The one who had received the five talents went off at once and traded with them, and made five more talents. In the same way, the one who had the two talents made two more talents. But the one who had received the one talent went off and dug a hole in the ground and hid his master's money.]

After a long time the master of those slaves came and settled accounts with them. Then the one who had received the five talents came forward, bringing five more talents, saying, 'Master, you handed over to me five talents; see, I have made five more talents.' His master said to him, 'Well done, good and trustworthy slave; you have been trustworthy in a few things, I will put you in charge of many things; enter into the joy of your master.'

[And the one with the two talents also came forward, saying, 'Master, you handed over to me two talents; see, I have made two more talents.' His master said to him, 'Well done, good and trustworthy slave; you have been trustworthy in a few things, I will put you in charge of many things; enter into the joy of your master.'

Then the one who had received the one talent also came forward, saying, 'Master, I knew that you were a harsh man, reaping where you did not sow, and gathering where you did not scatter seed; so I was afraid, and

I went and hid your talent in the ground. Here you have what is yours.'

But his master replied, 'You wicked and lazy slave! You knew, did you, that I reap where I did not sow, and gather where I did not scatter? Then you ought to have invested my money with the bankers, and on my return I would have received what was my own with interest. So take the talent from him, and give it to the one with the ten talents. For to all those who have, more will be given, and they will have an abundance; but from those who have nothing, even what they have will be taken away. As for this worthless slave, throw him into the outer darkness, where there will be weeping and gnashing of teeth.'"]

The Gospel of the Lord. ℟. **Praise to you, Lord Jesus Christ.**   ➔ No. 15, p. 18

PRAYER OVER THE OFFERINGS

[Everlasting Happiness]

Grant, O Lord, we pray,
that what we offer in the sight of your majesty
may obtain for us the grace of being devoted to
    you
and gain us the prize of everlasting happiness.
Through Christ our Lord.
℟. **Amen.**   ➔ No. 21, p. 22 (Pref. 29-36)

COMMUNION ANTIPHON Ps. 72.28   [Hope in God]
To be near God is my happiness, to place my hope in God the Lord. ↓

OR Mk. 11.23-24   [Believing Prayer]

Amen, I say to you: Whatever you ask in prayer, believe that you will receive, and it shall be given to you, says the Lord. ↓

PRAYER AFTER COMMUNION   [Growth in Charity]

We have partaken of the gifts of this sacred
    mystery,
humbly imploring, O Lord,
that what your Son commanded us to do
in memory of him
may bring us growth in charity.
Through Christ our Lord.
℟. **Amen.**   → No. 30, p. 77

Optional Solemn Blessings, p. 97, and Prayers over the People, p. 105

"The Son of Man . . . will sit on the throne of his glory.
All the nations will be gathered before him."

NOVEMBER 26

OUR LORD JESUS CHRIST, KING OF THE UNIVERSE

(34th Sunday in Ordinary Time)

Solemnity

ENTRANCE ANTIPHON Rev. 5.12; 1.6 [Christ's Glory]

How worthy is the Lamb who was slain, to receive power and divinity, and wisdom and strength and honour. To him belong glory and power for ever and ever.

→ No. 2, p. 10

COLLECT [King of the Universe]

Almighty ever-living God,
whose will is to restore all things
in your beloved Son, the King of the universe,
grant, we pray,
that the whole creation, set free from slavery,
may render your majesty service

and ceaselessly proclaim your praise.
Through our Lord Jesus Christ, your Son,
who lives and reigns with you in the unity of the
   Holy Spirit,
one God, for ever and ever. ℟. **Amen.** ↓

FIRST READING Ez. 34.11-12, 15-17   [The Lord's Care]

**The Lord looks after God's flock, takes them to pasture,
and rescues them. The Lord goes after those who are
lost. The Lord will also judge them.**

A reading from the book of the Prophet Ezekiel.

THUS says the Lord God: "I myself will search
for my sheep, and will seek them out. As a
shepherd seeks out his flock when he is among
his scattered sheep, so I will seek out my sheep. I
will rescue them from all the places to which they
have been scattered on a day of clouds and thick
darkness.

   I myself will be the shepherd of my sheep, and I
will make them lie down," says the Lord God. "I
will seek the lost, and I will bring back the strayed,
and I will bind up the injured, and I will strengthen
the weak, but the fat and the strong I will destroy. I
will feed my sheep with justice.

   As for you, my flock," thus says the Lord God: "I
shall judge between one sheep and another, between rams and goats."—The word of the Lord. ℟.
Thanks be to God. ↓

RESPONSORIAL PSALM Ps. 23   [Good Shepherd]

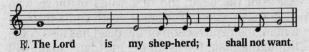

℟. **The Lord**   is   my **shep-herd; I**   shall **not want.**

The Lord is my shepherd, I shall not want.
He makes me lie down in green pastures;
he leads me beside still waters;
he restores my soul.

℟. **The Lord is my shepherd;**
    I shall not want.

He leads me in right paths for his name's sake.
Even though I walk through the darkest valley, I
    fear no evil;
for you are with me;
your rod and your staff—they comfort me.—℟.

You prepare a table before me
in the presence of my enemies;
you anoint my head with oil;
my cup overflows.—℟.

Surely goodness and mercy shall follow me
all the days of my life,
and I shall dwell in the house of the Lord
my whole life long.—℟. ↓

SECOND READING 1 Cor. 15.20-26, 28

[Christ the First Fruits]

**Christ has risen, and he is the first fruits of the dead. All
people have life in him. He will reign and all will be
subjected to him.**

A reading from the first Letter of Saint Paul
to the Corinthians.

BROTHERS and sisters: Christ has been raised
from the dead, the first fruits of those who
have fallen asleep. For since death came through
a man, the resurrection of the dead has also come
through a man; for as all die in Adam, so all will

be made alive in Christ. But each in his own order: Christ the first fruits, then at his coming those who belong to Christ.

Then comes the end, when he hands over the kingdom to God the Father, after he has destroyed every ruler and every authority and power. For he must reign until he has put all his enemies under his feet. The last enemy to be destroyed is death.

When all things are subjected to him, then the Son himself will also be subjected to the one who put all things in subjection under him, so that God may be all in all.—The word of the Lord. ℟. **Thanks be to God.** ↓

GOSPEL ACCLAMATION Mk. 11.9, 10   [Son of David]
(If the Alleluia is not sung, the acclamation is omitted.)

℣. Alleluia. ℟. **Alleluia.**
℣. Blessed is the one who comes in the name of the Lord.
Blessed is the coming kingdom of our father David.
℟. **Alleluia.** ↓

GOSPEL Mt. 25.31-46   [The Last Judgment]

All people will come to be judged by the Son of Man seated on his throne. The sheep will be on his right, the goats on his left. He will reward all good and punish all evil.

℣. The Lord be with you. ℟. **And with your spirit.**
✚ A reading from the holy Gospel according to Matthew. ℟. **Glory to you, O Lord.**

JESUS said to his disciples: "When the Son of Man comes in his glory, and all the Angels with him, then he will sit on the throne of his glory. All the nations will be gathered before him, and he will separate people one from another as a shepherd separates the sheep from the goats, and he will put the sheep at his right hand and the goats at the left.

Then the king will say to those at his right hand, 'Come, you that are blessed by my Father, inherit the kingdom prepared for you from the foundation of the world; for I was hungry and you gave me food, I was thirsty and you gave me something to drink, I was a stranger and you welcomed me, I was naked and you gave me clothing, I was sick and you took care of me, I was in prison and you visited me.'

Then the righteous will answer him, 'Lord, when was it that we saw you hungry and gave you food, or thirsty and gave you something to drink? And when was it that we saw you a stranger and welcomed you, or naked and gave you clothing? And when was it that we saw you sick or in prison and visited you?' And the king will answer them, 'Truly I tell you, just as you did it to one of the least of these brothers and sisters of mine, you did it to me.'

Then he will say to those at his left hand, 'You that are accursed, depart from me into the eternal fire prepared for the devil and his angels; for I was hungry and you gave me no food, I was thirsty and you gave me nothing to drink, I was a stranger and you did not welcome me, naked and you did not give me clothing, sick and in prison and you did not visit me.'

Then they also will answer, 'Lord, when was it that we saw you hungry or thirsty or a stranger or naked or sick or in prison, and did not take care of you?' Then he will answer them, 'Truly I tell you, just as you did not do it to one of the least of these, you did not do it to me.' And these will go away into eternal punishment, but the righteous into eternal life."—The Gospel of the Lord. ℟. **Praise to you, Lord Jesus Christ.**➔ No. 15, p. 18

PRAYER OVER THE OFFERINGS   [Unity and Peace]

As we offer you, O Lord, the sacrifice
by which the human race is reconciled to you,
we humbly pray
that your Son himself may bestow on all nations
the gifts of unity and peace.
Through Christ our Lord. ℟. **Amen.** ↓

PREFACE (51)   [Marks of Christ's Kingdom]

℣. The Lord be with you. ℟. **And with your spirit.**
℣. Lift up your hearts. ℟. **We lift them up to the Lord.**
℣. Let us give thanks to the Lord our God. ℟. **It is right and just.**

It is truly right and just, our duty and our salvation,
always and everywhere to give you thanks,
Lord, holy Father, almighty and eternal God.

For you anointed your Only Begotten Son,
our Lord Jesus Christ, with the oil of gladness
as eternal Priest and King of all creation,
so that, by offering himself on the altar of the Cross
as a spotless sacrifice to bring us peace,

he might accomplish the mysteries of human
    redemption
and, making all created things subject to his rule,
he might present to the immensity of your
    majesty
an eternal and universal kingdom,
a kingdom of truth and life,
a kingdom of holiness and grace,
a kingdom of justice, love and peace.

And so, with Angels and Archangels,
with Thrones and Dominions,
and with all the hosts and Powers of heaven,
we sing the hymn of your glory,
as without end we acclaim: ➔ No. 23, p. 23

COMMUNION ANTIPHON Ps. 28.10-11

[Blessing of Peace]

**The Lord sits as King for ever. The Lord will
bless his people with peace.** ↓

PRAYER AFTER COMMUNION

[Christ's Eternal Kingdom]

Having received the food of immortality,
we ask, O Lord,
that, glorying in obedience
to the commands of Christ, the King of the
    universe,
we may live with him eternally in his heavenly
    Kingdom.
Who lives and reigns for ever and ever.
℟. **Amen.**   ➔ No. 30, p. 77

Optional Solemn Blessings, p. 97, and Prayers over the People, p. 105

PASTORAL HELP

● The Liturgical Year and the History of Salvation

THE LITURGICAL YEAR
AND THE HISTORY OF SALVATION

1. THE LITURGICAL YEAR

Every Sunday the Church keeps the memory of our Lord's Paschal Mystery. She sanctifies time, consecrates it to God, and as it were inserts us into the History of Salvation. Within the cycle of a year she unfolds the whole mystery of Christ—from his foreshadowings in the Old Testament to his majestic Life and Work in the New Testament.

Thus, the feasts of the Liturgical Year are first of all celebrations of the History of Salvation. The mysteries of our Salvation are to be honoured not as something past but as something present, for while the act itself (e.g., Christ's birth, Death, Resurrection, Ascension, and the descent of the Holy Spirit) is past, its effects are present. Each feast puts before our mind the sign of some hidden sacred reality, which must be applied to us. We should celebrate the mysteries of our Salvation as happening now to us and we should undergo their mystical effect with an open heart. The best way to do so is by an active participation in Public Worship, aided by the Missal.

We can also be aided by the following summary of the major events of the History of Salvation.

2. ABRAHAM

a) The time around 1850 B.C. was a turning point in the long history of human beings. Almighty God interfered in the course of things and spoke to a man called Abraham. This man lived in what we call now the Fertile Crescent, i.e., the fertile countries along the Tigris and Euphrates rivers, the Jordan river and the Nile river, that surround the Syrian desert as a crescent. God gave the gift of faith to a simple bedouin, Abraham, who surrendered himself and his family entirely to God. Note that God blessed Abraham, promised to give the land of Canaan to his descendants, made a covenant (alliance) with him and wanted Abraham's faith to be sealed with a sign—circumcision (see Rom 4.11). This is the first establishment of the Kingdom of God on this earth. Read: Gen 11.27—12.9; Gen 17.1-14.

b) It is St. Paul who explains this simple beginning of God's dealings with humanity. Read: Gal 3.16, 26-29, 7-9; Rom 4.18-25. The Church considers Abraham the Father of all the faithful.

c) During the time that the Kingdom of God was restricted to Abraham's carnal offspring, initiation into it was achieved by the sign of circumcision. Now that it is open to all, through Christ's Death and Resurrection, Baptism and Confirmation are the signs (sacraments) of initiation into God's people on earth. Read: Acts 15.1-12; Col 2.11-14.

3. PASSOVER AND EXODUS

a) "Abraham was the father of Isaac, and Isaac the father of Jacob, and Jacob the father of Judah and his brothers" (Mt 1.2). The clan of Jacob emigrated to Egypt where it later fell into slavery. However, God did not forget his chosen people. He bestowed a leader upon the people of Israel (Moses) who led them out of slavery in Egypt. This is called the Exodus. Read: Gen 37; 41.37-46; 46.1-7, 28-34; Ex 1.1-14; 2.1-21; 3.1-14; 11; 12; 14.10-31.

b) God's people was saved from bondage and evil by the Passover sacrifice and its Sacrificial Repast—which foreshadowed the perfect Sacrifice of Jesus Christ on the Cross. Because Jesus was man, he could offer a sacrifice. Because he was also God, his Sacrifice symbolized an infinitely perfect obedience and self-surrender and was worthy of God the Father. We are saved from evil because of the blood of our Passover Lamb, Jesus Christ. We partake in this Sacrifice, made present to us under the signs of bread and wine, and eat the Sacrificial Repast. Read: Heb 10.4-10; Mk 14.12-16, 22-24; 1 Cor 5. 6-8.

4. GOD'S PROTECTION

a) Israel, God's people, went through the Red Sea and obtained their freedom from slavery in Egypt. Under the leadership of Moses they wandered in the desert for forty years and hoped to enter the Promised Land. Whatever they needed in the desert—water, meat, and bread—they received through the prayer of Moses. Read: Ex 16.4-15, 31-35; 17.1-7.

b) We, who are the new people of God, obtained our freedom from the bondage of Satan by going through the water of Baptism (best symbolized in the ancient Church by immersion). Under the leadership of Christ the Church passes through the desert of life, hoping to enter the Promised Land: heaven. All that the people need in order to reach their supreme goal is given through Christ, our Lord. Read: 1 Cor 10.1-11; 2 Cor 5.1-10; Jn 6.48-71.

5. THE COVENANT

a) Moses ascended Mount Sinai as the mediator between God and the people. It was on this mountain that God proclaimed the Ten Commandments. The Covenant of God with Abraham was then four hundred years old (see Gen 17.1-8). It is a perpetual Covenant, unfolded gradually and consummated with the blood of sacrifice, which reaches its final perfection in its renewed form on Calvary. Read: Ex 19.1-8, 16-25; 20.1-17; 24.4-8.

b) The Mediator of the New Covenant is Jesus Christ. It is established on Calvary with all peoples of the world. The New Covenant is consummated with the Sacrifice of Christ's Precious Blood. Read: Heb 3.1-6; 8.6-13; Lk 22.14-20.

6. FIRST FULFILLMENT OF GOD'S PROMISE

God promised Abraham to give the land of Canaan to his descendants (Gen 12.7). God began to fulfil his promise when the Jews crossed the river Jordan at Jericho under the leadership of Joshua. He realized it under the kingship of David and of Solomon. This great kingdom, ever more idealized in Jewish history, was actually the Kingdom of God. The king was merely his representative and servant (2 Sam 7.5). Since the kings were anointed to be king (2 Sam 5.3) they were called: "The anointed of Yahweh," which means in Hebrew: "Mashiah." Hence the Bible speaks of the "Messiah" or "Christ" (from the Greek) being the king of the great Kingdom of God to come. But this first fulfillment of God's promise contained a further promise, namely, of the Universal Kingdom of God, the Church. God gradually revealed that David's kingdom merely prefigured this great Kingdom to come. Read: 2 Sam 5.1-5; 7.1-17 (esp. 12-16); Ps 71.1-17; Lk 1.31-33; Mk 1.14-15; Mt 9.35-38; Lk 22.24-30; Jn 18.33-38.

7. THE EXILE (BABYLONIAN CAPTIVITY)

a) Israel knew that all the blessings and promises of God depended on faithfulness to the Covenant. But Israel was not faithful. God sent prophets to remind his people of the Covenant. He threatened them and finally had to punish them. Israel was carried away into exile. Read: 1 Kings 19.1-4; 21; Am 3; Isa 1.1-4; 5.1-7; Jer 2.4-7; 6.16-19; 15. 5-6; Bar 6, 1-6.

b) It was in the exile of Babylon that God's people started praying again. We should pray the psalms of God's chosen people and make them our prayer. Exile and punishment may be seen as separation from God, when we have sinned. We are now: Israel, House of Jacob, House of Judah, Zion or Jerusalem. Read: Ps 136.1-6; 78; 41; 125; 135.1-9, 26.

8. GOD'S PLAN OF SALVATION

a) The wise men of Israel, moved by the Holy Spirit (Gen 1.1—2.7) tell us that God created everything. To make "everything" more understandable for the people of their time, they divided it up in six portions, calling them "days," in order to suggest that the Jews had six days to work and were supposed to rest on the Sabbath. Compare this story about creation with the lesson about it by St. Paul to the Athenians. Read: Gen 1.1—2.7; Acts 17.22-34.

b) They give us God's plan: human beings would share in God's own life. They would be only a little less than the angels (Ps 8.6). They would live in happiness without pain, frustration, hard labor, or sickness and without dying would be admitted to see God in heaven. But this plan could not be realized, because Adam ate from the tree of knowledge of good and evil (committed sin). The Bible speaks of: "sin of the world" or simply: "sin." This is called "original sin"—the sinful condition in which all of us are born because of the sins of our first parents and everybody's sin. Read: Gen 1.26-30; 2.8-25.

c) God chose a people for himself. He began with Abraham. Patiently, he revealed his plans more clearly and finally established the Kingdom of God through Christ. God did not give up his original plan. He restored all things in Jesus. Read: Eph 1.3-10.

9. PREPARATION

a) The punishment of the exile was the punishment of a loving Father. The prophet Ezekiel, who was with the exiled Jews in Babylon, taught them these things. This punishment was to cleanse the people from evil and to prepare them gradually for the coming of the Universal Kingdom of God with the true "Anointed," Jesus Christ. Read: Ezek 36.24-28, 33-38.

b) In the past centuries before the coming of Christ, the pious Jews, called "The Holy Remnant" or sometimes "The Poor of Yahweh," fostered that waiting and desire for the Kingdom of God. They knew their Bible and prayed. Their prayer should be our prayer during our celebration of Advent. Read: Gen 3.14-15; Isa 7.14; 9.1-7; 11.1-9; 40.1-11; 53.1-7; Ps 21; Isa 45.8.

c) John the Baptist is the last of the prophets in the time of preparation. He introduced the Promised Messiah to his contemporaries. Read: Mt 3.

10. THE KINGDOM OF GOD IS AT HAND

a) When Jesus of Nazareth began preaching and establishing the Kingdom of God, he taught plainly: "I have come, not to abolish [the law and the prophets], but to fulfil them" (Mt 5.17). The kingdom of David was only a first fulfillment of God's promise to Abraham. It contained a further promise, which has been fulfilled in the Kingdom of the Anointed of Yahweh par excellence: Christ Jesus. Read: Mk 1.14-22; Mt 5.17-20; 4.23-25; Jn 1.35-51.

b) Christ Jesus explained that it was he of whom the prophets had spoken (see Jn 1.45) and he worked many miracles to manifest the glory and power of God in him. Read: Lk 4.14-22; Mt 11.16 and Isa 35.5 and 61.1; Lk 18.31-34; 24.13-35 (esp. 25-27); Jn 2.1-12 (esp. 11); 11.1-44 (esp. 42); 12.37-43.

c) With both plain words and parables Jesus explained the nature of the Kingdom and what it means to us. It is a universal Kingdom for all people of faith, who are henceforth the real children of Abraham (see Gal 3.7). It is a people cleansed from iniquity (see Eph 5.25-27) and sharing God's life as originally planned by him (see No. 8b). Read: Mt 22.1-4; 21.33-43; Jn 10.11-16; 15.1-11; 3.1-6; Mt 13.

d) Jesus established a hierarchy of bishops to rule the Kingdom, to teach and to distribute God's blessings in his name, while he resides in heaven, sitting at God's right hand, i.e., as Man sharing power with God, being King and High Priest, interceding for us at God's throne (see Heb 7.25). Read: Mt 28.16-20; Lk 10.1-16 (esp.16); Jn 20.19-23; Mt 16.13-20; Jn 21.15-17; 1 Cor 11.23-26 (esp. 24).

e) The gradually more perfect realization of the Kingdom in every person follows the universal law of birth and growth: through pain and death to life everlasting! But it is worthwhile to give up everything to gain it. Read: Jn 12.20-26; Mt 10.16-20; Lk 22.15-30; 12.22-34; 18.18-30; 24.25-27.

11. THE UNIVERSAL CHURCH

The History of our Salvation began with Abraham, reached a peak in the Death and Resurrection of our Lord and became complete with the descent of the Holy Spirit. But it goes on. Christ leads the Church through the Holy Spirit (see Jn 14.16 and Mt 10.20). He continues to teach us and to bless us through holy Signs, the Sacraments. And our grateful answer to God by good behavior is possible only with the help of Christ. Read: Acts 8.26-40; 8.14-17; 2.42-47; 2 Tim 1.6-9; Eph 5.22-33; Rom 8.26.

12. THE FINAL FULFILLMENT

When Christ Jesus established the Kingdom of God, the promise to Abraham was fulfilled. God's original plan was restored in human beings. Sin and evil were defeated. Human beings shared in God's life. But like David's kingdom (see No. 6) this first fulfillment contains a promise, namely, the glorious Kingdom of God in the future world. This will be realized when Jesus will surrender the Kingdom to the Father and God will be all in all. Read: Mt 25.33-46; 1 Cor 15.22-28; Rev 21.1-4; Titus 2.11-15; Mt 6.10.

HYMNAL

1

O Come, O Come, Emmanuel

Tr. J. M. Neale, 1816-66
and others

Veni Emmanuel
Melody adapted by
T. Helmore, 1811-90

1. O come, O come, Em - man - - u - el, And ran -
2. O come, thou rod of Jes - se, free Thine own
3. O come, thou day-spring, come and cheer Our spir -
4. O come, thou key of Da - vid, come, And o -
5. O come, O come, thou Lord of might, Who to

1. som cap - tive Is - ra - el, That mourns in
2. from Sa - tan's tyr - an - ny; From depths of
3. its by thine ad - vent here; Dis - perse the
4. pen wide our heav'n - ly home; Make safe the
5. thy tribes, from Si - nai's height, In an - cient

1. low - ly ex - ile here, Un - til the Son of
2. hell thy peo - ple save, And give them vic - t'ry
3. gloom - y clouds of night, And death's dark shad-ows
4. way that leads on high, And close the path to
5. times didst give the law In cloud, in ma - jes -

Refrain:

1. God ap-pear.
2. o'er the grave.
3. put to flight. Re - joice! Re-joice! O Is -
4. mis - er - y.
5. ty, and awe.

ra - el. To thee shall come Em - man - - u - el.

Hark, a Mystic Voice Is Sounding

Tr. E. Caswall, 1849

En Clara Vox
R.L. de Pearsall, 1795-1856

1.

Hark, a mystic voice is sounding;
"Christ is nigh," It seems to say;
"Cast away the dreams of darkness,
O ye children of the day."

2.

Startled at the solemn warning,
Let the earthbound soul arise;
Christ her sun, all sloth dispelling,
Shines upon the morning skies.

3.

Lo, the Lamb so long expected
Comes with pardon down from heav'n;
Let us haste, with tears of sorrow,
One and all, to be forgiv'n.

The Coming of Our God

1.

The coming of our Lord
Our thought must now employ;
Then let us meet him on the road.
With song of holy joy.

2.

The co-eternal Son
A maiden's offspring see;
A servant's form Christ putteth on;
To set his people free.

3.

Daughter of Sion, rise
To greet thine Infant King;
Not let thy thankless heart despise
The pardon he doth bring.

O Come, Divine Messiah

Anne Pellegrin, 1663-1745
Sr. St. Mary of St. Philip

Venez Divin Messie
16th Century French
Harm. G. Ridout, 1971

O come, divine Messiah!
The world in silence waits the day
When hope shall sing its triumph,
And sadness flee away.

Chorus: Sweet Saviour, haste,
Come, come to earth:
Dispel the night, and show thy face,
And bid us hail the dawn of grace.
O come, divine Messiah,
The world in silence waits the day
When hope shall sing its triumph,
And sadness flee away.

5. Hark! The Herald Angels Sing

1. Hark! The herald angels sing,
   "Glory to the newborn King.
   Peace on earth, and mercy mild,
   God and sinners reconciled."
   Joyful, all ye nations, rise,
   Join the triumph of the skies,
   With th'angelic host proclaim,
   "Christ is born in Bethlehem."

   —*Refrain*. Hark! The herald angels sing,
   "Glory to the newborn King."

2. Christ, by highest heav'n adored,
   Christ, the everlasting Lord.
   Late in time behold him come,
   Offspring of a virgin's womb.
   Veiled in flesh, the Godhead see;
   Hail th'incarnate Deity!
   Pleased as Man with men to appear,
   Jesus, our Emmanuel. —*Refrain*

6. Silent Night

Silent night, holy night!
   All is calm, all is bright.
'Round yon Virgin Mother and
   Child.
   Holy Infant so tender and
   mild:
Sleep in heavenly peace,
   Sleep in heavenly peace!

Silent night, holy night!
   Shepherds quake at the
   sight!
Glories stream from heaven
   afar.
   Heav'nly hosts sing Alleluia:
Christ, the Saviour is born,
   Christ, the Saviour is born!

7. We Three Kings

1. We three kings of Orient are
   Bearing gifts we traverse afar,
   Field and fountain, moor and mountain,
   Following yonder Star.

   Refrain: O Star of wonder, Star of night,
   Star with royal beauty bright,
   Westward leading, still proceeding,
   Guide us to thy perfect light.

2. Born a king on Bethlehem's plain,
   Gold I bring to crown Him again,
   King forever, ceasing never,
   Over us all to reign. —*Refrain*

O Come, All Ye Faithful

8

1. O come, all ye faithful, joyful and triumphant,
   O come ye, O come ye to Bethlehem;
   Come and behold him born the King of angels.

   —Refrain: O come, let us adore him,
   O come, let us adore him,
   O come, let us adore him, Christ the Lord.

2. Sing choirs of angels, Sing in exultation,
   Sing all ye citizens of Heav'n above;
   Glory to God in the highest. *—Refrain*

3. See how the shepherd summoned to his cradle,
   Leaving their flocks draw nigh with lowly fear;
   We too will thither bend our joyful footsteps. *—Refrain*

The First Noel

9

1. The first Noel the angel did say,
   Was to certain poor shepherds in fields as they lay;
   In fields where they lay keeping their sheep
   On a cold winter's night that was so deep.

   —Refrain: Noel, Noel, Noel, Noel,
   Born is the King of Israel.

2. They looked up and saw a star,
   Shining in the east, beyond them far,
   And to the earth it gave great light,
   And so it continued both day and night. *—Refrain*

3. This star drew nigh to the northwest,
   O'er Bethlehem it took its rest,
   And there it did both stop and stay,
   Right over the place where Jesus lay. *—Refrain*

4. Then entered in those wise men three,
   Full reverently upon their knee,
   And offered there in his presence,
   Their gold and myrrh and frankincense. *—Refrain*

10 · Angels We Have Heard on High

1. Angels we have heard on high,
   Sweetly singing o'er the plain,
   And the mountains in reply
   Echoing their joyous strain.

   Refrain: **Gloria in excelsis Deo.** (Repeat)

2. Shepherds, why this jubilee,
   Why your joyous strains prolong?
   Say, what may the tidings be
   Which inspire your heav'nly song? —*Refrain*

3. Come to Bethlehem and see
   Him whose birth the angels sing;
   Come, adore on bended knee
   Christ the Lord, the newborn King. —*Refrain*

11 · Joy to the World

1.
Joy to the world! The Lord is come;
   Let earth receive her King;
Let every heart prepare him room,
   And heav'n and nature sing,
And heav'n and nature sing,
   And heaven, and heaven and nature sing.

2.
Joy to the world! the Saviour reigns,
   Let men their songs employ,
While fields and floods,
   Rocks, hills, and plains,
Repeat the sounding joy,
   Repeat the sounding joy,
Repeat, repeat the sounding joy.

12 · O Sing a Joyous Carol

1. O sing a joyous carol
   Unto the Holy Child,
   And praise with gladsome voices
   His mother undefiled.
   Our gladsome voices greeting
   Shall hail our Infant King;
   And our sweet Lady listens
   When joyful voices sing.

2. Who is there meekly lying
   In yonder stable poor?
   Dear children, it is Jesus;
   He bids you now adore.
   Who is there kneeling by him?
   In Virgin beauty fair?
   It is our Mother Mary,
   She bids you all draw near.

Lord, Who throughout These 40 Days

1. Lord, Who throughout these forty days
   For us did fast and pray,
   Teach us to overcome our sins
   And close by you to stay.

2. As you with Satan did contend
   And did the vic'try win,
   O give us strength in you to fight,
   In you to conquer sin.

3. As you did hunger and did thirst,
   So teach us, gracious Lord,
   To die to self and so to live
   By your most holy word.

O Faithful Cross

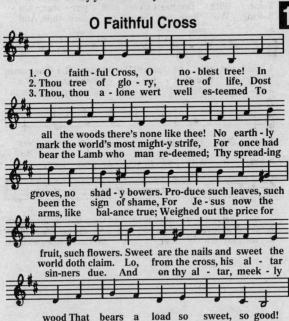

1. O faith-ful Cross, O no-blest tree! In
2. Thou tree of glo-ry, tree of life, Dost
3. Thou, thou a-lone wert well es-teemed To

all the woods there's none like thee! No earth-ly
mark the world's most might-y strife, For once had
bear the Lamb who man re-deemed; Thy spread-ing

groves, no shad-y bowers. Pro-duce such leaves, such
been the sign of shame, For Je-sus now the
arms, like bal-ance true; Weighed out the price for

fruit, such flowers. Sweet are the nails and sweet the
world doth claim. Lo, from the cross, his al-tar
sin-ners due. And on thy al-tar, meek-ly

wood That bears a load so sweet, so good!
throne, He gent-ly draws and rules his own.
laid, The lamb of God a-tone-ment made.

15 O Sacred Head, Surrounded

H.W. Baker, 1861
A.T. Russell, 1851, alt.

Passion Chorale
H. L. Hassler, 1601
Adapted, J.S. Bach, 1685-1750

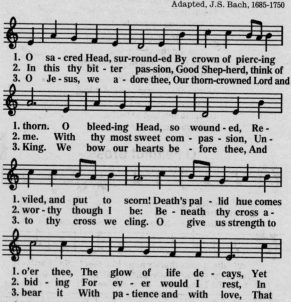

1. O sa - cred Head, sur-round-ed By crown of pierc-ing
2. In this thy bit - ter pas-sion, Good Shep-herd, think of
3. O Je - sus, we a - dore thee, Our thorn-crowned Lord and

1. thorn. O bleed-ing Head, so wound - ed, Re -
2. me. With thy most sweet com - pas - sion, Un -
3. King. We bow our hearts be - fore thee, And

1. viled, and put to scorn! Death's pal - lid hue comes
2. wor - thy though I be: Be - neath thy cross a -
3. to thy cross we cling. O give us strength to

1. o'er thee, The glow of life de - cays, Yet
2. bid - ing For ev - er would I rest, In
3. bear it With pa - tience and with love, That

1. an - gel hosts a - dore thee, And trem-ble as they gaze.
2. thy dear love con - fid - ing, And with thy pre-sence blest.
3. we may tru - ly mer - it A glo-rious crown a - bove.

All Glory, Laud and Honour

16

St. Theodulph of Orleans, c. 820
Tr. J.M. Neale, 1854, alt.

St. Theodulph
M. Teachner, 1615

1. All glo - ry, laud, and hon - our To thee, Re-deem-er,

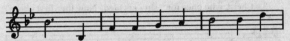

1. King, To whom the lips of chil - dren Made

Fine

1. sweet ho - san - nas ring. 2. Thou art the King of
3. The com - pa - ny of
4. The peo - ple of the
5. To thee be - fore thy
6. Thou didst ac - cept their

2. Is - rael, Thou Da - vid's roy - al Son. Who
3. an - gels Are prais - ing thee on high, And
4. He - brews With palms be - fore thee went; Our
5. pas - sion They sang their hymns of praise; To
6. prais - es, Ac - cept the pray'rs we bring, Who

D.C.

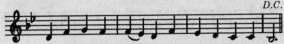

2. in the Lord's name com-est, The King and bles-sed One.
3. mor-tal men and all things Cre - a - ted make re - ply.
4. praise and pray'r and an - thems Be - fore thee we pre-sent.
5. thee now high ex - alt - ed Our mel - o - dy we raise.
6. in all good de - light-est, Thou good and gra-cious King.

603

17 Christ the Lord Is Ris'n Today

Jane E. Leeson, c. 1851,
based on Victimae Paschali

Victimae Paschali
Traditional

1. Christ, the Lord is   ris'n to - day, Chris-tians, haste your
2. Christ, the vic-tim   un - de-filed, Man to God has
3. Christ, who once for   sin - ers bled, Now the first - born

1. vows to pay;   Of - fer ye your   prais - es meet
2. rec - on - ciled; When in strange and aw - ful strife
3. from the dead, Thron'd in end - less might   and pow'r

1. At the pas - chal   vic-tim's feet.   For the sheep the
2. Met to - geth - er   death and life; Chris-tians, on this
3. Lives and reigns for   ev - er more. Hail, e - ter - nal

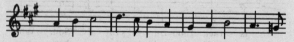

1. Lamb has bled, Sin-less in the sinners' stead; Christ, the
2. hap - py day Haste with joy your vows to pay. Christ, the
3. hope on high! Hail, thou King of vic- to - ry! Hail, thou

1. Lord, is ris'n on high, Now he lives, no more to die!
2. Lord, is ris'n on high, Now he lives, no more to die!
3. Prince of life a-dored! Help and save us, gra-cious Lord.

604

The Strife is O'er

Tr. F. Pott, 1861, alt.

Victory
Palestrina, 1591
Adapted W.H. Monk, 1861

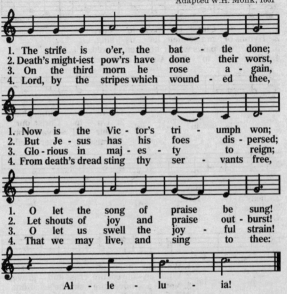

1. The strife is o'er, the bat - tle done;
2. Death's might-iest pow'rs have done their worst,
3. On the third morn he rose a - gain,
4. Lord, by the stripes which wound - ed thee,

1. Now is the Vic - tor's tri - umph won;
2. But Je - sus has his foes dis - persed;
3. Glo - rious in maj - es - ty to reign;
4. From death's dread sting thy ser - vants free,

1. O let the song of praise be sung!
2. Let shouts of joy and praise out - burst!
3. O let us swell the joy - ful strain!
4. That we may live, and sing to thee:

Al - le - lu - ia!

O God, Our Help in Ages Past

1.

O God, our help in ages past,
 Our hope for years to come,
Our shelter from the stormy blast,
 And our eternal home.

2.

Beneath the shadow of Thy throne,
 Thy saints have dwelt se-cure,
Sufficient is Thine arm alone,
 And our defence is sure.

3.

Before the hills in order stood,
 Or earth received her frame,
From éverlasting Thou art God,
 To endless years the same.

4.

A thousand ages in Thy sight,
 Are like an evening gone.
Short as the watch that ends the night,
 Before the rising sun.

Jesus Christ Is Ris'n Today

1. Je - sus Christ is ris'n to - day,
2. Hymns of praise then let us sing,
3. But the pains which he en - dured,
4. Sing we to our God a - bove,

Al - -

- le - lu - ia!

1. Our tri - um - phant
2. Un - to Christ our
3. Our sal - va - tion
4. Praise e - ter - nal

1. ho - ly day,
2. heav'n - ly King,
3. have pro - cured;
4. as his love.

Al - - - le -

1. Who did once up - on the cross,
2. Who en - dured the cross and grave,
3. Now a - bove the sky he's King,
4. Praise him, all ye heav'nly host,

lu - ia!

Al - - - le - lu - ia!

1. Suf - fer to re - deem our loss.
2. Sin - ners to re - deem and save.
3. Where the an - gels ev - er sing.
4. Fa - ther, Son and Ho - ly Ghost.

Al - - - le - lu - ia!

That Eastertide with Joy was Bright

Verses 1, 2: tr. J.M. Neale, 1851   Lasst   Uns Erfreuen
Verse 3: tr. J. Chambers, 1857, alt.   Geistliches Kirchengesang, 1623

21

1. That East-er-tide with joy was bright, The
2. He showed to them his hands, his side, Where
3. To God the Fa-ther let us sing, To

1. sun shone out with fair-er light, Al-le-
2. yet those glo-rious wounds a-bide, Al-le-
3. God the Son, our ris-en King, Al-le-

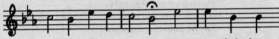

1. lu-ia, al-le-lu-ia, When, to their long-
2. lu-ia, al-le-lu-ia, The to-kens true
3. lu-ia, al-le-lu-ia, And e-qual-ly

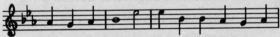

1. ing eyes re-stored, The glad a-pos-tles saw their
2. which made it plain. Their Lord in-deed was ris'n a-
3. let us a-dore The Ho-ly Spir-it ev-er-

1. Lord, Al-le-lu-ia, al-le-lu-ia, Al-le-
2. gain, Al-le-lu-ia, al-le-lu-ia, Al-le-
3. more, Al-le-lu-ia, al-le-lu-ia, Al-le-

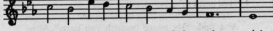

1. lu-ia, al-le-lu-ia, al-le-lu-ia!
2. lu-ia, al-le-lu-ia, al-le-lu-ia!
3. lu-ia, al-le-lu-ia, al-le-lu-ia!

22

At the Lamb's High Feast We Sing

1. At the Lamb's high feast we sing
    Praise to our victor'ous King.
   He has washed us in the tide
    Flowing from his opened side;
   Praise we him whose love divine
    Gives his sacred Blood for wine,
   Gives his Body for the feast,
    Christ the Victim, Christ the Priest.

2. When the Paschal blood is poured,
    Death's dark Angel sheathes his sword;
   Israel's hosts triumphant go
    Through the wave that drowns the foe.
   Christ the Lamb, whose Blood was shed,
    Paschal victim, Paschal bread;
   With sincerity and love
    Eat we Manna from above.

23

Ye Sons and Daughters, Let Us Sing

Alleluia! Alleluia! Alleluia!

1. Ye sons and daughters, let us sing!
    The King of heav'n, our glorious King,
   From death today rose triumphing. Alleluia!

2. That Easter morn, at break of day,
    The faithful women went their way
   To seek the tomb where Jesus lay. Alleluia!

3. An angel clothed in white they see,
    Who sat and spoke unto the three,
   "Your Lord has gone to Galilee." Alleluia!

4. That night th'apostles met in fear,
    And Christ did in their midst appear.
   And said, "My peace be with you here." Alleluia!

5. How blest are they who have not seen
    And yet whose faith has constant been,
   For they eternal life shall win. Alleluia!

All Hail, Adored Trinity

Verses 1, 2, 3: Anglo Saxon, 11th cent.
Praise God: Thomas Ken, 1709

Louis Bourgeois, 1551

1. All hail, a - dor - ed Trin - i - ty; All praise, e - ter - nal U - ni - ty: O God the Fa - ther, God the Son, And God the Spir - it, ev - er One.
2. Three Per - sons praise we ev - er - more, And thee th' E - ter - nal One a - dore: In thy sure mer - cy ev - er kind, May we our true pro - tec - tion find.
3. O Trin - i - ty, O U - ni - ty, Be pres - ent as we wor - ship thee; And to the an - gel's songs in light Our prayers and prais - es now u - nite.

Sing We Triumphant Hymns of Praise

1. Sing we triumphant hymns of praise
   To greet our Lord these festive days.
   Alleluia, alleluia!
   Who by a road before untrod
   Ascended to the throne of God.
   Alleluia, alleluia.
   Alleluia, alleluia, alleluia!

2. In wond'ring awe His faithful band
   Upon the Mount of Olives stand.
   Alleluia, alleluia!
   And with the Virgin Mother see
   Their Lord ascend in majesty.
   Alleluia, alleluia.
   Alleluia, alleluia, alleluia!

26 Praise God from Whom All Blessings Flow

1. Praise God, from whom all blessings flow;
    Praise him, all creatures here below;
   Praise him above, ye heav'nly host;
    Praise Father, Son, and Holy Ghost.

2. All people that on earth do dwell,
    Sing to the Lord with cheerful voice;
   Him serve with mirth, his praise forth tell,
    Come ye before him and rejoice.

3. Know that the Lord is God indeed:
    Without our aid he did us make;
   We are his folk, he doth us feed,
    And for his sheep he doth us take.

4. O enter then his gates with praise,
    Approach with joy his courts unto;
   Praise, laud, and bless his name always,
    For it is seemly so to do.

27 Come, Holy Ghost

1. Come, Holy Ghost, Creator blest,
   And in our hearts take up your rest;
   Come with your grace and heav'nly aid
   To fill the hearts which you have made,
   To fill the hearts which you have made.

2. O Comforter, to you we cry,
   The heav'nly gift of God most high;
   The fount of life and fire of love,
   And sweet anointing from above,
   And sweet anointing from above.

3. To every sense your light impart,
   And shed your love in ev'ry heart.
   To our weak flesh, your strength supply:
   Unfailing courage from on high,
   Unfailing courage from on high.

4. O grant that we through you may come
   To know the Father and the Son,
   And hold with firm, unchanging faith,
   That you are Spirit of them both,
   That you are Spirit of them both.

O Holy Spirit, Lord of Peace

28

Tr. J. Chandler, 1806-76, alt.

Jeremiah Clark, 1709

1. O Ho - ly Spir - it, Lord of grace, E -
2. As thou in bond of love dost join The
3. All glo - ry to the Fa - ther be, All

1. ter - nal fount of love, In - flame, we pray, our
2. Fa - ther and the Son, So fill us all with
3. glo - ry to the Son, And Ho - ly Spir - it

1. in-most hearts With fire from heav'n a - bove.
2. mu-tual love, U - nite our hearts as one.
3. ev - er more While end - less a - ges run.

Creator Spirit, Lord of Grace

29

1. Creator Spirit, Lord of grace
   Make thou our hearts thy dwelling place
   And with thy might celestial, aid
   The souls of those whom thou hast made.

2. O to our souls thy light impart;
   And give thy love to every heart;
   Turn all our weakness into might,
   O thou the source of life and light.

3. To God the Father let us sing
   To God the Son, our risen king;
   And equally with thee adore
   The Spirit, God forevermore.

30 Now Thank We All Our God

M. Rinkart, 1586-1649
Tr. Catherine Winkworth, 1858

Nun Danket
J. Crüger, 1647

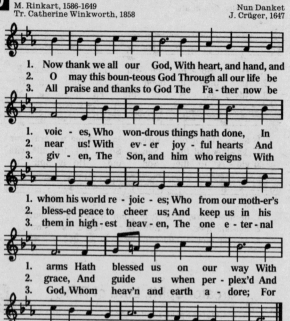

1. Now thank we all our God, With heart, and hand, and
2. O may this boun-teous God Through all our life be
3. All praise and thanks to God The Fa-ther now be

1. voic-es, Who won-drous things hath done, In
2. near us! With ev-er joy-ful hearts And
3. giv-en, The Son, and him who reigns With

1. whom his world re-joic-es; Who from our moth-er's
2. bless-ed peace to cheer us; And keep us in his
3. them in high-est heav-en, The one e-ter-nal

1. arms Hath blessed us on our way With
2. grace, And guide us when per-plex'd And
3. God, Whom heav'n and earth a-dore; For

1. count-less gifts of love, And still is ours to-day.
2. free us from all ills In this world and the next.
3. thus it was, is now, And shall be, ev-er-more.

31 We Gather Together

1. We gather together to ask the Lord's blessing;
   He chastens and hastens his will to make known;
   The wicked oppressing now cease from distressing:
   Sing praises to his name; he forgets not his own.

2. Beside us to guide us, our God with us joining,
   Ordaining, maintaining his kingdom divine;
   So from the beginning the fight we were winning:
   Thou, Lord, wast at our side; all glory be thine.

Holy, Holy, Holy

R. Heber, 1826, alt.

Nicaea
J. B. Dykes, 1861

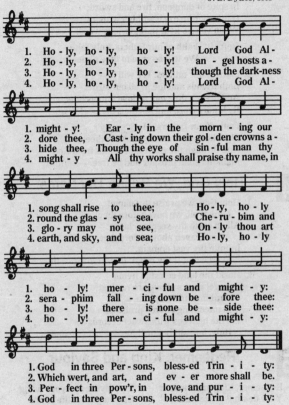

1. Ho - ly, ho - ly, ho - ly! Lord God Al - might - y! Ear - ly in the morn - ing our song shall rise to thee; Ho - ly, ho - ly ho - ly! mer - ci - ful and might - y: God in three Per - sons, bless-ed Trin - i - ty:

2. Ho - ly, ho - ly, ho - ly! an - gel hosts a - dore thee, Cast - ing down their gol - den crowns a - round the glas - sy sea. Che - ru - bim and sera - phim fall - ing down be - fore thee: Which wert, and art, and ev - er more shall be.

3. Ho - ly, ho - ly, ho - ly! though the dark-ness hide thee, Though the eye of sin - ful man thy glo - ry may not see, On - ly thou art ho - ly! there is none be - side thee: Per - fect in pow'r, in love, and pur - i - ty:

4. Ho - ly, ho - ly, ho - ly! Lord God Al - might - y All thy works shall praise thy name, in earth, and sky, and sea; Ho - ly, ho - ly ho - ly! mer - ci - ful and might - y: God in three Per - sons, bless-ed Trin - i - ty:

33

Faith of Our Fathers

1. Faith of our fathers, living still,
   In spite of dungeon, fire and sword;
   O how our hearts beat high with joy
   When'ver we hear that glorious word!

   Refrain: Faith of our fathers, holy faith,
   We will be true to thee til death.

2. Faith of our fathers! We will love
   Both friends and foe in all our strife.
   And preach thee too, as love knows how,
   By kindly word and virtuous life. —*Refrain*

3. Faith of our fathers! Mary's pray'r
   Shall keep our country close to thee;
   And through the truth that comes from God
   Mankind shall prosper and be free. —*Refrain*

34

Holy God, We Praise Thy Name

1. Holy God, we praise thy name!
   Lord of all, we bow before thee!
   All on earth thy sceptre claim,
   All in heaven above adore thee.
   Infinite thy vast domain,
   Everlasting is thy reign. *Repeat last two lines*

2. Hark! the loud celestial hymn
   Angel choirs above are raising;
   Cherubim and seraphim,
   In unceasing chorus praising,
   Fill the heavens with sweet accord;
   Holy, holy, holy Lord! *Repeat last two lines*

35

Redeemer, King and Saviour

1.

Redeemer, King and Saviour
Your death we celebrate
So good, yet born our brother,
You live in human state.
O Saviour, in your dying
You do your Father's will,
Give us the strength to suffer
To live for others still.

2.

Your dying and your rising
Give hope and life to all.
Your faithful way of giving
Embraces great and small.
Help us to make our journey,
to walk your glorious way,
And from the night of dying
To find a joy-filled day.

614

To Jesus Christ, Our Sovereign King

M.B. Hellriegel

Ich Glaub An Gott
Mainz, 1900

36

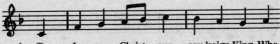

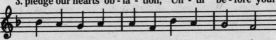

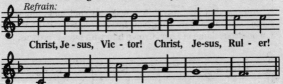

1. To Je-sus Christ, our sov-'reign King, Who is the world's sal-va-tion, All praise and hom-age do we bring And thanks and ad-o-ra-tion.
2. Your reign ex-tend, O King be-nign, To ev-'ry land and na-tion; For in your king-dom, Lord di-vine, A-lone we find sal-va-tion.
3. To you and to your Church, great King, We pledge our hearts' ob-la-tion; Un-til be-fore your throne we sing In end-less ju-bi-la-tion:

Refrain:

Christ, Je-sus, Vic-tor! Christ, Je-sus, Rul-er!

Christ, Je-sus, Lord and Re-deem—er!

O Lord, I Am Not Worthy

37

1. O Lord, I am not worthy,
   That thou shouldst come to me,
   But speak the word of comfort:
   My spirit healed shall be.

2. And humbly I'll receive thee,
   The bridegroom of my soul,
   No more by sin to grieve thee
   Or fly thy sweet control.

3. O Sacrament most holy,
   O Sacrament divine,
   All praise and all thanksgiving
   Be every moment thine.

38 Crown Him with Many Crowns

M. Bridges, 1851
and others

Diademata
G.J. Elvey, 1868

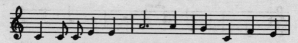

1. Crown him with man-y crowns. The Lamb up-on his
2. Crown him the Lord of Lords, Who o-ver all doth
3. Crown him the Lord of heav'n En-throned in worlds a-

1. throne: Hark, how the heav'n-ly an-them drowns All
2. reign, Who once on earth th'in-car-nate Word, For
3. bove; Crown him the King, to whom is giv'n The

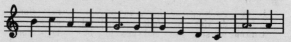

1. mu-sic but its own! A-wake my soul, and sing Of
2. ran-somed sin-ners slain, Now lives in realms of light, Where
3. won-drous name of Love. Crown him with man-y crowns. As

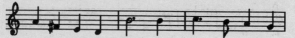

1. him who died for thee. And hail him as thy
2. saints with an-gels sing Their songs be-fore him
3. thrones be-fore him fall. Crown him, ye kings, with

1. match-less King Through all e-ter-ni-ty.
2. day and night, Their God, Re-deem-er, King.
3. man-y crowns, For he is King of all.

Taste and See

39

Tune: James E. Moore, Jr., b. 1951

Text: Psalm 34;
James E. Moore, Jr., b. 1951

Refrain

Taste and see, taste and see the good-ness of the
Lord. O taste and see, taste and see the
good - ness of the Lord, of the Lord.

Verses

1. I will bless the Lord at all times.
2. Glo - ri - fy the Lord with me,
3. Wor-ship the Lord, all you peo-ple.

Praise shall al-ways be on my lips;
To-geth-er let us all praise God's name.
You'll want for noth-ing if you ask.

my soul shall glo-ry in the Lord
I called the Lord who an - swered me;
Taste and see that the Lord is good;

D.C.

for God has been so good to me.
from all my trou-bles I was set free.
in God we need put all our trust.

40 Lord, Who at Your First Eucharist Did Pray

W.H. Turton, 1881, alt.

Song I
O. Gibbons, 1623

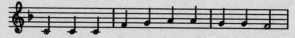

1. Lord, who at your first Eu - cha - rist did pray
2. For all your Church, O Lord, we in - ter - cede;
3. So, Lord, at length when sa - cra - ments shall cease,

1. That all your Church might be for ev - er one,
2. O make our lack of char - i - ty to cease;
3. May we be one with all your Church a - bove,

1. Grant us at ev - 'ry Eu - cha - rist to
2. Draw us the near - er each to each, we
3. One with your saints in one un - end - ing

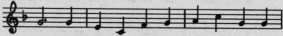

1. say With long - ing heart and soul, "Your will be
2. plead, By draw - ing all to you, O prince of
3. peace, One with your saints in one un - bound - ed

1. done." O may we all one bread, one bod - y be
2. peace; Thus may we all one bread, one bod - y be
3. love: More bless-ed still in peace and love to be

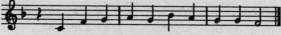

1. Through this blest Sa - cra-ment of u - ni - ty.
2. Through this blest Sa - cra-ment of u - ni - ty.
3. One with the Trin - i - ty in u - ni - ty.

618

Immaculate Mary

Anon.

Lourdes
Traditional Lourdes Melody

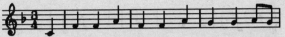

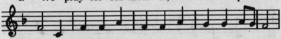

1.   Im - mac - u - late Ma - ry, your prais - es   we
2.   In heav - en, the bless - ed your glo - ry pro -
3.   Your name is our pow - er, your vir - tues our
4.   We pray for our moth - er, the Church up - on

1. sing, You reign now in heav-en with   Je - sus our King.
2. claim; On earth, we your chil-dren in - voke your fair name.
3. light, Your love is our com -fort, your plead-ing our might.
4. earth, And bless, dear-est la - dy, the   land of our birth.

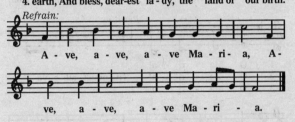

Refrain:

A - ve, a - ve, a - ve Ma - ri - a, A -

ve, a - ve, a - ve Ma - ri - a.

Hail, O Star of Ocean

1. Hail, O Star of Ocean,
   Portal of the sky!
   Ever Virgin Mother
   Of the Lord most high.

2. O by Gabriel's Ave
   Uttered long ago,
   Eva's name reversing
   Brought us peace below.

Hail, Holy Queen, Enthroned Above

Traditional

Salve Regina Caelitum
Traditional

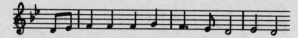

1. Hail, ho - ly Queen en - throned a - bove, O Ma -
2. Our life, our sweet-ness here be - low, O Ma -
3. We hon - our you for Christ, your son, O Ma -

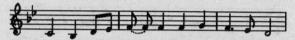

1. ri - a! Hail, moth-er of mer - cy and of love,
2. ri - a! Our hope in sor - row and in woe,
3. ri - a! Who has for us re - demp-tion won,

Refrain:

1. O Ma - ri - a!
2. O Ma - ri - a! Tri - umph all ye
3. O Ma - ri - a!

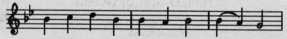

che - ru - bim, Sing with us, ye se - ra - phim,

Heav'n and earth re - sound the hymn: Sal - ve,

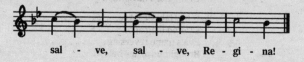

sal - ve, sal - ve, Re - gi - na!

For All the Saints

W.W. How, 1864

Sine Nomine
R. Vaughan Williams, 1906

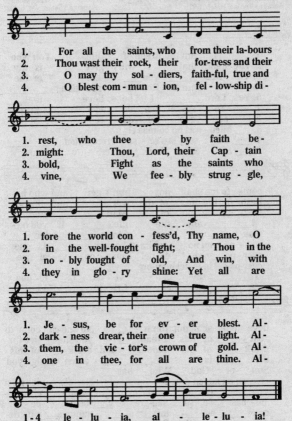

1. For all the saints, who   from their la-bours
2. Thou wast their rock, their   for-tress and their
3. O may thy sol - diers, faith-ful, true and
4. O blest com - mun - ion,   fel - low-ship di -

1. rest,   who   thee   by   faith be -
2. might: Thou, Lord, their   Cap - tain
3. bold,   Fight   as   the   saints who
4. vine,   We   fee - bly   strug - gle,

1. fore the world con - fess'd, Thy name,   O
2. in   the well-fought   fight;   Thou   in the
3. no - bly fought of   old,   And   win,   with
4. they in   glo - ry   shine: Yet   all   are

1. Je - sus,   be for   ev - er   blest. Al -
2. dark - ness drear, their   one true   light. Al -
3. them,   the   vic - tor's   crown of   gold. Al -
4. one   in   thee, for   all   are   thine. Al -

1 - 4   le - lu - ia,   al - le - lu - ia!

Music from the English Hymnal,
used by permission of Oxford University Press

I Am the Bread of Life

Tune: BREAD OF LIFE, Irreg. with refrain;
Suzanne Toolan, SM, b. 1927

Text: John 6;
Suzanne Toolan, SM, b. 1927

1. ___ I am the Bread of life. You who
2. The bread that___ I will give is my
3. Un - less_____ you eat of the
4. ___ I am the Res - ur - rec - tion,_____
5. Yes, Lord,_____ I be - lieve that___

1. ___ Yo soy el pan de vi - da. El que
2. El pan que___ yo da - ré____ es mi
3. ___ Mien - tras no co-mas el
4. ___ Yo soy la re - su - rrec - ción.___
5. ___ Sí, Se - ñor, yo cre - o que

come to me shall not hun - ger;___ and who be-
flesh for the life of the world,_____ and if you
flesh of the Son of Man_____ and___
I_____ am the life._____ If you be -
you_____ are the Christ, the____

vie - ne_a mí no ten-drá ham - bre.____ El que
cuer - po___ vi - da del mun - do,___ y el que
cuer-po del hi-jo del hom-bre, y
Yo_____ soy la vi - da. El que
tú e - res el Cris - to, _____ El

lieve in me shall not thirst._____ No one can come to
eat___ of this bread,_____ you shall__ live for
drink_____ of his blood,__ and drink___ of his
lieve ___ in___ me,_____ e-ven__ though you
Son__ of__ God,___ Who has___

cree_en mí no ten-drá sed.____ Na - die___ vie - ne_a
co - ma__ de mi car-ne_____ ten-drá___ vi - da_e-
be - bas __ de su san-gre y be-bas___ de su
cree_____ en___ mí,_____ aun-que___ mu - rie -
Hi - jo de Dios,___ que vi - no al

me   un - less the___ Fa - ther   beck-ons.
ev - er,_____ you shall__live for   ev - er.
blood,_____ you shall not have life with - in you.
die,_____   you shall__live for   ev - er.
come   in - to   the_____   world.___
mí_____   mien - tras el Pa - dre   lla - me.
ter - na,_____   ten - drá___ vi - da_e - ter - na.
san - gre,   no ten - drá___ vi - da   en ti.
ra,_____   ten - drá vi - da e - ter - na.
mun-do_____ pa - ra sal - var - nos.

And I will raise   you up,   and I will
Yo   le re - su - ci - ta - ré,   Yo lo re -

raise   you up,   and I will raise   you
su - ci - ta - ré,   Yo lo re - su - ci - ta -

up   on the last   day.
ré   el   di - a   de_El.

O Most Holy One

46

1. O most holy one, O most lowly one,
   Loving virgin, Maria!
   Mother, maid of fairest love,
   Lady, queen of all above,
   Ora, ora pro nobis.

2. Virgin ever fair, Mother, hear our prayer,
   Look upon us, Maria!
   Bring to us your treasure,
   Grace beyond all measure,
   Ora, ora pro nobis.

English text from the New St. Basil Hymnal
by permission of The Basillian Press, Toronto.

Send Us Your Spirit

Tune: David Haas, b. 1957
acc. by Jeanne Cotter, b. 1964

Text: David Haas, b. 1957

Refrain

Come Lord Je-sus, send us your Spir-it, re-new the face of the earth. Come Lord Je-sus, send us your Spir-it, re-new the face of the earth.

Verses

1. Come to us, Spir-it of God, breathe in us now, we sing to-geth-er. Spir-it of hope and of light, fill our lives, come to us, Spir-it of God.

2. Fill us with the fire of your love, burn in us now, bring us to-geth-er. Come to us, dwell in us, change our lives, O Lord, come to us, Spir-it of God.

3. Send us the wings of new birth, fill all the earth with the love you have taught us. Let all cre-a-tion now be shak-en with love, come to us, Spir-it of God.

May be sung in canon.

Praise to the Lord, the Almighty

J. Neander, 1950-80
Tr. Catherine Winkworth, 1863, alt.

Lobe Den Herren
Stralsund Gesangbuch, 1665

48

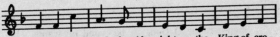

1. Praise to the Lord, the Al - might - y, the King of cre -
2. Praise to the Lord, let us of - fer our gifts at the
3. Praise to the Lord, who does pros-per our work and de -
4. Praise to the Lord, O let all that is in us a -

1. a - tion! O my soul, praise him for
2. al - tar. Let not our sins and of -
3. fend us; Sure - ly his good - ness and
4. dore him. All that has life and breath

1. he is your health and sal - va - tion.
2. fen - ces now cause us to fal - ter.
3. mer - cy here dai - ly at - tend us;
4. come now re - joi - cing be - fore him.

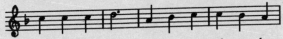

1. All you who hear, now to the al - tar draw
2. Christ the high priest, bids us all join in the
3. Pon - der a - new what the Al - might - y can
4. Let the A - men sound from his peo - ple a -

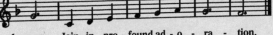

1. near; Join in pro - found ad - o - ra - tion.
2. feast, Vic - tims with him on the al - tar.
3. do, If with his love he be - friends us.
4. gain, As we here wor-ship be - fore him.

Psalm 23: Shepherd Me, O God

Music: Marty Haugen

Text: Psalm 23; Marty Haugen

Refrain

Shep-herd me, O God, be - yond my wants, be-

yond my fears, from death in-to life.

Verses

1. God is my shepherd, so nothing shall I want,
   I rest in the meadows of faithfulness and love,
   I walk by the quiet waters of peace.

2. Gently you raise me and heal my weary soul,
   you lead me by pathways of righteousness and truth,
   my spirit shall sing the music of your name.

3. Though I should wander the valley of death,
   I fear no evil, for you are at my side, your rod and your
   staff,
   my comfort and my hope.

4. Surely your kindness and mercy follow me all the days
   of my life;
   I will dwell in the house of my God for evermore.

Amazing Grace

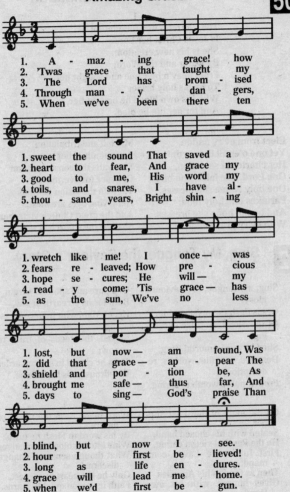

1. A - maz - ing grace! how
2. 'Twas grace that taught my
3. The Lord has prom - ised
4. Through man - y dan - gers,
5. When we've been there ten

1. sweet the sound That saved a
2. heart to fear, And grace my
3. good to me, His word my
4. toils, and snares, I have al -
5. thou - sand years, Bright shin - ing

1. wretch like me! I once — was
2. fears re - leaved; How pre - cious
3. hope se - cures; He will — my
4. read - y come; 'Tis grace — has
5. as the sun, We've no less

1. lost, but now — am found, Was
2. did that grace — ap - pear The
3. shield and por - tion be, As
4. brought me safe — thus far, And
5. days to sing — God's praise Than

1. blind, but now I see.
2. hour I first be - lieved!
3. long as life en - dures.
4. grace will lead me home.
5. when we'd first be - gun.

627

51 The Church's One Foundation

1.

The Church's one foundation
Is Jesus Christ her Lord.
She is his new creation,
By water and the Word;
From heav'n he came and sought her,
To be his holy bride;
With his own blood he bought her,
And for her life he died.

2.

Elect from ev'ry nation,
Yet one o'er all the earth.
Her charter of salvation,
One Lord, one faith, one birth;
One holy Name she blesses,
Partakes one holy food;
And to one hope she presses,
With ev'ry grace endued.

3.

Mid toil and tribulation,
And tumult of her war.
She waits the consummation
Of peace for evermore;
Till with the vision glorious
Her loving eyes are blest,
And the great Church victorious
Shall be the Church at rest.

52 Sing, My Tongue, the Saviour's Glory

1.

Sing, my tongue, the Saviour's glory,
Of his flesh the myst'ry sing;
Of the Blood, all price exceeding,
Shed by our immortal King,
Destined for the world's redemption,
From a noble womb to spring.

2.

Of a pure and spotless Virgin
Born for us on earth below,
He, as Man, with man conversing,
Stayed, the seeds of truth to sow;
Then he closed in solemn order
Wondrously his life of woe.

3.

On the night of that Last Supper,
Seated with his chosen band,
He the Paschal victim eating,
First fulfils the Law's command;
Then as food to his Apostles
Gives himself with his own Hand.

4.

Word made flesh the bread of nature
By his word to Flesh he turns;
Wine into his blood he changes
What though sense no change discerns?
Only be the heart in earnest,
Faith its lesson quickly learns.

(Tantum ergo)

5.

Down in adoration falling
Lo! the sacred Host we hail;
Lo! o'er ancient forms depart-
ing,
Newer rites of grace prevail;
Faith for all defects supplying,
Where the feeble senses fail.

6.

To the Everlasting Father,
And the Son who reigns on
high,
With the Holy Ghost proceed-
ing
Forth from each eternally
Be salvation, honour, blessing,
Might and endless majesty.
Amen.

Lord, Dismiss Us with Thy Blessing   53

1.

Lord, dismiss us with thy
blessing;
Fill our hearts with joy and
peace;
May we all, thy love possess-
ing,
Triumph in redeeming grace:
O refresh us, O refresh us,
And the world its turmoil
cease.

2.

Thanks to thee and adoration
For the scriptures' joyful
sound,
May the fruit of thy redemp-
tion
In our hearts and lives abound;
Ever faithful, ever faithful
To the ways of truth be found.

The King of Glory   54

W. F. Jabusch   Israeli Folksong

Refrain: The King of Glory comes,
the people rejoices;
Open the gates before him,
lift up your voices.

1. Who is the King of Glory;
how shall we call him?
He is Emmanuel,
the promised of ages.

2. In all of Galilee,
In city or village,
He goes among his people
Curing their illness.

Recorded on LP "Songs of Good News," © Copyright 1969 by ACTA
Foundations, 4848 N. Clark St., Chicago, IL.

55
Praise the Lord of Heaven

T.B. Browne, 1844, alt.

Une Vaine Crainte
French Carol Melody

1.

Praise the Lord of heaven; / Praise him in the height!
Praise him, all ye angels, / Praise him stars and light;
Praise him, earth and waters, / Praise him, all ye skies;
When his word commanded, / All things did arise.

2.

Praise the Lord, ye fountains / Of the depths and seas,
Rocks and hills and mountains, / Cedars and all trees;
Praise him, clouds and vapours, / Snow and hail and
    fire,
Nature all fulfilling / Only his desire.

3.

Praise him, all ye nations, / Rulers and all kings;
Praise him, men and maidens, / All created things;
Glorious and mighty / Is his name alone;
All the earth his footstool, / Heaven is his throne.

56
To Christ the Prince of Peace

1. To Christ the prince of Peace
   And the Son of God most high,
   The Father of the world to come,
   Sing we with holy joy.
   Deep in his heart for us
   The wound of love he bore;
   That love wherewith he
   Still inflames the hearts that him adore.

2. O Jesus, Victim blest,
   What else but love divine
   Could thou constrain to open thus
   That sacred Heart of thine.
   O fount of endless Life,
   O Spring of Waters Clear,
   O Flame Celestial,
   Cleansing all who unto thee draw near.

Praise, My Soul, The King of Heaven

F. Lyte

John Goss

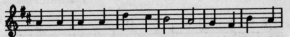

1. Praise, my soul, the King of hea - ven; To his feet thy
2. Praise him for his grace and fa - vour To our fa - thers
3. Fa - ther - like he tends and spares us; Well our fee - ble

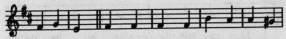

1. tri-bute bring; Ran-somed, healed, re-stored, for-giv - en,
2. in dis - tress; Praise him, still the same for ev - er,
3. frame he knows; In his hands he gen - tly bears us,

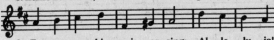

1. Ev - er-more his prais - es sing: Al - le - lu - ia!
2. Slow to chide, and swift to bless: Al - le - lu - ia!
3. Res - cues us from all our foes; Al - le - lu - ia!

1. Al - le - lu - ia! Praise the ev - er - last - ing King.
2. Al - le - lu - ia! Glo - rious in his faith - ful - ness.
3. Al - le - lu - ia! Wide - ly as his mer - cy flows.

Praise the Lord, Ye Heav'ns, Adore Him

1. Praise the Lord, ye heav'ns, adore him
Praise him, angels in the height.
Sun and moon, rejoice before him.
Praise him, all you stars of light.
Praise the Lord, for he has spoken:
Worlds his mighty voice obeyed.
Laws which never shall be broken
For their guidance he has made.

2. Praise the Lord, for he is glorious,
Never shall his promise fail.
God has made his saints victorious.
Sin and death shall not prevail.
Praise the God of our salvation.
Hosts on high, his pow'r proclaim:
Heav'n and earth and all creation,
Praise and magnify his name.

Alleluia! Sing to Jesus

Melody: Hymnal 1940, no. 347-b

W.C. Dix

Rowland H. Prichard

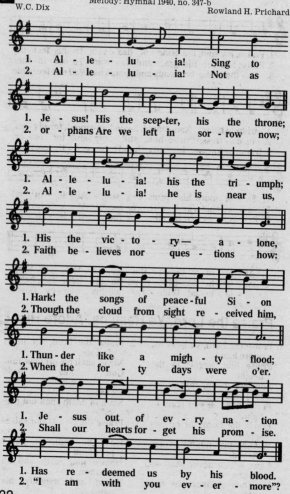

1. Al - le - lu - ia! Sing to Je - sus! His the scep-ter, his the throne; Al - le - lu - ia! his the tri - umph; His the vic - to - ry— a - lone, Hark! the songs of peace-ful Si - on Thun - der like a migh - ty flood; Je - sus out of ev - ry na - tion Has re - deemed us by his blood.

2. Al - le - lu - ia! Not as or - phans Are we left in sor - row now; Al - le - lu - ia! he is near us, Faith be - lieves nor ques - tions how: Though the cloud from sight re - ceived him, When the for - ty days were o'er, Shall our hearts for - get his prom - ise. "I am with you ev - er - more"?

Alleluia! Alleluia! Hearts and Voices

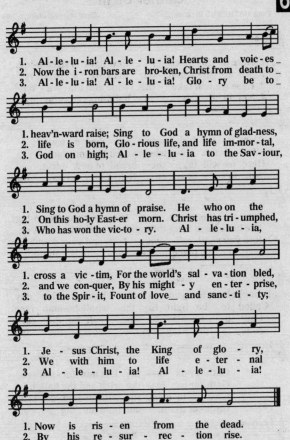

1. Al - le - lu - ia! Al - le - lu - ia! Hearts and voic - es
2. Now the i - ron bars are bro - ken, Christ from death to
3. Al - le - lu - ia! Al - le - lu - ia! Glo - ry be to

1. heav'n-ward raise; Sing to God a hymn of glad-ness,
2. life is born, Glo - rious life, and life im-mor - tal,
3. God on high; Al - le - lu - ia to the Sav - iour,

1. Sing to God a hymn of praise. He who on the
2. On this ho-ly East-er morn. Christ has tri - umphed,
3. Who has won the vic-to - ry. Al - le - lu - ia,

1. cross a vic - tim, For the world's sal - va - tion bled,
2. and we con-quer, By his might - y en - ter - prise,
3. to the Spir - it, Fount of love__ and sanc - ti - ty;

1. Je - sus Christ, the King of glo - ry,
2. We with him to life e - ter - nal
3. Al - le - lu - ia! Al - le - lu - ia!

1. Now is ris - en from the dead.
2. By his re - sur - rec - tion rise.
3. To the Tri - une Ma - jes - ty.

61 Gather Us In

Tune: GATHER US IN, Irreg.,
Marty Haugen, b. 1950

Text: Marty Haugen, b. 1950

1. Here in this place new light is stream-ing,
2. We are the young—our lives are a mys-t'ry,
3. Here we will take the wine and the wa - ter,
4. Not in the dark of build-ings con - fin -ing,

Now is the dark - ness van-ished a - way,
We are the old— who yearn for your face,
Here we will take the bread of new birth,
Not in some heav - en, light-years a -way, But

See in this space our fears and our dream-ings,
We have been sung through-out all of his - t'ry,
Here you shall call your sons and your daugh-ters,
here in this place the new light is shin-ing,

Brought here to you in the light of this day.
Called to be light to the whole hu-man race.
Call us a - new to be salt for the earth.
Now is the King-dom, now is the day.

Gath - er us in— the lost and for - sak - en,
Gath - er us in— the rich and the haugh-ty,
Give us to drink the wine of com - pas-sion,
Gath - er us in and hold us for ev - er,

Gath-er us in— the blind and the lame;
Gath-er us in— the proud and the strong;
Give us to eat the bread that is you;
Gath-er us in and make us your own;

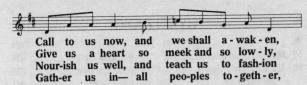

Call to us now, and we shall a - wak - en,
Nour-ish us well, and teach us to fash-ion
Give us a heart so meek and so low - ly,
Gath-er us in— all peo-ples to - geth - er,

We shall a-rise at the sound of our name.
Give us the cour-age to en - ter the song.
Lives that are ho-ly and hearts that are true.
Fire of love in our flesh and our bone.

Were You There

62

1. Were you there when they crucified my Lord?
Were you there when they crucified my Lord?
Oh! sometimes it causes me
To tremble, tremble, tremble.
Were you there when they crucified my Lord?

2. Were you there when they nailed him to the tree?
Were you there when they nailed him to the tree?
Oh! sometimes it causes me
To tremble, tremble, tremble.
Were you there when they nailed him to the tree?

3. Were you there when they laid him in the tomb?
Were you there when they laid him in the tomb?
Oh! sometimes it causes me
To tremble, tremble, tremble.
Were you there when they laid him in the tomb?

O Canada

63

R. S. Weir, 1908

A.B. Routhier

O Canada! Our home and na-tive land!
True patriot love in all thy sons command.
With glowing hearts we see thee rise.
The True North strong and free;
From far and wide, O Canada,
We stand on guard for thee.
God keep our land glorious and free!
O Canada! we stand on guard for thee.

O Canada! Terre de nos aieux,
Ton front est ceint de fleurons glorieux!
Car ton bras sait porter l'epee,
Il sait porter la croix!
Ton histoire est une epopee
Des plus briliants exploits.
Et ta valeur, de foi trempee,
Protegera nos foyers et nos droits.
Protegera nos foyers et nos droits.

HYMN INDEX

TREASURY OF PRAYERS

These prayers reflect the traditions of the Catholic Church. Individuals and families may find them helpful as they pray.

PRAISE AND THANKS

Blessed are you, Lord God:
blessed are you for ever.
Holy is your name:
blessed are you for ever.
Great is your mercy for your people:
blessed are you for ever. Amen!

Father, Son, and Holy Spirit,
we praise you and give you glory:
we bless you for calling us to be your holy people.

Remain in our hearts,
and guide us in our love and service.
Help us to let our light shine before others
and lead them to the way of faith.

Holy Trinity of love,
we praise you now and for ever. Amen!

We praise you, Father of all:
we thank you for calling us to be your people,
and for choosing us to give you glory.
In a special way we thank you for . . .

Cleanse our hearts and our lives
with your holy word
and make our prayer pleasing to you.
Guide us by your Spirit
as we follow in the paths of Jesus our brother.

All glory and praise are yours, Father,
for ever and ever. Amen!

Let us give glory to the Father
through the Son
in the Holy Spirit,
for God has made us his people, his Church,
and calls us to sing his praises.

All honor and glory and thanks are his,
and praise and worship belong to him.
To God be glory in his Church
for ever and ever! Amen!

   Thanks for a beautiful day: *On a beautiful day we may
thank God and praise him for his many gifts:*

Father of Jesus,
we praise you and give you glory
for the wonderful things you do for us:
for life and health,
for friends and family,
for this splendid day.

For these reasons, we pray as Jesus taught us:
Our Father . . .

MORNING PRAYERS

*With our risen Lord. we praise our Father and offer our day
and our work.*

**In the ✠ name of the Father, and of the Son,
and of the Holy Spirit. Amen!**

Father, help your people.
Be with us as we pray.

MORNING PSALM:

*We may pray one of these psalms, or last Sunday's respon-
sorial psalm, adding the* Glory (be) to the Father *at the
end.*

*Ps. 23—from Mass for Second Scrutiny (4th Sun. of Lent)
Ps. 95—from Mass for First Scrutiny (3rd Sun. of Lent)*

Ps. 97—from Mass of the Nativity (at Dawn)
Ps. 116—from Mass for Holy Thursday

On Sunday, it is appropriate to use Ps. 118 from Easter Sunday Mass.
On Friday, it is appropriate to use Ps. 51 from Ash Wednesday Mass.

PSALM OF PRAISE:

One of these Psalms may be prayed, adding the Glory (be) to the Father *at the end.*

Ps. 46(47)—from Mass for Palm Sunday of the Passion
Ps. 67—from Mass of January 1
Ps. 96—from Mass of the Nativity (During the Night)
Ps. 98—from Mass of the Nativity (During the Day)

READING:

One of the first two readings from last Sunday, or another appropriate text from God's word.

A moment of silent prayer follows the reading.

Canticle of Zechariah   Lk. 1.68-79

Blessed ✛ be the Lord, the God of Israel,
for he has looked favorably on his people and redeemed them.

He has raised up a mighty saviour for us
   in the house of his servant David,
as he spoke through the mouth of his holy prophets from of old,
   that we would be saved from our enemies and from the hand of all who hate us.
Thus he has shown the mercy promised to our ancestors,
   and has remembered his holy covenant,
the oath that he swore to our ancestor Abraham,
   to grant us that we, being rescued from the hands of our enemies,

might serve him without fear, in holiness and righteousness
  before him all our days.
And you, child, will be called the prophet of the
   Most High;
  for you will go before the Lord to prepare his ways,
to give knowledge of salvation to his people
  by the forgiveness of their sins.
By the tender mercy of our God,
  the dawn from on high will break upon us,
to give light to those who sit in darkness and in the
   shadow of death,
  to guide our feet into the way of peace.

Glory to the Father . . . .

Or Glory to God in the highest *(see page 14) may be
prayed or sung.*

Prayers for All People

Lord Jesus, we come to you for help:
Lord, have mercy.

Help us to love you more this day. ℟.
Teach us to see you in other people. ℟.
Help us to be ready to serve others. ℟.
Give us strength to carry our cross with you. ℟.
In moments of sorrow, be with us today. ℟.
Help us to do everything for the glory of your Father.
   ℟.
Help us to build the kingdom by our life today. ℟.

Other petitions may be added.

Lord Jesus, our brother,
hear our prayers for your people.
Help us to work with you today
to honour your Father and save the world.

Lord Jesus,
we praise you for ever and ever. Amen!

THE LORD'S PRAYER: *With Jesus and all his people on earth and in heaven, we sing or say:* Our Father . . . *(page 72).*

BLESSING: *The parents, one of the family, or all may say:*

May our loving God bless us,
Father, Son, and Holy Spirit. Amen!

All may share in a sign of peace and love.

EVENING PRAYERS

At the end of the day, we join Jesus and his Church in offering thanks to our loving God. A candle may be lighted.

In the ✠ name of the Father, and of the Son,
and of the Holy Spirit. Amen!

Father, help your people.
Be with us as we pray.

PSALMS:

We may pray one or two of these psalms, or last Sunday's responsorial psalm, adding the Glory (be) to the Father *after each psalm:*

Ps. 30—from Easter Vigil Service after Fourth Reading
Ps. 51—from Mass for Ash Wednesday
Ps. 104—from Mass for Pentecost Sunday
Ps. 130—from Mass for Third Scrutiny (5th Sun. of Lent)

READING:

One of the first two readings from last Sunday, or another appropriate text from God's word.

A moment of silent prayer follows the reading.

Canticle of Mary   Lk. 1.46-55

My soul ✠ proclaims the greatness of the Lord,
my spirit rejoices in God my Saviour
for he has looked with favour on his lowly servant.

From this day all generations will call me blessed:
the Almighty has done great things for me,
and holy is his Name.

He has mercy on those who fear him
in every generation.

He has shown the strength of his arm,
he has scattered the proud in their conceit.

He has cast down the mighty from their thrones,
and has lifted up the lowly.

He has filled the hungry with good things,
and the rich he has sent away empty.

He has come to the help of his servant Israel
for he has remembered his promise of mercy,
the promise he made to our fathers,
to Abraham and his children for ever.

Glory to the Father.

Or we may sing the Holy, Holy, Holy Lord, *from page 23.*

Prayers for all people:

Let us pray to God our Father:
Lord, hear our prayer.
For the people of God everywhere. ℟.
For peace in the world. ℟.
For the people who are suffering. ℟.
For the sick and the dying. ℟.
For our family, friends, and neighbours. ℟.
For . . .

                Other petitions may be added.

Prayer:

Blessed are you, Father of light,
Lord of all the universe:
in the name of Jesus our Lord we pray for your
    world.
Grant peace to your people,
strength to the weak,
courage to the downhearted,
and guidance to all in despair.
Send your Spirit to conquer evil,
and make your kingdom come among us.

Father, we ask this grace
through Jesus Christ our Lord. Amen!

THE LORD'S PRAYER: *With Jesus and all his people on earth and in heaven, we sing or say:* Our Father . . . *(page 72).*

BLESSING: *The parents, one of the family, or all may say:*

May our loving God bless us,
Father, Son, ✛ and Holy Spirit. Amen!

All may share a sign of peace and love.

BEFORE AND AFTER SCRIPTURE

Before:

Lord, open our hearts:
let your Spirit speak to us
as we read your word.

After:

Father, we thank you
for speaking to us today
through your holy word.

Or another prayer of thanks may be said (pages 637-638).

MEAL PRAYERS

When we are eating or drinking, or doing anything else, we can do it for the glory of God (1 Cor. 10.31). We may use these prayers or other familiar ones, or make up our own.

Before our meal:

Lord Jesus, our brother,
we praise you for saving us.
Bless ✛ us in your love
as we gather in your name,
and bless ✛ this meal that we share.

Jesus, we praise you for ever. Amen!

or:

Father of us all,
this meal is a sign of your love for us:
bless ✛ us and bless ✛ our food,
and help us to give you glory each day
through Jesus Christ our Lord. Amen!

After our meal:

Loving Father, we praise you
for all the gifts you give us:
for life and health,
for faith and love,
and for this meal we have shared together.

Father, we thank you
through Christ our Lord. Amen!

or:

Thank you, Father, for your gifts:
help us to love you more. Amen!

or:

Father, we thank you for your love
and for giving us food and drink.
Help us to praise you today
in the name of Jesus our Lord. Amen!

A PRAYER FOR OUR FAMILY

Blessed are you, loving Father,
ruler of the universe:

You have given us your Son as your leader,
and have made us temples of your Holy Spirit.

Fill our family with your light and peace.
Have mercy on all who suffer,
and bring us to everlasting joy with you.

Father,
we bless your name for ever and ever. Amen!

PARENT'S PRAYER

All praise to you, Lord Jesus, lover of children:
bless our family,
and help us to lead our children to you.

Give us light and strength,
and courage when our task is difficult.
Let your Spirit fill us with love and peace,
so that we may help our children to love you.

All glory and praise are yours, Lord Jesus,
for ever and ever. Amen!

PRAYER OF SORROW

Psalm 51: *from the Mass for Ash Wednesday.*

A prayer for mercy:

Lord Jesus, you have called us
to be children of light:

Lord, have mercy. **Lord, have mercy.**

Christ, you have suffered on the cross for us:
Christ, have mercy. **Christ, have mercy.**

Lord Jesus, you are the saviour of the world:
Lord, have mercy. **Lord, have mercy.**

Other prayers. We may sing or say Lamb of God *(see page 74), or* I confess to almighty God *(see page 12).*

JESUS PRAYER

We may use this simple prayer at any time.

Lord Jesus Christ, Son of God,
have mercy on me.

or:

Lord Jesus Christ, Son of God,
have mercy on us.

or:

Jesus, our Lord and our brother,
save us in your love.

MARIAN ANTHEM

Blessed are you, mother of my Lord,
for you have believed the word of God.

In faith and love,
you have pondered the words and actions of God
in your life and the life of God's people.

With Jesus we call you mother.
Pray for us,
and ask your Son to lead us to the Father. Amen!

PRAYER FOR PEACE

Lord Jesus Christ, we praise you:
bring peace into the world
by bringing your peace into the hearts of all.
Help us to turn away from sin
and to follow you in love and service.

Glory be yours, and honour,
for ever and ever. Amen!

A PRAYER FOR VOCATIONS

Heavenly Father, Lord of the harvest,
call many members of our community
to be generous workers for your people
and to gather in your harvest.
Send them to share the Good News of Jesus
with all the people of the earth.

Father,
we ask this prayer
through Christ our Lord. Amen!

THANKS FOR FAMILY AND FRIENDS

Blessed are you, loving Father,
for all your gifts to us.
Blessed are you for giving us family and friends
to be with us in times of joy and sorrow,
to help us in days of need,
and to rejoice with us in moments of celebration.

Father,
we praise you for your Son Jesus,
who knew the happiness of family and friends,
and in the love of your Holy Spirit.
Blessed are you for ever and ever. Amen!

FAMILY BLESSINGS

Family gathering: *When the family is gathered for a special occasion, a feast, a holiday, a reunion, or any other special time:*

Father in heaven,
we praise you for giving us your Son
to be our saviour and Lord.
Bless us all as we gather here today, [tonight,]
and let us live happily in your love.

Hear our prayer, loving Father,
for we ask this in Jesus' name. Amen!

Children: *Parents may bless their children each day, or on special occasions. These or similar words may be used:*

Simple form:

May God bless ✠ you, *N.,*
and keep you in love.

The child answers: **Amen!**

At bedtime:

Heavenly Father,
bless *N.,* and keep him/her in your love.
Grant him/her a good rest tonight,
and send your angels to protect him/her.
In the name of the Father, and of the ✠ Son,
and of the Holy Spirit.

The child answers: **Amen!**

PRAYER FOR A BIRTHDAY
OF A FAMILY MEMBER

This prayer may be offered at a meal or birthday party:

Heavenly Father,
we praise you for all your gifts to us.
In a special way, we thank you for *N.*
Bless him/her on this birthday,
and keep him/her always in your love.

Bless us too, holy Father,
and this food with which we celebrate.
Help us all to praise you and give you glory
through Jesus Christ our Lord.

All answer: Amen!

PRAYER FOR
A WEDDING ANNIVERSARY

N. and *N.,*
may God bless you and grant you joy.
May he deepen your love for each other.
May he bless ✠ you in your family and friends,
and lead you to unending happiness in heaven.

May almighty God,
Father, Son, ✠ and Holy Spirit,
bless us all, and keep us in his love for ever.

All answer: Amen!

WHEN VISITING A SICK PERSON

Heavenly Father,
look with mercy on *N.,*
and help him/her in this time of sickness.
Restore him/her to health, we pray,
through Christ our Lord.

All answer: Amen!

or:

Lord Jesus,
lover of the sick,
be with *N.* in his/her sickness.
Help him/her to accept this illness
as a sharer in your cross,
and bring him/her back to full health.

Lord Jesus,
we praise you,
for you are Lord for ever and ever.

All answer: **Amen!**

PRAYER FOR THE POPE

All praise and glory are yours, Lord Jesus:
you have made us your body, your Church,
and help us to bear fruit for our heavenly Father.

You chose St. Peter as the rock,
and sent him to feed your flock
and to strengthen his brothers and sisters.
Continue to help your Church
through the guidance of our pope,
and keep us faithful in your service.

Jesus, our brother,
you are Lord for ever and ever. Amen!

PRAYERS BEFORE MASS

Act of Faith

Lord Jesus Christ, I firmly believe that you are present in this Blessed Sacrament as true God and true Man, with your Body and Blood, Soul and Divinity. My Redeemer and my Judge, I adore your Divine Majesty together with the angels and saints. I believe, O Lord; increase my faith.

Act of Hope

Good Jesus, in you alone I place all my hope. You are my salvation and my strength, the Source of all good. Through your mercy, through your Passion and Death, I hope to obtain the pardon of my sins, the grace of final perseverance and a happy eternity.

Act of Love

Jesus, my God, I love you with my whole heart and above all things, because you are the one supreme Good and an infinitely perfect Being. You have given your life for me, a poor sinner, and in your mercy you have even offered yourself as food for my soul. My God, I love you. Inflame my heart so that I may love you more.

Act of Contrition

O my Saviour, I am truly sorry for having offended you because you are infinitely good and sin displeases you. I detest all the sins of my life and I desire to atone for them. Through the merits of your Precious Blood, wash from my soul all stain of sin, so that, cleansed in body and soul, I may worthily approach the Most Holy Sacrament of the Altar.

PRAYERS AFTER MASS

Act of Faith

Jesus, I firmly believe that you are present within me as God and Man, to enrich my soul with graces and to fill my heart with the happiness of the blessed. I believe that you are Christ, the Son of the living God!

Act of Adoration

With deepest humility, I adore you, my Lord and God; you have made my soul your dwelling place. I adore you as my Creator from whose hands I came and with whom I am to be happy forever.

Act of Love

Dear Jesus, I love you with my whole heart, my whole soul, and with all my strength. May the love of your own Sacred Heart fill my soul and purify it so that I may die to the world for love of you, as you died on the Cross for love of me. My God, you are all mine; grant that I may be all yours in time and in eternity.

Act of Thanksgiving

From the depths of my heart I thank you, dear Lord, for your infinite kindness in coming to me. How good you are to me! With your most holy Mother and all the angels, I praise your mercy and generosity toward me, a poor sinner. I thank you for nourishing my soul with your Sacred Body and Precious Blood. I will try to show my gratitude to you in the Sacrament of your love, by obedience to your holy commandments, by fidelity to my duties, by kindness to my neighbour and by an earnest endeavor to become like you in my daily conduct.

Act of Offering

Jesus, you have given yourself to me, now let me give myself to you; I give you my body, that it may be chaste and pure. I give you my soul, that it may be free from sin. I give you my heart, that it may always love you. I give you every thought, word, and deed of my life, and I offer all for your honour and glory.

Anima Christi

Partial indulgence (No. 10)

Soul of Christ, sanctify me.
Body of Christ, save me.
Blood of Christ, inebriate me.
Water from the side of Christ, wash me.
Passion of Christ, strengthen me.
O good Jesus, hear me.
Within your wounds hide me.
Separated from you let me never be.
From the malignant enemy, defend me.
At the hour of death, call me.
And close to you bid me.
That with your saints I may be
Praising you, for all eternity. Amen.

Indulgenced Prayer before a Crucifix

Look down upon me, good and gentle Jesus, while before your face I humbly kneel, and with a burning soul pray and beseech you to fix deep in my heart lively sentiments of faith, hope and charity, true contrition for my sins, and a firm purpose of amendment, while I contemplate with great love and tender pity your five wounds, pondering over them within me, calling to mind the words which David, your prophet, said of you, my good Jesus: "They have pierced my hands and my feet; they have numbered all my bones" (Ps 21.17-18).

A *plenary indulgence* is granted on each Friday of Lent and Passiontide to the faithful, who after Communion piously recite the above prayer before an image of Christ crucified; on other days of the year the indulgence is *partial (No. 22)*.

Stations of the Cross

The Way of the Cross is a devotion in which we meditate on Christ's Passion and Death in order to put their meaning into our lives.

Heavenly Father, grant that I who meditate on the Passion and Death of Your Son, Jesus Christ, may imitate in my life His love and self-giving to You and to others. Grant this through Christ our Lord. Amen.

STATIONS of the CROSS

1. Jesus Is Condemned to Death

O Jesus, help me to appreciate Your sanctifying grace more and more.

2. Jesus Bears His Cross

O Jesus, You chose to die for me. Help me to love You always with all my heart.

3. Jesus Falls the First Time

O Jesus, make me strong to conquer my wicked passions, and to rise quickly from sin.

4. Jesus Meets His Mother

O Jesus, grant me a tender love for Your Mother, who offered You for love of me.

STATIONS
of the
CROSS

5. Jesus Is Helped by Simon

O Jesus, like Simon lead me ever closer to You through my daily crosses and trials.

6. Jesus and Veronica

O Jesus, imprint Your image on my heart that I may be faithful to You all my life.

7. Jesus Falls a Second Time

O Jesus, I repent for having offended You. Grant me forgiveness of all my sins.

8. Jesus Speaks to the Women

O Jesus, grant me tears of compassion for Your sufferings and of sorrow for my sins.

STATIONS of the CROSS

9. Jesus Falls a Third Time

O Jesus, let me never yield to despair. Let me come to You in hardship and spiritual distress.

10. He Is Stripped of His Garments

O Jesus, let me sacrifice all my attachments rather than imperil the divine life of my soul.

11. Jesus Is Nailed to the Cross

O Jesus, strengthen my faith and increase my love for You. Help me to accept my crosses.

12. Jesus Dies on the Cross

O Jesus, I thank You for making me a child of God. Help me to forgive others.

STATIONS
of the
CROSS

13. Jesus Is Taken down from the Cross

O Jesus, through the intercession of Your holy Mother, let me be pleasing to You.

14. Jesus Is Laid in the Tomb

O Jesus, strengthen my will to live for You on earth and bring me to eternal bliss in heaven.

Prayer after the Stations

JESUS, You became an example of humility, obedience and patience, and preceded me on the way of life bearing Your Cross. Grant that, inflamed with Your love, I may cheerfully take upon myself the sweet yoke of Your Gospel together with the mortification of the Cross and follow You as a true disciple so that I may be united with You in heaven. Amen.

THE HOLY ROSARY

Prayer before the Rosary

QUEEN of the Holy Rosary, you have deigned to come to Fatima to reveal to the three shepherd children the treasures of grace hidden in the Rosary. Inspire my heart with a sincere love of this devotion, in order that by meditating on the Mysteries of our Redemption which are recalled in it, I may be enriched with its fruits and obtain peace for the world, the conversion of sinners, and the favor which I ask of you in this Rosary. *(Here mention your request.)* I ask it for the greater glory of God, for your own honor, and for the good of souls, especially for my own. Amen.

The Five

Joyful

Mysteries

Said on Mondays and Saturdays [except during Lent], and the Sundays from Advent to Lent.

3. The Nativity
For the spirit of poverty.

1. The Annunciation
For the love of humility.

4. The Presentation
For the virtue of obedience.

2. The Visitation
For charity toward my neighbor.

5. Finding in the Temple
For the virtue of piety.

1. The Baptism of Jesus
For living my Baptismal Promises.

The Five

Luminous

Mysteries*

Said on Thursdays [except during Lent].

*Added to the Mysteries of the Rosary by Pope John Paul II in his Apostolic Letter of October 16, 2002, entitled *The Rosary of the Virgin Mary.*

2. The Wedding at Cana
For doing whatever Jesus says.

4. The Transfiguration
Becoming a New Person in Christ.

3. Proclamation of the Kingdom
For seeking God's forgiveness.

5. Institution of the Eucharist
For active participation at Mass.

The Five Sorrowful Mysteries

Said on Tuesdays and Fridays throughout the year, and every day from Ash Wednesday until Easter.

3. Crowning with Thorns
For moral courage.

1. Agony in the Garden
For true contrition.

4. Carrying of the Cross
For the virtue of patience.

2. Scourging at the Pillar
For the virtue of purity.

5. The Crucifixion
For final perseverance.

The Five
Glorious
Mysteries

1. The Resurrection
For the virtue of faith.

Said on Wednesdays [except during Lent], and the Sundays from Easter to Advent.

2. The Ascension
For the virtue of hope.

4. Assumption of the B.V.M.
For devotion to Mary.

3. Descent of the Holy Spirit
For love of God.

5. Crowning of the B.V.M.
For eternal happiness.

VARIOUS PRAYERS

Prayer to St. Joseph

O Blessed St. Joseph, loving father and faithful guardian of Jesus, and devoted spouse of the Mother of God, I beg you to offer God the Father his divine Son, bathed in blood on the Cross. Through the holy Name of Jesus obtain for us from the Father the favor we implore.

For the Sick

Father, your Son accepted our sufferings to teach us the virtue of patience in human illness. Hear the prayers we offer for our sick brothers and sisters. May all who suffer pain, illness or disease realize that they are chosen to be saints, and know that they are joined to Christ in his suffering for the salvation of the world, who lives and reigns with you and the Holy Spirit, one God, for ever and ever.

For Religious Vocations

Father, you call all who believe in you to grow perfect in love by following in the footsteps of Christ your Son. May those whom you have chosen to serve you as religious provide by their way of life a convincing sign of your kingdom for the Church and the whole world.

For the Parliament

Father, you guide and govern everything with order and love. Look upon the assembly of our national leaders and fill them with the spirit of your wisdom. May they always act in accordance with your will, and may their decisions be for the peace and well-being of all.

PRAYERS IN ACCORD WITH THE LITURGICAL YEAR

ADVENT

Prayer to Help Others Find Christ

O Lord Jesus, I thank you for the gift of faith and for the continual grace you give me to nourish and strengthen it. Enable me to cultivate the genuine desire for you that lies beneath the zealous search for justice, truth, love, and peace found in our contemporaries. Encourage these searchings, O Lord, and grant that all true seekers may look beyond the present moment and catch sight of your countenance in the world.

Prayer for Christ's Triple Coming

Lamb of God, you once came to rid the world of sin; cleanse me now of every stain of sin. Lord, you came to save what was lost; come once again with your salvific power so that those you redeemed will not be punished. I have come to know you in faith; may I have unending joy when you come again in glory.

Prayer for Christ's Coming in Grace

O Lord Jesus, during this Advent come to us in your grace. Come to prepare our hearts, minds, and bodies to welcome you on Christmas Day. Come to comfort us in sadness, to cheer us in loneliness, to refresh us in weariness, to strengthen us in temptations, to lead us in time of doubt, and to exult with us in joy.

CHRISTMAS TIME

Prayer to Jesus, God's Greatest Gift

O Jesus, I believe that the greatest proof of God's love is His gift to us of you, His only Son. All love tends to become like that which it loves. You love human beings; therefore you became man. Infinite love and mercy caused you, the Second Person of the Blessed Trinity, to leave the Kingdom of eternal bliss, to descend from the throne of your majesty, and to become a helpless babe. Eventually you even suffered and died and rose that we might live.

You wished to enter the world as a child in order to show that you were true Man. But you become man also that we may become like God. In exchange for the humanity which you take from us you wish to make us share in your Divinity by sanctifying grace, so that you may take sole possession of us. Grant me the grace to love you in return with a deep, personal, and productive love.

Prayer for Christ's Rebirth in the Church

O Lord Jesus Christ, we ask you to incarnate in us your invisible Divinity. What you accomplished corporally in Mary accomplish now spiritually in your Church. May the Church's sure faith conceive you, its unstained intelligence give birth to you, and its soul united with the power of the Most High preserve you forever.

LENT

Prayer to be Freed of the Seven Deadly Sins

O meek Saviour and Prince of Peace, implant in me the virtues of gentleness and patience. Let me curb the fury of *anger* and restrain all resentment and impatience so as to overcome evil with good, attain your peace, and rejoice in your love.

O Model of humility, divest me of all *pride and arrogance.* Let me acknowledge my weakness and sinfulness, so that I may bear mockery and contempt for your sake and esteem myself as lowly in your sight.

O Teacher of abstinence, help me to serve you rather than my appetites. Keep me from *gluttony*—the inordinate love of food and drink—and let me hunger and thirst for your justice.

O Lover of purity, remove all *lust* from my heart, so that I may serve you with a pure mind and a chaste body.

O Father of the poor, help me to avoid all *covetousness* for earthly goods and give me a love for heavenly things. Inspire me to give to the needy, just as you gave your life that I might inherit eternal treasures.

O Exemplar of love, keep me from all *envy* and ill-will. Let the grace of your love dwell in me that I may rejoice in the happiness of others and bewail their adversities.

O zealous Lover of souls, keep me from all *sloth* of mind or body. Inspire me with zeal for your glory, so that I may do all things for you and in you.

Prayer of Contrition

Merciful Father, I am guilty of sin. I confess my sins before you and I am sorry for them. Your promises are just; therefore I trust that you will forgive me my sins and cleanse me from every stain of sin. Jesus himself is the propitiation for my sins and those of the whole world. I put my hope in his atonement. May my sins be forgiven through his name, and in his blood may my soul be made clean.

Prayer to Know Jesus Christ

O Lord Jesus, like St. Paul, may I count everything as loss in comparison with the supreme advantage of knowing you. I want to know you and what your Passion and Resurrection can do. I also want to share in your sufferings in the hope that if I resemble you in death I may somehow attain to the resurrection from the dead.

Give me grace to make every effort to supplement faith with moral courage, moral courage with knowledge, knowledge with self-control, self-control with patience, patience with piety, piety with affection, and affection with love for all my brothers and sisters in Christ. May these virtues keep me both active and fruitful and bring me to the deep knowledge of you, Lord Jesus Christ.

EASTER TIME

Prayer in Praise of Christ's Humanity

O risen Lord, your body was part of your power, rather than you a part of its weakness.

For this reason you could not but rise again, if you were to die—because your body, once taken by you, never was or could be separated from you even in the grave.

I keep your most holy body before me as the pledge of my own resurrection. Though I die, it only means that my life is changed, for I shall rise again.

Teach me to live as one who believes in the great dignity and sanctity of the material frame which you have given to me.

Prayer to the Holy Spirit

Holy Spirit of light and love, you are the substantial love of the Father and the Son; hear my prayer.

Bounteous bestower of most precious gifts, grant me a strong and living faith, which makes me accept all revealed truths and shape my conduct in accord with them. Give me a most confident hope in all divine promises which prompts me to abandon myself unreservedly to you and your guidance.

Infuse into me a love of perfect goodwill, which makes me accomplish God's will in all things and act according to God's least desires. Make me love not only my friends but my enemies as well in imitation of Jesus Christ who through you offered himself on the Cross for all people. Holy Spirit, animate, inspire, and guide me, and help me to be always a true follower of Jesus.

ORDINARY TIME

Prayer for a Productive Faith

O Lord, increase my faith and let it bear fruit in my life. Let it bind me fast to other Christians in the common certitude that our Master is the God-Man who gave his life for all. Let me listen in faith to the Divine word that challenges me.

Help me to strive wholeheartedly under the promptings of my faith in the building of a world ruled by love. Enable me to walk in faith toward the indescribable future that you have promised to all who possess a productive faith in you.

Prayer to Christ in the World

Lord Jesus, let us realize that every action of ours no matter how small or how secular enables us to be in touch with you. Let our interest lie in created things—but only in absolute dependence upon your presence in them. Let us pursue you and you alone through the reality of created things. Let this be our prayer—to become closer to you by becoming more human.

Let us become a true branch on the vine that is you, a branch that bears much fruit. Let us accept you in our lives in the way it pleases you to come into them: as Truth, to be spoken; as Life, to be lived; as Light, to be shared; as Love, to be followed; as Joy, to be given; as Peace, to be spread about; as Sacrifice, to be offered among our relatives and friends, among our neighbours and all people.

Prayer to be Generous in Giving

Lord Jesus, you came to tell us that the meaning of life consists in giving. You told us that those who cling too tightly to what they have—without thought for others—end up by losing everything. You gave us new values by which to measure the worth of a person's life.

Help me to realize it is not temporal success or riches or fame that necessarily gives life meaning. Rather it is the service rendered to others in your Name that brings fulfillment and makes my life worthwhile. May all my activity help build God's kingdom: my suffering bear genuine fruit, my obedience bring true freedom, and my death lead to eternal life.

Prayer to Discern God's Call

Heavenly Father, your call never comes to us in a vacuum; it comes to us in the circumstances of our ordinary lives.

Therefore, our response cannot be given only in the privacy of our own minds; it must overflow into our daily lives. You call us through our family, through our community or Church, and through the world.

Help me to see that when I say No to the legitimate requests of my family, my community, or my world, I say No to you. You have ordained that whatever advances the true progress of self, of the Church, and of the world is my way of saying Yes to your call. May I take advantage of the daily opportunities which you place at my disposal to answer your call affirmatively.

— OTHER POPULAR CATHOLIC BOOKS —